Nourishing Networks

NOURISHING NETWORKS

The Public Culture of Food
in New Orleans

ASHLEY ROSE YOUNG

OXFORD
UNIVERSITY PRESS

OXFORD
UNIVERSITY PRESS

Oxford University Press is a department of the University of Oxford.
It furthers the University's objective of excellence in research, scholarship,
and education by publishing worldwide. Oxford is a registered trade mark of
Oxford University Press in the UK and in certain other countries.

Published in the United States of America by Oxford University Press
198 Madison Avenue, New York, NY 10016, United States of America.

CIP data is on file at the Library of Congress.

ISBN 9780197794036

DOI: 10.1093/9780197794067.001.0001

Printed by Integrated Books International, United States of America

The manufacturer's authorized representative in the EU for product safety is
Oxford University Press España S.A. of Parque Empresarial San Fernando de Henares,
Avenida de Castilla, 2 – 28830 Madrid (www.oup.es/en or product.safety@oup.com).
OUP España S.A. also acts as importer into Spain of products made by the manufacturer.

To my parents, who have nourished me:
To my mother, whose lifelong love and commitment to her family were
inextricable from her inspiring culinary entrepreneurship;
And to my father, who sparked my passion for history at an early age and
who has kept that fire alight to this day.

Contents

Acknowledgments

MY PROJECT ORIGINATED in the sultry, sticky air of a New Orleans summer in 2009. Each day, I walked to my internship at the Southern Food & Beverage Museum with a chicory coffee in hand and a vague notion of an upcoming undergraduate thesis looming in my mind. I had little idea that the experience would shape not only my senior year at Yale but also the trajectory of my professional life. During that fateful summer, I developed a profound connection with Elizabeth Williams, the founder of the Southern Food & Beverage Museum as well as the National Food & Beverage Foundation. She recognized my passion for learning and my curiosity for New Orleans' history. She gave me a foundation upon which to build my academic career as well as my interest in public history. Rebecca Tannenbaum, my undergraduate senior thesis adviser at Yale, also helped me to crystallize my first thoughts about the significance of New Orleans' local food culture and economy. So, too, did Paul Freedman, who was kind enough to listen and provide feedback on some of my earliest historical analysis my senior year. Soon thereafter, I pursued my PhD in History at Duke University. There, I worked with Laura Edwards, Priscilla Wald, Laurent Dubois, and Adriane Lentz-Smith, who championed my project, encouraging me to write a dissertation of which I am proud. Together, these mentors supported my intellectual growth throughout this process, believing, like I do, that food is a crucial lens through which to explore history.

Over the course of my undergraduate and graduate work, something that had always been in my heart rose to my field of vision: This project was inspired by my own family's story. My maternal grandfather Elwood was a street food vendor, launching his produce business just after World War II in Pittsburgh, Pennsylvania. He and my grandmother Rosella worked their way up to owning a small grocery store, and then several others that my mother Sharon and aunts Bonnie and Noreen took over in the early 1980s. Together, these three sisters converted what was a series of mom-and-pop shops into award-winning gourmet grocery food stores under the name McGinnis Sisters Special Food Stores. I grew up in those businesses, working alongside my mother, aunts, grandparents, brothers, and cousins. Undoubtedly, my interest in food entrepreneurship and my passion for sharing the stories of women in the food industry were forged within the context of my family business. Pairing those experiences with the passion for history of my father Walter, a lifelong educator and teacher in the Baldwin–Whitehall School District in the Pittsburgh suburbs, it almost seems fated that I would become a food historian. I was perhaps the last person to realize this fact.

There are several institutions that have supported my research and writing efforts, especially during my PhD program. First and foremost, I must thank Duke University for providing me funding and professional opportunities throughout my graduate career. I would also like to thank the Southern Foodways Alliance as well as the Southern Food & Beverage Museum, where I served as a guest curator and research fellow. The former organization provided me experience developing, researching, and curating an oral history project, The Carrboro Farmers' Market Oral History Project. My work on that project piqued my interest in United States food markets, encouraging me to think about the complex dynamics at play within spaces of food provisioning. The Newcomb College Institute and the Radcliffe Institute for Advanced Study provided me with funds to expand the scope of my research to encompass a regional and then a national study of the nineteenth- and twentieth-century United States. The Friends of the Oxford Symposium awarded me the Cherwell Food History Studentship, which enabled me to examine the transatlantic connections between public markets in New Orleans and Europe. Their combined support gave me the intellectual freedom to explore larger themes, which have made this book stronger. I would also like to give thanks to several New Orleans- and DC-based archivists and librarians who have gone above and beyond to assist me with my research: Trina Brown, Florence Jumonville, Alexia MacClain, Jennifer Navarre, Eric Seiferth, Brittanny Silva, Bobby Ticknor, Susan Tucker, and Chloe Raub.

In my final semester of graduate school, I became the Historian of the Smithsonian Food History Project at the Smithsonian's National Museum of American History, where I co-curated the *FOOD: Transforming the American Table* exhibition and served as the project lead and host of the museum's live-cooking demonstration series, Cooking Up History. I also had the opportunity to continue my graduate research on Black Creole chef Lena Richard, amplifying her story through the highlights case, "The Only One in the Room: Women Achievers in Business and the Cost of Success," in the *American Enterprise* exhibition as well as through blog posts, panels, podcast episodes, and a number of other projects in concert with her granddaughter, Dr. Paula Rhodes. Through these dynamic curatorial and programming experiences, I solidified my love for public history while working alongside my fellow team members: Paula Johnson, Theresa McCulla, and Steve Velasquez. They provided invaluable insight and support as early portions of this book began to take shape during my tenure at the Smithsonian.

As they say, it takes a village, and many colleagues have read drafts of this work, first in the form of an undergraduate thesis, then as a dissertation, and most recently as a scholarly monograph. To all of you, I express my deepest appreciation. A special thanks to the most recent cohort of peer editors who helped strengthen the latest iterations of this book, chapter by chapter, sentence by sentence: Greg Beaman, Richard Campanella, Emily Contois, Mandy Cooper, Alisha Cromwell, Judie Evans, KC Hysmith, Beth Jacob, Josh Levy, Theresa McCulla, Justin Nystrom, Alex Piper, Abeer Saha, Sam Vong, and Oxford University Press' anonymous readers. Samantha Martin and Leila Farah gave essential editorial advice on Chapter 5 of this book, the first published version of which appeared as "Public Amenity or Public Threat?: Epidemiology and Grassroots Activism in the Food Markets of New Orleans, 1900–1940" in *Mobs and Microbes: Global Perspectives on Market Halls, Civic Order and Public Health*, edited by Leila Marie Farah and Samantha L. Martin (Leuven University Press, 2023).

I'm forever grateful to my editor, Nancy Toff, for recognizing the seed of a dynamic project back when she first heard me sing historic street cries at the 2015 Southern Historical Association Annual Meeting. As with New Orleans' street vendors and their community, those sonorous warbles brought us together to forge a connection that has lasted many years and proved both fruitful and meaningful. Nancy was a powerhouse reviewer of this work; after her retirement, Susan Ferber graciously and fearlessly stepped in to help me with the final polishes before publication.

Finally, and most importantly, I must thank my friends and family. My dearest friends from Yale, "The X-Plex" and "The Complex," are brilliant and sharp-witted. Equally supportive are my friends from the Yale Glee Club, especially Emily Howell and Stephen Wirth, whose dulcet tones and jokes have buoyed me along both the calm and tempestuous waters of my adult life. Together, this cohort has provided comments and suggestions on everything from my original graduate school application to research grant proposals, and from blog posts to drafts of this book. I feel an especially deep sense of gratitude toward Sarah Dewey, Celina Kirchner, Elisabeth Thomas, Allix Wilde, and Adrienne Wong, whose compassion and intellect enabled me to reach my fullest potential as both a person and a scholar. They have proven that a best friend isn't a person, but a tier.

Above all, this book is a product of my family's love and support. Daily phone calls and pep talks, regular discussions about the greater significance of my project, casual conversations over lunch, handwritten letters, and Zoom calls—these were the lifeblood of my academic process. My husband Christopher Coutin kept me smiling and laughing through the final years of writing and rewriting. He helped me realize that although this book is a part of me, I am more than this book. I wouldn't have made it across the finish line without his quiet strength, unwavering support, and inspiring work ethic or the humorous jingles he made up to bring levity to our daily lives. And from the start, my parents Sharon Rose Young and Walter Young have been there every step of the way, hand in hand, in this world and beyond. Their love for me is so strong, so powerful that I can feel it wherever I go. This book is as much theirs as it is mine.

Introduction: Food as Public Culture

ALL SUMMER LONG, Arthur James Robinson's 1988 brown-and-white Ford F-100 rumbled through the oak-lined streets of New Orleans at dawn. As tendrils of fog slowly evaporated with the rising sun, Robinson loaded up his truck with fruits and vegetables from wholesaler A. J.'s Produce and chatted with the proprietor and his staff. Robinson artfully arranged his bounty in his truck bed before setting off on his rounds, hawking the day's fresh fruits and vegetables across the French Quarter, Tremé, and Bywater neighborhoods, as well as the Lower 9th Ward and the Carrollton area.[1] This vast sales territory meant that his customer base was as diverse as the city itself, encompassing New Orleanians of different racial and ethnic backgrounds, and including everyone from economically disadvantaged to wealthy residents.

"I have oranges and bananas! I have eating pears and apples! I have cantaloupe! I have the mango! I have tangerine! I have collard greens! I have pineapples! I have mirlitons, sweet potatoes, orange potatoes!"[2] Robinson cried out his offerings using a CB radio microphone to amplify his voice so that it pierced through colorful wooden window shutters and thick walls to reach the inner sanctum of people's homes. When asked about his advertising strategy, he gave a matter-of-fact response: "I'm just telling people what I have. It comes out natural."[3] Yet Robinson's simple explanation belied the methods street vendors use to hone their cries into effective marketing tools.

Broadcasting his calls through the speakers gave them a gritty timbre, like the distortion caused by a megaphone at a rally or a sporting event. The *Times-Picayune* described his amplified voice as "thick" and "furry" and his cries as a "fuzzy squawk."[4] Robinson's voice became so well known that the average New Orleanian could easily imitate his iconic street cries, drawing out certain syllables to capture his vocal tone and singing style: "I have ooooranges and bananas! I have eeeeeating pears and apples!"[5]

In the early 2000s, before Hurricane Katrina, Robinson typically worked five to seven days a week, and during a good sales week, he could make around $500. There were many weeks when he made less. And the overhead costs of the business were steadily increasing. In previous years he spent ten dollars to fill up his gas tank, but in 2005 it was around twenty-five dollars. The rising costs of doing business did not deter him, though. He continued to expand his routes and grow his customer base to cover the increased overhead. Even after Katrina wreaked havoc on New Orleans, displacing so many people and destroying more than two hundred thousand homes, Robinson was eventually able to return to street food vending.

In post-Katrina New Orleans, Robinson's business grew as the city recovered. He gained customers along a new route through the Faubourg St. John, employing business tactics that had been used by generations of street vendors dating back to the colonial period. Those strategies were deeply tied to vendors' presence in the city streets and their ability to reach potential customers through creative street cries and mouthwatering visual displays. As Robinson rode along the new route, people came out of their houses to see who was selling fresh produce. He would tell them that he was going to come every day for the rest of that week so they would have a chance to get to know him not only as a vendor, but also as a person. Robinson understood that in the world of street food vending, relationships matter because the business model is predicated on cultivating and sustaining strong rapport with customers. As for how he built up his customer base, he explained, "Once people get to know you're coming, they'll be looking for you."[6] And he noted, "Once you start, you've got to keep it up," so he visited his new route almost every day.

Arthur Robinson's business acumen stemmed from generational knowledge, passed down from one family member to the next. He was born in New Orleans during World War II and grew up in St. Roch, a few neighborhoods downriver and a bit inland from the French Quarter. His father, Nathan Robinson, was also a street food vendor—but unlike his son, who used a truck, he had transported his fresh produce by wheelbarrow and horse and buggy.[7]

Arthur Robinson ultimately followed in his father's footsteps, like generations of street vendors before him, but he worked various jobs throughout his life before setting out to market his wares. He did everything from running a gas station to traveling with the Merchant Marine. In the 1990s, he began vending fruits and vegetables from a truck. He described his work, which had become increasingly known and celebrated in the city, in plain terms: "It's just an ordinary job. I'm just making a living, that's all." Certainly, that was how Robinson experienced the work. But he was also one of the last itinerant food vendors in the city, which made him and his business precious to his customers and to the broader community. As Robinson noted, "I'm about the only one that really goes around anymore," because "most all the old peddlers are dead now, just about." He went on to identify a few other peddlers still operating in the city, but as Robinson explained, "They don't go around the streets. I'm the only one that really goes around the streets."[8]

Robinson was simultaneously a food purveyor for local community members and part of the city's burgeoning food tourism economy post-Katrina. Robinson had "become as much a part of New Orleans' heritage as its architecture and music," according to Chris Bynum at the *Times-Picayune*.[9] He became a fixture of New Orleans Jazz Fest, the city's multiday music and culture festival.[10] He was such a well-known cultural figure that his face appeared on "Mr. Okra" T-shirts and other tourist trinkets. His street cries became so famous that they were featured on an audio keychain sold in places around the city, even next to the checkout line in the local grocery store.[11] With the press of a button, you could hear Mr. Okra's calls anywhere, anytime. Robinson also became the star character of a children's book, *Mr. Okra Sells Fresh Fruits and Vegetables*, and the singular subject of an award-winning documentary, *Mr. Okra*, which screened at film festivals including Sundance and Cannes, helping spread Robinson's story beyond the borders of the Crescent City.[12]

In homage to his larger-than-life persona, locals would dress up like Robinson.[13] During the 2014 Mardi Gras Season, community members created a Mr. Okra–themed group costume, featuring his brightly painted truck. Revelers in full-body produce costumes—a pea pod, a banana, and an orange—gathered around "Mr. Okra" and the replica of Robinson's truck, which had become as iconic as the man himself. By then, the old F-100's original paint job had been replaced with a spectrum of colors painted by New Orleans artist "Dr. Bob" Shaffer, featuring phrases like "Refresh yo'self," "Be Nice or Leave," and "Juiciest Fruits in the Hood."[14] Recognizing the group's tribute to a beloved public personality, many revelers stopped and took photos of the jovial Mardi Gras–goers, with some people even adding their own renditions of Mr. Okra's cries to the already raucous scene. Commenting on New Orleanians' feelings for Robinson, Josh Cohen, a local musician confirmed, "He was very loved. A lot of people who had never met him, just loved him."[15]

Robinson connected many New Orleanians back to a time when street vendors were more common, especially for the baby boomer generation that grew up in the 1950s and 1960s. That being said, the mid-century cohort was not nearly as robust as those of the nineteenth and early twentieth centuries, when the city relied heavily upon hundreds of street food and public market vendors for provisioning. For many boomers, Robinson's business reminded them of their childhoods, now seen through middle age's rose-colored glasses.

A documentary ripe with nostalgia, *New Orleans Food Memories*, opens with Robinson crying out, "I have okra, mustard greens, collard greens. I have spinach. I have broccoli. And I have oranges and bananas. I have New Orleans cucumbers."[16] In that initial scene, by the very virtue of his street-peddling trade, Robinson acts as the mechanism to draw viewers into the history and into the collective memory of the New Orleans community—a living time machine. And he could wield that power because street food had played such an important role in the city since its founding, although knowledge of that history has largely been lost to the broader public.

Robinson's ties to the community ran deeper than surface-level nostalgia. When his truck broke down in late 2009, people across the city banded together to raise funds for him to buy a new one so that he could continue operating his street-vending business. Several Bywater–based bands led the effort by hosting a benefit.[17] With their support, Robinson was able to resume his rounds once again in a Dr. Bob masterpiece truck, likely to the relief of customers who relied on him for access to fresh food, especially elderly people who did not have a car or easy access to a grocery store. As his daughter, Sergio Robinson, who worked alongside her father for years, observed, "For them, we're it. They need us."[18] A few years later, the community came to Robinson's aid again, raising over $12,000 through a GoFundMe campaign to help him pay his bills and make necessary repairs to his truck.[19]

When he died in 2018, many in the city and beyond mourned the loss, knowing that Robinson was one of the final strongholds for traditional street food vending in New Orleans. Brian Reaney—who supervised A. J.'s Produce where Robinson purchased his wares—told the *New York Times* that there "used to be a lot more peddlers like Okra.... I think he was the last of the neighborhood truck drivers."[20] In a Nola.com article, Ann Maloney confirmed the significance of losing Robinson, noting that many in the city called him "the last of the New Orleans street peddlers."[21]

What did it mean for New Orleans to lose its last street peddler? Who were the generations of vendors who came before Robinson and what role did they play in creating New Orleans' distinct food culture? How were their businesses connected to a broader network of urban food provisioning, and how did that system evolve over time to meet the needs of the city's ever-changing population? How and why did they compete for and use public space, including the city's streets and parks, to operate their businesses? For many, Robinson symbolized an earlier way of life, but he was also a product of, and participant in, a long history of the food culture and economy of New Orleans—a history that continues to shape the city to this day.

New Orleanians exercised agency and built community through the daily work of feeding the city. As Arthur Robinson's story demonstrates, that work was always about more than just sustenance. When vendors and their customers came together to buy and sell fresh products and prepared foods, they negotiated prices, discussed the quality of foodstuffs, and shared gossip and news. The regular exchange of food sat at the heart of community life in New Orleans, as it did in most cities that grew up around the trade of goods.

Throughout the nineteenth century and into the twentieth, street food businesses and public food markets played a crucial role in provisioning New Orleans. Between 1800 and 1950, the demographic makeup of street food and public market vendors shifted significantly. In the antebellum period, the majority of food vendors were enslaved women who sold goods on behalf of their enslavers both in the French Market—the city's central food retail space—and in the surrounding streets as itinerant vendors. Shopping on behalf of their enslavers, Black women also made up the majority of shoppers. The overarching cohort of vendors and shoppers was incredibly diverse, however, consisting of Indigenous people, migrants—voluntary and forced—from across Europe, Africa, the Caribbean, and around the world, as well as a growing number of Americans who moved to the city after the Louisiana Purchase of 1803. As European immigrants began arriving in large numbers in the 1830s and 1840s, especially from Germany and Ireland, they often found an economic toehold as food vendors because the trade had relatively low barriers to entry; this was especially the case among street vendors. Their immigration to New Orleans rapidly increased the city's population, making it the third largest city in the United States by 1840. In the decades leading up to the Civil War, New Orleans built more and more public markets to feed its growing urban population.

In the postbellum period, as the next generation took over their parents' businesses, American-born vendors' numbers grew. By 1880, they were joined by a large cohort of Italian immigrant vendors, who like the European immigrants who came before them, found footing in the city's food economy. As European immigrants and their descendants accrued wealth and property—capitalizing on the privileges their race afforded them—they dominated the city's public markets. The streets, however, remained a more egalitarian retail space where vendors of varied racial and ethnic backgrounds scrambled to make a living—that is, when they were able to work around the municipal laws enacted to control and stymie their businesses. Although Black New Orleanians were no longer the majority of public market vendors after the Civil War, they continued to have a strong presence as street food vendors and as shoppers, especially Black women who were employed in the domestic service industry.

Through the mid-twentieth century, the city's demographics and those of its food vendors and shoppers shifted in subtle ways, but the customer base of those vendors remained fairly consistent and reflected the ethnic and racial demographics of the city's population. Businesses housed within the public markets for the most part remained the domain of European immigrants and their descendants. The streets continued to provide opportunities, however challenging, to a motley group of itinerant vendors, including Black New Orleanians who worked to overcome the carefully erected structural barriers of the Jim Crow era meant to keep them and their businesses out of the public markets and on the margins of society in general.

Across the grand sweep of New Orleans' history, the preparation, sale, and consumption of food in the city streets and public markets played a central, yet often overlooked role in daily life. The construction of a public market symbolized the political and economic strength of existing communities and spurred the settlement and commercial development of new neighborhoods. The vast number of street food vendors sheds light on the barriers many small-scale food entrepreneurs faced to gain a coveted spot in one of those public markets, while at the same time highlighting their tenacity to carry on their businesses despite that lack of access. Vendors were considered a nuisance by some and essential to others. City officials listened to their constituents' needs and fought to create local laws that either curtailed or expanded opportunities for street vendors and other private food retailers operating outside of the municipal market facilities. Customers, above all, wanted affordable and safe food for their families and demanded the improvement of all food retail spaces, but reality regularly fell short of their high standards. Often at odds as they sought to create a food economy and culture that met their needs, the overt power plays and subversive behavior among vendors, their customers, and city officials shaped the trajectory of New Orleans in surprising ways. These people, the connections they forged among one another, and the goods they sold, consumed, and regulated, make up New Orleans' "nourishing networks."

Vendors and their customers—many of whom were otherwise politically marginalized because of their race, gender, ethnicity, socioeconomic status, and other identity and demographic factors—exercised considerable influence over the local food economy and the local laws that regulated it: negotiating prices, creating sites of distribution, shaping taste preferences, conducting research to inform policy, advocating for their businesses and personal interests, and openly defying ordinances they felt were unfair. This is a story of how power operates in unexpected and often overlooked ways through the networks of exchange that feed a city.

New Orleans vendors sold fresh and prepared foods, produce grown in urban garden plots or surrounding farmlands, and goods procured through foraging, fishing, hunting, and trapping. Theirs was a physically demanding trade, as were most in the food industry. Despite the bone-deep exhaustion and oppression that could define their occupation, growers and food vendors exercised remarkable creativity and ingenuity amid the harsh daily grind of their professions. They also cultivated power in the ways that they could, both subtle and profound. They were key players in the creation of one of the most iconic regional food cultures in the United States: Creole cuisine, which finds its origins as much in the city streets and marketplaces as it does in homes and restaurants.

Historically and through the present day, vendors sold wares in foot-traffic-heavy areas. Some gathered along riverfronts or streets, dispersing their displays along thoroughfares. Some gathered and created a center of commerce, or a market. In these often-crowded arenas of urban life, competition was fierce among vendors as they sought to capture the attention of passersby and cultivate customer loyalty. Their ability to make a sale and potentially incentivize a customer to return the next day could make or break their businesses. Perhaps nowhere more concentrated and fast-paced were these interactions than in New Orleans' public markets.

Public (or municipal) markets were the structures built for the use and benefit of the local population and were accessible to a community's diverse population. Public market structures often contained stalls or counters that vendors rented to sell their wares; some were pavilion-like structures, with screens and dividers, whereas others were enclosed buildings with solid walls. The activities of the public market often spilled out into the surrounding streets as vendors set up their displays not only within the market structure, but on the neighboring sidewalks and roads as well. These structures were not unique to the nineteenth century, but stem from a centuries-old tradition of public markets, often seen in Europe and European colonies.

What is unique, however, is the number of municipal markets in New Orleans and how long the city government operated them. By 1911, New Orleans had thirty public markets, more than any other city in the country. And by that time, most other major cities like New York and Philadelphia had opted to privatize their public markets, handing control over to private enterprise. For those cities that still operated public markets at the turn of the twentieth century, most had only one or two facilities. New Orleans' extensive public market system, therefore, was distinctive in the United States. Many neighborhoods developed around the facilities, spurring residential settlement and the opening of other businesses. In other words, the public markets were the seeds from which many of New Orleans' characteristic neighborhoods grew, and their history provides insights into how food retail spaces can kickstart and sustain the development of communities.

But stepping outside of the pavilions that defined the boundaries of the public markets did not remove marketgoers or vendors from the stream of commerce and food that sustained New Orleans. Beyond the markets, the city's thoroughfares teemed with street vendors selling their goods to passersby. Some displayed wares on the ground, in baskets, in makeshift stands, or under awnings; others were more mobile, carrying goods on their heads, in their arms, or transporting them by cart or vehicle. In many cases, street food vendors did not have access to the public markets or private shops because of structural barriers that made it difficult or impossible for people of color, women, recent migrants, and others from historically marginalized groups to obtain a stall in the public market or to rent or purchase private land. They had to vend in the streets, competing for and making claims upon public space to operate their businesses, because they had no other option.

Not until relatively recently have scholars begun to examine the lived experiences of vendors who sold goods in the streets or along waterfronts in the United States. And most scholars have not treated street vending as an integral and interconnected industry in local food economies but as distinct from the business practices of people vending in public markets or operating a store or shop. That treatment is, in many ways, a reflection of the available sources and records. Because public markets across the country were a source of income for local governments and entrepreneurs through rental fees and leases, a historical record exists that provides a glimpse into their past. Related materials also included city council minutes, reports from city engineers, construction and repair budgets, architectural plans, and annual profit records, among other written sources.

Unlike vendors in the public markets, however, there is little representation of nineteenth-century street vendors in the archival record. In cities with a strong bureaucratic presence and a commitment to regulating less formalized economy, there might be records of street vendor licenses as well as local laws regulating vendors' business practices. Additionally, some street vendors appeared in local courts and gave testimony including details about their personal lives that may still be housed in judicial archives. Most descriptions of street vendors, however, are found in manuscript diaries, correspondence, published travelogues, visual media, and literature that were written primarily by white authors and thus reflect a white (and often condescending and voyeuristic) perspective.

The limited representation of street vendors in the archival record can give the false impression that they were somehow not important to the development and sustainability of cities like New Orleans. Quite the opposite is true. In fact, the street is not merely a thoroughfare, but an arena in which vendors establish and carry out their businesses. The street is a market: a multidimensional space of exchange that extends throughout the city like a great cardiovascular system, keeping the city alive.

Nourishing Networks studies the exchange of food in New Orleans' municipal markets and their surrounding streets together, treating them as interconnected entities within a single local food economy and culture, defined as "the public food culture." Vendors in and outside of the municipal markets are powerful agents in the creation of food culture, specifically that which took place in public spaces—to which all people had access (as opposed to privately owned shops).[22] Street markets and public markets are examples of such public spaces where the movement of vendors and customers created the daily rhythms of urban life among a multifaceted urban populace.

Using the lens of food, we can see how otherwise marginalized groups exercised power over public culture. Although in theory public spaces were meant for everyone, they were not truly accessible to everyone. People competed with one another to access and to prevent access to public spaces, including city streets and municipal markets. Property owners, many of whom were white men, attempted to control and eliminate food vendors' businesses when they saw them as a threat to their own entrepreneurial endeavors. Some of these property owners lobbied for laws that would limit food vendors' access to public space, the kinds of food they sold, or at what times they were able to sell. Vendors thwarted their efforts through formal and informal channels. At times, vendors garnered support and tailored local laws to meet their needs. Other times, when formal channels were closed to them or said tactics proved unsuccessful, they skirted the law or outright broke it in order to keep their businesses going.

Tensions surrounding the public culture of food between elites and the rest of urban society reflect an ongoing battle for control over the city streets. Throughout the nineteenth and into the twentieth century, the legally disenfranchised—those without access to private property and the right to vote—shaped the public culture of food to their advantage in ways that thwarted the efforts of traditionally empowered people. In turn, those with access to the legal sphere sought to use local law and policing to control vendors' and customers' actions. All parties exercised power in meaningful ways through the first half of the twentieth century.

By the mid-twentieth century, however, New Orleans' nourishing networks began breaking down, and by 1950 the last of the city's once-numerous public food markets had closed. But it was not only public but also private entitles that stopped investing in urban food retail options, especially in economically disadvantaged neighborhoods. These communities were the hardest hit by the loss of many of the city's nourishing networks. In the second half of the twentieth century, they have become what are known as "food deserts"—areas that have limited access to food retail options, especially those businesses purveying affordable, fresh, nutrient-dense, and culturally meaningful foods. Yet even as food access became increasingly dire at the end of the twentieth century, new iterations of the city's historic public food culture emerged. They have not been so robust or inclusive as to revive New Orleans' nourishing networks completely, or even significantly, but they provide a glimmer of hope that by looking to the past, we might find a means to co-create a better food future.

The Growth of New Orleans' Public Food Culture, 1800–1850

FOR YEARS, CATHERINE had hawked foodstuffs on steamboats on behalf of her enslaver. A forty-year-old bondswoman, she was one of a cohort of enslaved Black vendors who were the principal food retailers in antebellum New Orleans. Her working relationships, perhaps even friendships, with steamboat operators secured her a prime spot for her itinerant business. When not on a steamboat, she circulated the city streets—likely near the port or the city's central French Market—to take advantage of high foot traffic areas. There, her business savvy shone as she made sales to passersby, regulars, and first-time customers alike. She became "well known in the city"—a recognizable figure of New Orleans' public food culture according to a published notice in the local newspaper.[1]

With this recognition came her gradual march to purchasing her own freedom. As was common in New Orleans for enslaved food vendors, Catherine was likely able to keep a portion of the profits she made, but a majority of those profits would have gone to her enslaver, at that time a free woman of color named Mlle. Belle.[2] Yet accruing the necessary funds to buy her freedom was a painfully slow process, one that could take decades and might never come to fruition, and so Catherine decided on another path: escape.[3]

On the morning of November 30, 1843, Catherine, as she would on any other day, donned a light blue print dress and a yellow striped apron, and wrapped a green and yellow handkerchief around her head. To keep off the autumn chill, she cloaked herself in a red shawl. At noon that day, she left the house of P. Reynaud on Tchoupitoulas Street and never returned—sustaining herself in the months that followed with funds earned from thousands of sales over years. She deployed her trade networks, including her knowledge of steamboats, to navigate the treacherous and uncertain path to freedom.

Those very same steamboats provided a haven for an escaped man named Wilson who, like Catherine, had worked as a food vendor and had been seen

on the vessels since running for his freedom the year prior.[4] Perhaps he supported himself by vending on those steamboats as Catherine had done before
her own emancipation, using the skills he cultivated as a retailer at one of the
city's public markets. Perhaps the two of them had even encountered each
other, exchanging words of advice, or sharing precious foodstuffs on their
shared route to freedom.[5] Their possible encounters would have been lost
amid the swirl of activity that defined the riverfront where, as the *Daily
Picayune* described it, "The fruit and book vendors, with their baskets, pass
hurriedly from boat to boat."[6] The frenetic movement of the waterfront
worked like a cloaking mechanism for those seeking anonymity, especially
those running for their freedom.

Many aspects of Catherine's and Wilson's lived experiences remain
unknowable because the archival record so often omits the stories of Black
food vendors. Rarely can one find first-person narratives created by the
people who were at the core of New Orleans' antebellum food-provisioning
system. What we do have access to, though, are the local laws that regulated their trade; the observations of their businesses made by visitors to
the city; published notices describing their skillsets, sometimes referred to
as "runaway slave advertisements"; as well as memories of previously
enslaved people, in the form of transcribed interviews recorded decades
after federal emancipation. Together, these sources provide a crude collage
by which to understand the history of New Orleans' food culture and
economy—often creating a slightly distorted and disjointed picture of the
past, but an important one, nonetheless. For threading through that patchwork lay the city's nourishing networks, created and sustained by a diverse
cohort of food vendors like Catherine, Wilson, and countless others from
throughout the Atlantic world.

The development of street food culture in antebellum New Orleans exemplifies the ways that disenfranchised groups, seemingly against all logic, integrated into the city's commercial core—and how their desires to realize full
citizenship through food entrepreneurship clashed with many city officials'
and some residents' views about who should enjoy social, economic, and
political power.

After the Louisiana Purchase in 1803, New Orleans' economy and population grew rapidly under American governance.[7] What was once a remote city
on the outskirts of European empire quickly became one of the busiest ports
in the world and a center for the export of agricultural goods. With city elites
focused on international and national trade, the business of feeding the
city—of distributing fresh food for everyday consumption—became the

domain of the disenfranchised: a racially and ethnically diverse population of Atlantic world migrants, free and enslaved.

Through their businesses, these entrepreneurs made themselves indispensable figures in New Orleans' food economy. Because many vendors were people of color, women, and recent migrants, they were subject to major structural inequalities and discrimination. Yet they developed ways to work around those barriers and integrate themselves into New Orleans' public food culture and, ultimately, shape it to their advantage. In doing so, they developed relationships and even exercised power over customers from a variety of racial and socioeconomic backgrounds. Some customers respected vendors' entrepreneurial efforts. Others derided them, not liking that they were beholden to people whose social and economic status was supposed to be limited within New Orleans' slave society.

Throughout the eighteenth century, early encounters and experimentation among Atlantic world peoples—Native Americans, Africans, and Europeans, among them—created a distinct public culture through food.[8] Regarding street food, these groups exercised considerable agency on the periphery of European empire, regularly depending on one another in ways that contradict traditional understandings of colonial power. Distance from colonial oversight and regulation created spaces in which the exchange and distribution of foods was spontaneous and often inclusive, involving both free and enslaved people. These interactions took place in informal spaces along bayous and rivers—the waterways and pathways along which people, goods, and cultures moved throughout the lower Mississippi Delta. During this period, Europeans reluctantly came to depend on Indigenous communities and people of color, free and enslaved, to survive the harsh conditions of colonial Louisiana. They appropriated the environmental and agricultural knowledge of these groups to survive. In turn, Indigenous and Black vendors became key players in the local food economy, exercising notable power within that realm through their role as food purveyors.

In order to capitalize on Europeans settlers' dependence on their food supplies, Indigenous groups, such as the Acolapissas, Chitimachas, and Houmas, moved from the Louisiana interior to burgeoning riverfront settlements such as New Orleans in the 1720s.[9] They were important figures at the informal market that developed along the levee in front of New Orleans' central square, or Place d'Armes, where trading took place. In the early colonial period, they supplied New Orleanians with staple foods such as corn and wild game in exchange for imported European goods such as axes, knives, kettles, mirrors, scissors, awls, needles, and clothing.[10] Their exchanges along the levee created a meeting space for the residents of New Orleans and its surrounding environs, drawing people together through the daily act of provisioning the city.

Enslaved Africans, forcibly brought to Louisiana by European colonists, largely relied on their own cultivation, hunting, and gathering skills to survive, providing them with a sense of agency through food procurement within the unjust hierarchy of New Orleans' slave society. Out of necessity, enslavers granted some freedoms to enslaved people because their plantations were generally not profitable enough to supply substantial provisions to their labor force. The same thing had happened in the 1720s and 1730s, when setbacks to Louisiana's nascent tobacco industry caused planters to scramble to cut costs. Some enslavers demanded that enslaved people plant gardens, assigning them plots of land to cultivate to sustain themselves. In turn, bondspeople tended to these gardens, raised domesticated fowl, wove baskets, made pottery, and sold surplus crops and craft goods at the levee market. Local laws pertaining to enslaved persons, the Code Noir, protected their right to earn income with their enslaver's permission on paper, although it was not always honored in practice. Some bondspeople moved with relative freedom between the plantation, hunting grounds, and the city center, and were not required to carry a pass to do so until 1751. This mobility and limited freedom from enslavers' direct oversight provided opportunities for bondspeople to engage in New Orleans' local food economy on their own terms without upsetting the overarching power dynamics of slave society.[11]

The knowledge, skills, and entrepreneurship of Indigenous and Black vendors contributed to the remarkably varied offerings of the market—an array of foodstuffs that European settlers marveled at in their writings. Marie-Madeleine Hachard, a member of the Ursuline Convent in New Orleans, for example, wrote of the abundance of game and fresh produce available in the city. She praised many fish unknown in France as well as a variety of fruits like pineapples and watermelons, and many others that she could not identify by name.[12] In the French colonial period, the exchange of these foodstuffs was relatively dispersed, although there was some regulation in the form of price setting for wild game and certain crops; otherwise, the French colonial government expected customers to independently assess the quality of foodstuffs for sale and barter with vendors to determine a reasonable price. Under Spanish colonial rule, however, regulations on provisioning increased as local officials centralized food exchange within a municipal market to protect the interests of customers.

Known for its strong regulatory presence throughout its empire, the Spanish colonial administration sought to impose order on colonial communities by regulating local commerce. It did so in the name of providing city residents with safe, affordable food. Regulation in the name of the "public good," however, had consequences for the existing public food culture and economy that had developed under French rule—one in which vendors exercised considerable mobility and freedom to sell when and where they liked. Spanish colonial officials, by contrast, almost immediately created laws after assuming power in 1769 that concentrated vending in the city center and also placed limits on when and to whom vendors could sell their wares. Major consequences of the laws were not only that local officials had greater oversight of the local economy, but also that city residents gathered in greater numbers and therefore had more opportunity to interact and build social bonds through economic exchange.

Through a series of laws passed in 1770, the Cabildo (the city council) created the first municipally regulated open-air market in New Orleans. The Cabildo began by addressing the somewhat sprawling nature of local trade in New Orleans, which took place at different points along the Mississippi River and surrounding bayous. One law made it illegal for city residents to travel up and down the river to buy provisions. They instead had to purchase wares at the river levee at the foot of the Place d'Armes (modern-day Jackson Square).[13] After this law's enactment, sales took place within plain sight of the administrative building of the Cabildo, which sat opposite the central plaza from the levee. As vendors entreated passersby to purchase their wares, the Cabildo offices were never out of view. The looming presence of the building foreshadowed local officials' growing oversight over daily provisioning in the coming years.[14]

That oversight reflected a deeply held belief in a moral economy, brought from Europe, defined by the practice of local governments regulating local economies for the benefit and well-being of residents.[15] One such law that mirrors this mentality required vendors to sell directly to customers for a period of four hours each day before they could sell their products wholesale to retailers, ensuring that residents had access to food during times of scarcity.[16] Embedded in this law is a distrust of vendors to do right by city residents—a fundamental concern that permeated New Orleans' market culture in its infancy and almost immediately placed the interests of vendors and customers in opposition. Like the French colonial authorities, the Cabildo also monitored the price of certain goods. Yet bartering between vendors and customers was the primary method of setting prices, at times furthering the tensions between the two parties.

To ensure that vendors and customers complied with these new rules, within a month of establishing the levee market, the Cabildo appointed two commissioners to regulate food provisioning in the city.[17] Their appointment enabled the city government to monitor the daily sale and distribution of food more closely. Also at this time, the attorney general recommended that the city purchase a set of scales and measures to periodically check the accuracy of the set used at the market.[18] These antifraud protections likely reflected some underlying suspicions about vendor practices; they also protected against potentially dangerous adulterated foods made to weigh more through additives.

Municipal oversight of market activities was funded through various means—vendor licenses for one, but also taxes derived from the sale of food and beverage items. Prior to the creation of the levee market, New Orleans official Alejandro O'Reilly created an annual tax of $40 on taverns and coffeehouses; $370 on butchers; and $1 on every barrel of brandy imported into the city. The tax on butchers cemented a practice of taxing food artisans to fund city projects. Within a few years, those butchers would be legally bound to conduct their businesses within the municipally regulated markets, no longer able to operate independent shops. These kinds of taxes were crucial in funding the local government's efforts to regulate food distribution and to its future efforts to create market buildings.[19]

It was not until 1779 that the city government decided to build a covered market at the levee where open-air provisioning had long taken place. The structure was basic: a wooden pavilion (sixty feet by twenty-two feet) about the size of a tennis court. It was designed to provide shelter from inclement weather, but its impact was far more significant. It physically demarcated who had and who did not have access to municipal facilities. Those vending within the pavilion enjoyed safety from harsh sunlight and violent rain and wind; those on the outside did not. The municipal government intended the market to function primarily as a meat market, although other products could be sold there. Many vendors, therefore, were butchers—a group consisting mainly of white men with recognized skill in an artisan trade.[20]

It is likely that the butchers lobbied for the construction of the levee market pavilion, a long colonnaded structure, demonstrating the active role that vendors could take in shaping the local food economy to meet their needs. In fact, the butchers had already successfully lobbied the Cabildo to construct a public meat market located in a different part of the city.[21] With the construction of the original meat market in 1770 and then the levee market in 1779, the butchers cemented their status as a privileged group of vendors; they continued to successfully lobby for greater investment in market facilities, further strengthening their influence over the local food economy. In 1782, the Cabildo replaced the original levee pavilion with a sturdier one. Women and people of color, however, did not have the same legal access to advocate for their needs. The levee market, then, became a physical manifestation of the legal marginalization of these vendors who were largely excluded from selling within the pavilion. Its robust wooden columns made visible the invisible barriers that barred many vendors from accessing a coveted spot within.

Although the butchers had successfully lobbied for access to better market facilities, the Cabildo maintained a healthy suspicion of vendors in and outside of the levee market. City officials continued to worry about peddlers who exploited city residents by selling at exorbitant prices or hawking adulterated goods, especially those who vended not at the levee market, but along waterways and pathways outside of the direct oversight of the market commissioners. They were all too aware of what a government record called "the great abuses committed in the sales of provisions" along the Mississippi and argued that a larger central market "would result in untold good to the public."[22] In 1784, the Cabildo chartered the construction of a second market that was large enough to house all the vendors, including the ones currently along the levee, so that city officials could inspect the quality and pricing of the fresh produce, meat, fish, and game that they sold.[23] Four years later, the levee market burned down, leaving New Orleans' 5,388 residents without a central market for several years.[24]

In 1791, the Cabildo constructed a new market where the French Market stands today. Over the next twenty years, the city remodeled and rebuilt the market several times. Additions were also made to what became known as the French Market "complex." Complex is an appropriate descriptor for the French Market because the municipal government expanded the retail space over time. Between 1798 and 1800, the Cabildo approved and constructed the Fish Market within the complex.[25] The complex eventually encompassed five separate markets: meat, fruit, vegetable, fish, and bazaar.

Between 1801 and 1803, New Orleans came under the jurisdiction of France once again. However, Napoleon Bonaparte sold the territory of Louisiana in 1803, and the French colony fell into the hands of yet another foreign power: the United States. Throughout these tumultuous years, the local food economy remained a centralizing force within New Orleans, consistently gathering the population together. That the city was now a part of the United States did not dampen the particularly strong sense of French and Spanish Atlantic culture that had marked New Orleans from its founding, nor did it stymie the important role that Indigenous and Black vendors played in the local economy.

As in the colonial period, the French Market remained a magnet for the city's population in the early antebellum period, in part due to local law. Legal codes mandated that city residents buy regulated food products in the municipal market and at specific times (usually in the morning) to prevent vendors from selling spoiled product to customers as the day wore on in an era before modern refrigeration; these early operating hours were seen across the country, including in major cities such as New York.[26] Regulated products included butchered meat like beef, veal, mutton, and pork. According to an ordinance passed by the New Orleans City Council in 1828, "The butchers' market shall open at the break of day, and will close at noon from the first of April to the first of November, and close at one of the clock in the afternoon, the remaining part of the year." The ordinance continues: "All persons who shall sell or cause to be sold the meats in the said market before ten of the clock in the morning shall pay for each offense, twenty-five dollars," meaning that, although the market was open sunrise to noon, the sale of meat was permissible only for two to three hours depending on the time of year.[27] These time constraints gave butchers several hours each morning to prepare for their customers, breaking down carcasses into different cuts of meat. That way, all butchers would have a reasonable amount of time to ready their stalls, with no one butcher gaining advantage over another by starting to sell product to customers at sunrise. Similarly, no one customer would gain advantage over another by accessing choice product before ten o'clock in the morning.

Although market laws like this one were written with the intent to protect vendors' and customers' interests, there was an unintended consequence: the creation of ritualized habits. For a few hours each morning, customers gathered to purchase wares. This legally enforced rhythm contributed to the market's role as a central shopping district and as a community meeting ground. Informal run-ins and social interaction between city residents within the formal realm of municipal regulation (i.e., the market) were the lifeblood of New Orleans' local community—a community forged through the act of daily food procurement.

It should be noted that in New Orleans, food shopping, or "making groceries" in local parlance, usually meant a morning trip to the public market, but also to the grocery store, the latter legally only able to sell dry goods. Grocers' wares included edibles like sugar, flour, and alcohol, but also clothing, soaps, and household tools. Their businesses were part of a broader network of provisioning in New Orleans, running adjacent to the enterprises of public market and street food vendors.

There were some stands designated for grocers within the French Market, bringing their dry goods trade into close proximity to the sale of perishables. Still, local officials gave preferential treatment to vendors of fresh food. In 1834, local officials restricted the presence of grocers to the vegetable market and required that they immediately vacate their stalls should a vegetable retailer need the space.[28] Vying for prime real estate in the covered market, vegetable vendors appear to have lobbied local lawmakers to further restrict grocers' access to stands; the next year, an ordinance passed confining grocers to the row of stalls next to Levee Street, presumably a less favorable location.[29] For many grocers, operating outside of the public market system was a more appealing option with greater flexibility and more autonomy.[30]

Because of the previously mentioned local law, market vendors operated their businesses during the prime hours of the early morning when climes were cooler and fresh foods spoiled less quickly. Those who did not have access to the market's shelter clustered nearby, seeking to catch the eye of passersby en route to the French Market. At times, the number of vendors in and around the market was almost overwhelming. Travel writer and journalist Anne Newport Royall, who visited New Orleans in the 1820s, noted how vendors' displays spilled out into the surrounding streets: "Besides several rows of benches, the floor and the outsides of the market are strewed so thick with vegetables and bowls of beans, as to render it difficult to walk through them."[31]

Products for sale in the French Market and along the neighboring levee could vary wildly, from onions to exotic creatures. The de Sale family, who were free people of color living south of Baton Rouge, raised pelicans that they sold at market in New Orleans, as recalled by their daughter decades later.[32] But pelicans were a relatively mundane animal compared to the ones Henry C. Knight observed on his 1824 trip to New Orleans, which were likely sold as pets: "Along the levee, hang cages of canary, and mocking birds, for sale. Here may you see the little Congoese parrots, not bigger than sparrows, of a fine shape, with their gaudy, but beautiful plumage. I saw here a China macaw, larger than a pheasant, with twelve inches of sweeping tail features, and a superb vivid plumage of red, yellow, green, blue, and their shades."[33]

Knight also marveled at the variety of foodstuff along the levee: "Here you see huge bulging octagonal pitchers, that would contain half a barrel of punch....At short intervals, you pass domes and pyramids of the largest, and most luscious melons." For him, the levee was a "novelty" and a bustling place that caught his attention as vendors and their customers conducted business.[34]

Under the eaves of the French Market itself, the products available were equally diverse and visually appealing. On a visit to the market in April 1828, Captain Basil Hall marveled at the agricultural abundance he encountered, which included cabbages, peas, beets, artichokes, beans, radishes, potatoes, tomatoes, corn, ginger, blackberries, oranges, bananas, apples, and fresh flowers like roses and violets. Behind every column and from one vendor stall to the next, the market scene unfurling around him assaulted his senses. In addition to the fresh produce, he made note of the game birds, hung three by the leg, as well as the salted fish and bottled beer available for sale—a seemingly endless array of gustatory delights.[35]

Vendors were as varied as the products available for sale in the French Market and its surrounding streets. James Stuart remarked upon that diversity: "Negroes, Mulattos, French, Spaniards, Germans, and Americans are all crying their several articles in their peculiar languages." European men—especially those from the Gascony region of France—and their descendants continued to dominate the butcher stands and were often among the wealthiest market vendors.[36] Working-class whites from throughout the Atlantic world sold fresh food at the French Market and surrounding streets as well, some of whom were able to accrue a modicum of wealth and open their own storefronts and restaurants. Indigenous peddlers also hawked herbs and spices and other goods from surrounding hinterlands, which they artfully displayed in baskets. Most vendors, however, were enslaved Black women. Stuart, too, took note of their presence, observing how women of color could be seen "carrying baskets of bread, and every thing on their head."[37]

Black women vendors in New Orleans drew upon economic tradition of West Africa, shaping the local food economy to mirror familiar ancestral customs. In West African cities, women held primary positions of small- and large-scale trade, dealing in such commodities as cloth, salt, gold, and enslaved people.[38] Women merchants with substantial businesses understood and shaped the dynamics of long-distance trade, while small-scale market vendors specialized in local food economies.[39] Black women in New Orleans engaged this ancestral economic knowledge to build up their businesses and inhabit their roles as key players in the local food scene, inside and outside of the public markets.

To sell their wares, vendors had to obtain a license from the city government, just as they did in the colonial period.[40] Enslavers purchased these licenses for the bondspeople they tasked with selling surplus produce and artisan goods.[41] License sales provided the city with necessary funds to maintain public amenities like the French Market complex and also to retain a workforce to monitor the sale and distribution of food for the public good. The implications of licenses for bondspeople's agency were significant, rendering them beholden to the economic support of enslavers who could more easily afford to purchase the licenses. The exception was Sundays and holidays, when bondspeople could sell fresh food from their gardens without a license.[42]

In the early antebellum period, the rate for licenses changed over time, but it hovered around one dollar per quarter within the calendar year.[43] Taxes played a large role in preventing economically marginalized communities from legally participating in the local food economy. In the 1830s and 1840s, the annual tax to vend wares was approximately forty dollars per year, or ten dollars per quarter. Many working poor could not afford to purchase licenses or pay taxes. There were some exceptions to the licensing requirements, however, creating space for certain marginalized groups to vend their wares. Indigenous vendors, for example, were legally able to sell their products without a license any day of the week; their trade, however, was restricted to the streets surrounding the Vegetable Market.[44] And enslaved people could sell wares without a license on Sundays and holidays, which removed an economic barrier and assisted enslaved people in operating their businesses legally.

There was some flexibility within local laws to distribute free licenses to certain people after they submitted a petition to the city council. In January 1832, for example, the local government made an exception for thirty-six vendors, stating that the listed persons "are and remain granted" thirty dollars "for the purpose of helping them pay peddlers' licenses."[45] Of the thirty-six people listed, sixteen appear to be women bearing first names commonly given to women at the time: Catherine, Antoinette, Emilie, Maria, and so on. Four of the listed people—Belmont, Rosalie, Thiat, and Pigeon—are identified only by their first names, which may indicate that they were enslaved or a free person of color. That same year, the city council extended or renewed free licenses for some of them.[46] Vendors with those licenses were at the mercy of the local government and had to wait to see if their licenses would be renewed. This situation destabilized their businesses as officials could easily revoke or defund their licenses.

Interestingly, there were exceptions built into the local law that enabled vendors to sell certain wares, such as prepared foods, without a license. Those prepared foods included baked goods and sweets, fruit in baskets, and domestic beers.[47] Black vendors typically carried these wares, including iconic treats like calas (sugary rice fritters) and pralines (pecan candies).[48] The exception made in the licensing ordinance enabled enslaved people and the working poor to occupy a space in the local food economy while still restricting their ability to sell most food, thereby protecting the interests of stall-keepers at the French Market. The provision may have been included in the law because those vendors, regardless of their ability to purchase a license, were integral to the local food culture and economy.

In this vein, the exception may have been made to recognize these vendors' contributions and indispensability—an acquiescence of sorts made by the municipal government acknowledging the importance of local food traditions and Black vendors' dominance in the prepared food and beverage market. Just as they do today, customers valued quality and likely wanted to be able to purchase piping hot calas from a vendor who knew how to make them well. The fritters, roughly the size of a golf ball, were made from a batter consisting of day-old rice, flour, milk, eggs, sugar, and aromatic spices such as cinnamon. After the batter had risen overnight, it became slightly fermented and sour tasting; it had a flavor profile similar to fermented beverages and porridges popular in Africa, such as buttermilk-like *lar* and *tchiakri* of Senegambia, and sourdough breads prevalent in Europe.[49] By the early nineteenth century, calas had become a much-beloved street food in New Orleans. The most skilled calas vendors at that time were Black women who had perfected their recipes through years of informal apprenticeship and experience.

The legal exception for prepared foods came with stipulations that limited the mobility of Black vendors. The law afforded vendors of prepared foods, fresh fruits, and domestic beer a financial break, yes, but it also restricted their ability to vend those specific foods to the river levee—the location of some of the earliest, informal markets in New Orleans. The implication of the law is that it contained the entrepreneurism of these Black vendors to a particular place, legally and physically separating their economic transactions from the ones occurring in the French Market.

Despite the redistribution of power, the French Market was a key center of business and community for Black people, free and enslaved. Within the market, they gathered in large numbers to engage in trade that was also deeply social.[50] Basil Hall, a visitor like Royall and Stuart, quickly recognized the central role that Black women played. During a trip in 1828, he observed that at "every second or third pillar sat one or more black women, chattering in French, selling coffee and chocolate." In addition to those wares, they sold curry with "smoking dishes of rice, white as snow," which Hall came to realize was Louisiana's iconic soupy stew, gumbo.[51] Royall, too, observed the tight-knit Black community in the French Market. She remarked upon the cease-less conversations among Black women, speaking in French or Creole, exchanging news, gossip, and all manner of information.[52] In this way, selling goods at the French Market became a means through which Black women could resist the social isolation of slavery.

So vibrant and public were the interactions among Black women in the French Market that Ellen Call Long, the daughter of a white Floridian politi-cian, described how they were "laughing and chatting, and apparently as free as the customer who ordered his omelet or fruit." In and outside of the mar-ket, she made note of the bondswomen selling "beer, cakes and fruit at street corners, or with baskets of fancy goods which they carried to the houses of patrons." In Long's estimation of this cohort of enslaved retailers, "a more free, frolicking set of creatures I never saw—slavery at least with them had little significance." She went on to amend her statement, acknowledging that bondswomen were responsible for selling goods on behalf of their enslavers and that their enterprises were not wholly their own.[53] Long's romanticized depiction of enslaved vendors is deeply problematic, as it glosses over the trauma of slavery and the freedom denied these women on a daily basis. Reading against the grain, though, we glimpse the strong social bonds that Black women forged with each other and the relationships they developed with their customers. These are some of the nourishing networks that under-girded the city's evolving food economy; they were strong enough that white visitors like Long, Hall, and Royall felt compelled to share them with their readers.

It was not just in New Orleans where Black women found community in the marketplace. In mid-eighteenth-century Charleston, a robust cohort of Black women, possibly numbering several hundred, built businesses and fostered social relationships within the city's public market. They did so often to the annoyance and dismay of white residents.[54] So, too, was this the case in Manhattan, where the Catherine Market served as stage for dance performances among enslaved and free people of color, attracting perform-ers and audiences from the urban core and rural surrounding. In this sense, Catherine Market was not only a central node through which food passed, but also a venue for collective cultural expression among Black community members.[55]

Although they were multidimensional spaces, marketplaces were economic centers at their core and created opportunities for some enslaved people to gain a modicum of economic independence. In New Orleans, enslaved
vendors, in many cases, were able to keep part or all the profits they accrued
from their food-vending businesses—a precedent set in the colonial period
and a reflection of enslavers' views of food vending as a skilled form of labor.
This practice was not unique to the Crescent City; it extended throughout
Louisiana and across other slaveholding regions. In their effort to capture
antebellum history and culture on the page, staff members of the Federal
Writers' Project (FWP) interviewed previously enslaved people and recorded
stories and other folklore in the late 1930s and early 1940s as part of a larger
federal documentation project that is collectively known as the WPA Slave
Narratives.

One such story, as told by Pierre Aucuin and transcribed by FWP staff
members, shares Aucuin's experiences on Madewood Plantation, near
Napoleonville, Louisiana. Although Aucuin did not mention food vending
specifically, he did mention how his enslaver, Victor Aucuin, granted enslaved
laborers a plot of land to cultivate foodstuffs. Victor Aucuin also permitted
"skill workers," or artisans, to keep part of their earnings for themselves.[56] Perhaps
some of the enslaved people who maintained their own gardens on Madewood
Plantation harvested surplus fruits and vegetables to peddle on neighboring
plantations or in nearby towns. As Catherine Cornelius recalled of her enslavement on Smithfield Plantation near Baton Rouge, she and her family had some
time to pursue their own tasks and also some mobility to visit other plantations.
At 103 years old, she remembered with striking clarity, "We had Saturday and
Sunday off, but we had to go to church. Saturday was de day we did our washing,
sewin', and cleaning up de house; dat was de day for ourselves. We all had certain
tasks to do. If we finished dem ahead of time, de rest of de day was ours." She
remembered, "visitin' among ourselves and on other plantations."[57] Perhaps on
those visits enslaved gardeners hawked their wares and accumulated some
money or possibly bartered for other essential goods.

Across slaveholding states, the nature of bondspeople's food businesses
varied; some were side hustles that brought in little money, and some were
larger than that. In an interview with the FWP in 1937, Willis Cozart, then
ninety-two years old, recalled how he and his North Carolina–based family
maintained a small garden in the antebellum period. Still, the only way for
them to make money was "pickin' berries an' sellin' 'em." Their vending was
sporadic. Cozart explained, "We ain't had much time to do dat, case we
wucked from sunup till sundown six days a week."[58]

In Georgia, Henry Wright's family was able to maintain a garden for their own sustenance and to sell product for a profit, if time permitted. In an FWP interview he gave when ninety-nine years old, Wright recalled that enslaved people could either sell their surplus product in town or directly to their enslaver, Mr. House. Sometimes, House would sell produce for them in town and give them the profits upon return to the plantation. Wright, though, felt that "they were being cheated when the master sold their goods," according to an FWP interviewer's notes.[59] Wright learned that to maximize their profits, it would be more advantageous to manage the sale oneself, if possible, taking out the middleman.

Some enslaved growers in New Orleans and across the country had more time than others to work in their gardens and grow produce for sale; these fresh products were regularly referred to as "garden truck." Marshal Butler recalled growing "lots of garden truck" in Georgia and noted, "Our boss-man give us Saturday as a holiday to work our four acres."[60] So, too, did Phil Towns, who recalled, "Every adult had an acre of ground which he might cultivate as he chose. Any money made from the sale of this produce was his own."[61] Conversely, Hal Hutson, at ninety, remembered how his enslaver in Tennessee "would not let us raise gardens of our own, but didn't mind us raising corn and a few other truck vegetables to sell for a little spending money."[62] That money could be used to purchase all manner of things from foodstuffs to clothing—items that could restore and foster a sense of humanity within slave society. Some of those purchases, however small or unassuming, were a form of self-expression and therefore a daily act of resistance to slavery.[63]

For some, the money they earned through selling garden truck or vending wares was more than a means of daily resistance; it was a means to change their life completely. Perhaps this was the case for Nancy, an enslaved woman in New Orleans who ran for her freedom in 1828. She "had the habit of selling cakes," and maybe had the chance to save money to buy essential items to support herself leading up to and after escape. These items possibly included ingredients to keep making and selling baked goods.[64] Similarly, George Bollinger remembered how in Missouri his father had saved money by making and selling baskets, using precious hours at night to weave his wares. Bollinger's father kept his life's savings under a loose stone in their fireplace, where he had slowly accumulated funds from his basket business. On the night he fled, he took that money purse with him.[65] "Self-manumitted" or "self-liberated" people—persons who either purchased their own freedom or escaped slavery by some other means—used similar skills. Those skills could sustain them in their pursuit of freedom as was the case for a man named

Barlow who supported himself in Georgia by making and vending "baskets, footmats, and brooms."[66]

Given the robust Black presence in public markets in the South and in New Orleans (which grew in number throughout the first half of the nineteenth century), these commercial centers could become a haven for some self-liberated people. Published notices from the period, sometimes referred to as runaway slave advertisements, made note that self-liberated persons frequented the public markets. This was the case for John in 1840, who had been "seen about the markets several times," and Jane in 1844, who had "been seen for two or three mornings past in the Poydras and St. Mary Market."[67] Theodore, a young boy, also sought refuge in the hustle and bustle of the Magazine Market.[68]

In these public spaces, amid a cohort of Black vendors and customers, people like John, Jane, and Theodore could blend in with the crowd and perhaps even find support among other bondspeople. In 1844, the *Daily Picayune* reported, a self-liberated woman named Judy strategically carried a market basket with her that added an extra layer of camouflage as passersby might "believe she did not run away," but was rather conducting business in the market as usual.[69] It was enslavers' very dependence on Black men and women to carry out selling and buying in the marketplace that protected Judy and the others from detection, at least for a time.

Although out of the shadow of the plantation, the presence of municipal policing and regulation was ever looming over these important spaces of Black sociability. As observed by Royall, two guards stood at each entrance of the French Market. She noted that they were "perfectly silent."[70] In this sense, they were a sonic foil to the gregarious market women Royall had observed. Their silent attendance was symbolic of ever-present white regulation in Black people's lives, however muted. Guards not only stood watch in the central market but also walked the streets—joining the constant flow of people and goods through the city.[71] Their watchful eyes grazed over thousands of economic transactions initiated largely by Black vendors. They also bore witness to the social culture that Black people had created through their businesses.

Black social networks at the French Market extended beyond the vendors themselves. Black women were also the majority of shoppers. They bought goods on behalf of enslavers. As proxies, they represented their enslavers' interests at the market—interests that the city government had sought to protect since the colonial period. And with that role, Black women accessed protections largely intended for white customers. The city government, therefore, ensured that Black women had access to fair prices, accurate measurements, and clean facilities. Thus, in a slave society in which bondspeople were supposed to be marginalized economically and legally, the French Market emerged as an exception. Black women's protected status as customers demonstrates the pliability of the concept of the "public" in public good to extend, in certain situations, to include enslaved people.[72]

Free New Orleanians noted the agency that Black people exercised through purveying and purchasing foods. They noticed that enslaved people were enacting a form of independence and daily resistance through their roles as producers, distributors, and consumers. One such frustrated white resident complained to a local newspaper, the *Bee*, writing that enslaved people were "at liberty to purchase what they please, and where they please, without the personal inspection of any member of the family [who enslaved them]."[73] The author was clearly bothered by the fact that enslaved shoppers regularly obtained wares without direct oversight from enslavers. Their ability to act as a consumer—with needs, expectations, and decision-making power—challenged their alleged status as completely subordinate to free people.

Legal protections granted to bondswomen shopping on behalf of enslavers did not necessarily extend to vendors. Legally, free and enslaved vendors had little protection and were at the mercy of city officials and, in some cases, nonmunicipal officials too. In 1806, the Code Noir, or Black Code, included a section that enabled "every person or persons" to stop any enslaved persons hawking fresh foods and demand to see their vending license. If the vendor could not produce one, the law enabled the person who stopped them to seize their goods or collect two dollars from the enslaver as their reward.[74] Presumably, people assessed the free or enslaved status of a vendor by sight, potentially targeting any vendor of African descent, including those who were free people of color. Black vendors, free and enslaved, therefore, were extremely vulnerable to harassment especially when people abused local laws like this one. This was especially true for Black peddlers who sold goods not from a market stall but out of baskets or temporary stands on the city streets and sidewalks, a significant number of whom vended without licenses. Through this law, the local government deputized vendors operating market stalls and other residents to police Black vendors.[75]

The tensions between vendors within and outside of the public markets was not unique to New Orleans but was rather a conflict that had shaped marketplaces across the country. Similar turf wars defined the commercial spaces of New York, where local laws also protected the interests of rent-paying market vendors and independent shopkeepers over those of itinerant

vendors. In Manhattan, it was common for hucksters—another term for itinerant vendors or peddlers—to purchase left-over product, often of a lesser
quality, from market vendors to resell in the city streets. The purchase,
markup, and resale of goods is what defined the huckstering trade; they were
middlemen and middlewomen in local food economies. To prevent direct
competition, the city government made it illegal for hucksters (and also other
retailers and shop owners) to purchase surplus market product during market
hours.[76] Instead, they had to wait until the markets officially closed in the
afternoon to purchase any remaining product for resale. The same market
laws outright banned most hawking and street peddling during the week, stating that retail goods could be sold only in shops, warehouses, or in the public
markets on "Market Days." The main city markets did not operate on Sundays,
allowing hucksters only one day a week to legally vend their wares.[77]

Across the country, small-scale food vendors found ways to voice their
concerns to local lawmakers when they felt their livelihoods were at stake
because laws favored property owners' interests. Submitting petitions was a
common way of formalizing their opinions and shaping local politics even
though they were denied the vote. On December 18, 1805, a group of nineteen
women hucksters in Philadelphia gathered to co-create and sign a petition
that offered local lawmakers a way to create more equitable conditions for
middlewomen and middlemen.[78]

The small-scale vending women of Philadelphia had scraped by for years
hawking wares in the public markets. By December 1805, however, they called
into question the viability of their businesses, noting that the previous year's
harsh winter and disease outbreaks over the summer drained them emotion-
ally, physically, and financially. Desperate and anxious, they turned to the city
council for help.

Huckstering had been banned in the public markets of Philadelphia since
1792, rendering brick-and-mortar retail spaces, including official market stalls,
the only legal place to sell food in the city. This law intended to protect the
businesses of people who had access to property, mainly white men, by eliminating competition from itinerant vendors like Elmore who set up smaller
retail spaces on overturned barrels and collapsible tables and out of baskets.
Some of these laws were eased in 1802, allowing hucksters to sell wares in the
public markets as long as they were sourced outside of the city limits. But if
hucksters purchased goods at a Philadelphia-based wholesaler or at a discount
at a retail shop and sold those items for a profit, they did so illegally and were
subject to fines, arrest, and the confiscation of their wares. Such were the circumstances of the women petitioners in 1805 who felt particularly targeted in
recent police efforts to crack down on illegal huckstering.

From their perspective, local laws disproportionally and unfairly harmed them and others like them, and they had a solution to the problem: They suggested that stands be designated in the public markets specifically for use by people who "labour under the infirmities of age or sickness, or are reduced by misfortunate, and have families depending on them." Not wanting to come off as a societal burden, but as legitimate entrepreneurs, they suggested that vendors pay reasonable rents for these stands. Equally eager to combat pervasive negative stereotypes of price-gouging vendors, they assured local lawmakers that they would sell their wares at fair rates "which may be deemed least disadvantageous to the buyer." In designating these stalls for them, they argued, the city council would prevent an entire cohort of Philadelphians from the "extremist miseries of cold and of hunger." It would also spare them from being forced, "as paupers, [to] seek an asylum, contrary to their inclinations and their feelings, in the poor house!"[79]

Through this petition, the women hucksters articulated a vision of a more equitable, inclusive public market where they could make an honest living alongside more economically advantaged and able-bodied vendors. The petition, however compelling, did not sway local lawmakers and no changes were made to support the petitioners. Women like Elmore were left with few options but to continue to vend wares illegally, hoping to evade the police and make enough sales and in around the marketplaces to put food on the table.

To the tempered relief of such vendors, city officials across the country struggled to consistently regulate street food culture. Laws like the ones passed in Philadelphia in 1792 and in New Orleans in 1807 seemed more like symbolic representations of property owners' power—and a way to ease their anxieties—than actual mechanisms to control vendors.[80] Whether vending legally or illegally, to the best of their abilities vendors navigated a treacherous legal landscape to make some semblance of a living.

In New Orleans, some vendors carried out their legitimate businesses in and around the French Market without facing displacement by the mayor or one of his cronies. Others vended illegally, without a license, or sold products outside of permissible hours. Still others created a subversive "black market" where they exchanged illegal goods and services in the municipal market and its surrounding streets and waterways.[81] These kinds of exchanges took place outside of the realm of formal regulation yet within the bounds of slave society. In this realm, marginalized people exercised greater agency, but they also contended with greater risk.

One such person who may have skirted local laws was John White, a twenty-five-year-old man who in 1846 had escaped from slavery and had for weeks been selling bread out of a cart to make ends meet.[82] His enslavers owned a bakery where White had likely honed his skills. Flour, water, and yeast became the mode through which he supported himself in the tenuous conditions of his freedom. He perhaps saved money to buy a license to legally peddle his wares, but registering with the city council would place him at greater risk of discovery. So instead, he likely vended unlicensed, joining the cohort of small-scale business people making do on the edges of legal economy.

One solution that city officials posed to combat unlicensed and illegal vending was to adopt a badge system, like the one implemented in Charleston, that would require vendors to wear their licenses in the form of metal badges. The proposed badge system further indicates that New Orleans vendors who chose to illegally sell their wares were agile enough to evade detection. The need for badges also indicates that authorities desired transparency in the local food economy: They wanted to see if a vendor was selling legally or illegally. However, the municipal government was not able to successfully implement the system as Charleston officials had. Instead of badges, the city continued to use the comparatively unsophisticated paper licensing system, keeping open a door for vendors to continue to skirt local laws.[83]

The French Market served as a nucleus of the local food economy and was surrounded by an expansive, overlapping network of itinerant food vendors, many of whom were also enslaved women. Writing about his travels in New Orleans around 1820, architect Benjamin Henry Latrobe observed, "In every street during the whole day black women are met, carrying baskets upon their heads calling at the doors of houses."[84] The fluid mechanics of city life defined their businesses. They faced a dynamic, ever-changing urban landscape—one marked by the construction of new roads, new buildings, and the arrival of new people. Between 1803 and 1840, the city's population increased twenty-fold, from around five thousand to one hundred thousand people, making it the third largest in the United States after New York and Baltimore. As an import-export center, the Port of New Orleans also grew exponentially in this period, competing with other major ports across the country. In 1830, New Orleans ranked second in commercial imports, with New York claiming first place; by 1840, New Orleans' exports surpassed Gotham's.[85] In the early 1830s, visitors to the city noticed that New Orleans not only imported massive amounts of goods but also drew in people: "Everything comes to her [New Orleans]. She goes abroad for nothing. Already the centre of attraction of the remotest parts of the globe, what will she be in a few years hence."[86] Catering to that growing population, street food vendors spread throughout the city on their daily routes, bringing fresh produce and prepared foods right to the doorsteps of New Orleanians.

To launch and strengthen their businesses, vendors had to employ strategies to find customers within the city's developing neighborhoods and build a client base from scratch. To do so, they moved through the city searching for particularly lucrative trade routes or street corners to set up shop. Theirs was a business sense defined by agility and adaptability. Among the first people walking through New Orleans every morning, itinerant vendors set the pace for how people moved through the city streets. According to Anne Newport Royall, they directed the parade of diverse people who occupied the urban center. As some of the earliest wanderers, the calas vendors led,

> while the little short-coat, wooden nutmeg fellows are close at their heels, in a run, the New Yorker, in a sleek coat, striding with his long legs; the white ladies, with a bandbox of ribbons on their bonnets, enveloped in lace down to their heels, the quateroon, with her flowing veil and glossy black silks; the colored lassy, with a wreath of flowers on their heads; the stately, slow walking foreigner; the neatly dressed guard, in uniform; with a long line of carts, make up the sum of the streets.[87]

The thumping of shoes on dirt and paved roads created a communal rhythm reflective of the interconnectivity of their urban experiences. The city was in constant motion.

But it was not only a parade of foot traffic that marked the public food culture of New Orleans, but also a small army of ambling of carts, wooden wheels creaking as they cut paths across the city. For street vendors seeking to transport more goods than could be carried on the body alone, carts proved essential tools for their businesses. This was the case for Juan Gomez, a free man of color, who lived about a half of a mile from the French Market and used his cart to deliver beer.[88] The same year that Gomez received his bond for a market cart, so too did Josephine Tassy Mathé, a free woman of color, who lived on Bayou Road in the Faubourg Tremé (the suburb of Tremé), about a mile from the French Market.[89] Unlike Gomez, Mathé possessed real estate and was an enslaver.[90] She likely assigned one of the people she enslaved to vend wares on her behalf, bringing in additional income by transporting and selling goods via cart either in one of the city's municipal markets or out in the streets.

The streets that vendors, enslaved and free, navigated by cart or by foot in the early antebellum period were not modem marvels, but primitive pathways that could make their daily trade routes challenging and difficult to navigate.[91] They were also dangerously dirty. Muck from rank street-level sewers leaked onto vendors' walking paths, clinging to their shoes and feet as they made their rounds; the stench of human waste and refuse, too, especially in the hotter months, pervaded the air, mixing with the sweet smell of ripe berries and other fresh produce for sale. This was the arena in which vendors made a living, carving out a space for themselves amid the sensory chaos of the city.

Whether traversing the sidewalks or the city streets, vendors had to dodge all manner of damage and debris even as local officials made efforts to create safer and more sanitary pathways. In 1817, the city finally invested in its first stone-paved street, but it would be another five years before municipal officials began a citywide initiative to do so; and in 1820, the city slowly began replacing the wooden sidewalks with brick ones.[92] But the improvements rarely met the needs of New Orleanians. In 1829, just a few years after the city government committed to replacing the sidewalks on Bourbon Street, they remained a sore point for locals: "The side walks on Bourbon st [sic] from one extremity to the other are in the most wretched state. The bricks are torn up, the gutters sunk and the edgings of the walks rotten, and in many places the walking at night is dangerous."[93] There seemed to be no reprieve in sight, no safe way to move throughout the city.

For street vendors, walking along those treacherous pathways was a means of knowing the city and the people who lived there. Their businesses did not require a storefront or renting a stall in the public market; instead, their entrepreneurial endeavors depended on their ability to navigate and establish themselves within the city's neighborhoods—each with their own set of cultural and social norms. The most successful vendors employed different business strategies to build strong relationships with customers in distinct communities.

Although the language of local law often pitted vendors and customers against one another, the realities of their interactions were more complex. In everyday practice, some vendors and customers had strong social relationships. Vendors employed specific strategies to gain and retain customers. Some had consistent routes or daily schedules that brought them into contact with clients on a regular basis. This regularity enabled them to build rapport and establish trust. That sense of trust was important to solidifying vendors' customer base, thus stabilizing their revenues, which they often kept track of via promissory notes from customers.[94]

Another way that vendors established long-term relationships with customers was by setting up temporary stands in familiar locations, enabling customers to come to them. They built a space for themselves in the local community, not by renting or purchasing a storefront but by building a mobile one that could have a similarly recognizable and consistent presence. Ultimately, street food vendors were some of the most recognized figures in New Orleans public spaces. As was the case with Catherine, an enslaved vendor; she became "well known in the city" because of her "habit of selling in the streets and on board of steam boats as a Marchande."[95] Those were her retail locations, and loyal customers knew to find her in those places.

In a city where hundreds of street vendors operated businesses, competition was fierce, and mobility was essential. Vendors like Catherine carried or used a pushcart to bring what they needed to run their pop-up businesses. Some adapted traditional business models, like restaurants, to mobile ones in public spaces. Others would set up entire kitchens, carrying furnaces, utensils, and other necessary accoutrements into the city center, where there was an abundance of customers.[96]

In homage to the adaptability and mobility of itinerant vendors, Royall wrote a fantastical and likely embellished story of one vendor who set up a mobile restaurant near the French Market. According to Royall's tale, the vendor took a table that seated four people, turned it upside down, and placed a full meal in its frame. The haul included "her coffee-pot, steak, plates, knives, and forks, cups and saucers." To carry the table, she had someone assist in hoisting it onto her head. Dodging people and carts, she made her way to the French Market, all the while maintaining her balance. Once there, she unloaded the table, and bought fresh ingredients at the market, including bread, butter, and cream, to supplement her offerings. Then she set the table and entreated pedestrians to dine at her roadside café. After serving the meal, she packed up her things, placed the table back on her head, and returned home. Although likely inflated for effect, Royall's story contains some grains of truth about the lengths to which vendors might go to cater to their customers.[97]

Royall's story also speaks to the sustained West African knowledge and technologies present in New Orleans' local food economy. Generations of Black women wove and used baskets to carry produce and other goods on their heads, skillfully balancing their wares as they walked within the city and in its surrounding rural landscape. This form of "head carrying" had deep roots in West Africa and was a crucial skill and tactic that sustained Black businesses by increasing vendors' mobility and extending their customer reach.[98]

What is perhaps even more striking about itinerant vendors, especially those who physically transported their businesses with them, is the visibility of their labor. People could see these vendors carrying goods down the street, shopping in the market, setting up their stands, and advertising their wares. This was work that took place not in a plantation field outside of the city center or in a domestic kitchen separated from the streets by a wall; it unfolded in the public sphere for all to see. In this way, the labor of street food could be thought of as spectacle or perhaps even performance. As Royall's profile demonstrates, there was a desire among her readership (and the author herself) to marvel at the ingenuity of some itinerant vendors even in a slave society that defined Black women, among other marginalized groups, as insignificant. The visible and performative labor of street food vending disrupted that marginalization, if only for a time.

As much as some vendors were known in their communities, there were others who seemed invisible, unable to establish strong business relations with customers, yet were still a part of the community fabric. These vendors were depicted as wandering listlessly, without purpose. The local newspaper, for example, described one such vendor, a mustard seller, as slowly trudging through the streets. It went on to say that "every one seems to know him, and as he walks his rounds many an honest housekeeper and bright-eyed dame nod familiarly to him if they do not buy his wares." Unlike the typical vocal street vendor, "he rarely speaks." He was an anomaly in a street food culture steeped in verbal engagements. "He is one of those strange beings," the paper explained, "that may be found in every crowded city, whom everybody sees and nobody knows anything about." Although community members acknowledged his presence, tipping their heads or waving to him, his relationships to them were weak because he engaged people neither in economic transactions nor conversation. His business, at least as depicted in the local paper, was unprofitable, and he likely struggled to make ends meet. But he seems to have been a rarity among New Orleans' cohort of entrepreneurial street food vendors who otherwise were known to be skilled at interacting with and building relationships with community members.[99]

So entrenched were the itinerant vendors that when local law disrupted their businesses, customers spoke out against the decision. For generations, oyster sellers had moved through the city streets selling their wares door to door or by setting up temporary stands and stalls in neighborhoods. In 1829, however, local officials passed a new law that required all oyster sellers to halt their itinerant vending and instead sell their wares in city-owned and city-operated oyster stands located on the levee and on the bank of the Carondelet Canal. According to the law, failure to comply would result in an initial fine between ten and twenty dollars, and a subsequent fine of five dollars a day if the vendor remained in place at the illegal location.[100]

For New Orleanians, door-to-door street food vending was a great convenience that brought food right to their doorsteps; the above law, however, required that many customers make a special trip to purchase the beloved bivalves. One New Orleanian expressed their frustration in the local paper: "We are not to have the privilege of buying sweet, fresh, and wholesome oysters from carts at our doors; but must take them at an extravagant price from the stalls on the Levee." The resident went on to explain that oyster sellers raised their prices at the levee stands to cover the rental fees they had to pay, thereby making customers shoulder the expense. What's more, the resident pointed out, many people who harvested oysters did not even have the means to a rent a stall from the city; instead, they had to sell their oysters to middlemen and middlewomen who could afford the stand rent, creating further separation between harvester and customer.[101]

In the vocal New Orleanian's estimation, the city-owned stands were primarily a means to fill the city's coffers and secondarily an effort to build up middlemen's and middlewomen's businesses, not protect the interest of oyster harvesters or consumers. Simply put, the New Orleanian argued, "This is 'robbing Peter to pay Paul' with a vengeance." Seeking some relief, the denizen proposed a solution: demolish the oyster stands and allow oyster harvesters to sell their product door to door. Said harvesters would then purchase licenses for their carts; that way, everyone would have "a chance to eat good oysters for a fair and reasonable price." Despite this resident's public outcry, the law remained in place; the practice of selling door to door, however, could continue as long as oyster sellers were willing to take the risk of defying the law. For some, the only viable choice was to do exactly that.[102]

Carving out a place for their businesses in public spaces, especially in high foot traffic areas, was key to vendors' success. Prime locations afforded vendors the ability to foster relationships with diverse customers, yes, but vendors supported their businesses in other ways. They employed a set of business skills and tactics including product display and vocal advertisements to strengthen their enterprises. Together, these elements worked to attract the attention of potential and existing customers and draw them into the vendors' retail space, where they might engage in conversation, start or build upon a relationship with a vendor, or make a purchase.

Just as with most retail spaces, alluring visual displays were part of food vendors' business strategies. Some vendors wore colorful clothing to attract potential customers, while others displayed the eye-catching tools of their trade. Some coffee vendors, for example, showcased brightly burning furnaces and shiny copper kettles at their roadside stands. Such ornamentation caught people's attention. Reflecting on a trip to New Orleans in 1848, Walt Whitman wrote that "one of my choice amusements during my stay in New Orleans was going down to the old French Market." He described to readers the paramount role of Indigenous and Black vendors in the market, and how he often patronized their businesses. Specifically, he cited his many trips to the stall of one Black woman vendor: "I remember I nearly always on these occasions got a large cup of delicious coffee with a biscuit, for my breakfast, from the immense shining copper kettle of a great Creole mulatto woman."[103] The copper kettles were a sight unto themselves. Because they were made of copper, a valuable material at the time, they could set this vendor's stand apart from other purveyors who might not be able to afford such an expensive vessel. The copper kettle could signify quality and distinguish this vendor's high-quality product from that of her competitors.

Visual display was but one means through which vendors enticed customers to purchase their wares. Street food culture has a dynamic sonic component—ones connecting musical traditions in New Orleans to those in West Africa, the Caribbean, and other regions in the Americas.[104] Street cries played a crucial role in supporting vendors' businesses, in particular. They were a way of marking one's territory in an overcrowded and competitive commercial landscape. They were a means to advertise one's wares and announce one's presence along new and well-worn walking routes. And, ultimately, they became symbolic of vendors' essential status in the city's public food culture.

With so many people, residents, and tourists alike, moving through the city, food vendors had to develop strategies to differentiate their movement from that of the masses, and also set their businesses apart from their competitors. Street cries were a distinguishing factor. Wasting not a sliver of daylight, many vendors began to hawk their wares just as the faintest hint of dawn colored the sky blackberry instead of pitch black. In 1824, Henry C. Knight made note of the "turbaned demoiselle" who "trips by every morning early, singing out in her Babel tongue" about her freshly made fruit-cakes, likely incorporating West African or Creole words and phrases.[105] Her cries, braided with those of her fellow vendors singing out in different Atlantic world languages, were a natural alarm clock for the city, rousing even the soundest sleepers.[106] Street cries, therefore, were part of an intricate sonic landscape that not only created a shared culture, but organized daily life.[107]

They were as constant and influential as other sounds such as the ringing of church bells to call people to worship, which was not only an expression of religious liberty but a way of cultivating a shared culture.[108] By the time sunlight skimmed over the placid waters of the Mississippi, vendors' sonorous warbles, especially of those clustered around the central market, grew to a dull roar. We can think of the dull roar of street cries as a sonic means of self-expression and an act of community creation akin to those of church bells.

Those same street cries captured the strong presence of food vendors in the city and reflected the relative autonomy and importance of vendors within the local food scene. For those chafed by their prominent presence, street cries became a relentless reminder of vendors' claims upon public lands. And their vocalization impressed upon listeners that although their voices may have been muffled in the legal system, they were not similarly silenced in the local food economy.

Vendors across the city commonly cried out in Creole or French, knowing that many city residents could understand them. Speaking the language of their customers reinforced cultural continuity between the two, solidifying a sense of shared culture—one born of the Atlantic world. Stationed by their furnace or with a basket of piping hot fritters perched on their heads, calas vendors often cried out a derivation of the following:

> Belles calas,
> Madame, mo gaignin calas,
> Madame, mo gaignin calas,
> Madame, mo gaignin calas;
> Mo guaranti vous ye bons
> Beeelles calas…Beeelles calas.

Or in English:

> Beautiful rice fritters,
> Madame, I have rice fritters,
> Madame, I have rice fritters,
> Madame, I have rice fritters;
> I guarantee you they are good
> Beautiful rice fritters…Beautiful rice fritters.

Catering to the French-speaking community was even more important as tensions rose between New Orleanians who identified with French and

Spanish Atlantic culture and those who did not. When New Orleans became part of the United States, English-speaking Americans from across the country migrated to the city in large numbers. Remarking on the vast migration, Benjamin Henry Latrobe claimed, "Americans are pouring in daily, not in families, but in large bodies." Many of them settled upriver from the French Market in what became known as the American Sector (the present-day Central Business District). Culturally this population stood in stark contrast to the francophone community that had lived in the French Quarter and surrounding neighborhoods for generations. In Latrobe's estimation, "In a few years therefore, this will be an American town."[109]

Despite the growth of the American Sector, French Atlantic cultural influences remained strong in New Orleans. Between 1809 and 1810, over ten thousand refugees from the former French colony of Saint-Domingue arrived in New Orleans following the Haitian Revolution. In rough estimates, their numbers were evenly divided among white, free people of color, and enslaved Black refugees. Their arrival doubled the city's population overall and contributed to the growth of New Orleans' population of free Blacks.[110] Many of the refugees from colonial Saint-Domingue, including a substantial number of free Blacks, settled in the Faubourg Tremé and in neighborhoods downriver of the French Quarter. This migration pattern concentrated the francophone community on the opposite side of town from the American Sector, physically separating them from the anglophone population uptown.

By 1810, almost one-third of the city's population was made up of free people of color, although that ratio slowly declined over the next several decades as white American migrants and European immigrants flocked to the city.[111] Free Blacks, many of whom were mixed race with some combination of Spanish, West Indian, French, and African ancestry, played key roles in the local economy.[112] They were entrepreneurs, innovators, members of the militia, and more, making their mark on the city's public food culture as street food and public market vendors.[113] They could accumulate wealth and own property, and some were enslavers like Josephine Tassy Mathé. Their robust presence contributed to a tripartite racial order in New Orleans that mirrored other Atlantic world port cities made up of free whites, free Blacks, and enslaved people. In New Orleans, free people of color, or *les gens de couleur libres*, were key contributors to the francophone culture of the city, keeping alive French Atlantic culture.[114]

Although the popularity of French and Creole street cries was indicative of that strong French Atlantic influence, even residents and visitors of the city (those not necessarily fluent in French or Creole) understood what calas vendors were selling; the street cry, when paired with visual display, still served its purpose as a vocal advertisement. A common feature of many calas vendors' cries was the description of their fritters as "tout chauds," or "very hot!" When Anne Newport Royall attempted to transcribe their cries, she phonetically recorded what we know as "Tout chauds calas" as "Toshow culler!" Her transcription was not linguistically accurate. Yet she was able to uncover the general meaning, inferring that the vendors were selling "nice hot cakes" either by observing the vendors' display or from getting an explanation from someone else.[115]

However, street vendor cries were not always effective communication tools. Some vendors sang in a way that made their cries difficult for some listeners to understand, as was the case with the Green Sass men who sold vegetables and cream cheeses. As described in the local newspaper, their cry, "as near as it can possibly be translated, is *'E-a-r-s yerfineniccartatics, artichokes, cantelopes feegs and arwicerkereama-cheeses! Ear! ear!*"[116] These cries, with almost indistinguishable descriptions of products for sale, did not actually prevent them from attracting business. In some cases, their distinctive calls made them more recognizable to regular customers.

Although the street cry was a prominent feature of food vendors' advertising strategies, not all vendors employed them. The *Daily Picayune* noted that a vendor known as the Candy Man, who sold "caraway comfits" and other sweets to children, caught the attention of his clientele by "incessantly play[ing] upon a triangle, and every afternoon his tink-tink-a-tink, tink-tink-a-tink may be heard in the streets." His music was similar to that of a modern ice cream truck. The paper described him as possessing a "musical turn of mind" like that of the other street vendors. The same article noted that like "all the other street-dealers," the Candy Man "understands but little English."[117] We can think of the musical street cry or street melody, whether it be sung or played, as a kind of universal language, understood by vendor and customer regardless of their ability to communicate through speech. The song, when paired with a compelling display, could communicate enough information to facilitate an economic transaction. This phenomenon was particularly advantageous to new migrants who may not have been able to communicate in Creole, French, or English, the predominant languages in New Orleans.

A vast majority of vendors, it seems, sang about their wares. Their cries were a marketing tactic, but Black vendors incorporated and braided African musical traditions, sensibilities, and culture into them, transforming them into something else entirely: a performance of Black cultural expression in the heart of New Orleans' slave society. The broader New Orleans community, for the most part, accepted these performances as an inescapable part of the public food culture. However, in other venues, white New Orleanians and visitors to the city found similar forms of Black cultural expression disconcerting and dangerous. For example, when Latrobe traveled to New Orleans between 1818 and 1820, he found himself returning again and again to Congo Square: a meeting ground in the rear of the French Quarter where many enslaved people gathered on Sundays to sing, dance, socialize, and even vend wares. For Latrobe, the "noise" of the square was unpleasant. He disdained, in racist terms, the chorus of Black voices singing, their feet stomping, and drums beating in synchronized rhythm:

> A Man sang an uncouth song to the dancing which I suppose was in some African language, for it was not french, and the Women screamed a detestable burthen on one single note. The allowed amusements of Sunday, have, it seems, perpetuated here, those of Africa among its inhabitants. I have never seen any thing more brutally savage, and at the same time dull and stupid than this whole exhibition. Continuing my walk about a mile along the Canal, and returning after Sunset near the same spot, the noise was still heard.[118]

Unlike the city streets, where Black vendors' presence was accepted or at least reluctantly endured, the frivolity of Congo Square chafed Latrobe. The actions that took place in the square were intended for members of New Orleans' Black community; everyone else was an outsider. In this way, Black sociability disrupted their sense of control over public space, incentivizing the local government to restrict Black people's access to the square. Like the songs and dances performed in Congo Square, the street cry can also be thought of as a subversive expression of Black culture, which undermined other people's sense of power and control. Street cries, however, were permissible and tolerated because of their connection to the street food economy and culture that served and benefited the entire New Orleans community. These distinctions demonstrate New Orleanians' conceptions of "acceptable" and "unacceptable" forms of self-expression, the blurred lines between them, and the unique context of the city's public food culture as a space for marginalized groups to exercise some form of power on a daily basis.

Perhaps the vendors Catherine and Wilson visited, engaged, and contributed to the culture of Congo Square much as they did aboard the steamboats of the Mississippi River. We know that they occupied other public spaces, exercising their business savvy and flexing their economic and social networks to their advantage to create an opportunity to escape the bonds of slavery, even if temporarily. Like many other public market and street vendors, they cultivated expertise in their corner of the food industry, building a customer base and extending their networks across the urban landscape of New Orleans. Likely, they crafted their own street cries or developed mouthwatering sales pitches to entice customers to patronize their businesses day after day—to inch them closer to a modicum of financial independence. The quality of their products, too, undoubtedly played a role in securing customer loyalty and strengthening their financial reserves. And through those skill sets and resources, they created an opportunity to chase freedom, ever uncertain of their ability to escape detection of enslavers, on the waterways and surrounding landscapes of the lower Mississippi Delta.

Vendors of diverse racial and ethnic backgrounds continued to occupy public spaces and employ various business tactics through the remainder of the antebellum period, growing their businesses alongside the explosive growth of the city's population. Local officials had to act quickly to supply growing neighborhoods with safe and affordable food. They did so by building new municipally regulated markets, extending the reach of regulation beyond the French Quarter, and establishing new economic and social hubs at which New Orleans' community could come together to feed the city. These new markets served not only as community meeting grounds but as the catalyst for the growth of entirely new neighborhoods outside of the city's central core. In turn, they became symbolic of a neighborhood's prosperity, moving far beyond their core roles as economic centers.

The Expansion of New Orleans' Public Market System, 1822–1865

THE SWEDISH ADVENTURIST Fredrika Bremer had no agenda in touring the French Market complex in 1851 except to observe the activity around her. The market's kaleidoscopic sights and vibrant atmosphere overwhelmed her senses. She wandered among stalls displaying colorful mountains of mouth-watering tropical fruits, stacks of aromatic breads still steaming from the oven, and neatly hung varieties of game ranging from hares to waterbirds. Time and time again, vendors called out greetings as she passed by, inviting her to peruse their wares. She concluded that the market was "one of the most lively and picturesque scenes of New Orleans."[1]

The market's population was a microcosm of the Crescent City and the broader Atlantic world. "Here are English, Irish, Germans, French, Spanish, Mexicans. Here are negroes and Indians. Most of those who offer articles for sale are black Creoles, or natives, who have the French animation and gayety, who speak French fluently," wrote Bremer. In her estimation, the market was akin to the grand markets of Europe: "One feels as if transported to a great Paris *marché*." Like the heterogeneous population that frequented Paris' public markets, the central market of New Orleans was a place where one "meets with various races of people [and] hears many different languages spoken."[2]

Although Bremer observed an astonishing number of people in the market that day, she also witnessed how there was synchronicity in their movements: "Between two and three thousand persons, partly purchasers and partly sellers, were here in movement, but through all there prevailed so much good order." Not only did New Orleanians synchronize the daily rhythms of provisioning, but they did so in a way that created a social atmosphere of "amiable vivacity." Again, Bremer could not help but compare New Orleans to Europe, noting with quite a bit of romanticization how New Orleanians "breakfasted, and talked, and laughed just as in the markets at Paris." From what Bremer witnessed, clearly shaped by her perspective as a white woman of means, the French Market was, at its core, an essential community space "full of sunshine, cheerful life, and good humor."[3]

Bremer's telling omits how the social bonds made among the men and women she observed were forged in the ever-looming shadow of slave society. Her story glosses over the trauma and oppression that existed alongside the laughter and conviviality of marketgoers and vendors, alike. But when recontextualized within the complex dynamics of slave society, we see that the French Market was a site upon which enslaved people, too, built resilience with each other through their food work. Their integral social bonds existed alongside and became entangled with those of free people in this central site of community formation.

From 1791 to 1822, the French Market was the only municipally owned and operated market in the greater New Orleans area. Bremer astutely observed that it became home to the businesses of new migrants who integrated into the existing public food culture—one shaped by a racially and ethnically diverse population, free and enslaved. As the city's population grew more rapidly, however, the French Market could no longer provision the entire city. Municipal officials did not want the expanding population to become even more dependent on itinerant vendors, whom they saw as already exercising too much influence over the local food economy.

To accommodate growing and diversifying needs, local officials began building a series of neighborhood-based public food markets to cater first to established neighborhoods surrounding the city's central core and then eventually to developing communities beyond that. Between 1822 and 1860, local officials approved the construction of fourteen markets, laying the groundwork for a local food distribution system that would look like no other in the United States. By the start of the Civil War, New Orleans would become a city of markets.

New Orleans' reliance on neighborhood markets in the antebellum period provides a rich case study on the subtle yet pervasive influence of food provisioning on conceptions of local identity in a nineteenth-century city; said reliance demonstrates that local identities remained strong even as a broader national consciousness developed. Whereas New Orleans' public food culture centered around a single public market for decades, starting in the 1820s, that centrality diffused as newly built public markets pulled New Orleanians away from the French Market complex.

Communities with significant political power were able to secure new markets for their residents, while those without it could not. Once constructed, the markets influenced where people settled and where commercial corridors developed, sculpting the physical and cultural geography of the city. Those business owners who were unable to access stalls within the public markets due to their general lack of privilege continued to operate near them despite local laws that sought to restrict street food vendors' movement and stifle their enterprises. A burgeoning nativist movement in local politics among New Orleanian–born residents shaped the policing of these peddlers, an increasing number of whom were recent immigrants from Europe. Largely understudied, the history of antebellum New Orleans' nourishing networks reinforces the organizing power of food distribution—a force that served as a catalyst of commercial and community development.

Although the French Market remained a crucial commercial center throughout the antebellum period, the gradual development of New Orleans' neighborhood public markets created alternative centers of influence. The construction of the first auxiliary market, the St. Mary's Market, demonstrates that these public amenities did far more than provide access to affordable fresh food; they also became symbolic of the economic and political power of the communities in which they were built—communities that had long been competing with each other for control of the city.

Rival interests fell between two major groups: French-speaking Creoles and Anglo-Americans, both of which consisted of racially diverse people, although whites controlled the political sphere.[4] The French-speaking Creoles, henceforth referred to as "French Creoles," consisted of New Orleanian natives and "foreign French," those who emigrated from France, colonial Saint-Domingue, and other francophone places, as well as immigrants from the Mediterranean, Caribbean, and Latin America. The French Creoles were unified by their Catholic faith and general Latin culture, and made up the majority of the population, enabling them to control local politics and shape the city's culture in the opening decades of the eighteenth century. They tended to live near one another and largely resided in the Vieux Carré, the Faubourg Tremé, and the faubourgs downriver from the city center, including the Faubourgs Marigny and Washington, the latter a part of what is known today as the Bywater neighborhood. The other group consisted of English-speaking transplants of Anglo-American ethnicity who were largely Protestants. Henceforth referred to as "Americans," this group sought economic dominion over New Orleans and garnered political power through partnerships with German and Irish immigrants. These groups tended to settle in the same area upriver of the city center.[5]

As Americans carved out more space for themselves in New Orleans' economy after the Louisiana Purchase in 1803, visitors took note of their endeavors in particular industries. In 1806, Irish travel writer Thomas Ashe observed that Americans "reign over the brokerage and commission business," whereas French Creoles and other Latin community members were involved in smaller-scale businesses, many of them tied to food distribution. He noted, "The French keep magazines and stores; and the Spaniards do all the small retail of grocers' shops, cabants [*sic*], and lowest orders of drinking houses. People of colour and free negroes, also keep inferior shops, and sell goods and fruits." In Ashe's eyes, the division between the two groups really came down to the scale of their businesses, with Americans investing in larger trades as the city's commercial center grew, and French Creoles operating smaller enterprises.[6]

Local politics became increasingly messy as the two culturally distinct groups competed for power: French Creoles fought to maintain their upper hand, while Americans gained support by liaising with immigrants who settled in their communities.[7] Like other major port cities in the United States, New Orleans took in large bodies of immigrants from Europe, mainly Germany and Ireland, during the antebellum period.[8] From 1800 to 1850, for example, fifty thousand people emigrated from Germany, many of whom settled upriver of the city center, increasing the American Sector's population and the representation of its interest in the city government. It was not uncommon for these recent immigrants to find their first economic toehold in New Orleans' public food culture; as German and Irish populations grew, so too, did their presence as food entrepreneurs.

To accommodate the American Sector's robust population, the city council constructed the St. Mary's Market around 1822; the market was named for the faubourg within which it was located. The decision to build the first auxiliary market was political as well as practical: While the growth of the American Sector made an additional market useful, the construction was also an effort by American Sector community members to create their own commercial and cultural center that would rival that of the French Creoles, that is, the French Market complex. Now residents in the American Sector could create a public culture around food at their own market; they would no longer be beholden to the entrenched traditions and peculiarities of the French Market.[9]

Even though the St. Mary's Market was in a part of town governed by American tastes, the market was designed in an architectural style similar to that of the French Market. For the cost of $22,000, the city built the 165-feet-long and 42-feet-wide wood-framed structure with a tiled interior at the intersection of Annunciation and Tchoupitoulas Streets—just over one mile upriver of the French Market. The St. Mary's Market's edifice was built of brick and was plastered to imitate granite, gesturing to Greco-Roman

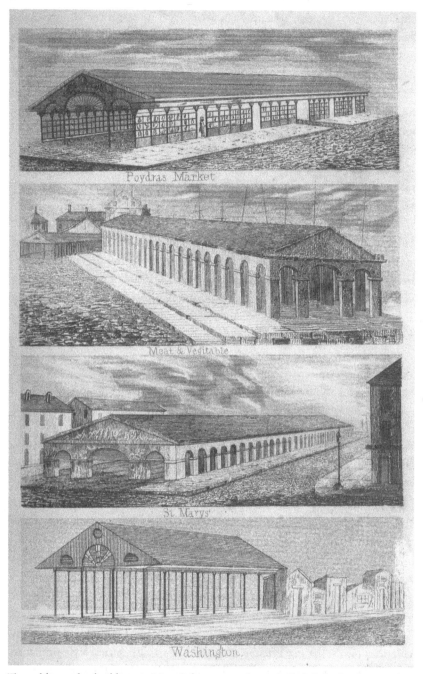

The public market buildings in New Orleans around 1838 included the Poydras Market, the meat and vegetable markets at the French Market complex, the St. Mary's Market, and the Washington Market. These structures served as commercial and cultural centers for their communities.

Gibson's Guide and Directory of the State of Louisiana, and the Cities of New Orleans and LaFayette, 1838. The Historic New Orleans Collection, Acc. No. 87-085-RL.

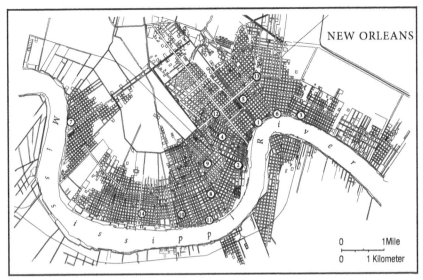

pre-Civil War

① French Market, 1791
② St. Mary's Market, 1822
③ Washington Market, 1836
④ Poydras Market, 1838
⑤ Treme Market, 1840
⑥ Port Market, 1840
⑦ Carrollton Market, 1846
⑧ Magazine Market, 1847
⑨ Dryades Market, 1848
⑩ Ninth Street Market, 1850
⑪ Soraparu Market, 1852
⑫ Claiborne Market, 1852
⑬ St. Bernard Market, 1856
⑭ Jefferson Market, 1860

This map shows the locations and approximate dates of construction for the public markets built in New Orleans before the Civil War. The first three markets were located near the historic heart of the city and the banks of the Mississippi River. As the city's neighborhoods expanded, radiating outward from the French Quarter, new public markets opened to cater to those growing populations.

Base map source: *New Encyclopedic Atlas and Gazetteer of the World* (New York: P. F. Collier & Son, 1917). Courtesy of the University of Texas Libraries, University of Texas at Austin.

classical architecture.[10] The architect of the structure was city surveyor Joseph Pilié, who also designed the vegetable market in the French Market complex, which was built around the same time as the St. Mary's Market.[11] The ample similarities between the two buildings signal the fact that the St. Mary's Market, and the community that frequented it, could never fully divorce itself from the overarching market culture developing in New Orleans, as much as it would like to; in other words, the cultural distinctions between the two dominant groups was not as stark in the public food culture as the political climate might suggest.

Continuing to respond to the needs of American Sector residents, the city expanded the market several times toward New Orleans' modern-day Convention Center abutting the river. Around 1830, local officials contracted with J. D. Paldwin to build a second section of the market, also 165 feet long, for $13,750. And in 1836, local officials extended the St. Mary's Market a third time, contracting with Paldwin once again to complete the 156-foot-long structure at a cost of $12,000.[12] The extension of the St. Mary's Market represented the growth of the American Sector's population, but also its economic strength and political influence.

Throughout the antebellum period, many American cities, from New Orleans to New York, operated public markets like the French Market complex and the St. Mary's Market to provision urban populations with affordable, safe food. A major component of public provisioning was addressing public health concerns and ensuring the quality of products. Historically, by concentrating exchange in a single place, city officials were better able to monitor the quality and pricing of goods to ensure that vendors were not taking advantage of customers. The centralization of food provisioning largely took place in two kinds of markets: "curb" and "pavilion." At curb markets, vendors set up displays on a street corner or sidewalk. At pavilion markets, like the French Market and St. Mary's Market, vendors set up stands or carts under a shed, which provided some shelter from inclement weather. These sheds could be constructed in a street or on a designated plot of land, similar in size and design to twenty-first-century covered farmers' markets.

As urban populations steadily increased throughout the nineteenth century, the activities of the public markets spilled out into the surrounding city streets, creating major public health and traffic issues. What's more, the overcrowded commercial centers became increasingly difficult to regulate because of the sheer volume of goods and people moving through them. City officials in and outside of the United States grew desperate for a new market model that would house more vendors and bring order to the chaos of public food provisioning.

The solution came in the form of the enclosed market hall, which was gaining popularity in European cities like Paris and London, where they were considered to embody the ideals of a modern and therefore orderly urban society.[13] The halls were devised to eliminate sprawl, unclutter city streets, and protect sellers and buyers from the smoke, dust, and soot characteristic of rapidly industrializing cities. Their architectural designs were ornate, with cavernous ceilings and multiple levels of retail space.[14] Whereas pavilion markets were typically constructed out of wood, market halls were regularly built out of brick, stone, stucco, marble, iron, and glass—materials meant to inspire and awe. The market hall, then, was intended as a space of enlightened economic exchange, where interactions between vendors and customers happened not in muddy streets but on terrazzo tile, not over makeshift wooden tables but over polished countertops. City official considered market halls to be symbols of civic progress like other municipal buildings such as courthouses, libraries, and museums.

Major cities like New York, Boston, and Philadelphia were early adopters of the modern market hall in the United States, experimenting with increasingly complex and nuanced market structures. Whereas in the opening decades of the nineteenth century, New Orleans had one central wholesale-retail market, the French Market complex, New York City had many. The Fly Market and Catherine Market catered to the East Side of Manhattan and the downtown Washington Market catered to what was then known as the Lower West Side and now known as Tribeca. Supplementing these larger markets were numerous smaller, neighborhood markets like the Centre, Grand Street, and Essex Markets. As with the French Market complex and St. Mary's Market, Manhattan's markets grew to meet the demands of a blossoming urban population; by the end of the eighteenth century, the Fly Market, for example, was made up of three separate market halls specializing in meat, produce, and fish. Those structures resembled the pavilion style of the French and St. Mary's Markets.[15]

Completed in 1812, the Washington Market, by contrast, looked different from the Fly Market and the French and St. Mary's Markets because most of its vendors operated in a walled wooden structure. The market was large, too, taking up an entire city block, and contained stalls to sell meat, seafood, and produce. It also had a central open-air courtyard dedicated solely to produce vendors' businesses. Part of the market had a second story that was used by the fire department as a watchhouse; this demonstrated that markets could be far more than places of public provisioning, and quite often housed other municipal services like police and fire stations and post offices. By sheer proximity, the presence of regulatory institutions like the police also added an element of increased surveillance of both free and enslaved people working in and around the markets; although often challenging to regulate, people working within the public food culture were all too aware of the possibility that law enforcement could be moments away from rounding the street corner.[16]

In the nineteenth century, the mixed-use market was a near-constant form across the country, including in some southern cities.[17] As was the case in relatively smaller cities like Athens, Georgia, these multipurpose, multifloor markets were not as expansive as the ones in Manhattan. As Nellie Smith, a previously enslaved woman, remembered it, "The Old Town Hall was standin' then right in the middle of Market (Washington) Street.... The lowest floor was the jail, and part of the ground floor was the old market place. Upstairs was the big hall where they held court, and that was where they had so many fine shows. Whenever any white folks had a big speech to make they went to that big old room upstairs in Town Hall and spoke it to the crowd."[18] As part of multiuse municipal spaces, public markets like the one in Athens sat at the heart of urban life, whether in Georgia or in New York.

Early antebellum-era changes in American public market architecture are perhaps best embodied in Manhattan's Fulton Market, opened in 1822, the same year that the St. Mary's Market opened in New Orleans. Built to replace the Fly Market, the new structure was massive compared to the supplementary neighborhood markets, some of which only had a dozen or so vendor stalls. Fulton Market, by contrast, sported eighty-eight butchers' stalls, thirty-four stands for produce and poultry, four stands dedicated to sausage, and sixteen stands outside of the market hall for vendors coming in from the surrounding countryside. The market also had an extensive basement made up of sixteen cellars to house grocers and coffee and cake sellers.[19] Construction costs reached $220,000, making Fulton Market one of the most expensive public projects in New York City's history at that time.[20] John Pintard, a New Yorker with a passion for food and market-going, marveled at the new structure. He boasted in a letter to his daughter that it was "superior in accommodation perhaps to any thing of the kind, probably even in Europe" and that the market vendors created an "abundant display of every variety of Meats, Fish & Game, exceed[ing] any thing that I Have [sic] witnessed in this city."[21]

Unlike the Fulton Market in New York, New Orleans' antebellum markets did not have cellars for grocers to purvey their wares; instead, most dry goods purveyors maintained independent small-scale shops around the city, although some did have stalls in the public markets. In the antebellum period, therefore, a majority of grocers' businesses were physically separated from the public markets and quite distinct from unpropertied itinerant vendors working in the streets. Legally, dry goods retailers could not sell fresh food and were therefore not "greengrocers," but rather just "grocers." They sold everything from sugar and flour to clothing and household tools.

By 1822, the year St. Mary's Market opened, there were, according to Paxton's city directory, 428 taverns and groceries around the city; these two establishments were likely grouped together because it was not uncommon for grocers to also operate as barkeeps.[22] Whereas the city's 260 wholesale merchants occupied prime real estate along the river and major throughways of the city, the small-scale grocers were embedded in neighborhoods themselves, catering to the many communities that made up the larger urban populace.[23] Often living and working in close proximity to the communities they served, grocers were agile and adaptive; although more adjacent than central to the public food culture, they played a notable role in provisioning the city with dry goods and other consumables that paired with the fresh ingredients and prepared foods offered by the city's market and street food vendors. Although they contributed to the local food economy, grocers operated largely on the periphery of New Orleans' public market system, a situation that distinguished the city's public food culture from those of other urban centers in the United States.

As the St. Mary's Market expanded to include new buildings to accommodate growing populations, so did the conflict between French Creoles and Americans. In between the second and third extensions of the market, tensions came to a head, forcing the Louisiana State Legislature to embark on an experiment that solidified rather than mitigated the differences between the two groups. In 1834, the legislature amended the 1805 charter of the city of New Orleans to create three distinct corporations. The mayor and General Council oversaw all three municipalities, but each one had its own council, police, schools, and amenities. Essentially, instead of trying to resolve the issues between the two dominant cultural groups in New Orleans, the state legislature gave them control over their own communities.[24]

Because members of particular ethnic groups tended to settle near one another in New Orleans, the three municipalities were each culturally cohesive. The First and Third Municipalities consisted mainly of French Creoles and the Second consisted of Americans and recent immigrants from Europe. The First Municipality sat between Canal and Esplanade and extended from the riverfront back toward Lake Pontchartrain, housing the Vieux Carré and the Faubourg Tremé. Upriver of the First Municipality, the Second Municipality ran between Canal Street and Felicity Street. And the Third Municipality, downriver from the First and Second, ran between Esplanade and the present-day St. Bernard Parish line, including the Faubourgs Marigny and Washington.

Each municipality was sectioned into wards, and elected aldermen represented the interests of residents in that ward. The councils of aldermen oversaw municipal affairs, including infrastructure, education, and, yes, the public markets within their municipality. Once a year, the three councils of aldermen would meet to form the General Council, which answered to a single mayor. Together, they addressed citywide legislation related to business licensing, port management, policing, and incarceration. What appeared to be a reasonable system on paper was in fact quite the opposite: It amplified the cultural and political differences among ethnic groups that dated back to the Louisiana Purchase of 1803.[25]

The experiment lasted for more than fifteen years, a time in which the New Orleans area's public market system grew quite rapidly. Between 1834 and 1852, local officials built nine more markets, bringing the area's total to eleven markets. Local community members and the officials who represented them understood that a public market—like the French Market complex— served not only as a community's commercial core but also as a cultural and social center. A public market, therefore, was an important municipal amenity, and without one, the municipality would be lacking.

Around 1836, the Third Municipality finally built its own market, the Washington Market, based on plans also drawn up by Joseph Pilié. Municipal officials constructed the market, consisting of several structures, near the river levee on Chartres Street, stretching from Louisa to Piety Streets.[26] It was located about one mile downriver of the French Market complex in the Faubourg Washington, taking its name from the faubourg it called home. French Creoles, Black and white, free and enslaved, and migrants from the Spanish colonial empire occupied the area at that time.[27] A historic community, the Third Municipality did not, however, hold as much power or wealth as the larger First and Second Municipalities. The latter two used up many municipal resources, leaving little for the Third. Consequently, the Third came to be referred to as the "old Third," "the dirty Third," and "the poor Third."[28]

The Washington Market became a significant symbol of the Third Municipality's emerging independence and self-reliance. It also represented the productivity and effectiveness of its municipal council. As the local paper noted, "Our fellow citizens of the lower part of the city are going ahead in fine style with their various improvements. Preparations are in active progress, we should judge from the proceedings of their Council, for creating the 'Washington Market.'"[29] The paper went on to include two other public works projects but listed the construction of the market as the first, and arguably the most important, investment. The market, then, was symbolic of the coming of age of the Third Municipality.

The Washington Market's design further emphasized this important moment of departure for the Third Municipality. The structure was somewhat distinct from the previous three in that it incorporated natural elements into its design by including small community gardens at the entrances. These served to demarcate community spaces, reinforcing the idea that the new neighborhood market was a meeting ground for residents; the small parks included "forest trees for shade" and "a fountain in the centre, designed to cleanse the building, and refresh the atmosphere." These elements suggest that Pilié desired the market to be not only a space of commerce but a space where people could find respite from the heat and socialize with one another.[30]

Now all three municipalities had their own community-based public markets, all of which abutted the Mississippi River. The demand for public markets, however, did not cease with the construction of the Washington Market. Petitions for new public markets continued to pour in as community members who lived farther away from the riverfront sought their own inland public markets.

Around 1838, the Second Municipality built a second public market, the Poydras Market, to accommodate the residents living in what is now known as the Central Business District. Like the St. Mary's Market, the Poydras Market was located on a median, or "neutral ground" in local parlance, this one on Poydras Street. That placement allowed market vendors to easily cart in product but also caused the activities of the market to spread out into the surrounding streets, disrupting the flow of foot and cart traffic. Like its antecedents, the market stretched along several city blocks. It was 42 feet wide and extended from Fortier to Circus Streets, running a total length of 402 feet. Phillippa Street intersected the market under an elliptical arch, taking everyday foot and cart traffic through the heart of the market itself.[31]

The Poydras Market was much more than a second commercial space: It was symbolic of the emerging political and economic dominance of the American Sector. Even its design sent a message that represented the Second Municipality's attempt to aesthetically distinguish itself from the two French Creole municipalities. Breaking away from the wood- and brick-covered stucco of the other markets, F. Wilkinson, the surveyor of the Second Municipality, designed the market largely out of metal, with fireproof iron pillars, an iron room frame, a zinc roof covering, and flagstone pavement. His design embodied the Second Municipality's financial strength and its ability to invest in expensive technologies and construction materials. Totaling a cost of roughly $40,000, the Poydras Market cost nearly twice as much as its first neighborhood market, St. Mary's Market, demonstrating the rising wealth of the community.[32]

The first five auxiliary markets were all constructed within a mile of the French Market complex, quite close together. After the opening of the Poydras

Market, the First Municipality furnished the Tremé neighborhood with a market around 1840, the fourth auxiliary market. That same year, officials in the Third Municipality built the Port Market along the levee in between the French Market and the Washington Market. It was at this time that New Orleans became the third largest city in the United States, with a population in 1840 of 102,193.[33] Around this time, the demographics of food vendors began to shift as a significant wave of European immigrants settled in the city. Although Black vendors still played a prominent role in the city's public food culture, especially in and around the French Market complex, the makeup of food vendors in the city's periphery began to reflect the influx of European migrants into those burgeoning residential areas.

As New Orleans' and the surrounding areas' population grew, city governments continued to build new public markets to accommodate residents' needs. In 1846, the Carrollton Market opened far upriver, past the current location of Tulane University. The Carrollton neighborhood, not yet a part of New Orleans, saw population growth with the help of the New Orleans & Carrollton Railroad, which opened in 1835.[34] The railroad brought greater mobility between the city center of New Orleans and neighboring communities like Lafayette, Jefferson, and Carrollton.[35] The market would become part of New Orleans' municipal market system in the future. Likewise, the Magazine Market, constructed in the city of Lafayette in 1847, would also join that system.

Through their work in the public markets, white food vendors sometimes had opportunities to acquire private property, which in turn enabled them to vote and fully exercise their rights as citizens.[36] There are countless examples of working-class white men in food industries steadily expanding their businesses and eventually accessing private property and realizing full citizenship.[37] For some, entrepreneurial efforts led to political connections and public service, further solidifying their status as citizens. Many of them started off as market vendors (some were even street vendors, at first) and grew their businesses over time into independent stores or restaurants. For them, occupying public space with their small-scale food businesses was merely a steppingstone to private property, which was not often the case for women and people of color who worked in the same food industry.

The story of brothers-in-law Bernard Maylié and Hypolite Esparbé, who owned a coffee stall in the Poydras Market, epitomizes that upward mobility. They had a successful business catering to butchers, milkmen, and other people who headed to the stockyards in the early morning hours to purchase cattle for their respective trades. Through their role as coffee vendors, they built crucial economic and social relationships that enabled them to accumulate wealth and purchase private property outside of the Poydras Market. With a flourishing coffee stand, Maylié and Esparbé decided to move their business to an independent café. They eventually transitioned to operating a full-service restaurant, La Maison Maylié et Esparbé or just "Maylié's," which became one of the most well-known establishments in New Orleans.[38]

Public market vendors like Maylié and Esparbé employed diverse strategies to build up their customer base and grow their businesses; often, their strategies looked quite different from those of street vendors because of greater educational opportunities and access to liquid assets. Some public market vendors took to the city's newspapers to build awareness of their enterprises. Butchers, for example—who had occupied a place of relative privilege within the city's market system from the colonial period because of their status as mainly white men—used the city newspapers to advertise to an educated (that is, literate) client base. Their form of advertising stood in stark contrast to that of itinerant vendors and even many public market vendors, who relied on oral communication to garner customers' loyalty.

For vendors privileged enough to work in recently opened public markets, print advertising was a way to find new clientele by communicating what they sold and the quality of their product. This was especially important given that new public market vendors were in competition with existing ones across the city, including those in the French Market. H. F. Pilster, who operated a stall in the newly opened Poydras Market, put out an advertisement in the local paper to inform "his friends and the public in general that he has taken" stall No. 7. His advertisement went on to tell readers that he sold, beef, pork, and veal, which he emphasized were "equal at least to any which can be procured in New Orleans." Of special note was "a very superior OX" that he intended to slaughter the evening the advertisement ran, denoting the freshness of his product and gesturing toward the demand it would likely incite from patrons. In addition to sharing wares he offered, Pilster emphasized the aesthetic properties of his stand: "The Stall is fitted up in a very superior manner, is neatly painted, and has a marble slab for the meat." In focusing on these material qualities, Pilster set apart his business from the more rudimentary stalls of other butchers and the mobile stalls of itinerant vendors. If the advertisement did its job, potential customers' interests would be piqued, and they would visit his stall.[39]

Unlike Pilster's solo marketing endeavor, some vendors pooled resources to print detailed advertisement about their offerings, enabling them to reach a wider audience through the newspaper. Establishing trust with new customers was key in an age when people regularly fell ill because of food poisoning and various foodborne diseases. Some vendors emphasized transparency, sharing detailed information about the products they sold to assure customers that they could consume the products safely and that they were not being cheated on quality. Several butchers in the Poydras Market advertised their partnership to slaughter three cattle. They proclaimed that the animals were "the best and fattest Beef ever offered for sale" in the Poydras Market. They notified potential customers that they could go and see the livestock at the slaughter-house until four o'clock that Saturday afternoon to inspect the quality of the animal or visit their stalls on Sunday morning and judge the beef itself.[40] Aspiring to reach as many readers as possible, they ran the advertisement for four days in a row—no small expense. Working together and combining resources enabled the butchers to reach many more consumers, shedding light on some of the collaborative efforts between public market vendors. Even "competitors" with separate businesses found mutual benefit in combining resources at times, especially when they were endeavoring to launch viable businesses that could compete with the already established butchers in markets across the city.

Food businesses also provided enslaved Black retailers opportunities to earn income, purchase their own freedom, and gain access to property. Most who were able to do so lived in New Orleans, rather than the rural interior of Louisiana, and had desirable skill sets, food retailing among them.[41] Although they did not have the right to vote, free people of color could own property and accrue wealth.[42] The ability to earn income was key, as it provided them the means to self-purchase and perhaps pay any legal fees should their efforts to manumit themselves be contested by their enslaver.[43] Such was the case for an enslaved woman named Fanny who successfully sued for her freedom in 1848 via the First District Court of New Orleans. She earned about twenty dollars per month selling bread on behalf of her enslaver, Desdunes Poincy, a baker. By comparison, Fanny earned nearly twice as much as enslaved people working in the domestic service industry.[44]

Similarly, François Naba relied on his income operating a grocery store to successfully sue for his freedom in the Second District Court. By the time he went to court in 1855, Naba had been operating a grocery store, presumably on behalf of his enslaver, for more than two years. The trade was lucrative for him. In his testimony, he noted that he sold between $300 and $400 in groceries each month, and that he paid for two-thirds of the grocery stock himself (his enslaver likely paying for the remainder). Although it was illegal for enslaved people to own any kind of property or learn to read at that time,

Naba admitted, "I can calculate and write a little" and expressed a desire to "go to night school."[45] Before and after his freedom, Naba used his business acumen and other skills to gain financial stability. So, too, did Fanny, although the archival record does not reveal whether she could read or write.

Although Fanny and Naba successfully sued for their freedom, that freedom was tenuous and could be questioned, so free people of color also used the courts to retain their liberty.[46] Throughout the antebellum period, when free people of color were able to sustain their freedom, a significant number became expert craftspeople and built prosperous businesses. Julien Adolphe LaCroix operated a grocery store on Frenchman Street prior to the Civil War, and his estate was valued at $130,000 in 1868.[47] He was among a cohort of free people of color, including women, who supported themselves and their families through food retailing in and outside of the public markets. Although the population of free people of color in New Orleans decreased by the mid-nineteenth century, shrinking to just 6 percent by 1860 from its peak of around 30 percent in 1810, their businesses continued to contribute to the evolution of the city's public food culture and provide support for their community.[48]

Whereas local officials constructed the first public markets in existing neighborhoods, they also approved the construction of public markets in areas that had not yet amassed a significant population on the developing semirural periphery of New Orleans. Those public markets were the catalyst for new population and commercial growth that led to the emergence of these neighborhoods. One such example was the Dryades Market, located at the intersection of Dryades and Melpomene Streets at the rear of the Second Municipality.[49]

In the antebellum period, recent European immigrants settled in developing communities like Dryades. Ethnic intermixing predominated, with immigrants from different countries living next to one another or even in the same dwelling (versus in distinct ethnic enclaves) and adjacent to manumitted Black neighbors.[50] All community members, regardless of race or ethnicity, had access to these new public markets and the offerings of vendors within, that is, if they could afford their wares; and whatever provisioning needs could not be met by public market vendors could be fulfilled by street food vendors or by personal urban gardens, often more economical options.

In the first decade of the nineteenth century, the neighborhood that would eventually become known as "Dryades Market" was undeveloped swampland—a patch of wetlands connecting expansive cotton fields to the city of New Orleans. A three-hundred-foot-long rope bridge was one of the first amenities in the Dryades neighborhood, acting as a vital lifeline between the cotton fields and the emergent community in the 1820s. The neighborhood sat "at the back door" of the American Sector.[51] The undeveloped land was wild and held a certain mystique that captured the imagination of New Orleans' residents. It is not difficult to picture people traversing the unstable rope bridge in the early morning as tendrils of fog slowly crept over the still, murky water and folded around the bases of ancient cypress and oak trees. The trees were (and still are) emblematic of Louisiana's native climes. It is unsurprising, then, that developers named the Dryades neighborhood after the mythological dryads—wood nymphs—whom they believed could have lived amid those ghostly trees.[52] How did this natural and dangerous hinterland eventually become a major residential area and shopping corridor in New Orleans?

In the first decade of the nineteenth century, the swampland captured the interests of property investors who sought to expand the American Sector out toward Lake Pontchartrain.[53] The municipal government drained the land to prepare for the growth of a residential and commercial sector. As city officials developed the area, they understood that a public market was necessary to sustain a growing urban population.[54] The local newspaper noted that, prior to the construction of the Dryades Market, the rear of the first district was underdeveloped and lacking infrastructure and community (good roads and residences). The newspaper clarified that "only a few scattering houses were to be seen in that portion of the city."[55] In the late 1840s, the municipal government began to plan for the construction of a "quasi-public" market in the Dryades neighborhood. The market was quasi-public in that the city did not bear the cost of its construction. Rather, individuals submitted bids to build the market, and the chosen person would bear the construction cost in exchange for full stall revenues for a defined period, usually twenty to thirty years. For all intents and purposes, though, these markets were treated as public ones and were subject to all the rules and regulations of a municipal market. After the contractual period ended, the city once again took full ownership of these markets. In this way, the quasi-public market model enabled the city government to furnish new neighborhoods with a public market without bearing the upfront cost of its construction. Patrick Irwin, a real estate developer and later millionaire and politician, entered into a contract with the city government to erect one such quasi-public market and several other buildings on Dryades Street.

Waiting with anticipation for the Dryades Market's official opening, community members gathered just outside of the new facility along Dryades and

Melpomene Streets on the morning of January 10, 1849. The market opened its stalls to the public at seven o'clock in the morning.[56] Vendors had worked tirelessly to prepare their displays, hoping to make strong first impressions with potential customers and solidify their reputations.

A walk through the pavilion a few hours prior to opening would have revealed stall keepers working with fierce efficiency to prepare their retail spaces as a near-constant flow of mule-drawn carts laden with fruits and vegetables arrived on the scene. Produce vendors would have taken care to artfully arrange their wares in baskets and on top of barrels to showcase the vibrant colors and rich textures of seasonal produce. Vendors would have likely halved winter citrus fruits or sliced them for display so that their cloying scent carried along the halls of the market. Bakers would have stacked steaming loaves of fragrant, German-style breads, still hot from the oven, in their stalls. The coffee stand keepers, too, would have showcased the robust aroma of their product by roasting, grinding, and brewing their coffee on site. These sensory delights would have been but a taste and a whiff of what was to come for the neighborhood.

From its very first hours, New Orleanians deemed the market as a place for the people of the Dryades neighborhood and a place that bolstered a belief in the importance of public welfare. Events at the opening were geared toward fostering a shared sense of ownership over the market. Local politicians, vendors, and community shoppers were all invited to participate. The opening ceremonies culminated at two o'clock in the afternoon with a luncheon. The elaborate feast signaled the market's opening as an important event not only for the surrounding neighborhood, but for the city of New Orleans as well. Fathers, mothers, children, and local aldermen attended the event, which transformed the market from a retail space into a community one. According to the *Daily Picayune*, "The long tables of the market house groaned beneath the weight of roast turkeys, ducks, chickens, beef, &c. champagne, claret, &c. were provided in profusion to wash the aforesaid articles down." The community lunched for a good hour. A series of toasts commemorated the market and wished market entrepreneurs future success. Spirits rose as the event continued (and as attendees consumed more champagne and other libations). Attendees reportedly danced around with turkey legs and wings waving above their heads in jubilation. This was a celebration of the coming transformation of the Dryades neighborhood and a beckoning of good fortune for local entrepreneurs.[57]

As the symbolic heart of many neighborhoods in New Orleans, and as a representation of municipal responsibility, the public markets—including the new Dryades Market—directly reflected the health and productivity of local communities and their governing bodies. New Orleans' officials, therefore, felt compelled to invest in the upkeep of these public spaces. In order to maintain their appearance, municipal officials assigned "negroes belonging to the city gang," and eventually prisoners in Orleans parish, to clean the markets.[58] The harsh Louisiana climate accelerated wear and tear on the structures, and the city government was not always able to keep up repairs, to the dismay of community members. It was not uncommon for city residents to petition the local government to improve a public market's roof, sidewalk, or some other part of the facility if it had fallen into disrepair or needed renovation or expansion. Most public market maintenance was fairly routine and involved repainting the posts and eaves as well as repairing leaks in the roofs.

Public market vendors, too, most often the butchers, would speak to their local government representative to address issues ranging from maintenance to equipment. They had the ear of local officials, as indicated by the regular improvements and equipment installed specifically to benefit their businesses. In 1840, the Second Municipality paid William Bell $480 to build thirty-two butcher stalls ($15 each) in the St. Mary's Market.[59] He also repaired a hose for $1.50.[60] B. T. K. Bennett made meat hooks for the St. Mary's Market butchers in the same year.[61] These vendor-initiated improvements highlight how the city's public food culture was entwined with the city's political culture too.

As anticipated, the construction of the Dryades Market ignited population growth, and the market's presence gave new residents a place to regularly convene for commercial and noncommercial activities. Whereas the Dryades neighborhood was still a nascent community through much of the 1840s, it boomed in the early 1850s. The residents demanded the enlargement of the Dryades Market to meet their needs. Their requests were brought in front of local officials, and construction began only a few weeks later. As noted in the local paper, it was "the enterprise of the population" that brought about the second market building, demonstrating the power of communities to organize and acquire the municipal resources they needed.[62] The second building was of the same size and appearance as the original one; it was located on the opposite side of the Melpomene Canal, one square up at the intersection of Dryades and Terpsichore Streets.[63]

Whereas the Dryades neighborhood had previously been a community defined by its scattered residences and dearth of public amenities, the construction of the market signaled a turning point in the neighborhood's economic role in the city. In acknowledging these upcoming developments, the local newspaper noted that the market provided a much-needed space for commercial activity while also increasing property values of the surrounding streets.[64] That uptick attracted other businesses to the area. As on Dryades Street, it was common for banks to open along streets on which a public market had recently been completed.[65] These bank branches, of which many of the buildings still stand today, often bore the name of the market with which they were associated.[66] The Canal Commercial Trust & Savings Bank, for example, had a Dryades Market branch. These bank branches provided the necessary financial assistance and infrastructure for other private enterprises to open near the commercial core of the public market. These other entities were diverse and included grocery stores, bakeries, restaurants, coffeehouses, taverns, saloons, drugstores, specialty shops, and eventually, department stores.[67]

It was advantageous for these businesses to cluster near the public markets because of the foot traffic around the central commercial and community space. This was the case not only for the Dryades Market but also for others around the city. An advertisement in the local paper, for example, described a recently opened grocery's location as "in the most thriving portion of Lafayette, near the New Magazine street Market."[68] Advertisements for dwellings, too, mentioned if homes were desirably located near the public markets—for example, "A good Dwelling House and Lot on Felicity street, near the Magazine street market."[69] The markets, whether in the Dryades neighborhood or Magazine Street corridor, were the desirable public amenities for potential retailers and residents alike, drawing people and businesses to their vicinity.

The commercial corridor that grew up around the Dryades Market created a village life for those living within close proximity to it, constantly reinforcing connections among community members in the Dryades neighborhood. That village life concentrated the movement of neighborhood residents who no longer had to venture to the city center for necessities; nearly everything they needed was within a few city blocks of where they lived. They could buy food, deposit money, or get fitted for a dress all within minutes of home. Schools, too, were built in relation to the market. After the Dryades Market's construction, the local government erected the Jefferson and Webster schools to accommodate the expanding number of children in the Dryades neighborhood.[70] The market—along with the resources that grew up around it—met the physical, social, and economic needs of its community.

From its conception, Patrick Irwin envisioned the Dryades commercial corridor as a shopping destination both for neighborhood residents and for those who lived in other parts of the city.[71] Irwin strategically invested not only in the construction and expansion of the market, but also in neighboring properties and a transportation service that would bring customers from outside the Dryades neighborhood to its commercial core.[72] He established an omnibus line—horse- or mule-drawn carriages that operated on major throughways—along Rampart Street from Julia Street to the Dryades Market. This line ran for fifteen years and acted as a key connector between downtown New Orleans and the Dryades commercial district.[73] Eventually, these omnibus lines were superseded by railroad lines, in which Irwin also invested, and from them he amassed most of his fortune.[74]

Omnibus lines played a key role in the growth of other neighborhoods as well, including the Magazine Street corridor, which was also supported by a line.[75] The combination of an omnibus line and a public market was a powerful draw for potential residents and business owners alike, as reflected in newspaper advertisements. One such advertisement for a dwelling near the Magazine Market described it as "a very desirable two-story DWELLING… contiguous to the Magazine Street Market and Omnibus line."[76] The expansion of the consumer base in each market district ultimately led to the growth of the residential base, encouraging new families and individuals to settle in the community and diversifying its population.[77] In turn, new residents supported the commercial activity around each market, grounding the shopping district in the local community. The markets and neighborhood residents were interdependent: One could not thrive without the other.

The Dryades Market was one of four markets constructed just upriver of the French Quarter between 1848 and 1852. The others were the Ninth Street Market, which opened in Lafayette in 1850; the Soraparu Market, which also opened in Lafayette in 1852; and the Claiborne Market, which opened in the Second Municipality in 1852. As in the past, these markets were in relatively close proximity to one another. The Dryades Market, for example, was within one mile's walking distance to the three closest public markets: the Poydras, St. Mary's, and Magazine Markets. Similarly close to one another, the Soraparu Market was about one mile away from its two neighboring markets, the Ninth Street and St. Mary's Markets. If they so desired, local residents could walk between one public market and the next in about twenty minutes. Additionally, they likely did not have as long a commute to the public market closest to their residence, especially in new communities where residences clustered around the recently constructed amenities.

Local officials approved the construction of these markets as the ethnic divisions and political rivalries between French Creoles and Americans came to a head. Their rivalries placed the city in massive debt, which ruined its credit rating and made it difficult to raise money for infrastructure projects by issuing government bonds. All too aware of the stagnant, messy political situation, in 1852 the Louisiana State Legislature repealed the 1836 act and reconsolidated the city.[78]

On the same day, the state legislature passed another act that had New Orleans annex the city of Lafayette, which brought the majority American, German, and Irish people living in that area into New Orleans, thus increasing the power of the Americans located upriver of the older French Creole communities. The former's economic and political power continued to grow after 1852, whereas the French Creole community and its largely working-class population would grow more slowly, causing it to lose its long-held upper hand in local politics. It was around this time that English began to replace French as the most common language of the city streets and that American cultural tastes (in architecture, literature, and more) became more prominent.

Once again consolidated under one city, local officials approved the construction of an additional market prior to the start of the Civil War: the St. Bernard Market (1856), located in the Faubourg Marigny, previously a part of the poorer and politically weaker Third Municipality. It's neighboring public market, the Tremé Market, was about one mile away. Jefferson Parish, upriver of New Orleans, also constructed its own market, the Jefferson Market, in 1860, one mile up the road from the Ninth Street Market. Both the Ninth Street Market and Jefferson Market were located upriver of the Magazine Market on the same street, demonstrating how urban populations that were spread out along main thoroughfares developed a community and a commercial center around each public market. Similarly, St. Bernard and Claiborne Markets both occupied positions on Broad Street, serving the communities that had developed on opposite ends of that major roadway.

Together, the markets built between 1848 and 1860 created a secondary ring around the first seven markets in the greater New Orleans area (except the Carrollton Market, which was far upriver). Those markets fed the nearly seventy thousand additional people who moved to New Orleans after 1840.[79] Distinct from the communities that formed in the city center, and now with their own markets, communities throughout the greater New Orleans area developed strong ties through the public culture of food in their immediate surroundings.

In the four years directly following consolidation, the city government passed around thirty-three hundred ordinances and resolutions.[80] Of particular interest are the extensive market ordinances that aggregated previously passed market ordinances in one place while eliminating redundancies and also resolving legal discrepancies between the defunct municipalities.[81] Examining them provides details about the standardization of the management of the public markets, their daily operations, and how the city protected them from outside competitors. These laws also helped solidify the public markets' monopoly over most fresh food provisioning in the city. Protecting the centrality of these public amenities ensured the continuation of the social and economic relationships that made up the city's nourishing networks.

On an annual basis, the city government leased out each public market to an individual referred to in the revised and compiled market ordinances as "the farmer." This model drew upon the traditional "farmer-of-the-market" model popular in Europe. After signing the lease, the farmer became eligible to collect all market revenues for the year. To earn these revenues, the farmer collected "duties" from butchers, including ninety cents for every head of cattle and twenty-five cents for every head of veal, mutton, pork, or venison sold. The revised and compiled ordinances standardized these duties across the city's public markets, eliminating variations within individual neighborhoods. Additionally, the farmer sublet stalls within the market to individual vendors, which provided further income. Butcher stalls (furnished with a table and frames with meat hooks) and fish stands could be rented for twenty-five cents a day. The city required that farmers keep detailed records of these fees; it was the responsibility of the farmer "to collect the above established duties, to keep an exact register of the persons to whom he lets the stalls, stands, tables, and frames with hooks, at market hours, and deliver certificates thereof to persons occupying the same."[82] Additionally, the farmer became responsible for the maintenance of the market in that year, including sweeping and whitewashing the building.

The process by which individuals competed to hold the position of farmer could be quite exhilarating—a spectacle, really—as was the case in December 1859 when the city comptroller conducted a public auction for the revenues of several of the city's public markets. The right to a public market's revenues went to the highest bidder. According to the local newspaper, a large crowd had gathered, and as each public market went up for auction the bidding became "animated" and a decision was made only after "a long series of bids of fifty and twenty-five dollars each." Given that the individual public markets went for an approximate range of $2,000 to $55,000, those bidding processes could indeed take some time. The bids were based on predictions for how profitable each public market would be in the coming year; according to the newspaper, prospective farmers had anticipated that sales in 1859 would be higher than those the previous year, leading to higher bids. For example, in 1858, a farmer leased the Poydras Market for $45,900, but in 1859, a farmer, possibly the same one, leased it for $46,200. Similarly, the Ninth Street Market leased for $2,600 in 1858 and $3,400 in 1859. The same article noted that the Claiborne Market, which had been built by an outside contractor around 1852 and was categorized as a quasi-public market, would "revert to the city for sale next May." Once the market was transferred back to the city in 1859, the comptroller could then open a public auction and find a farmer to manage it.[83]

Outlining the procedures related to the annual sale of the public market revenues to a farmer was one small part of what the revised and compiled market ordinances covered. Once a public market was leased out to the farmer, its cleanliness and order were of utmost concern to local lawmakers. They required that each vendor "scrape, wash, and cleanse their respective stalls and tables" immediately after the market closed at noon. Failure to close and clean a business resulted in a five-dollar fine, equivalent to twenty days' stall rent.[84] Sanitation and orderliness were important within the public market and its surroundings. The ordinances restricted any vending beyond the immediate covered area of the public market and noted that those vendors operating on the edges of the market could not obstruct pedestrian walkways. Local lawmakers, though, anticipated that vendors' businesses would inevitably creep onto the sidewalks. They specifically targeted fruit and vegetable vendors, noting that if "boxes, barrels, or other articles" blocked the sidewalks after the public market closed, they would pay a fine of five dollars.[85]

Food safety and the spread of disease were also of prime concern, as reflected in Revised City Ordinance No. 427. It stated that any person who sold "any blown, stale, imperfect, or unwholesome provisions, or meat of any animal that died of disease" would be fined ten dollars on the first offense, and on the second would be forbidden from vending in any public market.[86] That ordinance was amended in December 1856 to increase the penalty for selling adulterated or unsafe food to a $100 fine. Local lawmakers were concerned about not only the sale of rotten foods but also the disposal of foods at the end of each market day. Vendors had the habit of throwing refuse into the city's streets and gutters, which led to the spread of disease. To curtail this practice, the city forbade such actions, and those in violation faced a five- to twenty-dollar fine.[87]

The revised and compiled ordinances also introduced new restrictions on market vendors' enterprises, allowing specialized retailers to open businesses outside of the public market system. For example, the handful of public market vendors operating grocery stands (stocked with dry goods like flour and tea) in the public markets could no longer do so. Instead, grocers were legally bound to sell wares outside of the public markets in their own stores. This particular ordinance legally codified the bifurcation of food shopping in the city—a division that sustained well into the twentieth century. "Making groceries" now necessitated a trip to both the public market and the grocery store, shaping what food shopping looked like for the next several generations.

The city required that the revised and compiled ordinances be posted in French and English in six places within every market, clearly intending the rules to be widely known and understood. Even so, the printed regulations were not accessible to all, especially those who did not have access to education and were therefore likely illiterate or for recent immigrants who did not read French or English. The market ordinances contained no specification that laws had to be read out loud in a city square or public place, nor that they had to be translated into other languages commonly spoken in the city, like German. In this way, many vendors had limited access to the new laws, which further marginalized them within the traditional legal culture. Entrepreneurs not literate in French or English may have struggled to successfully manage their market stalls and stay within the bounds of the law, which also worked to stifle economic equality and limit social mobility for those people not already part of the privileged classes.

Inevitably, market and street vendors broke these laws, and it was the responsibility of the market commissary to write up fines and arrest people when necessary. Accountable for enforcing the ordinances, the commissaries were required to be on site every day during market operating hours. The commissary was also in charge of providing the approved scales and weights "to be used at the request of any person, who, at the time of purchase, may desire to prove the weight of any meat or other provision."[88] Like police officers, the commissaries represented the interests of the city government and worked to protect the well-being of customers. They helped maintain orderly, well-regulated municipal facilities that encouraged New Orleanians to take full advantage of these economic and community spaces.

Whereas the New Orleans city government doubled down on public provisioning in the second half of the antebellum period, codifying their commitment to the public market monopoly in local law, other cities such as Boston and Philadelphia increasingly embraced private food-retailing options. In fact, in cities across the United States, although not really in New

Orleans, more and more private markets opened to sell fresh and prepared foods. Some were small, private shops—greengrocers—that were simple in design. Between 1851 and 1870, the number of greengrocers in Boston increased from 330 to 739 shops, indicating the city's reliance on alternatives to the public markets, which were struggling to fulfill the needs of a growing population.[89] Unlike in New Orleans, where burgeoning neighborhoods petitioned the city government to construct a public market to meet their needs, most other cities had far fewer public markets. They were often located in the city center and were therefore not conveniently located for developing neighborhoods on the urban outskirts. Identifying their needs, greengrocers established businesses in these new communities, becoming key nodes of urban provisioning.

Although small food retailers were increasingly popular, so too were privately owned and operated market halls that rivaled and, in some cases, outdid public markets in terms of their size and ornate architectural designs. Philadelphia butchers, for example, financed the city's impressive Western Market, which opened in April 1859. A classically inspired pastiche, the market was "built of brick, ornamented with granite and brown stone, and externally presents a beautiful and tasteful appearance." It had 280 stalls with countertops hewn from Italian marble that had been polished until customers could see their reflection in them. The market was also equipped with the latest ventilation technologies to promote airflow and reduce the smell of meat, seafood, and produce.[90] It stood in sharp contrast to Philadelphia's public markets, which were comparatively simple in design, many of them pavilion-style structures.[91]

The butchers who privately financed this market felt that they were helping to launch an innovative approach to urban provisioning: market privatization. In fact, they felt that the Western Market was a model that, in time, could "be adopted by all the principal cities in our Great Union," according to Philip Lowry, the chairman of the committee of the Butchers' Association.[92] The mayor of Philadelphia supported the butchers' views, believing that private enterprises could better provision the city than the municipal government.[93] Their shared vision, however, was not one that New Orleans officials or their constituents wanted to adopt. Most New Orleanians in this period were content with and supportive of the city's public market system. Government officials in both cities, however, felt that their particular approach to urban provisioning contributed to their city's growth, civic progress, and public health. In New Orleans, municipal officials safeguarded that vision by creating and, to some degree, enforcing market ordinances.

The influx of people into New Orleans spurred cultural upheaval, as evidenced by the tripartite municipal experiment from 1834 to 1852. In that period, the city was not a veritable "gumbo pot," as so often described in historical and popular literature; it was, for lack of a better word, a "dump casserole"—a nonsensical, unplanned mélange of people and cultures. There was no end goal, no recipe in mind. That change incited a sense of instability for many residents and encouraged xenophobia, as expressed in nativist political movements, especially among those who had already established themselves in New Orleans for a generation or more.

Recent migrants worked to provide for themselves and their families often by starting small-scale food distribution businesses, which had relatively low barriers of entry, especially street food vending. Some new migrants who settled near the Dryades Market or those along Magazine Street, for example, were able to integrate into the public market culture. Others were not so lucky. They lacked the expendable income, credit, and networks to establish a business in the public market. Instead, they took to the streets, seeking to make their way amid the food and cart traffic. Some established community members saw the entrepreneurial efforts of both migrant market and street vendors as invasive or bothersome. They were fearful that migrants' businesses would disrupt their own enterprises.

One of the revised ordinances, No. 432, maintained earlier restrictions on street vendors, expressly forbidding them to sell all vegetables, game, and most seafood, reinforcing the public market monopoly. If they broke the laws, they would be fined ten dollars, a prohibitively large sum for them. Not only that, the same ordinance forbade all street vendors from selling their wares along the footways surrounding a public market, also under penalty of ten dollars for each offense.[94] Local officials did not want their temporary stalls and stands to block pedestrian traffic. This ordinance endeavored, at least on paper, to control the movement and stifle the diversification of street vendors' businesses. The repercussions of the regulations included the marginalization of street vendors within the city's public food culture, forcing some of them to vend illegally to make a living.

The regulation of street vendors exemplifies some New Orleanians' efforts to thwart the business endeavors of recent migrants, many of whom were white working poor. City employees, including any city guard, could approach hawkers or peddlers, demand to see their license, and if one was not present, discard all their goods and fine them between five and one hundred dollars.[95] Black vendors were susceptible to such policing as well. The law, however, appears to have targeted recent immigrants from Europe, as it was passed at a time when New Orleans residents regularly spoke out against immigrants' role in the local food economy and culture. The law also tied into larger nativist political movements in the city and across the country.

Although city officials had not always regulated food vendors very strictly, there were periods in which local law enforcement attempted to make examples of vendors who sold their wares illegally. In the 1840s, the local newspapers occasionally reported license infractions, as was the case on November 6, 1845, when Commissary Prados of the First Municipality seized the wares of a peddler who was selling without a permit. That vendor's wares included dry goods, beads, and umbrellas.[96] In December 1846, police seized two peddlers' goods because they were selling without a license in the Second Municipality.[97] Such arrests and seizures of goods were made public to elicit fear and prevent others from breaking the law.

The mobility and access that street vendors exercised in their everyday business transactions also proved a sore point for some New Orleanians. These residents were particularly averse to the business practices of seasonal vendors who visited New Orleans for a few weeks or months to take advantage of a peak season or harvest, then moved on to other cities or regions. Their mobility and transience irritated shopkeepers, who felt that their businesses suffered because of street vendors' presence. Municipal officials also took issue with these itinerant salesmen for more than just the complaints of constituents: The city could not easily require them to pay vendor licensing fees or taxes, meaning their presence in the city had no real economic advantage to those in power.

Tensions mounted in 1841 when the Second Municipality moved to ban most peddling and hawking within its borders. Alderman Lockett, chairman of the Police Committee, proposed the ordinance on January 5, 1841. He made several arguments against the "evils growing out of the present system of hawking and pedling [*sic*]," convinced that the practice should be abolished. He characterized itinerant peddlers as predatory for taking advantage of seasonality "without any outlay for store rent, clerk hire, or taxes, to the great injury of the regular dealer, whose expenses are necessarily heavy, and whose interests should be protected."[98] Lockett used food vending to define citizenship. For him citizenship was tied to an entrepreneur's ability to pay taxes and rents and create jobs for fellow citizens. Members of the Municipal Council found Lockett's notions of citizenship compelling and framed their critique of itinerant vendors in those terms. In their opinion, peddlers "fulfill none of the duties of citizens," and in fact "exert an influence on the business of the tax-paying store keepers, much to their prejudice." They thought of these vendors as "a nuisance."⁹⁹ Thus, the council approved the ordinance, preventing those whom they saw as noncitizens from partaking in local commerce.¹⁰⁰ Ordinance No. 117 read:

> Be it Ordained that from and after the passage of this ordinance, no person shall hawk or peddle within the limits of the Second Municipality, goods, wares, merchandise, or any other articles whatso-ever, except fruits, flowers, ice cream and cakes, under a penalty of not less than twenty-five nor more than one hundred dollars, for each offence, recoverable before any court of competent jurisdiction.¹⁰¹

The ordinance, then, was not merely about controlling the number of ped-dlers in the neighborhood or their interactions with residents, but a way of controlling who was included in their community. Itinerant vendors whose businesses competed with storekeepers did not belong, at least in the council's opinion.

Not all street vendors were excluded from the Second Municipality's vision of its community and who should have the right to move freely and conduct business within it. The new ordinance had a provision that created an exception for the vendors of "fruits, flowers, ice cream and cakes," many of whom were enslaved.¹⁰² Although these vendors were not barred from the Second Municipality, their permissible presence did not indicate that the council considered them citizens. Their presence, however, may indicate that the council, and the community it represented, envisioned enslaved Black vendors as an essential part of the public food culture of the Second Municipality. Their inclusion afforded Black entrepreneurs, enslaved and free, access to an exclusive area that shut out other street food vendors and an opportunity to build and maintain their food businesses in the municipality as long as they did not compete with storekeepers' interests.

For those who had permission to sell wares, there was a second set of restrictions within the ordinance that drew clear divisions between the public and private spheres, demarcating where vendors could and could not move within the municipality. This part of the ordinance made it illegal for any person to enter a house with articles for sale, or pretending to sell articles, without first "having obtained the permission of the tenants of said house."¹⁰³ This provision speaks to the somewhat more "aggressive" or "invasive" tactics employed by some vendors who would enter the homes of potential custom-ers in order to initiate a sale. It restricted their mobility within the residential parts of the Second Municipality. Those vendors who had established a strong connection to their customers could enter homes, bringing baskets of fresh produce right into the kitchens of their regular customers.[104] Their business acumen and ability to foster strong relationships with long-term customers afforded them greater mobility and access.

Vendors, Black and white, resisted the city government's attempts to limit their businesses. Some chose to vend illegally to their detriment. Within one month of passing the ordinance, arrests of vendors who had been trading illegally were made public. A police officer, for example, successfully seized the goods of a Dutch peddler only after the two had a scuffle.[105] Illegal peddling continued in the city, indicative of its ability to overwhelm the police by force of sheer numbers: It was difficult to keep track of all peddlers and hawkers working the city's crowded streets. Ten years after the 1841 ordinance passed, the newspaper continued to report issues of unlawful vending. It was not an occasional peddler here and there, but "scores" of peddlers, whom the newspaper identified as "interfering, prying, impertinent and lazy fellows."[106] In the eyes of some New Orleanians, the mobility of peddlers and their presence in the city was a pervasive problem. For street food vendors, though, it was a way of survival, especially when they faced so many barriers on a daily basis.

Some New Orleanians' general aversion to itinerant vendors played into much larger anxieties associated with the movement of people in and out of New Orleans in the antebellum period. When the Council of the Second Municipality approved the street-peddling ban in 1841, New Orleans was growing rapidly, its population having doubled from 1830 to 1840.[107] Controlling the flow of commerce in one's neighborhood was one way of coping with a sense of instability brought about by population change and rapid urban development.

For city administrators and their constituents, protecting and patronizing local food businesses was a means to preserve community identity. City newspapers were filled with pleas to support local businesses rather than purchase from out-of-region competitors. As reported in the *Daily Picayune* in 1842: "Peddling, or buying and selling western produce on the Levee is, as dear, departed Dickey Riker would say, 'carried to a great extent in this community.' The permission of such a course is a positive injustice to our permanently settled merchants and tax payers." The protagonists were portrayed as those who were "permanently settled" in New Orleans, people with a long-standing presence in the community and whose products were grown locally.[108] Urban nativism incentivized them to villainize not only the businesses that imported produce to New Orleans, but also the peddlers who chose to buy those products wholesale and distribute them throughout the city. In the eyes of these urban nativists, these peddlers had no loyalty to New Orleans.

Such nativist beliefs tied into the rise of the American Party, colloquially named the Know-Nothing Party, in the 1850s in New Orleans.[109] By 1853, the Know-Nothing Party's nativist sentiments appealed to more and more city residents, especially those frustrated by the impact of immigration and the increasing influence of recent migrants in the local economy and political scene, food vendors among them. As tensions and the influence of Know-Nothingism peaked, riots broke out in the city—a manifestation of the xenophobia that had taken root. Given the vast number of immigrants who made up the city's food vendors, it is not surprising that regulating street food vending became a point of interest among city officials trying to appeal to their nativist constituents.

Throughout the 1850s, New Orleans' population continued to grow as immigrants and migrants from across the United States moved into the city. In that decade alone, the city grew by 45 percent, which matched the growth of other key cities like Boston and Cincinnati and almost mirrored the expansive growth of New York City. The steady increase of its population fueled New Orleans' impressive local economy; it had the second largest per capita income in the country and the largest in the South. In the late antebellum period, New Orleans was unmistakably the economic capital of the region, which meant that it had farther to fall and more to lose as the pressures that led to the Civil War gripped the country.

Data from the 1860 US federal census illuminates how street vending was an occupation deeply influenced by immigrants during the height of the Know-Nothing movement. Of the 175 free people who listed their occupation as either "huckster" or "peddler" in the 1860 census, 87 percent were born outside of the United States. As hucksters and peddlers, these individuals retailed a diverse range of goods, and some, as recorded in the census, were food vendors.

Census data alone does not provide a complete picture of street vending and public market culture in New Orleans, as it does not take into account the large number of enslaved men and women vending on behalf of enslavers, nor Indigenous vendors. What it does reveal, though, is that more and more European immigrants were joining the trade. For those peddlers and hucksters who were free, a vast majority were white immigrant men. Of the immigrant vendors of all genders, many were either German (39 percent) or French (19 percent), followed by Spanish (9 percent) or Irish (7 percent). The remainder came from regions across Europe and the Mediterranean except for two retailers from Cuba and two from Venezuela.

In 1860, the hucksters and peddlers in the US census predominantly lived in three of New Orleans wards (the rather coarse electoral spaces by which census data was aggregated). The 11th Ward was home to 51 percent of the city's total number of hucksters and peddlers, while the 5th Ward had 28 percent, the 3rd Ward had 12 percent; and all eight other wards combined had less than 10 percent. The 11th Ward, located uptown, included the Garden District as well as parts of today's Central City and the Irish Channel, the latter of which was a hotspot for immigrant settlement, particularly German and Irish. Downriver, the 3rd Ward encompassed the American Sector (present-day Central Business District), by then the city's emerging political epicenter.[110] Last but not least, the 5th Ward encompassed the middle of the French Quarter and Faubourg Tremé, home to the heart of the francophone Creole population, largely Catholic, and including a substantial number of free people of color. Enslaved populations could be found in all wards, though in varying percentages. The Fifth Ward incorporated part of the French Market complex as well as the Tremé Market, two major food sources for the adjacent population, and also included the Carondelet (Old Basin) Canal, an important navigational waterway through which shellfish, finfish, game, and other food entered the city.

Of the entire pool of hucksters and peddlers recorded in the 1860 census, only eight (5 percent) were women, all of whom were white. It should be noted that there was likely a substantial group of women who worked alongside their husbands, or even ran the listed businesses, but were not identified as hucksters and peddlers in the census. Some of the census-listed women appeared to be widows, like J. N. Castola, who emigrated from Cuba with her husband and daughter Carmania. Years later, widowed and a mother of three, Castola retailed goods to support her children, who ranged in age from nine to sixteen years old. Similarly, a forty-eight-year-old widowed huckster named Mary Kurtmacker made ends meet to support her two children, Margaret and William, and had actually accumulated a modicum of personal wealth in the range of $250.

In some households, family members may have worked together as street vendors to support the larger family unit, which is perhaps the case for Elizabeth and Wilhelmena Cohn. At forty-six years old, Elizabeth Cohn—who is listed in the census not as a peddler or huckster but as a "fruiterer" (retailer of fruit)—owned $900 in real estate and claimed an additional $800 in personal wealth. Wilhelmena, twenty years old and likely her daughter or niece, worked as a huckster, perhaps selling fruit from Elizabeth's business to grow her own wealth, which at the time was around $400. Alternatively, Wilhelmina may have operated independently from Elizabeth, accumulating wealth outside of the family business.

Of that same pool of vendors, only two individuals (1 percent) were free people of color, both men and both born in New Orleans.[111] This low percentage, though, may not reflect the number of free people of color working as hucksters and peddlers. In this period, free people of color's rights were eroding.[112] Beginning with incremental changes in the 1830s and increasing more rapidly through the 1850s, New Orleans' tripartite racial structure began to shift. People of color, regardless of their status as free or enslaved, faced increasing limitations in legal, economic, and social spheres based on their race.[113] This was especially jarring for free people of color who had exercised relatively more power and liberties compared to their enslaved counterparts in decades prior. By 1860, as the gap between free and enslaved people of color shrank, free people of color grew more anxious about their wavering social status and diminishing rights overall. As a result, the low vendor numbers may have reflected their efforts to evade census takers or identify their occupational status in a different way to protect themselves against increased bias and structural inequalities.[114]

Of the two men that were listed, Augustin Ben, who was around forty-five years of age in 1860, lived in the 5th Ward, where he owned $2,000 in real estate and had $100 in personal wealth.[115] He built a life with his wife Mary, then around thirty-five, who was a washerwoman; together they lived with their five children (possibly some were in-laws).[116] Ben was identified as a "peddler" in the 1860 census and as a "marketman" in the previous 1850 census, suggesting that his business was, in fact, part of New Orleans' food economy.[117] Louis John, around fifty years old at the time of the 1860 census, also worked as a peddler; he lived with his wife Rosine and their daughter Zuline in the 5th Ward.[118] Unlike with Augustin Ben, we do not know if John owned property or what his personal wealth was, as that data was not recorded in the census. He passed away sometime between 1863 and 1880; Rosine worked as a cook to make ends meet after her husband's death.

As street vendors moved throughout the city and even into the surrounding rural communities, they were far more than economic interlocutors. Free and enslaved retailers alike were part of a vast network that transported goods, yes, but so much more as well, including information and ideas—some of which threatened the very tenets of New Orleans' slave society.

Just a few years later during the Civil War, the mobility of vendors across urban and rural landscapes caused concern among Confederate supporters. They feared that mobile hucksters might share news that went directly against their belief system, demonstrating the role that vendors played far beyond hawking foods. In an interview with Adella S. Dixon, a member of the Federal Writers' Project, Pierce Cody recalled how "Yankee peddlers" came to a plantation in Georgia selling various goods and shared word of the outbreak of war and updates on the conflict. Summarizing Cody's experiences, Dixon wrote, "When the master discovered how this information was being given out, these peddlers were forbidden to go near the quarters. This rule was strictly enforced."[119] The enslavers understood the potential power of the peddlers' knowledge and how news of the war might incite enslaved people to think differently about the permanence of their enslaved status. Vending, therefore, was more than just buying and selling goods; it was also about exchanging information and ideas, some of which had the ability to change the tides of history.[120]

In the years leading up to and during the Civil War, street food vendors would continue to play multidimensional roles in New Orleans' public food culture, braiding together economic and social relationships among city residents through the daily acts of provisioning the city. So, too, would their counterparts in the municipal markets, who played an equally dynamic role. Together, they proved to be formidable forces, often at odds with each other, but inexorably bound to each other and their customers by the Crescent City's nourishing networks. Those connections would undergo major changes as the country erupted into civil war.

As the country tore itself in two, every aspect of life, including how people fed themselves, dramatically shifted. During the war, food systems across the country experienced major disruptions due to road blockades, port closures, intentional crop destruction, and the eradication of slave labor in the Confederate states.[121] New Orleans' food economy was no exception. Its once-growing public market culture came to a screeching halt from 1861 to 1865. No new public markets were constructed, nor were any new market laws passed. In existing municipal markets, vendors struggled to survive; so, too, did street food vendors hawking wares on the markets' peripheries.

3

Market Privatization and Mythmaking in New Orleans, 1866–1910

ON A BALMY summer afternoon in 1894, Toto scanned the faces of the people who walked along Canal Street as she fanned herself with an old-fashioned turkey-tail duster. She was on the lookout for potential customers for the sweet pecan candies she was selling. Spotting a gaggle of youngsters, some of her most loyal customers, she crooned in French: "Belles pralines pour les belles petites filles." She entreated the children to buy her pecan confections, which she had artfully displayed in a cloth-lined basket. Spotting a woman whose gaze lingered on the tantalizing treats, Toto called out, "Oh! ma belle demoiselle, you go'ne buy some praline for sure; dey so pretty for de pretty lady." Sure enough, a few moments later, the woman left with one of Toto's pralines in hand.[1]

Later that day, Toto moved her business to Jackson Square in the heart of the French Quarter, which was bustling with locals and tourists. Children dodged in and around the flowers of the park, taking breaks from their play to purchase a praline from Toto. They could not resist the cloyingly sweet candies. After observing this summer scene unfold, a writer for the *Daily Picayune* paused to reflect; the moment stirred memories of "when you, too, were a little child and used to go with your nurse to the Old Creole square in the summer evenings, just to spend your 'picayune' [a small amount of money] for one of 'Toto's' pralines." Toto, had in fact, been vending pralines in New Orleans since shortly after the Civil War. So familiar was her presence and so integral to the local culture that the *Daily Picayune* author mused: "You dimly wonder how deserted the old square would seem without this ancient, familiar figure seated within its shadow."[2]

Toto was one of countless food vendors who eked out a living selling food in the city streets after the Civil War. Hers was a business built on a long-standing tradition of Black women and other marginalized groups carving out space for themselves in New Orleans' local food economy. That economy underwent significant changes in the postbellum era, when political power struggles changed the very laws that governed provisioning in the Crescent City. Like her fellow food vendors, Toto weathered that change, sustaining her praline business for decades even as the legal and cultural landscape shifted around her.

One of the major forces that transformed New Orleans' postbellum food economy was outside political influence at all levels of government. During Reconstruction (1862–1877), recently elected Republican officials, many from other parts of the country, were growing their political careers in New Orleans, which also operated as the state capital from 1866 to 1879.[3] To these Republicans, New Orleans' traditional public food culture needed to give way to the privatized market systems already common in cities like Philadelphia and others across the North and Midwest—models familiar to the nonnative politicians. In this period, Republican leaders butted heads with the failed Confederate rebels who were infuriated not only by their politics—including efforts to enfranchise Black voters and increase the number of Black elected officials—but also by their lack of ties to New Orleans and Louisiana.

Amid the political chaos and power struggles that often saw Republicans coming out on top, New Orleans experimented with market privatization and reduced restrictions on private food retailers, including street food vendors like Toto. While Republicans advocated for changes that made food systems resemble those in other parts of the country, New Orleanian food vendors and customers held varying opinions about deregulation and privatization and used what political and legal recourse they had to advocate for their best interests. Disagreements among vendors, customers, and politicians demonstrate the ways in which New Orleanians struggled to find consensus regarding the public food culture in the immediate aftermath of the Civil War. These local tensions reflected broader political conflicts reverberating across the country.

In the same period, a second outside force shaped public provisioning in New Orleans and had an impact on food vendors' businesses: an emergent tourist industry. Travel companies marketed the postbellum city as a destination to Americans living largely outside of the South. They employed vivid and descriptive language of the cityscape, the people, and its public food culture to capture the imaginations of tourists, who were primarily white Americans from the Northeast and Midwest. As a result, upon arriving in the city, these new customers craved "authentic" encounters with New Orleans' food vendors, like Toto, who were often referenced in the tourist literature.

Adapting their business practices to meet the needs and wants of a growing tourist client base, food vendors demonstrated agility and business savvy, setting up shop in key sightseeing areas and even donning historic garb to appeal to their sense of nostalgia for the antebellum South. Attuned to the desires of their evolving customer base, food vendors out in the city streets and in the public markets continued to play a vital role in feeding the city even as other American cities turned to alterative urban provisioning models in the second half of the nineteenth century.

In the wake of the Civil War, some New Orleanians looked around at the local food economy and felt a deep sense of frustration. They were essentially forced to shop at the public markets because local law prevented them from buying most fresh food elsewhere. Faced with limited options, some customers grew resentful of the public market monopoly and the food vendors who occupied stalls in the municipal facilities. Those vendors paid fees to rent stalls and adjusted the price of their wares to help cover the costs of doing so. Some customers saw these price increases as an unfair "tax" shoppers had to pay—a tax that hurt them and benefited public market vendors and municipal officials.[4] Some customers grew envious of other large cities like New York and Philadelphia where food was sold from private markets and stands, rather than just public markets. This situation was reported admiringly by the *Daily Picayune*, a major proponent of private markets and instigator of conversations around their adoption in the city. These customers felt that competition among public and private market vendors in other cities incentivized them to keep prices as low as possible, which was a great benefit to customers. They wanted similarly low prices in New Orleans.[5]

Some of these very same customers looked longingly across the waters of the Mississippi River to the neighboring community of Algiers, which had not yet been incorporated into New Orleans and was not beholden to the public market monopoly. In Algiers, as in cities like New York and Philadelphia, private markets and small retail food shops operated unrestricted. Some New Orleanians felt that the Algiers businesspeople continually strove "to furnish the best of meats and the freshest of vegetables at the lowest prices" for fear that if they did not, they would lose customers to their competitors. In these New Orleanians' estimation, competition was the key to creating a local food economy that benefited customers; they saw no other path forward than for the public market monopoly to end.[6]

During Reconstruction, the local laws that policed public provisioning significantly changed in a way that incentivized and invited the competition that some New Orleanians craved. In 1866, the majority Republican state legislature, urged by Republican politicians in New Orleans, passed a law opening New Orleans' food economy to private retailers. The law also reduced regulation on food retailing, in general, in the hopes of increasing competition and decreasing food prices for customers.[7] The law noted:

> It shall be lawful for persons, after they have obtained the license required for retailers of provisions, to open and to keep open at all proper hours of the day private markets, stores or stands in any part of the city of New Orleans, for the sale of meats, game, poultry, vegetables, fruit, and fresh fish, subject to the general sanitary ordinances of the city council.[8]

Significantly, this law broke the monopoly that the city government had held over local food distribution since the colonial period, providing an opportunity for entrepreneurs to opt out of the public market system and instead pursue food retailing on their own terms through private shops; those who could do so were mostly white men who had relatively unfettered access to private property.

As some vendors left the public markets to strike out on their own, new opportunities arose for marginalized vendors—including recent migrants, women, and people of color. Take, for example, Rose Nicaud, a coffee vendor, who had been operating a stand in the Vegetable Market within the French Market complex since the 1850s. Some of her clientele included fellow market vendors like Mrs. Simon, another woman vendor of color, who operated a vegetable stand nearby. Simon was known take breaks from her own selling duties to sit down and enjoy a cup of coffee and catch up on gossip and news with Nicaud. Sometimes Charles Fox, a white man who operated a neighboring vegetable stall, also joined them. So, too, did Mrs. Christian and Mrs. LaCaze, both women of color, who sold dairy products at the market.[9] In fact, it was a regular occurrence for fellow French Market vendors, Black and white, men and women, to frequent Nicaud's stand along with a broader cohort of customers. Nicaud herself remarked in 1868 that "everybody takes coffee at my stand."[10] Perhaps during one or more of these exchanges, Nicaud and her fellow vendors discussed the laws transforming the very nature of food vending in New Orleans by allowing private markets. Perhaps even some from her cohort discussed the pros and cons and leaving the market to strike out on their own.[11]

The first legally operating private markets opened in 1867.[12] They were small shops, simple in design, providing shelter for purveyors who chose not to sell in the public markets. Like public market vendors, private market vendors created eye-catching displays of recently butchered meats, freshly caught fish, and ripe produce so that shoppers could come and assess the quality of their products. Grocery stores that began to sell fresh produce (i.e., greengrocers) were also legally defined as private markets. In addition to fresh food, these stores sold dry goods such as coffee, tea, sugar, tobacco, and animal feed, in addition to liquor.

Supporters of the private markets reported out that their prices were significantly more affordable than those of their competitors in the public markets. In December 1867, the *Daily Picayune* noted that "choice beef" was available in recently opened private markets "at fifteen cents per pound, while for the same cuts in the public market twenty and twenty-five cents is demanded." The paper claimed that similarly low prices were available for vegetables, poultry, and game.[13]

For proponents of the private markets, the benefits of these enterprises stretched far beyond access to affordable food. They believed, the *Daily Picayune* reported, that "the system of private markets will be apt to revolutionize the culinary department of housekeeping in New Orleans and place it, as it has done in New York and other Northern cities, upon a much more agreeable footing." Not beholden to the local laws that governed the public markets, private markets could sell products at any time of the day, creating potentially more convenient shopping experiences for their customer. The paper stated, "It is not always the pleasantest thing in the world to be obliged to go or send one's servants at unreasonable hours in the morning to market houses." What's more, the article went on to claim that the public markets, compared to their private counterparts, could be quite a trek from one's home and overcrowded on top of that. The article enticed readers to imagine a future in which there was a private market "upon almost every square, as in other large cities" so that the housekeeper "can send at any time and order, without fear of disappointment" all that she needs to create a meal.[14]

A few months later, in February 1868, the *Daily Picayune* admitted that the private markets were not the perfect solution to the city's public provisioning problems, noting that some private markets overcharged for their wares. "The depreciation in our currency may have something to do with this, but not all," the article surmised. It went on to argue that if more private markets open in the city, "and they are well encouraged and spring up near one another, there will be such competition that we shall have our meat and vegetables, aye, and our fruit and fish also, given us at very moderate terms." Once again, the *Daily Picayune* hammered home the point that competition was key to the future of food provisioning in New Orleans.[15]

As private retailers slowly spread throughout the city, municipal officials passed a comprehensive revision of the city's market ordinances. As in the past, they delineated everything from operating hours and maintenance procedures to what products could be sold within and outside of the public markets. Retaining an antebellum practice, the Republican government leased out the public markets to private entrepreneurs or "farmers." They were then responsible for the annual care and upkeep of the municipal facilities, thereby relieving municipal officials of the obligation.

Overall, the reimagined market laws sought to reduce regulation on food provisioning, affording food retailers opportunities to sell new products. A major departure from antebellum-era law, the ordinances allowed for the sale of fish, fruit, and vegetables in the city streets as long as vendors purchased licenses. In enacting this law, the municipal government created more room for street vendors to build businesses outside of the public markets—the very same businesses it had previously tried to stifle to protect the public markets' monopoly in the antebellum period.

The revised market ordinances, along with the 1866 ruling to open up the city's economy, had noticeable impacts on the profitability of individual public market vendors' businesses and the overarching municipal market system's revenues. According to the 1874 city directory, there were 1,374 grocery stores operating in the city, all of which could legally sell fresh food, and some of which were competing directly with the public markets by virtue of their proximity to the municipal amenities.[16] That proximity, and the sheer number of greengrocers, was damaging to public market business. Witness to these losses, some city lobbyists, along with the constituents they represented, pushed back against the Republican state legislature's deregulation and privatization experiment. Less than a decade into the changes, they wanted to return to their traditional food-provisioning system that protected public market vendors from competition.

In 1874, demonstrating how deeply rooted these beliefs were among certain New Orleans populations, lobbyists' arguments made headway in the Republican state legislature. In January, legislators proposed House bill No. 30, which would once again restrict and regulate private markets in New Orleans. The bill was not without its naysayers, who were in favor of maintaining a deregulated food economy supported by private retailers—a provisioning model, they argued, that city residents preferred. Some opponents of the bill actually "believed in abolishing the public markets, as they were at present mismanaged, and had been mismanaged for the past four or five years."[17] That opinion, however, remained in the minority in the House.

Community meetings shed light on how critical House bill No. 30 was for some business owners whose success was tied to that of the public markets. On a brisk winter night in 1874, "property-holders, butchers and citizens generally of New Orleans" gathered at the Magazine Market to discuss the proposed piece of legislation that might mean the public markets' rescue.[18] That evening, the Nineteenth Infantry band played at the entrance of the market—its "sweet music" alerting neighboring residents that something important was happening. From the February darkness shone lamps like beacons, which organizers had erected, and which cast a warm and steady glow on the butchers, customers, local officials, and several state senators and representatives from the Republican Party who gathered "intent upon getting the opinions of the public upon this bill."[19]

That evening, the Magazine Market, normally a forum for trading ripe produce and choice cuts of meat, transformed into a political meeting ground where a shared vision emerged for the future of New Orleans' public food culture. Reconstruction-era legislation had left public market vendors' businesses devastated and with them their neighbors' businesses as well. Peter Kaiser, who owned property adjacent to the Magazine Market, noted how the market's decline impacted the value of his property and countless others on the Magazine Street corridor. The 1866 law "had brought grievous injury to the city," said Kaiser, and caused the entire market system's revenues to decline by more than half in under a decade, "all on account of private markets" that outcompeted them.[20]

Stepping up to support Kaiser, Louisiana House Representative L. Sewall added that "the markets had done much to build up the city." He found it despicable that opponents of the newly proposed bill had suggested that the city dissolve its public market system. He pointed out that their disestablishment "would seriously and unjustly injure these property-holders." Instead, he supported the proposed legislation that would restore antebellum-era restrictions on private markets. Republican Representative William Murrell backed Sewall's arguments. So, too, did city resident Anthony Sambola, who publicly grieved the loss of a once robust public market system, lamenting that "the markets of the city were its pride," but no longer.

For Sambola, Murrell, Sewall, Kaiser, and the rest of the group gathered in the market that night against the chills of winter and economic slump, it was time for city residents and local officials to support the public market vendors who had provisioned them for generations; they called upon fellow New Orleanians to demonstrate loyalty to the city's traditional food system and work in tandem with politicians to protect and revive what they saw as essential economic spaces.

So powerful were the arguments against deregulation and market privatization that the state legislature acquiesced that same year to lobbyists from New Orleans and passed House bill No. 30, which prevented private markets from operating within twelve blocks of any public market.[21] The lobbyists' victory reveals how public market vendors reinstated their antebellum status as a protected class of entrepreneurs because of their connections to government officials. Their political networks remained intact despite the experimental and unstable period of Reconstruction, enabling them to shape local law to their advantage: in this instance, repealing postwar laws that deeply affected their businesses.

After the bill became law, private markets essentially became illegal because there were so many public markets in the city, many of which were fewer than twelve blocks apart. The extent to which the government officials enforced the radius rule, shutting down illegally operating private markets, is another matter entirely. In fact, private markets went mostly unregulated and operated across the city and in close proximity to the public markets.[22] Perhaps what mattered most in this moment was the legal codification of pro-public market lobbyists' desires.

In this period of economic experimentation, the municipal government also approved the construction of several new public markets, bringing the total number to nineteen.[23] Some of these new facilities were quasi-public markets—ones built by and at the expense of private entrepreneurs who then held a contract for that market for a twenty-year period before the city took back full control. These establishments were still subject to all public market rules and regulations, so local officials considered them public markets.[24] Joseph Raymond, for example, won the bid to build the Second Street Market, and seeking to create the most profitable market possible, searched for an ideal plot of land. As the local paper noted in 1873, "Mr. Raymond, an enterprising gentleman, conceived the happy idea some time ago of looking for some desirable central location, which would be convenient to the residents of all the north of St. Charles [Avenue], and the major part of the south side." Raymond built the "magnificent market" on that location soon afterward.[25]

The construction of these new public markets and the legal restriction of private enterprise in New Orleans' food economy coincided with major political turmoil in New Orleans and the state of Louisiana. In 1874, white

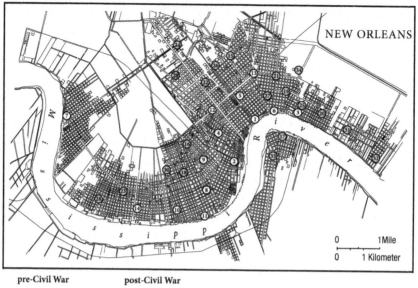

pre-Civil War	post-Civil War	
① French Market, 1791	⑮ Le Breton Market, 1867	㉙ Memory Market, 1907
② St. Mary's Market, 1822	⑯ Keller Market, 1867	㉚ Mehle Market, 1907
③ Washington Market, 1836	⑰ St. John Market, 1872	㉛ Doullut Market, 1907
④ Poydras Market, 1838	⑱ Second Street Market, 1873	㉜ Behrman Market, 1909
⑤ Treme Market, 1840	⑲ St. Roch Market, 1882	㉝ Foto Market, 1910
⑥ Port Market, 1840	⑳ Guillotte Market, 1882	㉞ McCue Market, 1910
⑦ Carrollton Market, 1846	㉑ Delamore Market, 1882	
⑧ Magazine Market, 1847	㉒ Rocheblave Market, 1882	
⑨ Dryades Market, 1848	㉓ Prytania Market, 1890	
⑩ Ninth Street Market, 1850	㉔ Suburban Market, 1896	
⑪ Soraparu Market, 1852	㉕ Zengel Market, 1900	
⑫ Claiborne Market, 1852	㉖ Maestri Market, 1900	
⑬ St. Bernard Market, 1856	㉗ Lautenschlaeger Market, 1902	
⑭ Jefferson Market, 1860	㉘ Ewing Market, 1907	

This map shows the locations and approximate dates of construction for the public markets built in New Orleans after the Civil War. Their locations mirror the outward expansion of New Orleans' urban footprint in the decades following the war. The public markets were so abundant that local law, which prevented private markets from operating near them, essentially created a public market monopoly over fresh food provisioning in New Orleans.

Base map source: *New Encyclopedic Atlas and Gazetteer of the World* (New York: P. F. Collier & Son, 1917). Courtesy of the University of Texas Libraries, University of Texas at Austin.

supremacists in New Orleans formed the White League, which was set on dismantling Republican control in the region and disenfranchising Black Americans.[26] So strong was their presence and their ability to gain support among local residents that in September 1874, White League members successfully carried out a violent political coup. They unseated Republican Governor William Pitt Kellogg from his office in New Orleans for several days before President Ulysses S. Grant sent federal troops into the city to reinstall the governor. In the aftermath, not a single White League member faced criminal prosecution for participating in the coup, which had led to the death of several people, innocent bystanders among them. This inaction and the lack of an outcry against the White League on a national level reflected an increasing number of Americans' dissatisfaction with Republican Reconstruction policy and Americans' corroding conviction to protect Black civil rights.[27]

In the eyes of a growing number of people in New Orleans, the state of Louisiana, and the United States as whole, the White League's discontent and resentment and their attempts to violently re-empower Democrats on a white supremacist platform was justified. It is not surprising, then, that in the national midterm election of 1874, Americans voted in so many Democrats as to give them control of the US House of Representatives. Louisiana soon followed, with Republican control unraveling in early 1877 as the White League and the Democratic Party tightened their hold on New Orleans. Former Confederate general Francis Tillou Nicholls became governor, realizing Louisianan Democrats' long-standing desire to ascend to power once again and begin an era of "Redemption." However, enacting their vision in the wake of Reconstruction proved difficult as infighting among conservative white politicians, which eventually ended up dissolving the White League coalition, impeded the Democratic Party. Discontent spread among their constituents, who began questioning the party's rise to power, some abandoning it all together.[28]

In 1878, members of the fringe National Party spoke out in the *Daily Picayune* about how they were dissatisfied with the "so-called Democratic and Conservative party of Louisiana." According to their printed testimony, National Party members had voted in the Democrats in order to remove the Republican Party from power with the "assurances that all the abuses, corruptions, derelictions and malpractices in the administration of our public affairs, the stagnation in business, depreciation of property, all of which were charged upon the Republican party, were to disappear, and we were to enjoy the inestimable blessing of good government prosperity."[29] Those political promises were not fulfilled. Instead, National Party members, and many other New Orleanians not associated with the party, saw corruption and waste all around them.[30] The ineffectiveness of the Democratic government was no more apparent than in its bungling of the 1878 yellow fever epidemic, which killed nearly five thousand residents. A viral disease spread by mosquitos, yellow fever thrived in the warm and damp conditions of New Orleans' summer and fall seasons and crowded public spaces. New Orleanians associated the high death toll with the intolerable and unhealthy conditions of the city and its public amenities, the public markets among them. In their eyes, the Democratic-controlled municipal government had failed to protect them.[31]

Just as the yellow fever epidemic came to an end in November, discontented city residents took issue with the municipal government's decision to lease the public markets to private businessmen, or "farmers of the market." They felt that the contractors had neglected necessary repairs to the structures and failed to provide sanitary conditions for vendors and their customers. The markets no longer felt safe. Further, they argued that leasing the markets to the highest bidder created an indirect tax for all customers and disproportionately affected the poorest people in the city, who struggled to purchase affordable food. In their estimation, New Orleans' public markets no longer served the needs of the people but served market managers' interest in financial gain.[32]

New Orleanians' growing dissatisfaction worked in the favor of street food vendors operating outside of the public markets who did not have to significantly raise the price of their products to accommodate overhead costs like stall rental fees. As in earlier periods, street vendors remained a crucial part of New Orleans' public food culture, continually adapting their businesses to the changing regulatory conditions around them. But the shifting legal landscape was not the only thing they had to navigate in the postbellum period. They also had to adapt to an ever-changing consumer base, populated more and more by American tourists who came with their own expectations of street vendors and their businesses—expectations shaped by tourist literature created for major events like the 1884 World's Fair.

The 1884 World's Fair in New Orleans—officially known as the World's Industrial and Cotton Centennial Exposition—celebrated American unity and progress in the postbellum period. For city officials and local businesses alike, the goal of the fair was to showcase New Orleans' cotton industry and to demonstrate on the world stage that after the Civil War and Reconstruction, the city was very much a part of and contributing to a modern, progressive American society.[33] As the host city, New Orleans found itself and its local food economy and culture in the national limelight.

Philadelphia had been the last American city to host the World's Fair in 1876, celebrating the centennial of the Declaration of Independence and the birth of the United States. That event reinforced in the American imagination the idea that Philadelphia was central to how Americans understood themselves as citizens and patriots. Americans undoubtedly compared New

Orleans, the subsequent host of a World's Fair in America, to Philadelphia—not only juxtaposing the two cities' roles in American history, but also their success in hosting the fair. As an 1884 fair promotional pamphlet stated, "Those who visited Philadelphia in 1876, will need no words to recall the rich and varied treasures of the Government Department, but remarkable as that exhibit was, it is thrown into the shadow by that of 1884." Later, the pamphlet noted, "It was said that had the visitors to the Centennial of 1876 conscientiously given but five minutes of time to each object of interest, he would have spent 265 years in the task. In some particulars, the Centennial of 1884 is more rich and varied than its predecessor."[34] The Fair organizers' desires to highlight New Orleans' modernity, therefore, contradicted many Americans' attitudes and expectations of the city shaped by a growing tourism industry—one built on the idea that New Orleans' antebellum agrarian culture stalwartly persisted and was unfazed by the forces of modernity gripping other parts of the country.

After the Civil War, tourism became an important industry not only in New Orleans but throughout the American South. Eager tourists crisscrossed the region on rail to visit major battlefields and "charming" plantations. Wanting to share their experiences, they sent postcards to family and friends. Those postcards captured an emerging tourism industry's fascination with antebellum slave society and often featured palatial plantation homes flanked by craggy oak trees hung with Spanish moss. These images represent a particular vision of the American South as a region in stasis and one defined by an unchanged agrarian society; that vision of the South was part of an ever-changing American mythology. The idea of stasis appealed to Americans anxious about the rapid industrialization of cities in the Northeast and Midwest, where change marked so many aspects of life.[35]

Since New Orleans was a major southern city, the development of its postbellum tourism industry occurred within this paradigm of southern stasis. However, the city's role in the American and global economy, as a crucial port with a diverse population, complicated its position within the southern archetype. Unlike the rural South, which people cast as isolated, New Orleans was embedded in a complex economic network that stretched all over the world.

Americans associated New Orleans with a strange kind of cosmopolitanism rooted in the past. One tourist pamphlet described it as "a most cosmopolitan city; and its ways partake largely of the traditional habits of both Spanish and French towns. It is gay, yet sad; sparkling as champagne, yet sedate as Quakerdom. Its people are fond of idleness, yet build up and sustain a great commerce. It is an enigma."[36] New Orleans' cosmopolitanism did not prevent Americans from imagining the city as an antebellum relic, but they were also forced to acknowledge the city's interconnectivity and fusion culture born of the Atlantic world. Thus, New Orleans was simultaneously part of the larger southern regional tourism complex but also distinct within that model. No more apparent were these complicated and seemingly incongruent depictions than in the era of the 1884 World's Fair.

The fair played an important role in launching New Orleans' postbellum tourism industry. For the first time in world's fair history, railroads, hotels, and other tourism-based industries endorsed the event, which gave birth to new strategies to promote regional tourism in America. Companies created marketing campaigns that fueled the city's burgeoning tourism industry, while stirring up excitement about the fair.[37] They also aimed to transform New Orleans into an ideal urban destination.[38]

To generate interest among tourists, companies distributed flyers and advertisements painted with idyllic images of the fairgrounds and vivid descriptions of New Orleans' Creole culture.[39] Promotional literature depicted the city as a balm for the anxieties of the hard-working American. One such pamphlet implored tourists "to turn your back resolutely on the plow, the desk, the office and the quiet home, and seek in the New South and her Exposition grounds an invigorated frame, and a mind enriched and broadened as it could be in no other way."[40] The pamphlet cast New Orleans as an adult playground of sorts where tourists could forget the pressures of their daily work and get lost in a city commonly referred to as "the Paris of America"—one whose foreignness enabled them to escape the mundane and the difficult.[41]

How did the city account for its distinctiveness? A succinct explanation, and one that reflects popular understandings, was provided in a guidebook created for the 1884 World's Fair:

> New Orleans—by its cosmopolitan character, and having been so far removed in its early history from the rest of the colonies, and during its occupancy by the Spanish and French—took to itself usages, customs and even patois of its own, the story of which has furnished material for romances equaled by few other cities in this country.[42]

The writer and translator Lafcadio Hearn, who lived and worked in New Orleans in the 1870s and 1880s, similarly noted that it "resembles no other city upon the face of the earth, yet it recalls vague memories of a hundred cities." The city, he wrote, "owns suggestions of towns in Italy, and in Spain, of cities in England and in Germany, of seaports in the Mediterranean, and of seaports in the tropics."[43] Likewise, an article published in the *New York Commercial Advertiser* claimed that New Orleans resembled "a town in the South of Europe rather than anything American."[44]

New Orleans' uniqueness lay in its kaleidoscopic culture—one that seemed to be made up of innumerable traditions from communities throughout the Atlantic world yet was a distinct unit within that world. Perhaps therein lies its appeal to tourists attending the World's Fair. The city's fusion landscape enabled one to liken it to innumerable overseas destinations to which the average middle-class white American would probably never travel. Yet by visiting New Orleans, and by engaging in its multivalent culture steeped in tradition, visitors could feel as though they had traveled the world.

Not all of New Orleans' cityscape, though, conjured a sense of foreignness for outside visitors. For Hearn, the American Sector (present-day Central Business District) was a modern neighborhood that therefore suffered from the afflictions of modernization quite familiar to northern tourists. This was a part of the city that was constantly growing and bustling with commercial activity. Conversely, Hearn saw the French Quarter as more stable and resilient with a slower pace of life that soothed anxieties brought on by rapid industrialization. He characterized this neighborhood as a bastion of quietude in an otherwise electric American city: Whereas the "American city is all alive—a blaze of gas and a whirl of pleasure," the French Quarter "is asleep; the streets are deserted."[45]

This dichotomy, however, broke down when Hearn described the street food culture of New Orleans and, in particular, when he spoke of the sounds of the city's markets. In contrast to the rest of the French Quarter, the French Market and its surrounding streets were rarely quiet. The "musical announcements" of food vendors harmonized with the thwack of meat cleavers and the hum of pleasure seekers gossiping over steaming cups of chicory coffee in the market halls. "Noisiness," though, for Hearn, was an acceptable trait of the French Market because it was associated not with industrialization, but with antebellum New Orleans—a period reimagined to be more akin to the ideal of the rural picturesque than to northern industry.[46] Even so, the emphasis on sound in an otherwise muted neighborhood signals that the French Market was different; it was in this place where people of different races, ethnicities, and nationalities came together on a daily basis to conduct business. People accepted that cosmopolitanism as well as the boisterous economic exchange of goods taking place in the market. There, race, gender, and ethnic identity operated differently. The line that divided the Anglo-American and French Creole parts of the city—the new-age industrialism from the romanticized antebellum past—blurred amid the economic activity of a motley crew of vendors and customers from across the United States and around the globe.[47]

The soundscape of New Orleans' public food culture played a powerful role in shaping Americans' understandings of the city as both foreign and anti-quated. Authors writing for broader American audiences regularly featured food vendors' cries. They shared those cries through diverse media ranging from postcards to cookbooks. Some writers likely modified street cries or invented their own to fit the vision of New Orleans that they sought to create in their works. These sources must be treated with care because they can both distort and preserve the city's historic soundscape. This duality affords us an opportunity to hypothesize about the lived experiences of New Orleans' residents while also scrutinizing the ways in which writers altered those experiences to further their own literary agendas. Conversely, one must keep in mind that many of the writers who came to New Orleans around the time of the World's Fair sought to capture reality on the page. Their transcriptions of street cries, then, cannot be completely fabricated; rather, it is likely that they are to a certain extent representative of the miscellany of vendor calls that marked the city's soundscape.

The voices of vendors, so often silent in mainstream representations of American culture, dominated the soundscape of New Orleans. Vendor cries, which commonly combined numerous languages and regional phrases, repre-sented the cultural fusion taking place in New Orleans. Those same cries also reinforced the city's connections to places outside of the United States, thus underpinning the city's "foreign" feel. Writers like Hearn often specified the ethnic and racial identity of vendors and sought to capture that identity in their voices. For example, Hearn drew attention to the strong Italian accent of an immigrant vendor selling odds and ends in the street. This vendor had adopted the common New Orleanian term "lagniappe" to describe his assort-ment of wares. Hearn was fascinated by the cultural hybridity embodied in this vendor's "war-cry," in which he pronounced "lagniappe," a word belong-ing to Creole culture, "Italianwise." By adopting this phrase, the Italian ven-dor integrated himself into New Orleans' preexisting culture, which, in turn, was shaped by his presence. His hybrid street cry became a metaphor for the city's fusion culture and reinforced New Orleans' reputation as an interna-tional city.[48]

Seeking to capitalize on the potent association of Black women vendors with places outside US borders, writers regularly featured sellers of pralines and calas in their works about New Orleans. These vendors stood in sharp contrast to Italian vendors who had made their major mark on New Orleans' local food culture in the second half of the nineteenth century. Instead of Italian, their calls were typically sung out in French, Creole, or heavily accented English, all of which associate these vendors with distant places and foreign cultures, particularly those of West Africa and the Caribbean.[49] Calas vendors' cries were some of the most consistently included in postbellum writings, often a variation of *"Bons petits calas! Tout chauds! Tout chauds!"* or "Beautiful little *calas*! Very hot! Very hot!"[50] For readers, their long-standing presence in New Orleans illuminated the continuities between the city's antebellum and postbellum street-vending practices, both profoundly shaped by migration and global trade networks.

In attempting to capture and preserve such street cries, writers took something that was at its core part of a larger, sonic whole and separated it into a distinct unit—decontextualizing the sound bite and imposing order on the sonic landscape. They are archived on the page as well-ordered snippets of sound, which, in many ways, were misleading to readers. In reality, numerous street vendors would have vocalized their cries at the same time, thus braiding their calls together. In their new literary form, these street cries often look and read like stand-alone poems or song lyrics. By separating those sounds and making them orderly in printed text, writers were symbolically controlling the voices and bodies of vendors who were notoriously difficult for city officials to regulate.

Through transcribed vendor cries, we can see an attempt on behalf of writers to share a largely Afro-Caribbean sonic culture with white American tourists who would likely be unfamiliar with it. Their attempts to do so were often creative, albeit likely lacking in accuracy. Primitive sound-recording technology at that time made it difficult to share street cries. Thus, writers had to improvise. They often used hyphens, capital letters, italics, and the repetition of syllables to indicate inflection and phrasing. For example, in a newspaper article titled "Voices of Dawn," Hearn described the cries and selling strategies of "Italians, negroes, Frenchmen, and Spaniards." In this scene, Hearn noted that "The peddlers of 'Ap-PULLS!' of 'Straw-BARE-eries!' and 'Black-Brees!'—all own sonorous voices."[51] The focus on individual vendors' inflection and phrasing suggests that these qualities mattered to their recital, making street cries more distinctive and memorable.

Street cries as poems and song also rendered a raucous, in-your-face action into something less threatening, more controllable and portable, and thus easier for American audiences to consume. In essence, their transposition onto the page was a means of making "the other" more palatable to white

Americans.[52] That transposition, however, was not merely textual; it was also musical. Given the melodic and percussive nature of street cries, some authors transposed them onto sheet music. Instead of using hyphens, italics, and creative punctuation, authors used notes and keys. In doing so, they took a non-material cultural form and forced it into the rigid structure of Western music, complete with time signatures, key signatures, bar lines, and perfectly subdivided rhythms.

The translation of street cries, especially those of people of color, into Western musical notation was a form of whitewashing that made Blackness less threatening. The cookbook *Cooking in the Old Créole Days* (1903), for example, contains several vendor songs. The sheet music provides information that would allow one to sing (out loud or in one's head) in a particular key, and to understand the rhythm and emphasis of certain syllables, in addition to the melody of the song. One featured street cry is that of the French mustard seller, notated in the key of G:

> Tout le monde me regarde mais person ne n'achète rien.
> Achetez de la moutarde çela vous fera du bien.[53]

Or in English:

> Everyone is looking at me, but nobody is buying anything.
> Buy mustard it will do you good.[54]

Transcribing his song was not merely about capturing his lyrics and preserving the musical qualities of his voice; it was also about reducing the perceived threat of Black voices. In this instance, because of his association with a predominantly Black cohort of street food vendors, the French mustard seller, too, is a Black figure. It is not his skin tone that determines his Blackness, but his position as a street food vendor—an occupation popularly depicted and understood as one of the lowest forms of labor. His lyrics, as written, describe his lack of business acumen and his inability to succeed. That narrative further associates him with the derogatory understandings that some white Americans held of Black Americans. The other figures included in the cookbook consist of a cartoon frog and several Black children and adults. One of them is identified as the "young callas girl," who sang out in French, "Bel callas tout chauds!"—an unsurprising presence considering writers' tendencies to connect New Orleans with far-off places through the inclusion of Black women vendors.[55]

Transposed street vendors cries were also a means through which white Americans could act out the culture of Black Americans and attempt to experience their physicality and emotions—characteristics that were, of course, stereotypes.[56] This racialized play enabled white Americans to further reduce the threat that Black people posed to white supremacy by making a mockery of Black traditions and business practices.[57] At a time when white Americans continued to police their behaviors and limit emotional expression and physical intimacy, the stereotypical street vendor did not heed those same societal expectations. Expressive vendors, therefore, stood in sharp contrast to white middle-class Americans.[58]

Perhaps therein lies the appeal to white readers of the transposed street vendor cries in *Cooking in the Old Créole Days*. For the length of a street cry, anywhere from a few seconds to a minute, a white person could, as Tanya Sheehan so succinctly stated, "safely indulge in the so-called primitive nature of the black."[59] The performance was a form of entertainment, like Black minstrelsy, that served to erase the historical reality of slavery—a reality that gave rise to the Black food vendors of New Orleans in the first place. The "strange" yet "quaint" song that poured out of white singers' mouths sought not to acknowledge the labor, business acumen, or resiliency of Black vendors, but evoke the exotic and antiquated vision of New Orleans in the listeners' imagination. Through song, New Orleans' culture was no longer out of reach for white Americans living outside of the city. Ultimately, the transposed street cry, like a recipe for a dish, transformed something ephemeral and mysterious into something indelible and accessible, and therefore controllable.

Many of the older vendors depicted on postcards and whose stories were told in newspapers had lived through slavery and survived the Civil War. They had been part of a devastating slave economy that treated their bodies and labor as a commodity. Even the mode through which slave auctioneers sold enslaved people had an eerie auditory parallel to the how food vendors made a sale: through a cry. At eighty-eight years old, W. L. Bost remembered the slave auctioneers' cries that he heard in North Carolina when he was young: "Lord child, I remember when I was a little boy, 'bout ten years, the speculators come through Newton with droves of slaves." He went on, "I remember when they put 'em on the block to sell 'em…. The auctioneer he stand off at a distance and cry 'em off as they stand on the block. I can hear his voice as long as I live."[60] At eighty-seven years old, Perry McGee, too, remembered how in Missouri, where he grew up enslaved people, were auctioned off like "a hog or cow" and how slave auctioneers "would put slaves on de block and 'cry them off.'"[61]

In the antebellum and postbellum periods, many street vendors hawked wares mere blocks away from where they themselves had been sold into slavery and where their status as enslaved people rather than as citizens had been reified. Their cries mapped on top of the silent echoes of the auctioneer's cries from days, weeks, or years before, becoming part of the same sonic landscape. The Black vendor Toto was all too familiar with the chafing proximity of the slave auction block. According to an article published in the *Daily Picayune* in 1894, Toto's enslaver killed himself after squandering his money through gambling, at which point his plantation and the people he enslaved—including Toto, her husband, and her son—were put up for auction in the lobby of the St. Louis Hotel on the corner of St. Louis and Chartres Streets.[62] On that auction block, her family was separated. Her husband and son were forced to move to Tennessee without her, and she never saw them again. A man identified as Monsieur John purchased Toto and "gifted" her back to her original enslaver. The arrangement, according to the article, was amenable to Toto, although she might have told the tale differently, if given a chance. It was at that time that Toto began selling pralines, distributing them in front of St. Louis Cathedral in Jackson Square, just two blocks away from where she and her family were similarly sold back into slavery.[63]

That auction block represented Toto's disenfranchisement. On that block, she was presented as a commodity, as a piece of property, to be bought and sold by other people. Yet the cathedral steps upon which she vended foods represented something else—her ability, as an entrepreneur, to engage with other city residents, build relationships, and support herself economically. Vending ultimately became a means of resisting the totalizing impacts of slavery, the loss of her loved ones, and a sense of isolation among them.[64] Similarly, in the postbellum period, vending enabled her to support herself despite the failures of Reconstruction to protect the interests of newly freed Black Americans. In a way, her dependency on traditional vending practices in the postwar period signified those failures. Had the Reconstruction government created a more equitable economy, she might have been able to take up a more lucrative trade or apply for financial support that would have enabled her to retire from street vending. It was the government's failure to enact those changes that fueled some of the cultural continuity in the food economy before and after the war.

Toto's story of resilience did not align with white American tourists' expectations of what and whom they would encounter upon arriving in New Orleans. Tourist literature and other ephemera, by contrast, regularly depicted Black women vendors as passive characters. Those materials conflated Black women vendors with the stereotype of the "mammy," so popular in romanti-cized renderings of the South.[65] Doing so served a widespread movement to reinforce feelings of nostalgia, remembrance, loss, and spectacle around southern culture.[66] Some vendors were even identified as mammy-like figures by name. One postcard featuring a Black praline vendor read: "One of the quaintest characters of old New Orleans is the Praline Mammy."[67] Another postcard noted, "The praline vendor, now almost a figure of the past, although one may find an old Mammy sitting at the gates of the Place d'Armes, now Jackson Square, or by the front of the 'Patio Royal.' "[68]

Creole cookbooks, themselves objects that circulated in the public sphere, regularly referenced New Orleans' street food vendors in their pages. As in *A Book of Famous Old New Orleans Recipes Used in the South for More than 200 Years* (1900), image and text worked together to associate Black women ven-dors with the seemingly timeless magnetism of New Orleans—permanently marrying these street vendors to a romanticized antebellum past:

> The praline vendor remains a fixture in New Orleans street-life. On Canal Street, one still sees them, very old sometimes, and bent almost double, sitting by a basket of pecan and coconut pralines. In the old quarter, too, they sit in friendly doorways and call, "Praline!" all day. By evening the basket is empty, and they hobble home to cook another basketful for the next day.[69]

One of the strongest links between these laborers and the antebellum period was their advanced age. One postcard described a very old praline ven-dor: "Praline Vender, age 109, sitting in her 'Place in the Sun' in the court yard of the Green Shutter, 633 Royal Street, in the French Quarter at New Orleans, LA."[70] Many of these women were old enough to have actually lived through the antebellum period. Toto herself had labored in the fields of a plantation down the coast prior to emancipation, tying her story directly to the roman-ticized agrarian past that so many tourists read about.[71] For them, older pra-line vendors seemed like living relics from a time gone by.

Locals and tourists alike saw vendors' aging as a sign of impending loss, a metaphor for the eventual decline of traditional southern cultures. In fact, the article in which Toto's story was told described her in its opening paragraphs as "the old shrunken figure seated before a little old table, on which are spread out dainty pink and white pralines." The article went on to say that passersby looked at Toto with "half pity, half amusement"—a mix of emotions that mir-rored many tourists' opinions of New Orleans during the 1884 World's Fair.[72]

It was a potent combination of feelings too. American tourists could feel empowered by comparison, seeing New Orleans as lacking, yet deriving a satisfaction from that malnourishment, from the dearth of forward progress that other parts of America were experiencing.

American tourists' growing interest in street vendors coincided with the rising popularity of "people watching" in the late nineteenth century.[73] Seeking to partake in this activity, visitors were eager to spot the iconic set of vendors working the city streets.[74] Street food vendors, then, had an integral role to play in drawing tourists' attention away from the 1884 World's Fair and its message of American unity and progress, and toward Creole food culture and its association with an exoticized antebellum past. In this way, the fair had failed. Although organizers had conceived of New Orleans' exposition as one to rival Philadelphia's and as a way to announce postwar New Orleans' progress on the world stage, New Orleans, and its public food culture in particular, represented something else entirely to the American people: a gateway to the past and a symbol of cultural stasis.

The rise of people watching tied to this particular vision of antebellum New Orleans would not have been possible without the participation of the men and women who actually produced and distributed Creole cuisine. They were well aware of their position in the limelight and assumed a double role as both food purveyors and performers. Street vendors, for example, carefully crafted their behavior and appearance to embody the Creole culture that tourists sought to encounter. In doing so, they demonstrated business savvy by adapting the stereotypes of a racist economic system to their advantage.[75]

Although the *Daily Picayune* article depicted Toto in a romanticized and derogatory fashion, it also caught something important about Toto: her resilience, and her tenacity as a businesswoman. The author stated, "There is something in the old woman's face which tells its own tale of heroism and suffering and unswerving fidelity, and thinking to make her talk about herself you purchase some more of her pralines." Like the city in which Toto vended, she was mysterious to the American visitor, seemingly unknowable and somewhat closed off. As the article observed, the visitor was compelled not to abandon the interaction, but to draw closer, just as tourists wanted to draw closer to New Orleans and immerse themselves in the local culture to discover the city's true essence. But Toto "resolutely resists all attempts to be drawn into conversation, answering you always, 'You want for buy some more?'" For her, interactions with potential customers came down to quickly building business relationships. She was likely all too aware of their expectations of her and so she shared the parts of her personal story that would make the sale; she expertly narrated "a history with a soft, mournful beauty that seems like a romantic tradition in these prosaic days."[76]

Moreover, praline vendors like Toto strategically dressed in antebellum-era costumes to appeal to white tourists' romanticized perceptions of slave society and culture.[77] Their dresses, described in a Boston newspaper as deep guinea or purple, were "cut in just the far-away fashion" popular before the Civil War, encouraging tourists to associate these Black women vendors with antebellum New Orleans.[78] Toto herself wore "a dark guinea blue" outfit with "a white apron tied about her waist and a white handkerchief folded across her bosom," according to the *Daily Picayune*. She also tied a "bright bandana handkerchief" around her hair, what the newspaper article went on to describe as a "picturesque 'tignon'" that "only the old Creole darkies know how to tie."[79] Vendors like Toto continued to wear these uniforms well into the twentieth century, at a time when the outfits were clearly antiquated by nearly a century.[80] The decision to dress in them is akin to a twenty-first-century candy salesman wearing a red-striped shirt and straw hat. It provides a certain air of authenticity and romanticism that can potentially attract more customers than if they were dressed in contemporary clothes. The decision to wear historic ensembles also hints at the preferences of the customers. Presumably, white tourists wanted to interact with the antebellum past; or, at least, it was what they expected to interact with when they traveled to New Orleans.

Also key to the success of vendors' businesses was location, especially ones emphasized in tourist literature; they understood that many tourists came to the city with a checklist of attractions to see to get a sense of the city's culture. Postcards and guidebooks from the era spotlight iconic community meeting grounds like Jackson Square and landmarks like St. Louis Cathedral and the French Market complex; and these are the places that some Black women vendors set up their businesses, knowing that they would more likely be able to make a sale. Toto and Praline Zizi sold pralines in Jackson Square, and the former was also known to vend just a few blocks away on Canal Street, another major commercial corridor and favorite tourist destination.[81] Another one of the city's praline vendors, Tante Titine, sold her wares near the cathedral on Royal Street, and another vendor, Gâteaux Bon Marché, set up in the Place Washington.[82] Like Toto and Praline Zizi, they established themselves in places frequented by tourists, ready to engage these potential customers in an "authentic" New Orleans experience; it was in these iconic arenas that the praline vendors themselves also became iconic figures, known even outside of New Orleans.

The city's praline vendors were not the only figures to gain a strong reputation for their culinary craft in key tourist areas. So, too, did the city's coffee vendors. Black women vendors such as Rose Nicaud and Manette had locations in the French Market, and Zabette and others kept stands in front of St. Louis Cathedral and Canal Street.[83] Nicaud, who was known as Old Rose, had such a presence at the French Market that Catherine Cole, writing for a national audience to promote French Market brand coffee, described her memory as one "embalmed in the amber of many a song and picture."[84] A number of these women were known and romanticized figures in their communities and beyond, memorialized in the city's newspapers and even in folklore compendiums published after their deaths.[85]

The strength of New Orleanians' memories of them and the appeal of their stories to audiences outside of New Orleans is testament to their business savvy and the tenacity in which they pursued their food enterprises despite the major structural barriers and discrimination they faced in the Jim Crow South. They used New Orleans' burgeoning tourist industry to their advantage, carving out a niche in the hyper-competitive and contentious arena that was New Orleans' public food culture. At the same time, they also sustained long-standing relationships with fellow New Orleanians whose shopping habits existed outside the bounds of the city's tourist industry.

Despite tourism's growth, street food vendors demonstrated a strong commitment to sustaining relationships with fellow New Orleanians, going to great lengths to satisfy their local customers. Take, for example, Anita Fonvergne, who was born a free woman of color in New Orleans in 1861 and who peddled vegetables in the postbellum period. She spoke of her relationship with customers in an interview with the Louisiana Writers' Project, the state-based arm of the Federal Writers' Project. In that interview, Fonvergne noted, "I had regular customers"—ones whose business she would go to certain lengths to retain, including when they moved outside of her immediate business area. She explained, "When the people started to move uptown, I would take the Ferret Street Car and get out on Audubon Street, and then I'd walk on to all my customers." On these trips uptown to see her clientele, she would touch base with them on their needs: "They would tell me what they wanted for the next day, and then I'd go to the French Market and buy my vegetables. I brought them meat too. They would tell me what kind of meat they wanted, and I'd get their meat at Treme's Market. From there I would walk to the French Market and get the vegetables." Central to her business strategy was reducing shopping stress for her customers. Reflecting on her enterprise, she noted, "I'd make a little profit on the meat 'cause I brought them what they wanted, and I saved them the trouble of getting it." For Fonvergne and countless other vendors in the postbellum period, creating a shopping culture of convenience for her clients was key to sustaining long-term relationships with them.[86]

Sustaining strong relationships with customers could also be physically demanding. Even twenty years after she stopped peddling vegetables, Fonvergne remembered all too well her daily labor and its impact on her health: "I'm telling you that's hard work." She went on to explain, "I think that's why my legs are so bad now—because you have to carry those baskets that are filled with vegetables—you know how heavy they are—and carry one on your head." She recalled, "The heaviest baskets were the cabbages. When four or five of my customers wanted cabbage in one day, it made it pretty hard." Eventually, she gave up selling vegetables, plainly stating, "I couldn't make enough money." For Fonvergne, it was too difficult to make a profit hawking produce, unlike her meat-peddling business, which she felt was successful and worth the effort. Reflecting on her life, she proclaimed, "I'm poor but I'm proud."[87]

Fonvergne was among a robust cohort of food vendors who operated street-vending and public market businesses during a time of social, economic, and political upheaval. While these vendors shifted their strategies to sustain existing relationships with fellow New Orleanians and or appeal to new bodies of tourists, they also navigated the changing legal landscape of the city's public food culture.

Several years before New Orleans hosted the 1884 World's Fair, debates over the regulation and management of public and private markets gripped the city as Reconstruction came to an end in 1877; vendors in both realms fought for the existence of their businesses. Acquiescing to the outcries of public market vendors, the city council petitioned the state government for the right to regulate private markets, the public markets' major competitor.[88] Food vendors working in public and private markets navigated these political and legal battles and shifts in power dynamics as best they could. Those with direct access to the political realm in the post-Reconstruction era, mainly white men, wielded their political influence to shape the public food culture, and the laws that governed it, to their advantage. Others who were largely barred from that realm, like many street food vendors, had to find alternative ways to keep their businesses alive, including skirting local laws and defending themselves and their livelihoods in court when public market vendors sued them.

State legislators were willing to empower the city council to regulate private markets with one stipulation; they wanted municipal officials to abide by an amendment to the market ordinances that reduced the twelve-block radius rule to six blocks, which the state legislature passed in March 1878.[89] State officials understood that once the city council was empowered to regulate private markets, it would enforce whatever radius law was in a place with great fervor to protect the city's financial investment in the public markets. By reducing the radius law from twelve to six blocks, state legislators hoped to mitigate the fallout and help save some private market operators' businesses from forced relocation or closure.[90] The six-block radius was a legacy of the now gutted Republican Party, demonstrating how early Reconstruction-era policies had a life beyond their partisan origins. The belief in deregulation and market privatization, at least vestiges of it, had permanently rooted itself in New Orleans' public food culture despite its politicized start.

In April 1878, the New Orleans chief of police, as requested by the administrator of commerce, shut down private butcher shops across the city. In the Fourth Precinct alone, seven shops were forced to close.[91] A private shopkeeper named Bernard Barthe sued the city for attempting to close his shop, which housed his business and his residence, and which was less than six blocks from the Magazine Market.[92] Originally from France, Barthe was a naturalized citizen and with his wife Josephine had four children. Seeking to defend his livelihood, he argued that the amended market ordinance allowed private markets to operate "in some portions of the city and not in others portions of the city, and by which the privileges and labor and the rights of property are denied in violation of the Constitution of the United States and of the State of Louisiana."[93] The case went to the Louisiana Supreme Court. In April 1879, the court ruled in favor of maintaining the six-block radius rule, noting that the New Orleans administrator of commerce "was required to close them [private markets in violation] up."[94]

That ruling rendered Barthe's private business illegal. From his perspective, the upheld law denied him access to private property in proximity to the markets; and that access was a major way he exercised his rights as a citizen. After losing the case, one of his remaining options would be to relocate his business outside of the six-block radius of any market. That option was not appealing in that it would move him away from the commercial corridors that built up around each public market, pushing him into a less commercially viable location. Alternatively, he could move his business to a public market. In doing so, he would have to build new relationships with community members, forged through the exchange of foods on public rather than private property. Having previously enjoyed unfettered access to private property, neither of his remaining options was appealing.

As written, the six-block radius rule "protected" public market vendors' businesses from private retailers operating outside of the markets. By 1880, there were nineteen public markets and eighty-five licensed private markets in New Orleans.[95] The public markets' competitors included not only people who wanted to set up their own greengrocers, butcher shops, and fishmonger stalls, but also those who sold fresh food, ranging from meat to vegetables, out of carts in the city streets. Some of those street vendors were actually farmers and growers who were once public market vendors themselves.

During Reconstruction, the makeup of vendors working within the public markets changed to include more middlemen and middlewomen and fewer farmers and growers, referred to in the New Orleans papers as "gardeners."[96] The Vegetable Market in the French Market complex, for example, was originally intended "solely for the gardeners" who could sell the products they grew directly to customers. Those gardeners got in the habit of selling leftover produce to small retailers who would then vend those wares after the market's peak morning hours. According to the local paper, by 1878 those small retailers continued to buy more and more fresh product directly from gardeners; eventually they held most stalls in the Vegetable Market, even during peak operating hours. The gardeners, therefore, could no longer find stalls in the market and were forced out into the city streets to vend their wares.[97]

Horace Capron, the US commissioner of agriculture from 1867 to 1871, conducted the first national study of public markets. The study sheds light on tensions between gardeners, many of whom were now street vendors, and the public market vendors in New Orleans. In many ways, it was an issue of scale with larger cities like New Orleans facing problems that smaller cities did not. His study showed that cities with populations under one hundred thousand had maintained public market systems that benefited both the producer (e.g., the farmers and growers) and the consumer.[98] In these cities, it was common for farmers and growers to sell directly to consumers, thereby making a reasonable profit. At the same time, customers had direct access to the producers of their food. In other words, they were sustaining local agriculture and provisioning people with safe food at an affordable price.

In contrast to small- and medium-sized cities, Capron saw many problems in the public markets of large cities with populations over one hundred thousand, including New Orleans. According to Capron's report, a major problem with market halls was that farmers and growers rarely sold directly to consumers, a shift from colonial and antebellum distribution practices. Instead, as seen in New Orleans, more and more vendors served as middlemen and middlewomen in larger urban food economies, buying wholesale from farmers and growers and then reselling those goods at higher retail prices.[99] In some cities like Charleston and Mobile, these middlemen and middlewomen reportedly made a 100 to 200 percent profit, which Capron considered an egregious practice.[100]

In New Orleans, tensions between public market vendors and street vendors erupted in 1878, the former accusing the latter of illegally vending fresh foods from carts during the markets' operating hours from nine o'clock in the morning to noon. To justify their case, public market vendors referred to Section 9 of the market ordinances, which provided "that every cart or wagon conveying supplies to any public market for sale by persons not occupying a stall in said market, shall pay for each and every load twenty-five cents. The carts owned by occupants of stalls are exempt from the tax." Section 9 elaborated that "no cart or wagon shall remain at any of the public markets except between the hours of midnight and 5 o'clock A.M., and between the hours of 2 and 6 P.M." Public market vendors argued that any street vendors selling produce from carts near the markets during their operating hours were violating the law. They demanded that the administrator of commerce punish the street vendors, but to no avail.[101] In late January 1878, those market vendors asked "for a mandamus," or court order, "to compel Mr. [Charles] Cavanac, Administrator of Commerce, to enforce the market ordinance for their protection."[102]

Conversely, street food vendors took great issue with Section 9 of the market ordinances, some of whom were gardeners that had lost access to stands in the Vegetable Market. They saw the twenty-five-cent tax as "unlawful and oppressive" and as of April 1, 1878, members of the Gardeners' Association refused to pay it. They felt that they should not have to pay a tax to vend on public land (i.e., the street).[103] Their protest added fuel to the fire around debates of lawful and unlawful street vending. Public market vendors who felt that the gardeners who were now operating as street food vendors threatened their businesses, continued to report them to local officials, and in some cases took them to court.

A lawsuit involving gardener Victor Ansemon signals that in some cases, the market ordinances actually hurt the livelihoods of people they were intended to protect. Ansemon was born in Louisiana in 1842 and was the son of French immigrants.[104] In 1878, at age thirty-six, he had been married to his wife Madeline, a French native, for over a decade and they had several children whom he supported through his food business.[105] As a gardener,

Ansemon should have had access to a stall within the Vegetable Market. The growing power of non-gardener retailers in that market, however, made it nearly impossible for him to rent a stall. Instead, he built business relationships with the very retailers that pushed him out, allowing them to preorder produce from him, which he then brought into the city via cart. Parked on the neighboring road median, one of Ansemon's staff, who was African American, walked the vegetable orders to stall operators and middlemen and middlewomen like Mrs. H. Dumestre.[106] Some of Dumestre's fellow stall holders went so far as to sue Ansemon, claiming that he was illegally operating as a private retailer—a street food vendor—on market grounds and doing so outside of official market hours.[107]

Ansemon's attorneys successfully defended him against such accusations. They began by arguing that "the ordinance itself was a violation of human rights as expressed in the constitution of the United States, that everyone has the inalienable right to 'life, liberty, and the pursuit of happiness.'" The ordinance, in effect, was actively preventing Ansemon from fully accessing his rights as a citizen and as a member of the New Orleans community. They went on to explain that Ansemon's cart was not on market grounds but was parked on the median in the public street. Judge Ernest Miltenberger, who heard the case, ruled in favor of Ansemon, noting that "he thought the ordinance had not been violated."[108] Ansemon's case was not the only one that went to trial. In fact, a few days prior to his case, M. Agneli, Gaspard Belet, and James G. Baerer also appeared in court to defend their street-vending businesses against the manager of the Vegetable Market; Dumestre testified against them as well, noting that they were illegally selling their wares on the street. As with Ansemon, Judge Miltenberger dismissed the case, arguing no law had been broken.[109]

The city government did, however, crack down on street vendors without licenses. For example, in the same month, the local newspaper reported "the arresting of the owners of floats and other vehicles for non-payment of licenses" and "brought great numbers of them to the City Hall on Thursday," where "as many as 300 licenses" were issued at the total cost of $2,000.[110] Because unlicensed vendors did not contribute funds to the city's general fund to improve public amenities, city officials saw their businesses as harming the overall well-being of New Orleans' community.

People of color and women, groups already politically marginalized in New Orleans and beyond, often suffered under market ordinances implemented in the post–Civil War era that increased the costs of vending legally in city centers. Zooming out beyond New Orleans demonstrates the wider context for their grievances. Postbellum regulation of food provisioning deeply impacted small-scale food entrepreneurs dealing with seemingly insurmountable barriers and discrimination in the years following the Civil War. Faced with new economic barriers to sustaining their businesses, street vendors across the country spoke out against these changes and sought help through what legal channels they did have access to despite the structures in place to keep them on the margins.

Unable to bear the astronomical and unrealistic taxes and fees newly demanded of street vendors by the city government in Portsmouth, Virginia, in 1866, for example, a group of nine Black women vendors gathered to talk over their shared predicament. Together, they sought to devise a course of action to advocate for their livelihoods and "lift this intolerable burden from their shoulders." Although the group did not name itself officially in the letter, it had an organizational structure and internal leadership.[111]

President Sarah Nash and Vice President Nancy Hodges presided over the meeting, with Nash opening the floor in exasperation as she exclaimed, "My friends we meet here to consult each other and talk our troubles over. So much is being done against us in this city that I don't know where to begin, nor what to say. I know we are left all alone and no one to give us any advice." She went on to outline the challenges they were facing as newly freed women without institutional support from the local or national government. "Our old rebel masters," she reflected, "say our freedom shan't do us any good." Exasperated she asked her fellow vendors, "Don't it seem like it?" Equally frustrated, they confirmed, "Yes!"[112]

The meeting attendees came to the quick understanding that they had to rely on each other if there was any hope to effect change; knowing that their message would be stronger if presented in a united front, they planned to record their grievances in a single document and then send them to the head of the Freedman's Bureau, General Oliver Otis Howard, in a plea for advice and support. Their intention with that document was to share the grievances of the "many hundreds here who huckster for a living" in Portsmouth, whose experiences undoubtedly mirrored countless others' throughout the country including street vendors in New Orleans.[113]

Continuing with her opening remarks, Nash noted, "We don't know nothing about the laws," which was a direct result of empowered enslavers barring bondspeople from learning about legal culture to hinder their abilities to defend themselves against the injustices and abuses of slavery. What Nash was intimately familiar with, however, were the impossibly high fees and taxes vendors now had to pay to sell their wares legally in the city. She explained in detail the new licensing and taxing system that made it impossible for her and her fellow vendors to continue to operate their businesses. Making the vendors' situation even more dire, although somewhat outside of the realm of market ordinances, was the fact that rents had also gone up 40 to 50 percent in Portsmouth.[114]

As Nash continued to share her story, she revealed how her own entrepreneurial endeavors operating an eatery for several decades had been thwarted by newly raised taxes. She explained, "For the last 30 odd years, when many of you were children I have been keeping a cook shop, and now I must stop because I ain't got fifty dollars to pay into the hands of the collector for one year's taxes, and I don't make that much in two years." Anxious and on the brink of losing her business, she exclaimed, "Now let them break me up, put me in jail, or do what they please with me, I say I am done serving them, by the help of God and the U.S. Army."[115]

As the meeting continued, we come to learn that the recently instated taxes were created by a newly elected leaders who, in the opinion of meeting attendees, had no sympathy for Black vendors. As in New Orleans, changes to the markets' laws reflected larger power struggles within the city's political system; in the case of Portsmouth, previous Confederates still bitter with the loss of the Civil War were clawing their way back to power, and they did not care if Black businesspeople suffered as a result. Black New Orleanians, too, faced similar bias and prejudice from Democratic politicians, many of them failed rebels, seeking to disenfranchise Black voters in the second half of the nineteenth century. Though it was certainly not just white Democrats who created this pressure, but rather a diverse cohort of white residents—native to Louisiana and migrants to the region—that sought to capitalize on Black labor while limiting their political influence.[116]

Meeting attendees noted how the situation was made even more unbearable because they, the vendors, were never consulted by the newly elected government officials on any of the changes made to the licensing and tax systems for food distribution. They did not have a chance to share their experiences as small-scale businesswomen and the impact raised fees and taxes would have on their livelihoods. Such an omission was a manifestation of the purposeful disenfranchisement of African American people historically and in the immediate aftermath of the Civil War.[117]

Making a plea through the Freedmen's Bureau, the meeting attendees vouched for their loyalty to the country. They shared their commitment to the Union during the Civil War, in which they had "often given their little alls to comfort a Union Soldier distressed, with bleeding wounds and dying groans; and that for the deliverance of our Republican government, they have laid their children, some their only child upon the altar of the country." In other words, these women had sacrificed for a dream—a country they believed would build a better future for all—and in this moment, that country was failing them and their community as Reconstruction failed to live up to its vision of a more equitable and just America.[118]

With few legal options available to them, the meeting attendees sent their letter through the Freedmen's Bureau in hopes of gaining support from General Howard. In the meantime, they were left to find their own path forward through the treacherous landscape of local politics, law, and economy. What some of them may have had to resort to was vending without a license or leaving the industry entirely—paths that vendors in New Orleans also resorted to when the market ordinances raised fees and taxes.[119]

As street vendors in New Orleans found ways to operate their businesses within and outside of the law, the city government continued to invest in the construction of new public markets in neighborhoods downriver of Canal Street. In 1882, the St. Roch and Delamore Market opened in the lower city, downriver of the French Quarter, where French Creoles, especially those of color, continued to reside. The same year, the Guillotte Market opened farther downriver in Faubourg Washington, a neighborhood nicknamed "Little Saxony" after the mid-century arrival of German immigrants.[120] And the Rocheblave Market, which also opened to the public in 1882, served community members in one of the new "garden suburbs," a suburb-style neighborhood, adjacent to City Park.[121]

As the new public markets opened downriver of Canal Street, another wave of immigrants, largely from Southern and Eastern Europe, but also places like China and Russia, arrived in New Orleans (1880s–1920s). This second major wave of immigrants settled on the periphery of the city's commercial core, creating a belt of immigrant communities. And as in the antebellum period, New Orleans' postbellum neighborhoods were not rigidly defined by race and ethnicity, as seen in some other cities in the United States. Even as ethnic enclaves developed, Sicilians still lived next to African Americans, Irish and Greek families shared duplexes, and Filipinos lived on the same streets as Mexicans.[122]

In the late nineteenth century, Italian immigrants, mainly from Sicily, came in relatively large numbers to Louisiana compared to other migrant groups. Whereas in 1882, there were three thousand Italians living in the state, by 1910, there were forty-five thousand.[123] In fact, Italians were the largest migrant group to settle in New Orleans since the mass migration of Germans and Irish in the 1830s and 1840s.[124] Many of them worked in food and agriculture industries. Some worked on surrounding plantations, while others found jobs in the city itself.[125] The public food culture, as for past immigrant groups, provided an economic toehold.

Federal census data from 1880 and 1860 for immigrants who identified as "hucksters" or "peddlers" reflects the beginnings of these demographic shifts influenced by Italian immigration. Whereas in 1860 roughly 3 percent of this pool was Italian, by 1880 nearly 39 percent were Italian, making them the largest cohort of immigrant vendors from one country. They were followed by German (25 percent) and French (18 percent) vendors. Bringing American-born and immigrant hucksters and peddlers together in one group, the largest cohort were American-born vendors, a majority of whom were born in Louisiana, making up 33 percent of hucksters and peddlers in the city; this was a major increase from the antebellum period, in which a vast majority of free vendors were immigrants. Italian vendors followed second, making up 26 percent of the overarching pool of these vendors.

Two such Italian vendors, Torre and Lina Gracia, lived near the French Market complex and vended vegetables to support their three young children.[126] Similarly, Nenette Lecausse, who was widowed, also sold vegetables to provide for her son and daughter.[127] For the Luccassio family, by contrast, selling vegetables was a multigenerational family affair with numerous members contributing to the business. While her husband and son drove for a living, Lucie Luccassio peddled vegetables with her daughter Mary and her son-in-law, Nicolas Clesi, who was also the child of two Italian parents.[128]

Building upon the work they did early in their marriage, Nicolas and Mary went on to own a vegetable stand together by 1910, and ten years after that, they were running a general market store, presumably near their home uptown.[129] Their story demonstrates how food retailing was a means for Italian American families to build economic stability over generations, gaining critical access to private property. Italian and Italian Americans' economic success, however, proved a point of contention among some New Orleans residents.

Often the target of xenophobia, Italian vendors faced various forms of discrimination at the turn of the twentieth century. They were depicted in the worst of terms in the local papers, contributing to some New Orleanians' efforts to marginalize them in the public food culture. Many New Orleanians had preconceived notions of Italian immigrants, fearing that they were part of criminal networks that could disrupt their peace.[130] In other words, they were afraid of the Mob, its influence over New Orleans' food distribution networks, and the possibility that their neighborhood Italian food vendor might be connected to organized crime. As was the case in the antebellum period, recent migrants were once again perceived as a threat and danger to existing power dynamics within the local food economy. Established vendors and wary customers, therefore, sought to shape public opinion of Italian vendors to discredit their businesses.

In local writings, Italian vendors were often described as verbally accosting potential customers and as invading their privacy. Lafcadio Hearn, an immigrant himself, described a scene where an Italian vendor thrust his body partly through the window of a potential customer to project his voice into the inner sanctum of the home. As portrayed by Hearn, "The vendor of fowls pokes in his head at every open window with cries of 'Chick-EN, Madamma, Chick-en!' "[131] In a different piece of writing, Hearn described the deceitful vending practices of another Italian vendor. This vendor tricked patrons into buying damaged apples by turning the bruised side face down.[132] The pages of the local newspaper were also peppered with articles reporting the disagreeable selling practices of Italian vendors, corroborating the premise of Hearn's article. In the spring of 1889, for example, the *Daily Picayune* noted the "aggressive" selling strategies of itinerant fishmongers, primarily Italian. The article reported that these vendors, who went door to door,

> are generally sensible enough to speak politely when there are any males about the house, but if not they are just the contrary. They ring at door bells and if not promptly answered, jerk the wire as though they would pull the ball from its fastenings. A simple refusal to purchase incenses them, and they thrust their offensive smelling fish in the faces of the persons, and if still refused frequently give vent to curses and abuse of those whom they seek to impose on.[133]

The title of the article, "Peddling Pests," speaks to the concerns and biases that some community members had about Italian vendors, whom they stereotyped as hostile and unwanted.

In 1900, the *Daily Picayune* reported that "the police have started a war upon the early morning street vendors of fruits and vegetables," arresting two Italian men: Merle Vacarro and Marlane Tofare. They were charged with "making boisterous outcry in violation of the city ordinance 1487." The paper went on to report that "in addition to shouting loudly in the streets the two offenders rang the doorbells in the neighborhood, necessitating the rising of the occupants of the houses to respond to the call at the unearthly hour of 6 o'clock." This complaint mirrored ones made a decade earlier. Homing in on their immigrant status and Italian heritage to vilify them, the article emphasized that Vacarro "was not conversant with the English language" and that Tofare was "a young Italian."[134]

The aforementioned Italian male vendors worked in the streets, a profession that associated them with the street food labor and businesses of Black entrepreneurs. When thinking of the Italian male vendor as a figure whose racial identity was not necessarily white, we see similarities in the ways in which white authors wrote about Black men and Italian vendors.[135] In the late nineteenth century, scholars have documented white Americans' fears that Black men might intimately or violently interact with white women.[136] As a result, white authors regularly depicted Black men as aggressive and intrusive. With this comparison in mind, when one reads the previously mentioned articles profiling "boisterous" Italian male vendors' interactions with their customers, we see parallels in the descriptions of Italian vendors and Black men. The white housekeeper, by contrast, was cast in the 1889 article as the helpless victim in an economic exchange. These misrepresentations worked against people who identified as Italian and as African American, but to varying degrees.

New Orleans' fixation on the "problematic" vocalizations and behavior of Italian male vendors continued in the early twentieth century. Their sonic presence became something on which the city government attempted to weaken and even eradicate through local law. In 1900, the city government passed Ordinance 356 N.C.S., which made it illegal for street vendors, specifically those who sold "market produce, vegetables, meat, fish, game, fruit and oysters" to cry out about their wares or to initiative a sale by knocking on customers' doors or ringing their doorbells.[137] The ordinance did not go uncontested. One vendor, Emile Fargot, who was convicted and imprisoned for violating the ordinance, appealed his conviction all the way to the Louisiana Supreme Court, although the court did not rule in his favor. Fargot argued that "the ordinance is unreasonable and oppressive, partial, and unfair, unlawful, and in restraint of trade," demonstrating how crucial vendors saw their street cries to the success of their businesses. The court determined that the law did not restrict vendors' trade, but just the manner in which they went about their trade: "A person engaged in peddling and hawking fruits has not right to bawl away in a manner that is annoying to others." By controlling the vocalizations of street vendors, the court reasoned, the city was not only protecting trade but allowing it to grow. However, in reality, the law seemed more likely to have protected the interests of public and private market vendors who saw roving street vendors crying out about their wares as direct competition. The court also reasoned that the street cry ordinance applied equally "to all persons engaged in the business of peddling and hawking." In practice, however, police officer could pick and choose which vendors they sought to arrest, creating opportunities for bias, including against Italian community members, to run rampant.[138]

Largely ignoring that street cry law and other food-vending ordinances, street vendors of diverse racial and ethnic backgrounds continued their business practices.[139] Occasionally, the city would make a public example of street vendors in an effort to bring order to the city streets. It appears that attention often fell upon the arrests of Italian vendors, in particular. Such was the case in 1904, when the First Recorder's Court fined six peddlers, some of whom were Italian descent, for being "too boisterous," as the *New Orleans Item* headline read, and for selling wares without a permit. As reported in the article, Recorder James Hughes "said that complaints against violators of this kind had been too numerous and that from now on he intended to deal severely with any brought before him."[140] The court records corroborate the newspaper's telling, with Recorder Hughes stating, "I am going to make an example of you people, and teach you that nobody can peddle throughout my jurisdiction, without having the necessary requirements according to the law."[141] Publicly naming the violators was key to the city's strategy of deterring future violations; the *New Orleans Item* dutifully noted: "The names of the hucksters fined this morning are: Tony Remfero, Nicola Arando, Tony Lotriglio, Sam Caruso and Emile Martin."[142]

The *Daily Picayune* reported a similar instance just under a year later when the city arrested numerous vendors for various volitions of local laws governing food purveying including "peddling during market hours, crying out wares aloud in the streets, boisterous outcry, etc." Recorder's courts across the city fined most of the vendors, except for one, an Italian vendor who "was excused on the plea that he did not know the law and had never been warned." The paper went on to describe the court proceedings in a harmfully humorous and pitying tone, claiming that some of the "excuses" given by vendors were "quite funny." The reporting was ripe with prejudice against several Italian vendors, using affected dialect when quoting them, as was the case for Mr. Salvador who had been arrested for illegally selling peaches on the streets during market hours. Salvador, according to the paper explained the situation as follows, "I drive da wagon, and a ledday she calla me and wanta buy 5 centa peacha. I tella her I no sell, and she tella me: 'Woman seek, and wanta da peach and getta well,' and I sells her 5 centa peacha." From Salvador's telling, he was merely meeting the demands of his customer, an equal party in violating the law. Judge J. J. Fogarty responded, "That's a very nice excuse, Salvador, but it won't go. I am going to be lenient with you, though, and fine you $2.50."[143]

Within that cohort of arrested vendors was also Angelo Newman, who that day was selling watermelons from a wagon. The police officer who testified against him described what had taken place in simple terms: "Your Honor, he was making a boisterous outcry, and I arrested him for that." But, according to the newspaper, Newman did not understand what "boisterous outcry" meant, perhaps indicating the opacity of local law especially to recent migrants for whom English was not their first language. Judge Fogarty was not forgiving, though, despite Newman's professed ignorance; he fined Newman along with the other vendors.[144]

As was the case with Germans and Irish and other immigrants who were eventually categorized as "white," some Italian vendors, despite facing discrimination, used street and market vending to gain access to private property and open their own businesses outside of the public food culture. This remained a difficult, if not impossible, prospect for people of color and many white women. Italian immigrant entrepreneurs, like Nicolas and Mary Clesi, eventually opened grocery stores, wholesale produce companies, macaroni factories, and restaurants, among other food enterprises in the French Quarter and surrounding areas.[145]

Although many government officials at the local and state levels had fought hard to protect the public markets in the wake of Reconstruction, the city council's investment in these municipal facilities waned after 1878. In fact, in the final decades of the nineteenth century, local officials neglected more and more the basic upkeep of market facilities. Vendors and their customers grew increasingly concerned about their worsening conditions as they dealt with frequent disease outbreaks, some of which residents tied back to the poor sanitary conditions around food distribution. Over the course of the nineteenth century, thousands of New Orleanians died from these diseases, as was the case with the 1878 yellow fever outbreak; the public markets, therefore, became associated with that loss of life.[146]

Concerned residents lobbied city officials to reinvest in the public markets' maintenance and the regulation of food vendors operating within and outside of them. Some residents even suggested that the city abandon its historic market structures and instead invest in the enclosed market halls popular across the country. Despite their outcries, the city government grew increasingly apathetic about public market upkeep as the turn of the century approached. Desperate to save their businesses, vendors launched campaigns to reassure customers that their food stalls were safe and that they could be trusted, all the while continuing to push for improvements. Their fight would last several decades.

4

Public Market Monopoly and Public Health Reform in New Orleans, 1878–1911

ON AN UNBEARABLY humid day in July 1884, the *Daily Picayune* published a scathing exposé, "Inviting the Cholera," about the deteriorating public health conditions of the municipal markets. Historically, summer was already a time of year when people, at least those with the means to do so, tended to flee New Orleans given the spike in infectious diseases during warmer months. That the local paper tied disease specifically to the public markets spoke to their woeful state. Capturing the fetid and "horrible" conditions, the article described how the floors of the Dryades Market were sticky and the thick air was ripe with the foul aroma of spoiled meat, fish, and produce; and how the wall paint had peeled, and the wooden eaves had rotted. The market, just like the fresh food it distributed, was slowly decomposing.[1]

Neglect was a key theme in the piece, which went on to describe how the market had not been washed out for almost two weeks and how "a filthier place" could hardly be imagined. Desperate, market vendors made complaints to city officials, but they went unaddressed. With seemingly no other recourse, those vendors turned to the *Daily Picayune* to make a public condemnation of their workplace. They chose to risk furthering the markets' bad reputation and potentially hemorrhaging more customers in the hopes that city officials might finally invest in the upkeep and cleanliness of the facilities. City officials, however, largely ignored the increasingly decrepit state of the existing facilities and instead focused on building even more public markets until their numbers peaked in 1911.[2]

At the turn of the twentieth century, New Orleans' municipal markets sat at the center of debates around public health and the spread of foodborne diseases, both of which tied into larger conversations about what constituted an "ideal" American city. Focused on maximizing profits while reducing overhead costs, the city government neglected the upkeep of existing markets, knowing that city residents would continue to patronize them regardless of their dilapidated status. That neglect was not a new phenomenon, but one that built on top of a long habit of mismanaging the markets' upkeep when city government priorities lay elsewhere. Throughout the nineteenth century, the local papers reported on public health concerns and maintenance issues at the public markets. But the situation seemed even more problematic in the latter years of the century as governing bodies and the public developed better understandings of how diseases spread and how to prevent unnecessary illness and death associated with these sites of food distribution.

The continuation of the city government's general apathy toward maintaining the structures created a bleak situation for public market vendors and customers alike. Because local laws restricted the sale of most fresh food to the public markets, customers were forced to patronize them, while vendors struggled to maintain their customers' trust as market conditions worsened. Some parties protested the government-created monopoly over public provisioning, while others embraced it. The reach of that monopoly spread as city officials approved the construction of additional structures in suburb-style neighborhoods; these were simple, cheap facilities that kept overhead costs low while introducing new market revenue streams through stall rentals. For the city government, maximizing its profit was the priority.

Those market vendors who sought to make the best of their situation turned to the city's newspapers to win over or maintain customer loyalty. In an era also marked by racism and xenophobia, they not only highlighted the cleanliness of their stalls, but also their whiteness and long-standing connections and cultural ties to New Orleans. Nonfood businesses that operated in the commercial corridors surrounding the markets joined in on this marketing strategy. All the while, private markets (including greengrocers) and street food vendors desperately sought to keep their businesses afloat under the crushing conditions of the municipal market monopoly, which only grew stronger in the years leading up to 1911.

As the central nodes of economic and social life across the city, the public markets reflected the overall well-being of the communities to which they catered. Their physical decline disrupted historic provisioning. Frustrated, customers instead turned to private markets, many of them operating illegally, and street food vendors. In fact, the number of peddling licenses steadily increased throughout the late nineteenth century. In 1893, the city government issued 533 permits; by 1899, the city government had issued 685; and by 1900, it was estimated that there were up to 1,000 peddlers with permits. New

Orleanians' reliance on these alternative food distributors was testament to the pervasive problems within the municipal market system.[3]

But when did city officials' neglect of the public markets start? Their negligence started after Reconstruction when the city council began regulating private markets in 1878. To reduce competition and ensure the public markets' profitability, which was a major priority, local officials closed private markets within six blocks of any public market. Also at that time, city officials decided to continue leasing the public markets out to individuals who would then manage the markets, bearing the responsibilities of their cleanliness and upkeep, in exchange for retaining all their profits. In doing so, city officials reasoned, the municipal government would be able to keep open a necessary public amenity without having to bear the cost or time of their management and upkeep.[4] After all, the leases would still deposit money into the city's coffers. The markets' contractual period lasted roughly between 1878 and 1900, and the contractors, for the most part, neglected the structures and the people who worked and shopped within them. They were interested in short-term profit and not in the long-term life of the public markets, demonstrating how in the contractual period (1878–1900), privatization harmed New Orleans' nourishing networks.

The existing public markets stood in stark contrast to the new ones the city built in burgeoning neighborhoods, which had not yet fallen into disrepair simply by virtue of their nascency. The last two markets constructed in the nineteenth century were the Prytania and the Suburban Markets, bringing the city's total number of built markets to twenty-four, twenty-three of which were still operational.[5] The Prytania Market was located uptown near Tulane's campus. According to the local paper, the market was a much-anticipated public amenity for the "large and rapidly improving neighborhood" where it was built.[6] The Suburban Market, indicative of its name, was located out in a suburb-style neighborhood heading toward Lake Pontchartrain. Representative of the typical pavilion-style markets of New Orleans, the shed-like structure was constructed primarily of wood that was painted, as reported in the *Daily Picayune*, "a light shade of green and trimmed with other harmonious colors." The floors were concrete, a practical choice that allowed for easy cleaning. In total, the market had ninety-six stalls, half of them for butchers and half for vegetable vendors. When the market began leasing stalls, the city received more applications than the management anticipated; in time for its opening, all the vegetable stalls and nearly half the butcher stalls were already leased.[7]

At first glance, these new markets seemed to signal that the public provisioning system in New Orleans was thriving and that city officials were dedicated to
providing food access for urban residents. However, a closer reading reveals that
city officials were clearly focused on other municipal projects, which led them to
overlook necessary repairs in existing public markets. As a result, the public markets became a constant topic of criticism in the city's newspapers during the contractual period. Complaint columns documented issues such as roof collapses,
which seemed to have happened with disturbing frequency.[8]

So terrible were the conditions of the public markets that in the late 1890s,
many lessees refused to renew their contracts. They no longer saw the markets
they had been managing as viable businesses. And they were not. The public
markets, which at their peak had drawn in nearly half a million dollars, were
only making "a few tens of thousands," the papers reported. Lessees went
before the US courts to obtain financial relief.[9] Upon the expiration of their
contracts around 1900, the markets defaulted back to the city, no longer public centers of food retailing, but marginalized, undesirable places that people
were forced to patronize. In sum, the markets had become a failed civic project corrupted by privatization and neglect.

Yet the city government, after years of disinterest, and seemingly against all
logic, was willing to resurrect the public markets even with one foot in the
grave.[10] In 1900, in the eyes of local officials, the markets were like the piece of
beef that was used to flavor the New Orleans breakfast staple, *bouilli*, or beef
soup. Largely seen as an ingredient that was better thrown away than repurposed after it had boiled all day, most Americans would have discarded the
beef just as they would have discarded the neighborhood markets. Yet like the
New Orleanian cooks who proudly claimed that they could convert that old
piece of beef into a delicious entrée, the municipal government tried to transform the unpalatable public markets into something enticing.[11] But why? To
put it simply: money.

City officials believed that the public markets could be quite profitable.
After all, the public market lessees had allegedly been profiting off the markets for decades. Why shouldn't the city do the same by collecting the market
revenues directly instead of leasing them out to the highest bidder as they had
done in the contractual period? With the support of the state legislature, city
officials took steps ranging from legal action to public marketing campaigns
to secure the municipal markets' financial success. With the markets back
under their full control in 1900, city officials believed their profit streams had
the potential to increase dramatically. They hoped that by pushing vendors

and customers back into the markets, sales would rise and boost revenues flowing into the city's general fund.[12]

The public markets became a key component in the city government's plan to bring New Orleans into the new century. Counter to the systems in other American cities, New Orleans officials sought not to completely revamp the public market system to symbolize the city's civic progress. Instead they sought to use the markets to earn revenue that they could put toward other needs in the city like improving roads and levees and building schools. Public market revenues and rental fees were meant to be invested back into the markets' upkeep. They were meant to pay a number of municipal employees to regulate the quality of produce, maintain the properties, and clean the markets. The municipal government of New Orleans, however, had the option, and it took it, to funnel a majority of those funds into other civic projects, while investing just enough in the markets so as not to cause a riot.

City officials were careful to control narratives about their reinstated control over the public markets. They knew the actions they were taking would likely upset private market operators and customers who might turn to the local newspapers to present their case against the local government. Their strategy was to focus on progress narratives, publicly naming the municipal markets as part of their strategic plan to shepherd New Orleans into the twentieth century—a golden age of progress. Newspapers covering the city government's actions reported stories that spoke of civic advancement and a renewed investment in the public markets. These narratives served to mask what the municipal government intended to do with market revenues. Meanwhile, they would do patchwork renovations on the existing markets and continue building inexpensive pavilion markets in new neighborhoods to create additional revenue streams for the city government at a minimal cost.

Concerned with saving the public markets' reputations, which would ensure their future economic success, city officials shifted the blame for their decline. According to newspaper reports, the government's long-term neglectfulness was not to blame. Rather, it was the predatory and, at times, illegal business practices of the public markets' direct competitors: private markets and street food vendors. In a city council meeting convened to discuss the renewal of the public markets, council members narrated the story of New Orleans' local food economy. The *Daily Picayune* reported:

> The public markets belong to the city, but for years have been leased out to private parties. The private markets are owned and operated by private persons. In addition to the private markets there are numerous

hucksters and peddlers who hawk their wares from door to door. The result is that people who formerly hired stalls in the public markets and sold their products there, now operate private markets and peddle, and the result is that the public markets, which formerly were large sources of revenue to the city, now give greatly reduced returns, while little or nothing comes to the city from the private market people and the peddlers.[13]

Additionally, city officials argued that the private markets and street food vendors were harder to regulate and therefore more likely to operate businesses that were a risk to public health.[14] They sought to convince New Orleanians that shopping outside of the public markets was not only detrimental to the city government's finances but harmful to the well-being of New Orleanian families too.

City council members proposed a solution in the form of two ordinances drawn from petitions submitted by local business owners.[15] As reported in the *Daily Picayune*, prior to the city council's decision, a group of merchants asked the governing body to "prohibit the establishment of private markets within nine squares or 3,200 feet of a public market, after the expiration of the present lease." Members of that same cohort asked the city council to "memorialize the legislature to adopt a law prohibiting or regulating peddling and hawking goods in the city." Seeing their petitions and noting how they aligned with the goals of the city government to increase public market revenues by quashing competition, the city council readily embraced the resident-originated ideas by taking steps to make them into law.[16]

The city council's first proposed ordinance banned the establishment of private markets within nine blocks of any public market, and once enforced, was estimated to bring an additional $200,000 annually to the city government's coffers.[17] Throughout the city's history, the municipal government had passed regulations prohibiting private retailers from operating within a certain radius of public markets. The distance fluctuated over the years, the most recent ordinance having been passed in 1888, which reinforced a previously instated six-block radius rule. The 1900 ordinance would extend the radius to nine blocks, forcing any vendors who had operated legally outside of the six-block radius, but illegally within the nine-block radius, to relocate or shut down. In this sense, the law aligned with legal precedent and was not a major departure from previous iterations.

The second proposed ordinance would enable the city government to regulate peddlers and hawkers, giving local officials more control over mobile food vendors, including the ability to restrict when and where they sold their wares. Doing so might incentivize itinerant peddlers to abandon their work on the sidewalks, streets, and city parks, and instead operate stands in the public markets.[18] Once within the markets, those vendors would have to pay a licensing fee in addition to monthly rent, increasing the profits that the municipal government skimmed from the public markets.

Residents of New Orleans, most of them white, spoke at a city council meeting addressing the two proposed ordinances. They voiced their opinions to the council and delineated their support and concerns for the recommended renewal plan for the public markets and the city government's particular vision of civic progress. Major supporters of the nine-block ordinance included existing vendors in the public markets whose businesses would benefit from the law. Those who opposed it included private retailers who owned and operated greengrocers that sold fresh produce among other goods, and who would be forced to stop selling fresh food, relocate, or shut down if the law were passed.

Frank Zengel, a lawyer who represented the interests of the public market vendors and their desire for both proposed laws to pass, agreed with the city council. He boldly claimed that "public and private markets could not exist at the same time, nor could public markets be profitable as long as peddling was permitted."[19] He also argued that "peddling is out of date" and, on behalf of his clients, encouraged local lawmakers to ban street food vending all together. Zengel reasoned, "Where you have a grocery at every corner and markets all around, there is no need for peddling and hawking."[20] Previously, he had also stated that street food vendors hurt other businesses, noting that "hundreds of hucksters and peddlers were going about the street without any license, to the detriment of regularly licensed and established merchants."[21]

Anthony Rabito, originally born in Italy and a resident of New Orleans for more than thirty years, made a class-based argument in favor of the nine-block radius rule. He observed that "the private market was only patronized by the rich," and therefore was not accessible to all New Orleanians.[22] In his estimation, speaking as a vendor of fresh fish and game at the Poydras Market, the public markets were the more affordable and accessible option, and therefore the one that local laws should protect.[23] What Rabito did not acknowledge is the fact that some street food vendors sold slightly damaged or leftover produce at prices far lower than those in the public and private markets (at least a third cheaper, as reported by one customer).[24] They were the vendors who often provided truly affordable and accessible products to economically disadvantaged community members.

Opposed to shutting down the private markets that were critical to the livelihood of his clients, lawyer E. Howard McCaleb Jr. argued that "the nine-block ordinance was built for revenue only" and was not fair to private market owners who had legally established their businesses in decades prior. He claimed that it was street food vendors, not the private markets, that rendered the public markets unprofitable and proposed that vendor licenses increase from $5 to $100. Mr. Merou, McCaleb's partner, backed him up, noting that "hundreds of people were dependent upon the private markets for a livelihood" and if the nine-block radius became law, it would "legislate the private markets out of existence." He went on to urge the city council to slow down because "the counsel for the private market men had no time to prepare their side of the case as fully as they desired." In other words, the fight was not being fairly fought.[25]

The *Daily Picayune* did not report any speakers in opposition to the second ordinance (which would place greater restrictions on peddling). The voices of street food vendors, of which there were an estimated seven hundred to one thousand operating on free permits, were suspiciously absent from the conversation, reflecting the fact that many of them were Black, recent immigrants, and women, and therefore politically disenfranchised.[26] Their iconic voices, marked by their distinct calls, were largely confined to the streets. During this city council meeting, they became the scapegoats for both public and private entrepreneurs, many of them white men who had both established political networks in the city and the privilege to voice their opinions. The particular vision of modernization held by city officials, public market vendors, and private retailers, and embedded within the second ordinance, did not have room for street peddlers whose livelihoods and racial, ethnic, and gender identities did not fit their vision of a controlled and contained local food economy.

Although Zengel endeavored to convince local lawmakers to ban street peddling all together, he was ultimately unsuccessful. The second ordinance, however, did pass, and it enabled the city government to restrict the time and place of iterant vendors' businesses.[27] The final version of the ordinance prohibited all street peddling in New Orleans between six o'clock in the morning and noon, the traditional operating hours of the city's public markets.[28] These same hours were crucial selling hours for street peddlers, whose iconic cries began at sunrise and who often clustered on street corners surrounding the public markets during their operating hours. These were the hours in which New Orleans' residents were accustomed to purchasing their fresh ingredients for the day. They were also the coolest hours, slowing the spoilage of fresh food and enabling roaming vendors to work in more comfortable and temperate conditions.

On top of the time restrictions, the new ordinance also made it illegal for peddlers to cry out about their wares and to knock on customers' doors to initiate a sale; essentially, it cut off their go-to marketing strategy. This law cast peddlers as urban nuisances, ones whose movements and "noise" did not align with notions of the ideal American city, a quiet place where residents would not be confronted with salespeople.

Although the modified law did not technically ban street peddling completely, the restrictions on time, movement, and verbal advertising made it difficult for itinerant vendors to operate successful businesses. In a rare instance in which peddlers' voices were reported in the *Daily Picayune*, one spoke about his grievances:

> I have a wife, five children and a horse to feed. If my sales are cut down by half [because of the time restrictions] and my profits, small as they are, are 50 per cent less, how can I get along? We poor people ask that the good and just mayor, whom we all admire and respect, will take an interest in us and help us to make a fair living.[29]

Further, the newspaper reported, the price for a peddling license was raised from five to forty dollars, making it difficult or impossible for peddlers, many already impoverished, to purchase one.[30] The new ordinance and licensing fees hurt both the peddlers and their poor and working-class clients. The latter depended on the former for affordable produce, which street vendors often sold at comparatively lower prices than their counterparts in the public markets. Perhaps recognizing these impacts, the city government eventually modified part of the ordinance to, once again, allow street food vendors to sing out about the goods they were selling. The initial ban, though, had lasted for more than a decade.[31]

Greengrocers were also not a part of the city government's particular vision of civic progress in 1900, demonstrating that competing ideas of modernization not only existed between different segments of the population in New Orleans, but also between New Orleans and other American cities where greengrocers flourished.[32] As a result, greengrocers and other private retail businesses suffered losses.

The municipal government began enforcing the nine-block radius law, discussed at the previous city council meeting, in January 1901.[33] Just as they had done when previous radius laws were enforced in the nineteenth century, private retailers sued the city government. That case went to the Louisiana Supreme Court. The court upheld the law's legality, reasoning that the city and state governments had the right to regulate the markets as they saw fit and that the nine-block radius rule did not violate any clause of the US Constitution.[34]

Of the approximately two hundred greengrocers operating in New Orleans in 1901, only thirty-eight were unaffected by the law because their businesses were positioned outside of the nine-block radius.[35] After all was said and done, 207 private markets operating within the radius were forced to discontinue the sale of fresh foods, relocate, or close. The city government defended its actions by clarifying that, of the 207 retailers, "there is no single one of this number that cannot, by removal beyond the nine-square limit, be located in the same neighborhood and in a populous district of the city."[36] This was an unusual attack on private markets without precedent in the United States; most other cities believed that public and private markets could coexist, provisioning urban populations through a symbiotic relationship that benefited the local government, purveyors, and customers.[37]

The new ordinances did not go unquestioned by some New Orleanians who approached the city government's plan for civic progress with great skepticism. Rumors spread, inciting customers' anxiety and fueling suspicion of the local government, the public markets, and the vendors who worked within them. Some people claimed that the municipal government was reinstating a monopoly over the city's food economy. Others insisted that vendors were colluding to raise prices that would make it nearly impossible for the laboring classes to afford fresh food.[38] As reported in the *Daily Picayune*, many New Orleanians were unhappy with the consequences of the public market ordinance, while others were misinformed about the legal extent of the peddling ordinance:

> It is loudly contended that this act has already operated greatly to raise the price of provisions in the markets; that it inflicts additional taxes upon the people; that it has broken up all the private markets in the city; that the provisions to be found in the public markets are not only higher in price, but are inferior in quality to what was kept in the private markets, and that, finally, under the law, all peddling and huckstering of fruit, vegetables and other articles being wholly prohibited, the people who lived by such huckstering and peddling of food are driven from business, while the people who depend on them are deprived

except at great cost of expense and exertion, of the necessary supplies to which they are accustomed.[39]

That same day, the *Daily Picayune* published another article recapping two meetings with Mayor Paul Capdevielle that cleared up confusion over the two new ordinances. In the first, the mayor described the legal history of the city's private markets; clarified that the peddling ordinance did not prohibit peddling all together; and noted that the city government passed these ordinances for public health reasons. As was always the case with public provisioning, it was easier for city officials to regulate the sale of food when it was concentrated in one place, he explained. In the second meeting where the mayor talked with merchants opposed to the nine-block radius rule, he stated that he believed the ordinance was good for the city's businesses, that "the city is improving," and that "we are not only on the eve of great prosperity, but we are already prosperous."[40]

As these conversations took place, the city government continued to grow its public market system, expanding its reach and tapping into burgeoning consumer markets on the outer rim of the city. Catering to those growing communities meant more money for the city. In 1900, the Zengel and Maestri Markets opened, and in 1902 the Lautenschlaeger Market opened. Local officials approved the construction of the Zengel Market only after community members complained about the dilapidated conditions of the existing market in their neighborhood: the Washington Market, which had originally been constructed in 1836. Charles A. Anderson, who sat on the city council, played a crucial role in advocating for his constituents and expediting the approval of the Zengel Market's construction.[41] The market operated as a quasi-public market and was contracted out to Frank Zengel—the very same man who supported the nine-block radius rule and the banning of all street vending— for a period of twenty-five years. As noted in the *Daily Picayune*, "The only difference between [quasi-public markets] and the public markets is that the dues are collected by the contractors, and not by the city." They were beholden to the same laws as the public markets and so the city treated them similarly.[42]

After the Zengel Market opened to the public, it quickly filled with butchers and vegetable vendors, many of whom were women. Their presence reflected how the public markets were a place for women to find an economic toehold. In fact, of the nine vegetable vendors operating in January 1900, six were women. By contrast, the twelve butchers and two fishmongers were men, demonstrating that men still typically dominated meat and fish trades.[43]

Women market vendors, many of them white and married or widowed, oper-
ated throughout the city. Agatha Bertucci, who was a vegetable vendor in the
Dryades Market for twenty-five years, was described in her obituary as a
"Well-known and Beloved Figure" at the market.[44] She went by the name
Hattie and, after emigrating from Sicily, operated the stall with her husband
Anthony.[45] Throughout their decades-long marriage, they earned enough to
support their family of ten. Another vendor, Annie Rabito—the wife of
Anthony Rabito, who spoke out against the private markets—owned and
operated a fishmonger stall at the Poydras Market. She was politically active,
joining her fellow fishmongers in protests against the city government's regulation of certain seafood.[46] She took over her husband's business after he
passed away in 1903.[47] For these women, the public markets were not merely
a place to exercise economic independence, but also a space to express their
political opinions, especially as they related to the protection of their business
interests. Whether an established markets, or a newer one, these municipal
spaces were dynamic arenas of self-expression for the men and women who
worked within them.

Another of the new markets, the Maestri Market, located in a suburb-style
neighborhood heading out toward Lake Pontchartrain, occupied a less
densely populated area than the Zengel Market. As with markets in the past,
city officials approved the construction of the market with the intent that it
would spur both domestic and commercial growth in the nascent neighborhood. Like the Zengel Market, it was also a quasi-public market and the city
contracted it out to C. N. Maestri for a period of thirty years. Whereas the
contract for the Zengel Market, located in an established neighborhood,
sold for $3,600, the one for the Maestri Market, located in a less developed
area, only sold for $250. Maestri was banking on the idea that, as noted in the
local newspaper, "every public market in the city has sprung up a business
center, where the property has largely increased in value, and the building of
markets in remote sections has helped to build them up." The market was
similar in size to the Zengel Market, consisting of thirty-two eight-foot stalls.
After building the market, Maestri also constructed five or six stores, creating
the retail space necessary to attract and enable private retailers to operate
nearby. Within a year, he began to see the fruits of his labor and noted that
"many houses have been built" where previously "no houses" had existed in
the immediate area. His was a long-term investment, though. He admitted
that within the first year, "The receipts [of the market] have not been very
good yet, but are improving." Those slowly increasing profits, though, would
benefit not only Maestri but also the city from which market vendors had to
purchase licenses.[48]

The profits across the city's public (and quasi-public) markets varied depending on the size and the location of each building. In this period, the quasi-public markets tended to be smaller than the public markets, and their profits much smaller by comparison. The local newspaper made a sampling of the daily profits of each market available in January 1901, which was part of an effort to create greater transparency around the markets. As important as they were to individual neighborhoods, some city residents did not understand the larger public market system feeding their city. In fact, the local paper cited one woman who believed there were only four public markets in all of New Orleans.[49]

In order to mitigate these misunderstandings, one local reporter sought to clarify both the number and geographic distribution of the public markets, as well as their profitability. The reporter listed out the receipts on a single day for each public market, which included the humble $4.10 profit at St. Mary's Market and the more robust $130 profit of the French Market complex. Their article went on to explain the differences in average profits among quasi- and non-quasi-public markets: "The five quasi-public markets, according to the figures given, which seem to be accurate, average $8.80 a day, and the nineteen public markets average $27.50 a day."[50] Such explanations played an important role in educating the New Orleans public about the expansive system that sustained them. Marketgoers' ignorance demonstrates how insulated neighborhoods could be from one another. Residents certainly knew the significance of their local market in their daily lives, while at the same time not understanding the larger whole. City officials, by contrast, very much understood the wider picture of the public markets and how those amenities supported their future aims and goals for New Orleans.

After securing their hold over the local food economy, thereby ensuring a steady stream of profits for the city government's general fund, the municipal government began to make conservative improvements to some of the market structures to alleviate customers' public health concerns. The city only remodeled a few key markets, though. Alexander Pujol, the commissioner of the Police and Public Buildings Committee, headed the renovations. He began with the Dryades Market because of its popularity, size, and historical significance. In 1903, Pujol fitted the Dryades Market for electricity, and more renovations followed.[51] In 1905, for example, Pujol resolved to repair and rebuild the sidewalks around the market. As noted in the local paper, Pujol was a force to be reckoned with: "When the Commissioner goes into any market with his force everything old and worn has to come out and new paint must show everywhere."[52] Many city residents viewed him as a reputable and efficient public servant. Pujol then moved on to the Claiborne and Tremé Markets, seeking to bring those public amenities up to par with the Dryades Market. With these improvements, the city government's plan to make the markets profitable was on its way.

With the local laws and structural improvements now working for them, public market vendors sought to win back the loyalties of customers who had grown distrustful and critical of them during the contractual period when the conditions of the markets deteriorated rapidly.[53] Although public market vendors saw themselves as central to New Orleans' food economy, customers did not necessarily share that same vision and needed convincing to support the public markets' continuation. Vendors at the Dryades Market made their case in the *Daily States*, a local newspaper aligning with Progressive politics. In October 1903, after initial market renovations were complete, they began running a two-page advertising spread in the Sunday paper. Other businesses in the Dryades commercial district were also included in the spread. The advertisement, then, became a microcosm of the neighborhood's economy— one that depended on the draw of the public market to bring shoppers to the neighborhood.[54] Revitalizing the market, therefore, was more than fixing dilapidated buildings and market stalls; it was a project about revitalizing an entire shopping district and its reputation.

Acutely aware of customers' fears of unsanitary markets, vendors not only at Dryades but also in other municipal markets made efforts to speak to the cleanliness of their businesses in the *Daily States*. They understood that cleanliness was directly tied to the successful renewal of the markets. Proving their commitment to sanitation in the local paper was also a step toward redemption, and toward saving their reputations and their businesses. Vendors from the Ninth Street Market, for example, advertised that their market was "the cleanest and best conducted in the city and that the quality of goods is not surpassed anywhere."[55] Individual entrepreneurs also placed advertisements that spoke to the good conditions of their particular businesses. At the Dryades Market, for example, Bernard Trapp of the Union Coffee stand claimed that he "offers everything in the line served up in clean and prompt style."[56] Similarly, John Flettrich at the Poydras Market, noted that "everything is neat and clean" at Lawrence's Coffee Stand.[57] In addition to addressing sanitation concerns, vendors also made references to their commitment to modern business practices so as to reassure customers that the public markets were the best place to purchase fresh food in the city. Although vendors had made some inroads through the *Daily States*, the markets continued to be the subject of much debate around public health concerns in the years leading up to World War I.

New Orleanians' dissatisfaction with the conditions of the markets and urban provisioning, in general, were not unique to the city, but indicative of issues with urban food economies throughout the United States. Regardless of how modern and up-to-date facilities were, fresh food, once harvested, foraged, or slaughtered was in a constant state of decay. It invited insects, vermin, germs, and disease even when kept under ice or placed in refrigerated storage. In addition to the natural state of deterioration, preparing and selling fresh food produced waste. When not managed properly, that waste contributed to public health issues by contaminating waterways and blocking sewage systems, among other issues. On top of these problems, there were also widespread issues with the adulteration of both fresh and preserved foods like canned goods. Although it had been customary for customers to take on a major role in regulating food distribution, views on this responsibility began to change with the industrialization of food production and the all-too-common adulteration of packaged foods.[58]

Nationwide, people began to push for federal regulation of food production and distribution and insisted upon greater transparency in those processes.[59] That movement, known as the Pure Food Movement, had roots in the late nineteenth century.[60] The efforts of this decades-long campaign led the federal government to take action in food regulation, which had historically been under the jurisdiction of the state and policed at the local level. Reports in the *Daily Picayune* were less than supportive of proposed legislation that would empower the federal government to assume this responsibility: the Pure Food and Drug Bill. Although in agreement that the quality of food should be regulated, some Louisianans believed the regulation of the sale of adulterated food and drugs was not the responsibility of the federal government, but that of the state governments.[61]

The centralization of food regulation brought on by the federal government's intervention in local and interstate food distribution impacted New Orleans' market culture in subtle but important ways. Those impacts signaled the increasingly powerful presence of a nationally recognized vision of modern provisioning that prioritized public health. In 1906, the federal government passed the Pure Food and Drug Act, which declared that the adulteration of food was dangerous and fraudulent. The act itself did not dramatically change the day-to-day activities of businesses that sold canned goods, mainly grocery stores. As described in the *Daily Picayune*, "The effects of the law will not, in all probability, be very prominent on the shelves of grocery stores, and the layman might not know from the looks of the goods he was buying that there had been any change at all; but it is said that the law will result in a much better quality of food, drinks and condiments being sold, and that the people will get what they pay for, and not something else that looks like it."[62] The act did, however, change the goings-on at the city's municipal markets in much more dramatic and public ways.

Beginning in 1906, the local government's plan to modernize New Orleans' public markets came to encompass a long-term campaign against adulterated food. The Pure Food and Drug Act and the Federal Meat Inspection Act spurred on a kind of "war on bad meat"—a campaign fueled by militaristic language and marked by impromptu inspections conducted by city police. These acts sought to prevent the adulteration of meat and ensure the quality of meat products sold in fresh food markets, both public and private. Dr. E. A. White, chief of the food department of the City Board of Health, was a major player in policing meat vendors in New Orleans. As part of a pure food campaign, White organized random health inspections, or "raids," of the markets. During one such raid in November of 1906, the *Daily Picayune* reported, White "swooped down on several of the local markets unexpectedly."[63] During his inspection, he found thirty-five pounds of decomposed meat in the icebox of George Bohm, a butcher at the Dryades Market. Bohm had started turning that bad meat into sausage, deceptively selling it as a high-quality product.[64] Customers were upset, yet not shocked by the news. White noted that the city government would " 'fight the thing [adulterated meat] until every one of them [vendors] is forced to comply with the law. The sale of inferior meats in New Orleans must stop.' "[65] When vendors prioritized the success of their individual business by selling bad meat over the city's project to modernize New Orleans' public markets, the municipal government penalized them with large fines and public condemnation in the local papers.[66]

At the turn of the twentieth century, public health was not the only issue on people's minds regarding the public markets. The marketing campaigns in the *Daily States* touch on the centrality of community, as cultivated in the public markets, that had long shaped New Orleanians' understandings of themselves. In fact, local businesspersons used the paper to garner support by appealing directly to residents' sense of loyalty to the communities of which they were a part. Businesspeople in the Dryades commercial district were the first to run a section in the newspaper. As noted in the October 25, 1903 issue of the *Daily States*, "For the next few weeks the States has arranged to assist the business men of the Dryades street market and vicinity in an effort to bring prominently before the public of New Orleans the advantages to be derived by trading in this locality."[67] As was the case throughout the nineteenth century, the local food economy, in many ways, was still grounded in the antebellum system of neighborhood-based food provisioning.[68]

Although the Dryades Market advertisement was the first to appear, others soon followed. Entrepreneurs from the Ninth Street Market contacted the newspaper asking that they too have representation in the Sunday paper. By mid-November, they had a spread that proudly stated, "This page is the outcome, and it is a most creditable exposition of the importance of the neighborhood as a commercial center."[69] Then the Poydras Market advertisement appeared on December 13, 1903 and the French Market published a grand multipage display just a few days before Christmas, on December 20. Throughout 1904 several more neighborhood markets joined the Sunday *Daily States* advertising campaign. In total, featured market spreads included the French Market as well as the Dryades, Ninth Street, Poydras, Tremé, Suburban, Zengel, and Jefferson Markets.

The Dryades Market newspaper spreads were diverse, but they focused on the personal lives of vendors, thus reinforcing the idea that these retail spaces were community spaces. They included an introductory essay and an image of the market as well as advertisements specific to the commerce of that particular neighborhood, giving insights into what individual vendors sold at the neighborhood markets. In an attempt to supplement advertisements with a more personal story, the *Daily States* proposed to publish a portrait and short profile detailing the life, character, and business practices of one or more of its advertisers each week. The profiles were designed to function as character references. They assured readers that the men and women who ran businesses in or around the Dryades Market were trustworthy and deserving of patronage. Aside from assurances, the content also often included vendors' place of birth and family connections in the city; where they received their education; how they got their start in their respective industry; the benevolent societies or social clubs to which they belonged; the name of their spouse and the number of children they had; and their home address.

The retailers who advertised in the *Daily States* defined community in terms of the entire commercial district that grew up around the market. This gesture of inclusivity indicates that community relationships were not bounded within the walls of the market, but rather stretched from door to door along the Dryades neighborhood's main commercial corridor, for example. In addition to the vendors selling fresh foods, meat, and game in the markets, the Dryades Market commercial district was home to several dry goods stores, saloons, coffee stands, grocers, clothing and shoe stores, furniture stores, a cookery store, and a bookstore. The area also had a jeweler, a tinsmith, an undertaker, and a baker. The district stretched several blocks—a behemoth presence in an otherwise residential neighborhood. Admiring the breadth of the neighborhood economy, an introductory essay in the *Daily States* paints a vivid scene: "Lined along both sides of the Dryades street, from Clio to Philip streets, is a succession of stores were every article of necessity or luxury may be found in great profusion: Indeed no part of the city offers a wider opportunity for the supply of every desire."[70] The entrepreneurs who ran these businesses bolstered the already tight-knit community created by the Dryades Market.

The proximity of these entrepreneurs' homes and businesses helped to create an environment in which commercial and residential life was almost inseparable. For many, in fact, their place of residence was the same as their business. Marshall M. Bradburn, who lived and worked at 1901 Jackson Avenue, at the corner of Dryades Street, was a druggist for the Dryades Market neighborhood.[71] George H. Leidenheimer, a Bavarian baker, also lived and worked at the same address at 1835 Melpomene.[72] Others lived in close proximity to their businesses, but not in the same building. Charles A. Kaufman, for example, lived just three blocks from the Kaufman's Department Store of which he was president.[73] Given the success of Kaufman's business, it is not surprising that he lived at 1707 St. Charles Avenue, one of the wealthier streets in New Orleans. New Orleans was set up in such a way that wealthier entrepreneurs like Kaufman could live on grand throughways like St. Charles Avenue and still be near one of the neighborhood commercial corridors. In preindustrial cities, it was not uncommon for wealthy people to live in the inner city. The enslaved people and domestic servants who maintained their estates lived in adjacent buildings and middle- and working-class families resided in bordering neighborhoods.[74] This antebellum trend echoed in the twentieth century, explaining the socioeconomic diversity of the Dryades neighborhood where everyone from street peddlers to department store moguls lived within a few blocks of one another.[75]

Commercial and residential activity were further entangled because family members regularly lived together and worked in the same industry. Nathan and Morris Dreyfus owned and operated a dry goods store on Dryades Street called Dreyfus Brothers. They resided together at 1629 Erato Street, as did William Dreyfus, who was a clerk at the store.[76] The importance of family networks in these local commercial corridors is also evident in the story of Lawrence Flettrich, who owned and operated a coffee stand at the Poydras

Market with his brother John. John also owned a saloon on Dryades Street. Eventually, Lawrence took over operations of the Lalla's Coffee Stand in the Dryades Market, expanding his Poydras Market business into the commercial corridor where John already had a food- and beverage-related business established.[77]

Familial business networks solidified community relations, yet even within those communities there were tensions that created in-groups and out-groups among entrepreneurs. Heterogeneous neighborhoods like the one surrounding the Dryades Market were rife with racial tensions, especially as migrant African American families settled near immigrant and white American families at the turn of the century. This proximity created competition among different racial and ethnic groups. Tensions were especially high between Black and white entrepreneurs and their customers, many of whom were Black women working in the domestic service industry for middle-class and wealthier white families. The *Daily States* became a mechanism to support white businesspersons and a device through which to identify who was and who was not a part of the community. Their notions of community decidedly excluded African American neighbors by omitting their businesses from the publication and from the potential patronage of their readers.

"Americanness" and, by extension, whiteness, became a critical criterion of community for many entrepreneurs who published profiles in the *Daily States*. Fittingly, the paper was progressive, but decidedly white supremacist in its progressive views. Market vendors' profiles reflected the publication's political sentiments; its readership and customer base, too, likely found their political views as well as their racist and xenophobic perspectives mirrored in the *Daily States* and vendors' profiles. Fighting for customer support and working to strengthen their particular vision of community, some vendors staked out their turf in ethnic terms, weaving their xenophobia into the public market profiles.

In 1900, New Orleans had one of the largest Sicilian immigrant populations in the world, and the largest in the United States, and many of those migrants integrated into the local economy and community through food businesses. Although strong fraternal relationships developed within New Orleans' Italian community, there existed tensions between Italian immigrants and "native" New Orleanians of diverse racial and ethnic backgrounds. In fact, those tensions had a history of turning violent, and the local papers, including the *Daily States*, helped stoke the fire. In 1891, for example, all the city papers supported the public gathering of angry city residents that led to the 1891 lynching of eleven Sicilian men. Several of the mob's victims worked in New Orleans' food industry, including one fruit importer and three fruit peddlers; another victim was a street vendor.[78] It was the *Daily States* that took the vocal lead, fueling the xenophobia that led to this horrendous public murder.

A decade later, the paper continued to sow the seeds of exclusion and marginalization of recent immigrants through the seemingly innocuous public market profiles. Entrepreneurs of the Dryades Market district appealed to their neighbors and patrons to support what they identified as "local" and "native born" businessmen. Vendor profiles in the *Daily States*, for example, demonstrated a strong sense of loyalty to New Orleans and tied that localism to the progressive ideas purported in the newspaper. J. J. Guinle's profile in the Poydras Market spread mentioned his birth in New Orleans and his education in the city's public schools.[79] A. Dobard's profile also noted that he was born in New Orleans and further mentioned that he came from an "old and well-known family of this section."[80] John H. Hunsinger's biographical sketch delved deeper and stated that the Dryades Market vendor was born in the Dryades neighborhood itself and had childhood memories of the market.[81] Dozens of vendor profiles tout these kinds of credentials—ones that allude to a birthright claim to their neighborhood's and city's culture. Their repetitive mention across different market spreads suggests a strong commitment to "American" entrepreneurs, which is unsurprising considering the widespread xenophobia characteristic of New Orleans at that time.

Although the *Daily States* and its readers supported native vendors, they were also willing to support immigrant vendors if they had established themselves in the community and ascribed to its sense of "Americanness"; their profiles often emphasized the immigrant vendors' long-term residence and commitment to their adopted city. H. B. Guinle was born in France and immigrated in 1865 to the United States, where he began a family and opened a meat stall in the Poydras Market. His profile noted that he was a "patriotic citizen," emphasizing his political and personal loyalty and ties to the city. To further emphasize the roots he put down, the *Daily States* published his profile alongside that of his son, J. J. Guinle, born and raised in the Crescent City.[82]

Other profiles seemed to de-emphasize immigrant vendors' foreign-born status and focused instead on how they were raised in New Orleans. Paul St. Philip, a vendor at the French Market, was born in Italy, but had lived in New Orleans for more than forty years.[83] His profile carefully notes that he was brought to the city as a boy and that he attended the public schools, growing up among New Orleanians. Similarly, the *Daily States* reported that

Henry J. Schenck was born in Alsace but was "brought to America at the early age of three, and reared in New Orleans," where he received a "liberal education, primarily in the public schools." These profiles stress that, although these men were immigrants, they grew up and were educated in the city and were thus privy to the city's culture and worthy of the city's support and patronage.[84]

Men like St. Philip and Schenck, however, may not have felt that they were fully accepted because of their immigrant status; if this were true, perhaps the *Daily States* profiles reveal a yet unrealized desire among immigrant vendors like them to become full-fledged members of New Orleans' community. Such desire may have been felt even more keenly by relatively recent immigrants like Charles Palermo. Unlike St. Philip, who had spent four decades living in New Orleans cultivating relationships with neighbors and customers, Palermo, a comparatively younger vendor at twenty years of age, did not have the same amount of time to build up his customer base. He had been living in the United States for only about ten years and had been working as a fish and game vendor for an even shorter period. The *Daily States* profile gave him a chance to rewrite his narrative to appeal to the paper's nativist readership suspicious of unvetted or unconnected immigrants; and he made sure to emphasize his social network: "He is a native of sunny Italy, but has been in New Orleans many years and has made a great many friends." His identity as an Italian immigrant may have also raised suspicions among the *Daily States* readership who may have ascribed to pervasive stereotypes of Italian food vendors as "aggressive." Perhaps in an effort to combat those misconceptions, Palermo chose to emphasize that "polite service" was a hallmark of his business.[85]

Profiles like Palermo's reveal the volatility of community acceptance at the turn of the century; it was not necessarily enough that an immigrant vendor worked their way up to own or operate a food stand in one of the city's commercial districts; their acceptance could still come into question despite their relative economic success and centrality in the local food scene. So, people like Palermo, and even St. Philip and Schenck, fought to solidify their standing by making an appeal for their worthiness and the support and economic patronage of their neighbors in print. The *Daily States'* willingness to share these pleas also suggests that its readership was open to hearing them and accepting immigrant vendors as part of the community as long as they bought into their particular vision of "Americanness"—one steeped in white supremacy.

What *Daily States* readers were not open to, if the paper's contents reflected readers' sense of community, were profiles of Black business owners

of large- or small-scale enterprises. The white supremacy that permeated the
pages of the newspaper mirrored New Orleans' broader racial dynamics and
structural inequalities. At the turn of the twentieth century, white supremacy
continued to have profound and lasting impacts on the job opportunities of
people of color, especially the working poor, whose employment options were
severely limited. Eugenia Marine Lacarra, a Black woman who grew up in
early twentieth-century New Orleans, reflected on the impact of racial segregation on the African American community's ability to make a living at the
turn of the twentieth century:

> I stop to think sometimes, and I wonder how the poor colored people
> got along. You couldn't work in the department stores, the men
> couldn't drive a bus, you couldn't work for the telephone company,
> you couldn't work for the Public Service, so if you didn't do menial
> labor, or housework, or learn to be a cigar maker, or you weren't lucky
> enough to get an education to teach, well, you were in very bad luck.[86]

One of the areas where Black working poor could find an economic
toehold was in street food vending, where there were fewer barriers to entry.
Black women, in particular, continued to carve out a space for themselves on
the streets of New Orleans as they had done since the colonial period.
Although some women like Rose Nicaud, who had a famous coffee stand in
the French Market, made a name for themselves on a national level for their
offerings, a vast majority of vendors barely scraped by. Although they built
crucial relationships with their customers in New Orleans, beyond the city's
bounds, they were largely anonymous.

Black women not only faced racism, but sexism—the two harmful forces
inextricably bound. At the turn of the twentieth century, the ideal of the
middle-class housewife had taken root, impacting women's abilities to open
and operate food businesses. That ideal housewife was someone who did
not work outside of the home, and certainly not someone who operated a
public-facing food business. So strong was the middle-class housewife ideal
that married women were known to minimize the work they did after marriage, as did their family members. When James M. Montoya, a Black New
Orleanian, responded to the question if his mother worked, Montoya
replied:

> Never. She worked in the home when the family got large....when
> work [for my father] was scarce, my mother would sew. She would also

make *calas* and we [the children] would sell the *calas* in order to buy bread to eat. That's the only work she did—in the house. She never went outside one day to work.[87]

But Montoya's mother did work. And her business, by virtue of her children's contributions, took her work into the public sphere. By today's standards she would be considered a small-scale entrepreneur operating a food business to contribute to the economic stability of her family. Making calas, sewing, and also operating a small store in the front room of their house, as her son later revealed, were the means in which she did so. And her children also worked, as many economically disadvantaged young people did, to help support the family. Together, they cultivated a customer base, built economic networks, and kept their family afloat when it was challenging or near impossible for her husband to find work in the segregated city. This is just one of the many stories of entrepreneurship not covered by the *Daily States* and other media shaped by white supremacy, but which took place in the same neighborhoods as the vendors and businesspeople profiled in the paper. The Montoya family's enterprise was as much of the fabric of the public culture of food as Palermo's or that of the Flettrich brothers.

Around the time Congress passed the Pure Food and Drug Act in 1906, the city government of New Orleans began its final push to grow the public market system. Between 1907 and 1910, city officials approved the construction of seven more markets: the Ewing, Memory, Mehle, Doullut, Behrman, Foto, and McCue Markets. Together, these markets pushed the boundaries and the local government's monopoly over local food provisioning out into the emerging communities along the city's outer rim. That monopoly even crossed the Mississippi River onto Algiers Point (located across the river from the French Quarter).

Some city residents were desperate for these markets to open, looking for the convenience they offered. When the Ewing Market's opening was delayed, concerned residents took to the local paper to express their dismay. On October 16, 1907, one such potential customer wrote to the editor of the *Daily Picayune* asking, "Dear Sir—Why is the Ewing Market not opened? It's completed, after taking six months to do so." They went on to ask who stood in the way of its opening, conjecturing that person was likely in favor of protecting "the miserable private ones" in the area. Lastly, the writer stated they were tired of trekking all the way to the Prytania Market and felt that "surely something ought to be done soon" to open the new market.[88]

When the Ewing Market finally opened on October 23, it did so to a great reception from city officials and many residents. The evening's ceremonies kicked off with a brass band, fireworks, a cannon, crackers, and a resounding speech given by Hon. George F. Bartley "explaining the many benefits and the great convenience the market would be to the ladies of the Sixth District." The mayor also attended the event to christen the structure in honor of its namesake, Councilmen David Ewing. The new amenity, which the city expected to make solid profits, embodied local officials' hopes for New Orleans' modern market system. So much so that Bartley was bold enough to note, "If the President of the United States, Theodore Roosevelt, could see the hundreds of pretty smiling, happy faces of the children who surrounded the platform, and were mounted on the stalls, his heart would open to them, and he would indeed be delighted. The presence of so many children proved beyond a doubt that the Ewing Market would be a success."[89]

Although the Ewing Market appeared a triumph, it and other markets built in the same year proved problematic. An unnamed person submitted a complaint to the City Board of Health within weeks of the Ewing Market's opening, noting that it was in "a bad sanitary condition" and needed "an immediate cleaning up." That same day, it came to the city council's attention that the water hydrant at the newly opened Memory Market had been cut off and as a result "the place was practically without water supply, necessarily resulting in a rather bad situation, where frequent washings are necessary in order to maintain cleanliness." City officials responded by sending a team to investigate.[90]

The markets' poor conditions hinted at the ugly underbelly of New Orleans' public market system, consisting of structures old and new that contributed to the poor public health of the city. Their conditions were made all the more frightening by a tuberculosis outbreak in the city's dairy supply that occurred at the same time.[91] Fear and a sense of helplessness permeated food distribution cultures across the city as officials and residents sought to better understand exactly how contagious diseases spread through animal-human contact and through the consumption of animal products.

The final four markets were all quasi-public, with the Doullut and Behrman contracted out to the same entrepreneur, Captain M. P. Doullut.[92] Contractors constructed the markets according to city regulations, and the markets were only allowed to open to the public once city officials had conducted thorough inspections of the new facilities. The structures, as a result, all looked quite similar.[93] The uniformity of the design of the late markets reflected the unified approach of local officials in expanding the public market system—a system designed to generate money for the city's general fund.

By 1911, the city government had approved the construction of thirty-three public and quasi-public neighborhood markets to supplement the French Market, and thirty of them were still operating.[94] At its peak, New Orleans' public market system looked nothing like any other system in the country because of the sheer number of markets and individual communities to which they catered. Additionally, the system looked distinct within the United States because of the monopoly that the city government maintained on local food provisioning.

Although unusual within the United States, New Orleans' market system did mirror market systems in Europe and specifically that of Paris, which municipal governments throughout Europe and the United States saw as exemplary.[95] Around 1910, Paris' market system consisted of one central market, Les Halles, and thirty-three auxiliary markets, almost the same number as in New Orleans by 1911.[96] The parallels between New Orleans' and Paris' systems in the nineteenth and twentieth centuries suggests that the former likely drew inspiration from the latter. City residents openly acknowledged this transatlantic connection and Europe's long-standing influence on New Orleans. In a speech recounting the history of the city's market system, one New Orleanian noted, "The French Market, if not physically as old as the city, was one of the European ideas brought over by the first settlers, and it has been along European lines of government that our market system has been run."[97] And so, more than a hundred years since being under French rule, the city still maintained a significant cultural connection to the public food culture of France in an era where the presence of the US federal government became stronger over time. Overlapping connections demonstrate the complex nature of culture in a city that had been governed by three different nation-states, all the while developing its own unique sense of community through a food-provisioning system that shaped and was shaped by the urban landscape.

Tensions and interactions between local, national, and historic influences from throughout the Atlantic world continued to shape New Orleans' public food culture after the opening decade of the twentieth century. In fact, those influences came into conflict with one another in later decades as city officials—pressured by activists tired of poor sanitary conditions in the public markets—finally began implementing a complete overhaul of the public market system. The debates among vendors, customers, and city officials about when and how to renovate the markets reflect deep-seated notions of community within the public food culture of the city.

Those debates reveal some customers' growing acceptance and desire for a local food economy that resembled a broader American food culture and departed from local food traditions grounded in the public markets and street food vending. Those conversations also shed light on the long-standing interest of some food vendors to embrace a deregulated food economy and privatized market system that mirrored those of cities across the United States, while other vendors held tight to local traditions of a monopolistic public market system. Local officials tried to navigate these competing ideas and find a middle path that preserved the unique nature of New Orleans' public food culture, while at the same time integrating national standards. They understood all too well that residents committed to retaining the city's traditional model were fighting to preserve a historic economic system that had sustained their livelihoods and contributed to their sense of self and community for generations.

5

Building "Model Markets" in Progressive Era New Orleans, 1911–1940

ONE DAY IN September 1912, Lucia Sargent arrived at the Dryades Market cloaked in a strong sense of purpose.[1] She was there on behalf of the Era Club, a white women's social and civic organization, to provide guidance and make suggestions on how best to operate the facility. For months, she had been working with fellow Era Club members to research best practices for the municipal markets, with a focus on public health, and she had more than a few ideas to share to help transform New Orleans' structures into "model markets."[2]

Sargent spent much of her site visit trying to convince vendors of the advantages of rearranging appliances. Specifically, she wanted them to move the shared refrigerator that was against a side wall of the market to the middle aisle; that way, she argued, butchers would have to take fewer steps to reach the appliance. Overall, the proposed rearrangement would reduce the amount of time butchers spent carrying product to their stands, which would reduce the likelihood that the meat would become contaminated. It would also shorten customer wait times, something from which she and her fellow shoppers would benefit. In her estimation, the minor adjustment was a win-win for all parties.[3]

Although people often think of public health reforms as top-down, in the case of New Orleans' historic public markets, these improvements emerged from decades-long grassroots activism by women like Sargent, highlighting the struggles and eventual successes of community activist groups. For decades, these engaged and committed city residents worked hand in hand with local officials to eventually overhaul the municipal market system. Although the rehabilitation of the public market structures began in the 1910s, they were not completed until 1940, after the federal government stepped in to provide financial support.

Together, local officials and their constituents, with assistance from the federal government, articulated a vision of a disease-free, modern society through new and renovated public market buildings. The facilities married the latest understandings of public health and epidemiology with emerging architectural styles and a national movement to preserve and celebrate regional cultures. Ranging from art deco to Spanish Colonial Revival, the varying aesthetics of the refreshed public markets signaled New Orleanians' embrace of diverse regional cultures throughout the United States. By adopting these aesthetics and marrying them to their traditional public market system, they boldly expressed their overlapping identity as American and Creole and created a distinct brand of American progressivism conveyed in the very structures of urban provisioning.

However, the reimagining of the municipal market system was also an attempt to further marginalize street food vendors within the public food culture. When the structures were enclosed to mitigate the presence of disease-carrying insects and vermin, street vendors were physically cut off from these commercial hubs. Products of the Jim Crow era, these new public market buildings embodied white supremacy to the detriment and exclusion of street vendors, many of whom were people of color. As in the past, street vendors improvised and innovated to keep their businesses alive despite the changes to their commercial environment, luring customers with their cries— "Watermelon, Lady! Come and git your nice red watermelon, Lady! Red to the rind, Lady!"[4]

In 1911, just as New Orleans' public market system swelled to its peak size, the city faced an alarming infestation of flies as spring arrived. These insects thrived in cities with heavy horse- and mule-drawn cart traffic and whose streets were covered in manure—an ideal environment to lay their eggs in warmer months. By early March, flies had found their way into every nook and cranny of public and private life, and the city seemed to echo with the grating buzz of their chaotic wingbeats. The public markets' open-air designs exacerbated the issue. With no screens or walls, flies could easily swarm over the ornate and fragrant displays of fruits, vegetables, meat, and seafood. The small army of mule-drawn carts that clustered around the markets made conditions worse. Scientists were all too aware that common flies, which hatched in manure, gravitated toward uncovered food on display in public markets. In the process, they flitted from a pile of dung to a barrel of apples, carrying bacteria on their bodies and transferring it to different surfaces and foodstuffs.[5]

During the fly infestation, New Orleans' public markets were dramatically and directly tied to the spread of disease, and specifically salmonella, a potentially deadly bacterial disease that affects the digestive tract.[6] In the twentieth century, salmonella was a major cause of food poisoning not only in the United States but worldwide. As scientists came to better understand the role of flies in the spread of salmonella, public health campaigns emerged to educate the public about how an everyday nuisance was also hazardous to one's health.[7] Witness to the swarms of flies in and around the public markets, city residents became wary of shopping in them.

When fear of salmonella peaked at the turn of the century, public market vendors felt that they had little option but to stay in the unsanitary public market structures where they were legally obligated to sell their wares. To make matters worse, their personal health was also at stake. Public market vendors were incredibly vulnerable to the spread of the disease because their businesses necessitated daily engagement and close contact with the public; they interacted with hundreds of marketgoers each day. In doing so, they risked their personal health to keep putting food not only on the tables of other New Orleanians, but on their own tables as well.

During the fly infestation of 1911, public market vendors openly expressed frustration over the terrible conditions of the municipal facilities. At that time, most public market vendors were white, and many were immigrants from Europe. Some in their cohort openly criticized the laws that forced them to vend fresh foods within the public markets. Several said they felt trapped by the public market system and argued that they could provide better services, higher-quality products, and safer conditions in their own stores if municipal laws allowed private markets to sell meat, seafood, and fresh produce.[8]

Flies were not the only problem that New Orleanians faced. Paul Cendon, a butcher in one of the public markets and an active member of several trade and civic groups, informed the city council that while the fly problem was unbearable, flies were but one of several creatures spreading foodborne illness. He noted that if the city officials visited the markets in the early morning, they would find dozens of feral cats and innumerable rats scampering over the meat that butchers were meant to sell to customers later that day. He criticized the City Board of Health for ignoring these conditions and for expressing little or no interest in the health of vendors, customers, or the entire city, for that matter. A fellow butcher added to the argument, stating that the City Board of Health's proposed solution—to screen in each individual stall with metal mesh—was a terrible idea; it would further endanger the health of vendors and would, in fact, "make them sick." Frustrated and seeking resolution, Cendon and his fellow vendors argued that the markets were "unfit to be used and that they ought to be torn down and remodeled."[9]

City councilmen took the concerns of these vocal vendors into consideration. According to the *Daily Picayune*, at a public forum held in March 1911, city councilmen had

> been considerably moved by the argument of the market people that the city forces them into the markets at a high rental when they might, if left to themselves, get fine shops with modern improvements outside, and as it is they are obliged to charge the public high and give inefficient service because they are up against high rents and poor facilities.[10]

Privately owned markets (i.e., greengrocers) seemed like an increasingly better option than the public markets, but in early twentieth-century New Orleans, they were still largely illegal because of the ordinance banning their operation within nine blocks of any public market. Arguably, the private markets afforded entrepreneurs greater control over the sanitary conditions of their businesses; whereas in the public markets, vendors were at the mercy of the city government to make improvements and maintain structures. More and more vendors in the public markets wanted that freedom.

To combat the growing clamor for private greengrocery stores, city officials rushed to make patchwork improvements to the municipal market structures to ease public concern, afraid that if they lost vendors' support, the entire public market system would collapse. City officials pushed to screen in some public markets (but not individual stalls) with metal mesh to keep insects and vermin at bay, starting with the McCue Market in 1912.[11] However, their efforts were halfhearted, and most of the public market structures remained unscreened and exposed in the years to come.

When the city screened in some of the public markets, the very nature of those spaces changed because screening necessitated the erection of walls. Contractors and city officials implemented their enclosure for public health reasons—to shut out dangerous insects and vermin, thus ensuring the sale of quality products, and to prevent the outbreak of disease. However, there were ulterior motives underpinning the renovations. The public market enclosures also shut out roving vendors who previously clustered right at the edge of the markets, hoping to catch passersby as they moved into the structures at various points along their perimeters. Historically, their itinerant businesses had operated as unsanctioned extensions of the public market—ones that the city government derided, but which customers found generally useful for procuring foodstuffs often at a discounted price. The public markets' newly erected walls limited the largely unimpeded interactions among street vendors, public market vendors, and customers in and around the markets—ones that had for generations contributed to the city's public food culture.

The 1912 screening in of some of the public markets was not the first effort to shut people out of these crucial commercial and community spaces. In fact, Captain M. P. Doullut, who contracted and built the Doullut Market, purposely built a gated entrance to his facility in 1907. That type of barrier was unprecedented in New Orleans' public market history and captured the attention of a local reporter: "In order to enter the market, it is necessary to pass through the gate of an Iron fence, this fence being the only one separating a market from the street in the whole city." The article goes on to note that Doullut designed the gate "for the purpose of keeping out the loafers and idlers that frequent similar places in other parts of New Orleans." Doullut, therefore, intentionally broke away from the traditional open-air pavilion-style market to make it more difficult for people who were not public market vendors to enter the grounds. Although Doullut used coded language ("loafers and idlers"), he was likely aiming to prevent itinerant vendors, many of whom were women, people of color, and recent migrants, among other working poor community members, from accessing the public market grounds.[12] Screening in some of the public markets in 1912 had a similar effect of blocking out street vendors who were deemed unwanted in the area. Peddlers, therefore, did not benefit from the renovated public markets. If anything, those renovations damaged their livelihoods.

While city officials were screening in a few public markets, they also considered making more substantial building renovations to mitigate the spread of disease. They began this process with the Dryades Market, opening discussions about renovating the structure in 1910 and eventually completing those improvements in 1913.[13] Their vision for the facility married federal standards for public markets established by the United States Department of Agriculture (USDA) with Classical Revival architecture. In the early twentieth century, the USDA envisioned the ideal American city as one that operated modern market halls for the benefit of the people and for the overall health of the community. This vision was tied to the City Beautiful movement, which sought to foster civic pride and engagement among city residents through architectural design and urban planning.[14] Combining these principles, the reimagined Dryades Market would embody the federal government's epidemiology guidelines and the City Beautiful movement's belief that a well-ordered, progressive society would thrive in an aesthetically pleasing built environment. As a result, in the early 1910s, New Orleans' public markets became a melting pot for American progressivism that drew upon European traditions.

To jumpstart the renovation process, New Orleans officials assessed the current conditions of the Dryades Market, which had served as the keystone of its neighborhood since 1849. Outfitted a few years prior with electricity and other structural improvements, the Dryades Market had long been a location in which the municipal government experimented with upgrades it sought to incorporate across the public market system. A heterogeneous community comprising white and Black residents of varying socioeconomic backgrounds, the Dryades neighborhood relied on the two-building market for provisioning. Each building carried specific products. Vendors sold butchered meat, game, and seafood in the first building, known by locals as the Meat Market and referred to as "Building A" in architectural plans. Meanwhile vendors sold fruits and vegetables in the second building, known as the Vegetable Market and referred to as "Building B" in architectural plans. The two buildings were connected by a covered walkway.

Ultimately, city officials decided to demolish and completely rebuild the Dryades Market because the condition of the existing structures was so poor. As much as Dryades neighborhood residents derided the unsanitary conditions of the old market structures and were thrilled that new, more sanitary ones were to be built, they were saddened by the loss of such an important and historic community center. Upon hearing the news that the market buildings would be razed to make way for the modern market, they proposed to place a commemorative tablet to honor the buildings.[15] Their sense of loss and compulsion to memorialize the old, dilapidated structures speaks to the fundamental dichotomy that lay at the heart of many historic urban markets: that they were simultaneously cultural centers and vectors of disease.

City officials wanted to build one of the finest markets in the country and make it a symbol of New Orleans' commitment to national standards of public health and provisioning. The mayor and William J. Hardee, the city engineer, saw the renovation of the market as a means to improve the overall reputation of the city. They sought to shed any traits that tied the public markets, and thus New Orleans, to antiquated stereotypes prevalent in the postbellum period. Hardee understood that the markets were a popular place for tourists to visit and a crucial spot where people formed impressions of the city. He therefore argued that the new markets needed to be "ornamental and up-to-date such that they may be admired by the many visitors who go to see them." All in all, their concerns reflect the growing desire of New Orleanians to fit within rather than outside of a larger national narrative of progress. City officials' vow to renovate the Dryades Market, therefore, affirmed their aspiration to belong to a larger national community by modifying their local public food culture.[16]

In order to fulfill those commitments, they strove to furnish the new Dryades Market with the latest technologies, including modern lighting, ventilation, and refrigeration systems.[17] For instance, city architects planned for thirty-two skylights and numerous windows to enable natural light to illuminate the retail space. They also planned to have eight twenty-four-inch galvanized iron vents along the center line of the roof to allow rising air perfumed with the smell of the marketplace to escape.[18] Further, they included screened, pivoted transom windows to encourage airflow.[19] Screens were not the only way to keep insects and vermin at bay. City architects planned to enclose the market, constructing brick walls where once wooden columns had existed—a departure from the colonnaded style of the pavilion market predominant throughout the city.[20]

New Orleans officials' commitment to technologies and architectural elements that improved public health mirrored the commitments of officials in other cities across the nation. For instance, when the West Side Market opened in Cleveland, Ohio, in November 1912, newspapers focused on narratives of improved public health. One article starts off: "Sanitation. That is going to be the watchword at the new West Side market house." According to the article, the aesthetic design of the West Side Market was reminiscent of cleanly, sterile hospitals: "The building is lined with white tile from the gleaming white counters to the lofty roof." Architects chose these elements to distinguish the new market from the old and to reaffirm the cleanliness of the new facility: "Everything has been eliminated which would tend to breed noxious germs." Like the West Side Market, the new Dryades Market buildings had white interiors that reflected the city's commitment to the new aesthetic of cleanliness and sanitation. The West Side and Dryades Markets not only strove for national standards of public health through architectural design but also came to exemplify them.[21]

Although the New Orleans government was willing to make strategic renovations as a symbolic gesture toward its commitment to improving public health, it stopped short of broader action. It neither had nor allotted funds to overhaul the entire market system—a widespread renovation that residents desperately needed. Behind the celebrations of the new Dryades Market, pervasive public health issues threatened the sustainability of the public markets and made private markets—which, in some cases, were more sanitary and modern—an increasingly appealing option for residents.

In the midst of implementing the Dryades Market renovation, unrest contin-ued to brew among the city's populace, much of it a carryover from the debates over the fly infestation and market screening debacle of 1911. Although generally supportive of the initial efforts with Dryades, customers wanted to see a renovation of the entire system, not just one or two select markets. They wanted a system that, across the board, eliminated the threat of foodborne illnesses. When the Louisiana State Board of Health stepped in to assess the public markets in 1912, the results were abysmal. The Poydras and Prytania Markets had dirty refrigerators, the Ninth Street Market had a rat infestation, and the Tremé Market had dysfunctional iceboxes. These public health infrac-tions exemplified the terrible condition of the entire public market system. State Board of Health officials were finally catching on to what angry and concerned residents had been expressing for decades. At a meeting with the State Board of Health in September 1912, New Orleans resident Raymond de Lord argued that a city that could not take care of its markets should not have them. De Lord's opinion reflected an increasingly popular sentiment: The public markets should be shut down or privatized.[22]

Concerned city residents realized that shutting down the public market system in the 1910s was a longshot. The markets were too entrenched in the politics of the city, and too critical to the city government's general fund. Not only that, for some New Orleanians they were too important as economic and community centers, however dysfunctional they had been for over a gen-eration. City residents, though, had other strategies in mind to ameliorate issues in the local food system. For inspiration, they looked to other American cities like New York, where modern market halls and grocery stores coexisted. In these cities, both public and private markets were fitted with electricity and refrigeration—necessary amenities and appliances for safe provisioning. In the eyes of New Orleanians, people in those other cities had choices of where to shop, whereas New Orleans customers did not. They were legally bound to shop in the subpar public markets. So, they began organizing to petition the local government to give them more options.

Women consumer-activists were key players in New Orleans' public mar-ket reform in the 1910s, creating leverage and shaping narratives about the markets that influenced public health policy.[23] Their efforts in New Orleans mirrored Progressive Era women's activism across the country, indicative of the political awakening more and more women experienced at the turn of the century. This awakening was often tied to the push for women's suffrage. Even before securing the right to vote, women had long lobbied for their interests by shaping the actions of those in power.[24] Between 1880 and 1920, American women exercised considerable influence over local politics, addressing core tenants of the Progressive movement ranging from education to public health.

Women in New Orleans, like those around the country, effectively organized and lobbied politicians to create real change in their communities, including in the public markets. In the Crescent City, however, the founding principles of the women's Progressive Era movement were forged within the context of the Jim Crow South, racial segregation, and the systematic disenfranchisement of people of color.[25] New Orleanian women's voices rang out alongside the voices of city officials, public market vendors, and private market operators and vendors—almost all men—whose involvement in the public markets were reported in the major city newspapers. Given the structural racism entrenched in New Orleans' segregated society at the time, the city's main newspaper, the *Times-Picayune*, and others such as the *New Orleans States* and *New Orleans Item*, privileged white women's voices over Black women's. In fact, Black women's voices were almost, if not completely, absent in the major newspapers' coverage of the public markets even though the papers' readership was fairly diverse. This is not to suggest that Black women did not act to improve the conditions of the public markets; but the archival record does not readily reveal their efforts.

Those same newspapers, though, did shed light on white women's activism, providing some insight, however incomplete, into the role of women consumer-activists in the shaping of New Orleans' public food culture in the 1910s. Ironically, many of these women consumer-activists, who were middle class or wealthy, did not shop at the public markets themselves. Instead, they employed Black women in the domestic service industry to "make groceries," as they called food shopping in New Orleans. The record of white women's efforts demonstrates how important grassroots organizations remained in shaping public health at a time when the federal government was becoming increasingly involved in the regulation of food in America.[26] That same record demonstrates how white women shaped public health and public food culture to their advantage, but too often to the disadvantage of people of color. In doing so, they embedded principles of white supremacy into influential Progressive Era reforms.[27]

One such group of white women activists belonged to the Era Club, which worked with Dr. Oscar Dowling, the president of the State Board of Health, to incentivize public market vendors to invest in the cleanliness of their stands. Together, they conceived a plan to pressure retailers through sheer force of consumer choice. The strategy was simple: refuse to buy products from vendors "who did not keep and handle their food products according to sanitary rules." Club members shared scenarios to help illustrate the strategy: If a butcher's stall was dirty, refuse to buy, and substitute beans as protein; if a baker's bread delivery arrived unwrapped, send it back and serve biscuits with dinner instead.[28] These women consumer-activists understood that their influence over the public markets lay in their potential collective purchasing power; and that power could be amplified if they worked in tandem with other white women's social and civic groups, which had a collective membership of thousands of people.[29]

Another group of white women activists involved in the creation of model markets was the Market Committee formed by the Housewives' League Division of the City Federation Clubs. The Market Committee members' ideal vision of New Orleans' local food economy was one based on an American model of deregulation and market privatization that would give shoppers a choice about where they acquired their food. They believed that such an arrangement would enable more sanitary and modern private markets to open in the city. These markets, direct competitors of the public markets, would encourage the city government to renovate the city's public markets to stay competitive, thus improving overall public health within the local food economy.[30]

In order to make their vision a reality, members of the Market Committee needed to convince public officials that private markets were essential to the city's success and that they were in fact necessary to the survival of New Orleans. One of the ways the committee members sought to gain officials' favor was to demonstrate the poor conditions of the public markets by conducting inspections that listed public health infractions, which they reported to the city government. They also collected data from heating, lighting, ventilation, and refrigeration experts about best practices in market facilities across America, comparing and contrasting the conditions in New Orleans with those in other American cities.[31]

Members of the Market Committee were particularly keen on providing greater opportunity for private markets to operate within the city, and often lobbied on behalf of private retailers. For example, at a Housewives' League board meeting, Miss Hudson objected to a drafted market ordinance that required private markets to have "holes in the roofs" to provide ventilation. Said ordinance would make it impossible for retailers to live above their stores. Members of the Housewives' League proposed a slightly modified architectural approach with "transoms or openings in the walls, up close to the roof" that would ensure airflow while also allowing for living space. They strengthened their argument by citing examples of other markets whose upper floors served as community and municipal office spaces. Harriet Barton noted a structure in Dayton, Ohio, "where above [the market] were the club-rooms of one of the prominent men's clubs of the day." Helen McCants drew upon another example in Houston, "which is climatically not unlike New Orleans," where the "city administration offices were erected over the public market." Such efforts demonstrate that the Housewives' League's activism included direct engagement with and suggestions about architectural design of marketplaces, both private and public. Their focus on market architecture was just one angle in their efforts to transform the public food culture of New Orleans by shaping local law.[32]

In the spring of 1914, the efforts of the Housewives' League paid off when the city government passed two new ordinances pertaining to the public markets.[33] The first governed the construction of private and public markets, and the second repealed a prior ordinance barring private markets from operating within nine blocks of the St. Mary's, Delamore, Soraparu, Guillotte, St. John, and Carrolton Markets.[34] At that time, city officials deemed these markets "not worth remodeling," and therefore not worth protecting against the competition of private markets.[35] With the exceptions of the St. Mary's Market, which sat at the heart of New Orleans' commercial district, and the Soraparu Market located close to downtown, these facilities were largely located on the edges of the city. The other public markets nearer to the city center and abutting established residential neighborhoods, by contrast, were still protected by the nine-block rule.

The Housewives' League also had a hand in a third ordinance, which Commissioner E. E. Lafaye of the Department of Public Property would propose to the city council in December 1914. The proposed ordinance, which the city council eventually passed, expanded private markets' operating hours throughout the day and it went into effect in January 1915.[36] Together, these three laws were a major victory for the women-operated committee, bringing it one step closer to its vision of a modern New Orleans free of the public markets' monopoly over local provisioning.

A report drafted by the Market Committee drew attention to aspects of the laws that its members identified as important.[37] One of those ordinances focused on improving public health through the built environment of the public markets and the amenities installed within. Creating space for the movement of fresh air was key. Market structures were required to stand alone, separate from any other structures, and had to be constructed of iron-concrete or brick-concrete. Alleys between buildings had to be at least five feet wide to allow for ventilation. The ordinance also required metal ventilators to provide adequate airflow in any attic space of the market—despite the Housewives' League's previous objections—and mandated that each market have at least one electric fan over each entrance. To maximize airflow while keeping flies and other creatures at bay, any openings in the market walls had to be screened in with 18 mesh bronze wire, which is still a standard mesh option today.[38]

The interior designs of the markets were made to resemble sterile, cleanly places akin more to a hospital than the city's markets of old. The ordinance required laid stone or tile flooring graded to drain into city sewers. The interior surfaces of all foundation walls had to be full-glazed white enamel brick or tile.[39] All other interior walls as well as the ceiling had to be plastered "perfectly smooth" and given three coats of white paint.[40] These interiors would plainly show any speck or splatter, making the market's cleanliness readily apparent to vendors and customers.

Guidelines for the construction of markets were just one piece of the legal reform that drew the attention of the Market Committee. Another element of special importance to them was the lifting of the nine-block-radius rule around public market facilities that were in poor condition and that the city might never bother to renovate. According to the ordinance, as long as those newly legalized private markets "comply with the sanitary provisions" outlined in the other market ordinance, they were clear to operate. The new law gave residents more choices in where they shopped by allowing "the modern sanitary grocery, restaurant, fruit-store, or department store to sell fresh meat, fish, or game, as in other cities."[41]

Celebrating their contributions to these major changes, the committee noted that "in framing the three ordinances, the suggestions made by our committee members were freely used. . . . and in almost every case the specifications suggested were inserted." The efforts of concerned residents led to one of the most significant changes in the city's food economy in decades. The women on this committee knew, however, that these ordinances would achieve real change only if the city enforced them.[42]

Soon after they became law, the Market Committee met with Commissioner Lafaye to make a strategic plan for the future. During this meeting, Lafaye noted that these ordinances were the first step in completely revolutionizing New Orleans' local food economy. He then stated, "I confidently hope that these changes will bring new blood into our market business, and that both local and Northern capital will open retail greengroceries here similar to those in other cities."[43] Later that year, after the market ordinances had been in place for several months, Lafaye once again publicly acknowledged the critical role that the Housewives' League played in improving market conditions in New Orleans, and he pledged to continue his support of their activism.[44]

The 1914 ordinances made inroads for modern private markets, enabling them to embed themselves into the changing food culture of the city. That culture was beginning to resemble those of other American cities, where private markets faced fewer restrictions. At this time, suburb-style neighborhoods such as Lakeview and Gentilly were growing, stretching out toward Lake Pontchartrain, creating new residential communities. These areas provided opportunities for private markets to legally operate outside of the nine-block radius concentrated in the historic heart of the city. Suburbs lying farther west and outside of the city limits, like Metairie and Jefferson, also created new business opportunities for private markets.[45] Able to tailor their business practices to the needs and the desires of their customers, most of whom were white, private retailers invested in refrigeration technologies, allowing them to keep longer operating hours and improve the quality and shelf life of their products.[46] This was the beginning of the transformation of small-scale private markets into supermarkets—ones that would eventually develop on the outskirts of New Orleans proper as suburban populations grew. As was the case in the antebellum period with the construction of the first auxiliary market, St. Mary's Market, an important geographic shift in power and influence occurred with the construction of each new food distribution space. Inevitably, as new private markets opened and built a customer base in the suburbs, the position of the public markets as crucial economic and community centers weakened.

In contrast to the suburbs, at the city center, public health crises persisted within and outside of the public markets. In 1914, there was an outbreak of bubonic plague, infecting approximately thirty people and killing ten of them. The rise in oceanic trade routes at the turn of the century brought infected fleas on the backs of rats (and people, too) to the ports of North and South America, and a disease that had largely been considered an Old World problem. Given the location of some of New Orleans' largest public markets near the epicenter of the plague—the city's ports—rat infestations were of grave concern. In the months following the outbreak, police officers carefully monitored food distribution centers such as the French Market to ensure that vendors did not throw any food waste into the stalls or gutters that might attract rats.[47] Behavioral modification could only go so far in stopping the plague, though; the city was in desperate need of a multipronged approach supported by the entire community.[48]

The localized plague caused enough panic to capture the attention of the federal government, ultimately involving the assistant surgeon general of the United States, Dr. W. C. Rucker. Given New Orleans' status as a major American port, the federal government could not afford for the plague to shut down the port's operations; nor was the federal government willing to risk the plague spreading from New Orleans to other key areas of trade in the country and elsewhere. Exasperated by the dire situation and seeking to garner support, Rucker exclaimed, "The time has come when New Orleans must say whether she will take her place as the most progressive of cities or stand shamed before the world as a laggard in a great duty she owes humanity." Answering the call to action, local officials worked together with state and national officials to enact a wide-sweeping aggressive campaign to identify infected specimens and eradicate the disease throughout the city, and especially at the ports. Fumigation, burning, and the leveling of some structures paired with the "rat proofing" of buildings the following year became a national example for how to manage a plague outbreak quickly and effectively.[49]

City officials' dedication to eradicating the plague, however, did not match their efforts to address long-standing public health issues in the municipal markets. These facilities regularly had problems throughout the 1920s and into the early 1930s because of the city government's decision, once again, to place market profits into its general fund rather than into market upkeep.[50] The issues, laid bare by the city newspapers, were eerily similar to those of the preceding decades due, in large part, to the municipal government's refusal to invest in overhauling the entire market system to improve public health. In 1920, the State Board of Health issued an injunction against several of New Orleans' public markets, most of which remained unscreened and therefore open to insects, vermin, and dangerous forms of nature that spread disease.[51] They were also condemned for their poor sanitary conditions because refuse and food debris had not been washed out of the markets.[52]

In 1930, Dr. Dowling, now retired as president of the State Board of Health, described the conditions of the market as "unspeakably filthy." He noted that he had condemned the public markets in 1911 and that conditions had improved, "but not much," over the last twenty years.[53] The threat of disease was still very much a reality for vendors and customers alike. New Orleans' public provisioning was stuck, unchanging for the most part, as new technologies and improvements thrived in privatized supermarkets on the city's periphery.

Earlier that year, in the spring of 1930, Commission Council member John Klorer proposed a solution to the public market problem: convert the public markets into public utilities controlled by a single private entrepreneur. Essentially, Klorer sought to privatize the public markets, releasing the city council from the burden of operating and maintaining them. In a proposed ordinance outlining his plan, he designated Andrew Fitzpatrick, a private entrepreneur, to take over the entire public market system. Although based in Chicago, Fitzpatrick had ties to New Orleans' slaughterhouse industry and, the press reported, enjoyed "the friendship and good will of many of the local butchers." Through those ties, Fitzpatrick came to the conclusion that he wanted to help improve the conditions of "fresh meat selling" in New Orleans' public markets.[54] Klorer later remarked that no New Orleanian entrepreneurs were interested in taking on the public market utilities, so he had to look outside of the city for capital.[55] With a hand on the pulse of New Orleans' public food culture, perhaps they realized Klorer was doomed to fail.

By contrast, Klorer and Fitzpatrick were confident in their public utility scheme and were eager to garner public support.[56] On March 20, 1930, Fitzpatrick ran the entire proposed ordinance on a full-page spread in the *New Orleans States* along with a letter boldly stating that its "fairness and advantages to the city speak for themselves."[57] Fitzpatrick plainly set forth their solution to fund the renovation or rebuilding of the city's twenty-three operating public markets, which would cost approximately $3.5 million.[58] "A local Company, headed by myself, has worked out this plan to give New Orleans, WITHOUT THE EXPENDITURE OF ANY PUBLIC FUNDS, new, permanent, up-to-date Public Market buildings, fully equipped with the most modern devices for keeping all perishable foods clean, fresh, wholesome and sanitary." He went on, "The city receives $40,000.00 per year for the use of its market sites, and in addition, 60% of the annual earnings of the Company thereafter. Furthermore, in approximately twenty-five years, the cost of the markets will have been repaid from the market rentals, and the city can then, without paying one cent, take over the new markets, free and clear of any indebtedness." In his estimation, it was a clear, concise, and conceivable plan. If only city residents felt the same way.[59]

As news spread, New Orleans erupted in fierce backlash against the so-called "Klorer ordinance." City residents' abhorrence of the plan made front-page news for weeks.[60] At the first public hearing for the proposed ordinance, New Orleanians came out en masse to protest. As reported in the *Times-Picayune,* "The council chamber was packed an hour before the scheduled beginning of the hearings, hundreds of those present wearing white badges on which the single word 'Against' was printed in red." In their ranks, according to the newspaper, were people representing "capital and labor, commerce and industry, seller and buyer," women consumer-activists among them.[61] What became clear in the ensuing public debates was that a vast majority of New Orleanians, at least the ones whose voices were covered in the major local newspapers, were completely against market privatization.

Many saw the Klorer ordinance as creating "a monopoly of an essential utility directly affecting every man, woman and child in the community," as the *New Orleans States* argued. The proposed ordinance reinstated the radius rule preventing greengrocers from legally selling fresh food within nine blocks of any public market, including public markets on the periphery of the city. Opposed to the idea, the *States* claimed, "The city cannot afford to turn over to any private corporation absolute control of the food and health of the people."[62] Influential civic and labor organizations around the city, including white women's groups like the Housewives' League, also voiced their concerns. The *States* reported, "A double-barreled denunciation was fired Monday afternoon at the Klorer ordinance proposing the leasing of public market to 'private enterprise' at the meeting of the New Orleans Federation of Women's Clubs."[63] In the following days, dozens of organizations would denounce Klorer's plan.

The success of the proposed ordinance hinged upon the public's support. Fitzpatrick's attorney, Henry H. Chaffe confessed, "We don't want to come in with the opposition of the butchers or of the public because we know that this venture in such circumstances would not be a success. We want good will, the good will of everyone affected, because without it we cannot succeed."[64] No matter how hard Fitzpatrick and Klorer tried, they could not convince New Orleanians to embrace their plan, and so, defeated, they withdrew the proposed ordinance. Although it was a victory for many New Orleanians, the larger problem of how to fund and fix the public markets remained.

The vehement defense of the public markets convinced the city council that there was still cultural and, therefore, economic value to be extracted from the public markets. So, the city council decided to abandon all thoughts of market privatization and double down on keeping the markets public and under its purview. With renewed vigor and an aim to maximize profits, local officials began brainstorming ways to once and for all repair the broken public market system. Renovation and total reconstruction of the municipal facilities were options certainly on the table.

The city council's decision to invest in the public markets mirrored its earlier efforts to improve the buildings in the early 1910s, when the public markets were in similarly poor condition and a state of financial duress.[65] This time, though, city officials were willing to overhaul the entire system, providing residents with the amenities they had so desperately needed for generations. They believed that with the market overhaul, they had the potential to see threefold profits, thereby justifying their investment in the markets' renovations.[66]

Yet conditions were slightly different in the 1930s from what they had been nearly twenty years earlier. Stronger external pressures from the federal government likely weighed on city officials, who had shown a commitment (albeit a wavering one) to meeting national standards. When the municipal government completed the reimagined Dryades Market in 1913, the first "modern" market in the city, the USDA was just a year away from establishing the Office of Markets, whose purpose was to identify model market systems and create standards for their construction and management. The creation of the office in 1913, and the elevation of its status to a bureau in 1917, testified to the federal government's belief in the 1910s that modern cities needed modern market halls.[67] Across the country, city governments heeded the call and reinvested in their historic market halls in the 1910s, many of which had been originally constructed in the nineteenth century. They invested in public markets for the economic and commercial advantage of both city government and local entrepreneurs. Ultimately, twenty years late to the game, the New Orleans City Council wanted to do the same.

In 1930, the municipal government tasked Theodore Grunewald, a native New Orleanian, with evaluating the city's current public market system. Grunewald's connection to the city was important as the public markets, however problematic, were key threads in the fabric of New Orleans' culture; a local like him would perhaps better understand the markets' cultural significance in addition to their historic economic centrality than someone brought from another city or state. Further, Grunewald could perhaps work better with Mayor T. Semmes Walmsley's market survey committee, which he formed to help "study the market problem with a view to making recommendations that will properly solve our difficulties." The original group consisted of more than twenty-five members, all of whom were white and most of whom were men from various sectors of the food industry. Four women sat on the committee representing the interests of various white women's social and civic organizations, making sure that Grunewald and other city officials heard their views and acted to protect the interests of customers.[68]

Grunewald originally made his name in New Orleans' hotel industry, building and operating the Grunewald Hotel, which would become one of the most iconic respites in the city (and today still stands as the Roosevelt

Hotel). The hotel gained a national and even global reputation, attracting US presidents and other elite clientele.[69] While in the hotel business, he launched several food-related enterprises, including a catering company, a mail-order praline company, a soft drink company, and a dairy business that supplied much of the city with milk; he also went into the warehouse and grocery business to supply his hotel, among several other non-food-related ventures.[70] Grunewald contributed to New Orleans' growth in meaningful ways, supporting the local economy through job creation, building up the city's reputation in the tourist industry, and implementing innovative business practices.

Juggling so many businesses, though, affected Grunewald's health, and on the recommendation of his doctor he retired from the hospitality industry around 1925. Seeking an environment conducive for health, he adopted an agrarian lifestyle, establishing Mascot Farms in neighboring St. Bernard Parish. There he raised "high grade chickens, oranges and vegetables," and became even more intimately aware of the particulars of the regional agriculture and food industries. Perhaps through his farm venture, he came to know the plight of the public markets.[71] His prescribed retirement was short-lived, as noted in the *New Orleans Item*, as "the placid calm of rural existence was incompatible with the temperament of a born builder."[72] When the city council asked him to study the market situation he readily agreed, eager to find purpose in a new project.[73]

Grunewald worked in tandem with Mayor Walmsley's market survey committee, listening to the thoughts and suggestions of its couple dozen members, including Aurelie Benedict.[74] She became a key figure in the public market overhaul over the next several years, representing the interests of the Housewives' League Division of the City Federation Clubs, of which she was president. She convened regular meetings to consult with its members to come up with unified messaging about various issues surrounding the public markets. One such debate that continued to circle among New Orleans' population was how profits from the public markets should be used; some people argued that the city council could use those profits for whatever it wished, while others felt that the funds should be used to directly support the public markets' upkeep. Speaking on behalf of the Housewives' League, Benedict declared that she and her fellow members "believe that the revenues derived from these markets should be used only to rehabilitate and build new markets as the necessity arises."[75] She carried that argument with her, and many others, as she assumed her role on the mayor's market survey committee. Eventually, the mayor would pare down and retitle the market survey committee as a temporary "Public Markets Commission" with Finance Commissioner

Miles A. Pratt as its head. The mayor appointed Benedict as one of the nine members who would work closely with Grunewald as he led the assessment of the public market system.

To fully immerse himself in his new role, in the spring of 1930, Grunewald visited markets located in Washington, DC, Detroit, Baltimore, Philadelphia, New York, and Chicago to observe their systems and devise a plan to bring New Orleans' system up to date.[76] There he began to take note of the disparities between New Orleans—where twenty-three public markets operated alongside several quasi-public markets—and New York, which operated eight public markets, and Detroit, which operated three.[77] He also spent several weeks working with market experts at the USDA, learning the federal government's views of what a well-operating public market system looked like and how it functioned.[78] Grunewald determined that "an enclosed retail market operating in conjunction with an open farmer's market is the most successful type." He went on to explain that this type "consists of an adequate modern building in which a great variety of foodstuff and other commodities are sold while adjoining the structure is an open or shed-covered lot on which farmers' products are sold from trucks or stands."[79]

After conducting his fieldwork, Grunewald began drafting a plan that would consolidate the city's public market system. In December 1930, at a community meeting at the Orleans Club—an elite white women's club located uptown on St. Charles Avenue—he shared his preliminary recommendations with the public for the first time. Instead of operating its remaining twenty-three public markets, he recommended that the city government focus on operating just three major facilities: a central wholesale-retail market and two retail markets, one uptown and one downtown. He suggested that the city completely remodel the French Market, located in the heart of the French Quarter, so that it retained its status as the central wholesale-retail market. He even proposed that the city relocate the French Market from the French Quarter to a more "suitable location in the city's business center." Regarding the two auxiliary retail markets, he felt accessibility was of the utmost concern and insisted that their locations have "good street car service, broad street approaches for automobiles and ample parking space" for the growing number of motor vehicles in the city. In his opinion, the municipal government should lease or sell all other public markets, which would then become private markets. Ultimately, Grunewald proposed that New Orleans completely abandon its traditional, neighborhood-based market system.[80]

In an attempt to capture the meeting attendees' support, Grunewald began painting a picture of what the two new auxiliary markets could look and feel like for the women who so desperately craved a transformed shopping experience. He started off by describing the wide variety of vendors who would occupy market stalls: bakers, butchers, fishmongers, dry grocers, greengrocers, and delicatessens. At each stand, Grunewald proudly noted, vendors would wear white uniforms or clean white aprons. Their work stations would sport the latest refrigeration technologies as well as hot- and cold-water taps. "The housewife," Grunewald proclaimed, "could safely purchase all of her food requirements in these attractive, clean, sanitary, comfortable market places." Not only that, Grunewald declared, "She can rest assured that the necessary and proper supervision and responsibility for the carrying on of the business would be maintained, thereby insuring her continuously correct weights and measures, lowest prices and a better selection of foodstuffs than is obtainable elsewhere."[81]

Grunewald understood that in order for his plan to take hold, he would need the support of the white women of New Orleans who had long been active in shaping the city's public food culture. That is why he made a concerted effort to first share his plan with a white women's club. Attendees of the Orleans Club meeting, too, felt that their opinions mattered. Henrietta Porteous, chairman of the civic committee of the Orleans Club, argued that when the city finally created the permanent Public Market Commission to supervise the markets, women should sit on it.[82] With conviction, she stated, "It is the women who go to the markets, do the purchasing and see conditions." She continued, "The men have been given a chance to better conditions, and now I think the women should be given an opportunity," implying that the men she spoke of had failed to resolve the public market issue. Grunewald's work with Aurelie Benedict on the temporary Public Market Commission demonstrated that he was already working with women consumer-activists. For Porteous, though, the question clearly remained as to whether Grunewald was taking women consumer-activists' opinions seriously.[83]

To drive home his vision in the final moments of his report to the Orleans Club, Grunewald also plainly pointed out the city government's damaging financial interests in the public markets. He declared to the women in that meeting, "The public markets have been political stepchildren. The revenue collected by the city government from the public markets does not go for the rehabilitation or upkeep of the markets. It goes into the general fund and is diverted to other uses."[84] Grunewald wanted to depoliticize the markets. Like many others, including women consumer-activists like Benedict who had already spoken out publicly on the subject, he wanted market revenues to support market upkeep and rehabilitation.[85] If this alignment were any indication, perhaps Grunewald was taking seriously the arguments and contributions of Benedict and other women leaders who were dedicated to the improvement of New Orleans' public market system.

Grunewald's proposal to shrink New Orleans' public market system incited major outcries not only from city residents who did not want to lose their neighborhood public market, but from government officials as well.[86] Commissioner Pratt assured concerned New Orleanians that they would not be shut out from conversations about the proposed public market plan. He affirmed, "I believe in frank, open discussions on all matters affecting the public welfare."[87] So Pratt and other city officials set out to slow down Grunewald and allow public discussion of this sensitive topic. The next morning, the *Times-Picayune* reported that city officials opposed many of Grunewald's recommendations, saying they "would not be taken seriously," indicating that there would, indeed, be time for the public to weigh in.[88]

Grunewald's draft plan involved implementing the best national standards in New Orleans. Those standards, however, conflicted with some local officials', shoppers', and food entrepreneurs' commitment to the city's distinct economic culture. That dispute demonstrated the staying power of local custom—and the influence of the people who support it—in a period marked by the popularization of national standards and mass consumer culture.

Women consumer-activists like Benedict were dead set on retaining the city's existing neighborhood-based public markets system. She convened the Housewives' League in early January 1931 to create consensus on their core beliefs to then share with the temporary Public Market Commission. Together, Housewives' League members confirmed that they did not accept Grunewald's draft plan for just three markets but wanted to see the neighborhood-based public market system sustained. Further, they wanted the existing public market buildings to be rebuilt, incorporating the most modern technologies and sanitation practices. Regarding updating the municipal facilities, their opinions aligned with Grunewald, and they were not the only ones to find some shared ground with him or to support his position as head of the public market study.

In a public letter published in the *Times-Picayune*, Sam Blum, a produce broker who supplied public market vendors, argued that the public markets "are essential in the neighborhood which they are located" and should not be converted into private markets. Instead, like the Housewives' League, he suggested that the current public markets "should be made modern in every respect, and all sanitary laws carried out." Despite his disagreement with

Grunewald's plan, Blum still felt that he was the best person to direct the public markets moving forward.[89]

Many food industry workers like Blum, concerned for their livelihoods, supported market retention and renovation, rather than complete consolidation. In December 1930, farmers who supplied the markets with goods, for example, shared their worries about job loss at the annual meeting of the agriculture bureau of the Association of Commerce.[90] At that gathering, the secretary of the New Orleans Live Stock Exchange, Major John S. South, pointed out that Grunewald's plan did not take into account the unique cultural makeup of the city: "The people of New Orleans are different from people of the cities Mr. Grunewald visited in making his market study."[91] Acknowledging those sentiments, and agreeing with residents who spoke out against Grunewald's plan, Commissioner Pratt, still head of the temporary Public Markets Commission, noted that "the council's intention [is] to preserve the public markets system for the public."[92]

The various objections to Grunewald's proposal did not come as all that much of a surprise given the city's tendency to resist change; throughout New Orleans' postbellum history, there seemed to be a culture of reaction toward "progress"—or, framed differently, a culture of commitment toward tradition. This aversion to change existed simultaneously alongside efforts to demonstrate the city's embrace of new ideas, industries, and technologies. Such efforts were evident in the propaganda of the 1884 World's Fair and in consumer-activists' attempts to modernize the public markets at the turn of the twentieth century. But the tenacity of the city's traditions ultimately seemed the stronger force. Who reinforced that tradition? Was it the will of the population, a result of local politics, or a combination thereof?

In the case of New Orleans' public market renovations in the 1930s, the power struggles were tangled. What is clear, though, is that local officials were more than happy to defend tradition if it suited their larger goals of obtaining money for the city's coffers. Similarly, food entrepreneurs, who believed their personal economic security depended on the continued existence of neighborhood public markets, fought hard to retain tradition. They did not, as Association of Commerce member Paul Habans stated, want to "see their public markets bartered away for the interests of the chain stores."[93] The underlying and powerful economic incentives of local officials and food entrepreneurs suggest that in the case of the public markets' 1930s renovation, the city's resistance to certain change was driven in large part by political forces. But the will of the broader public mattered too. At least it did to an extent, as evidenced by the women consumer-activists' who spoke out in favor of retaining and improving the existing neighborhood-based public market system and the city council's gestures to include white women in advisory positions.

Largely ignoring the preliminary recommendations Grunewald laid out at the Orleans Club, the city council adopted a hybrid renovation plan. It preserved elements from New Orleans' historic market system while adopting modern amenities and architectural designs that reflected national public health standards. The council also wanted to keep open as many public markets as possible to address food entrepreneurs' concerns regarding employment and financial security and women consumer-activists' similar desire to retain the expansive system. Accordingly, Grunewald adjusted his plan to meet the needs of the city council and its constituents. An initial bond issue of one million dollars from the city government helped initiate the market renovations.

In July 1931, the city council made Grunewald the supervisor of public markets under the rehabilitation program. That same month, the council also created a permanent Public Markets Commission comprising the mayor, the commissioner of public finances, and seven additional members. Benedict retained her former position as the representative of the Housewives' League. She continued to share white women's opinions by ensuring that their interests were looked after.[94] Working alongside Mayor Walmsley, the nine-member board was tasked with drafting rules and regulations for the operation of the public markets and would serve as an advisory group to the commissioner of public property.[95]

Over the next several years, Benedict sat on the Public Markets Commission and also retained her position as president of the Housewives' League, where she continued to organize meetings to discuss various issues that came up about the public markets. One such issue was whether the public markets should allow the sale of dry groceries—a debate that gripped the city in the spring of 1932. Ultimately, the Housewives' League, under Benedict's leadership, opposed the sale of dry goods in the markets. She and her fellow members supported grocers like Alfred A. Larose, secretary of the New Orleans Retail Grocers' Association, who argued that the sale of dry goods in the public markets would hurt their existing grocery businesses, which operated outside of the public market system. As customers, members of the Housewives' League were willing to continue making two stops to complete their shopping, however inconvenient, if it meant that they could support local grocers' interests. The bifurcation of "making groceries" would hold out for a while longer as the city council enforced the grocery ban in the public markets.[96]

Through their work with the Housewives' League, women consumer-activists continued to shape the public culture of food to their advantage; key to their success was Benedict's role as a member of the Public Market Commission, which gave her direct access to important political players like the Mayor Walmsley and Grunewald. Under Benedict, the Housewives' League also functioned as an additional set of eyes and ears on the ground, supporting local officials' efforts to ensure safe conditions in the public markets. In October 1933, for instance, the Housewives' League submitted a complaint about the quality of bread available for purchase, some of which was sold at bakery stands in the public markets. After several of its members had been sold spoiled shrimp at the markets, the Housewives' League also asked Grunewald to investigate shrimp purveyors.[97] Benedict would continue to hold her position on the Public Market Commission and represent her fellow Housewives' League members' interests as president until her untimely death in January 1934. During her tenure, and as a result of her activism and those of her fellow consumer-activists, the city made tangible moves to improve public health across the municipal market system.[98]

After decades of failed promises, the New Orleans city government finally rebuilt or renovated the public markets throughout the 1930s, transforming them into the impressive, clean, modern structures that city residents had wanted for generations. Many of the reimagined markets were aesthetically stunning, with terrazzo tile, wrought iron detailing, flowerbeds, flagstone patios, fireplaces, and men's and women's lounges. They were smaller than the market halls in most other American cities, but that reflected the architectural norms within New Orleans' historic market culture.

The first of the refreshed public markets opened to the public in 1931. The Public Works Administration (PWA) and the Works Progress Administration (WPA), the latter particularly interested in sustaining and celebrating regional cultures, funded the completion of the public market renewal project through the late 1930s. Their involvement illustrated the ever-increasing participation of the federal government in local affairs.[99] The city government, with the financial assistance of the PWA and the WPA, rebuilt the Ewing, Lautenschlaeger, Magazine, Maestri, Memory, Ninth Street, St. Bernard, Suburban, Tremé, and Zengel Markets. The city also completed a comprehensive renovation of the French Market complex and to varying degrees implemented improvements to the Dryades, Jefferson, Keller, Le Breton,

Rocheblave, St. Roch Markets, and possibly the Foto Market.[100] Finally, the city demolished the Claiborne, Second Street, Guillotte, and Poydras Markets, and in 1939 abandoned the Mehle and Behrman Markets, putting the land up for auction.[101] All told, by the end of the public markets overhaul in 1940, the city still operated at least sixteen public markets.[102] Their rehabilitation was a central aspect of a larger citywide urban planning effort, and their completion, along with that of other urban planning projects, signaled to city residents that "New Orleans has rebuilt itself," as proudly proclaimed in the *Times-Picayune* in 1939.[103]

City officials consolidated the markets' management and regulation under one department, the Department of Public Markets, appointing Theodore Grunewald as director—a post he would hold for seventeen years.[104] In time, his name would become synonymous with the development of modern New Orleans.[105] With the new market amenities in place and a centralized department to regulate the markets, the city managed the maintenance and cleanliness of the facilities. The department employed a team of janitors who were hired to prevent the markets from transforming back into neglected, unsanitary spaces. Janitors cleaned a number of market amenities, including stalls, refrigerators, toilets, ceilings, walls, sidewalks, windows, doors, and light fixtures. They were also in charge of garbage and repair issues related to plumbing, electricity, furniture, and hardware. These centralized maintenance efforts proved crucial in upholding the city's promise to keep disease out of the public markets.[106]

The rebuilt or renovated markets became some of the finest examples of public markets in the country. They sported functional designs that enabled vendors to safely handle and prepare food for sale. Detailed architectural plans remain for at least eight of the renovated public markets.[107] Those eight were fitted with hot- and cold-water lines and electricity and were furnished with the latest refrigeration and ventilation technologies. Stalls were equipped with expansive counters for food preparation as well as large display cases to showcase vendors' wares. Plans for the Dryades Market Building A, for example, indicate that there were twenty-three vendor stalls in total. Twenty were designated for the sale of meat and game and three were designated for the sale of fish. Of those twenty-three stalls, eight were equipped with walk-in coolers (six feet by eight feet) for easy access to refrigerated items. Display cases were twelve feet long in the meat department and six feet long in the fish department. The fish department also had a separate shared preparation area for fishmongers behind the display cases. In a plan for the Suburban Market, which was smaller than Dryades, there were eleven vendor spaces to vend meat, fish, and vegetables. Six of the stalls, presumably for meat, had refrigerators. The one fish stall had two fish boxes to keep seafood cold. The vegetable stalls, however, did not seem to require refrigeration. The architects also took into consideration the needs of vendors by equipping them not only with refrigeration and display cases but also flexible work environments that could be changed to suit the individual needs of each vendor. Another proposed architectural plan displayed layouts of vegetable vendors' stalls in six different public markets; movable counters at each workstation allowed for spatial flexibility.[108]

For New Orleanians, the public markets represented the city's arrival into the modern age of America and its renewed commitment to public health. City officials promoted the new public markets with great gusto, claiming that they "rival in complete detail and efficiency as well as artistic design any public market in the country."[109] They were the opposite of the unsanitary pavilion markets that had faced constant encroachment from Louisiana's natural environment, including insects and vermin, and the deleterious byproducts of New Orleans' industrial sector. The designs of Sam Stone Jr. & Co.—the firm hired by the city government to design the new public markets—eradicated all evidence of debris, dust, dankness, and disease that had plagued the markets for generations. The firm's namesake, Sam Stone Jr., a former New Orleans commissioner of public property, led their transformation. People who frequented these once decrepit spaces had to interact with these newly renovated spaces and with each other in different ways. The feel of the market was different in that it moved from dilapidated to sterling, from dark to light, as captured in photographs of the interior of St. Roch Market before and after its renovation.

Aesthetically, the new markets' architecture reflected styles that, while not historically representative of New Orleans, were popular throughout the United States in the 1930s; they were inspired by a variety of distinctive architectural movements including, but not limited to, art deco, PWA Modern, Italian Renaissance Revival, and Spanish Colonial Revival. The entrances to the Ninth, Zengel, Ewing, and Suburban Markets, for example, show influence from art deco, especially in the ornate aluminum grilles located above the main entrance of the markets. The Tremé Market, too, shows influences from the art deco movement, as seen in the fluted door surrounds, stepped vertical projections above each entrance, and geometric patterns incorporated in the glass entrance doors and transoms.

Among the cohort of renovated markets, there was also an example of PWA Modern, a blend of art deco and neoclassical architectural elements, seen in the Maestri Market. The style was also known as "Depression Modern,"

Several butchers and other food vendors in well-worn aprons attend to their stalls in the St. Roch Market as customers patronize their businesses. Taken on October 1, 1937, this image depicts the market before the PWA/WPA renovations, when it still had relatively poor lighting and ventilation and other outdated technologies.

Works Progress Administration Photograph Collection: Image 11602. Courtesy of City Archives & Special Collections, New Orleans Public Library.

"WPA Modern," and "stripped classical modern" and was characteristic of many public works projects that made up President Franklin Roosevelt's New Deal relief initiative.[110] Representative of the architectural style, the Maestri Market had smooth stucco surfaces, metal windows recessed within openings, horizontal banding at the base and sill course, and entrances framed by tall surrounds extending above the roofline.[111]

The Dryades Market's renovations from the 1930s fell under a different architectural style than the cohort of art deco markets and the PWA Modern Maestri Market. The architects modified the Dryades Market's Classical Revival elements from its early 1910s renovation; they incorporated influences from Italian Renaissance Revival architecture, most easily identified in the partial hipped clay tile roofs, which replaced the parapet, and the mirrored arcaded walkways along Melpomene Street.

The Magazine Market, in contrast, was modeled heavily after Spanish Colonial Revival architecture, with its terracotta tiled roof, round-arched arcade, and stucco exterior walls and ornaments. So, too, was the St. Bernard

St. Roch Market vendors dressed in pristine white aprons prepare their stalls at the renovated PWA/WPA market on June 30, 1938. In contrast to the previous iteration of the
market, this one had good lighting and ventilation and was outfitted with walk-in refrigerators and enclosed display cases. Additionally, the new light fixtures and decorative cast
iron columns created an elegant market interior.

Works Progress Administration Photograph Collection: Image 11631. Courtesy of City Archives
& Special Collections, New Orleans Public Library.

Market, which also had a copper-embellished copula and wood rosettes on
the arcade ceiling of its tower. These architectural elements were not only
popular in commercial spaces, but also in new residential buildings. Spanish
Colonial Revival–inspired homes peppered the uptown and Gentilly neighborhoods at this time; so too did California Craftsman–style bungalows and
English cottages, among other historic styles.

Sam Stone's incorporation of such varying architectural styles demonstrates the experimental nature of the 1930s market renovations. The architects then grafted these popular styles onto existing building types born of
New Orleans' historic public food culture: the public markets. In this sense,
the renovated markets found a middle path between sustaining traditional
building types distinct to New Orleans and embracing contemporary architectural movements popular across the country. Stone himself plainly stated
his intentions to find that middle path after people expressed concern that the

A street corner view of the Ewing Market in New Orleans around 1940. The building's architecture has art deco elements including an ornate aluminum grill above the market's entrance as well as aluminum framed windows and doors. These exterior features were paired with decorative tile accents in vibrant blues and greens to catch the eye of passersby.

Charles L. Franck Studio Collection at The Historic New Orleans Collection, Acc. No. 1979.325.3962.

renovated French Market buildings would be unrecognizable: "Some people are under the impression that we are going to erect some ultra-modern buildings, but we are going to keep all the old charm possible."[112] Although he was speaking about the French Market, this sentiment reflected his broader approach to the public markets' renovations. His aim, which also mirrored the desires of the city government, was for the renovated markets to marry the past with the present, and fuse Creole culture and American culture in physical spaces. These renovated market buildings, therefore, reverberated with the tensions that defined New Orleans in the mid-twentieth century as it fought to retain its cultural uniqueness while at the same time embracing a broader national culture.

The individual architectural styles—art deco, PWA Modern, Italian Renaissance Revival, Spanish Colonial Revival, and so on—of the renovated public markets also embodied certain beliefs and ideals. Art deco was an

A street corner view of the Maestri Market in New Orleans around 1938. The building is an example of PWA Modern architecture that can be seen in the structure's symmetrical exterior and recessed windows in vertical panels, which illuminated the interior with abundant natural light. This architectural style represented the federal government's growing investment in public amenities during the Great Depression.

Works Progress Administration Photograph Collection: Image 11452. Courtesy of City Archives & Special Collections, New Orleans Public Library.

architectural movement defined by underlying themes of opulence and faith in social progress.[113] PWA Modern, which so often featured durable materials and symmetrical designs, was meant to represent permanence and stability during the upheaval of the Great Depression and also what was "new" in American civic culture.[114] Italian Renaissance Revival, as the name suggests, drew inspiration from fifteenth-century Florence and other Italian cities at the heart of the early Renaissance; it sought to revive the past era's spirit of cultural innovation in the arts and sciences in a modern American context.[115] Spanish Colonial Revival, too, romanticized European and Mediterranean history and culture and gestured to historic Spanish colonial rule in regions now part of the United States.

New Orleans, which had historically been othered by Americans as an "exotic" and "antiquated" city, was now itself participating in that process of othering through the incorporation of Spanish Colonial Revival architecture.

A street view of Dryades Market Building A (*left*) and Building B (*right*) in New Orleans around 1940. These structures blend Classical Revival and Italian Renaissance Revival architectural styles, which can be seen in their brick exterior with high transom windows as well as the facing arcaded walkways between the two buildings (partially obscured by the angle of this image). This impressive aesthetic embodied the market's long-standing role as a cultural and economic center in the Dryades neighborhood.

Charles L. Franck Studio Collection at The Historic New Orleans Collection, Acc. No. 1979.325.3960.

The style became especially popular in California but had very little historic connection to the West Coast.[116] In fact, the architectural movement was created in California by newcomers to the area. These people helped construct a mythic architectural past, not unlike the writers who flocked to New Orleans in the postbellum period and crafted romanticized depictions of the Crescent City's culture. By building Spanish Colonial Revival–style markets in the 1930s, New Orleans embraced an architectural style that romanticized and mythologized California's past and the country's past. New Orleans, therefore, contributed to the popularization of an aesthetic form that othered a state and the West Coast, more broadly. And by doing so, the city symbolically reinforced its position as central to and exemplary of the modern American experience—one that so heavily relied on finding commonality by juxtaposing itself against othered places and people.

A street view of the Magazine Market in New Orleans around 1940. The building's Spanish Colonial Revival architecture is reflected in its terra-cotta tiled roof and stucco exterior walls. In addition to commercial space, the market also had meeting and community spaces on its first and second floors.

Charles L. Franck Studio Collection at The Historic New Orleans Collection, Acc. No. 1979.325.3987.

The local government's participation in cultural othering through market designs further bolstered racial dynamics already at play throughout the city. White residents relied on prevalent racist rhetoric in order to justify their views on modernization and so-called "ordered society"—rhetoric that was already systemically employed in such public spaces as streetcars, schools, pools, parks, and restaurants to enforce racial segregation.[117] For segregationists, the act of consumption, the ritual of the communal meal, and the bonds formed over a single table were too intimate and sensual for white and Black diners to share. Still, of the neighborhood markets that we have detailed architectural plans for, the Dryades Market is one of two markets that shows evidence of spaces designed for racial segregation, specifically in Building B, which had a lunch counter. The early plans for Building B had four bathrooms that were segregated by race.[118] In the original plan, the white women's and Black women's restrooms were similar sizes and were right next to each other (the same for white and Black men's restrooms). Later, however, the Black

A street view of the St. Bernard Market in New Orleans around 1940. Spanish Colonial Revival architectural elements are represented in the building's terra-cotta tiled roof, arched arcade, and stucco exterior walls—together, they created a distinct, eye-catching exterior on the corner lot upon which the market stood.

Charles L. Franck Studio Collection at The Historic New Orleans Collection, Acc. No. 1979.325.3987.

men's and Black women's restrooms were placed next to each other, and those two restroom designs were much smaller than those designed for white customers and staff. The lunch counter in the earliest architectural plan was not a racially segregated space; at least it was not specified as such in writing. This early plan was relatively minimal, with limited notations. Over the course of implementing changes to the architectural plans, however, the architects eventually defined the lunch counter, in writing, as a racially segregated space. As with the public restrooms, the lunch counter became a space modified to fit the culture of racial segregation in 1930s New Orleans.[119]

The final layouts of the Dryades Market drawn up by the Sam Stone Jr. & Co. architects racially segregated both the lunch counter and the bathrooms in Building B. Because dining was associated with a certain physicality—consumption being considered an intimate bodily activity—the "segregationist instinct" was to racially segregate eateries.[120] The building was also constructed at a time when race relations in the city were increasingly marked with violence and local officials sought to control people's movement and behavior through a seemingly benign medium: architecture. The design of Building B and its impacts on social interactions and cultural formation,

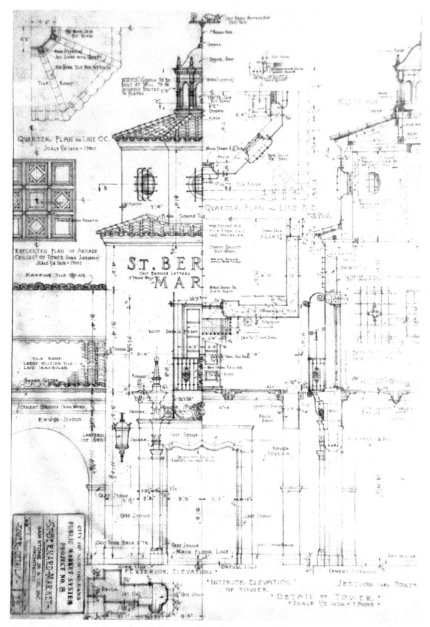

An elevation, or architectural plan, created by Sam Stone Jr. & Co., detailing the St. Bernard Market in New Orleans around 1931–1932. The copper-embellished cupola and wood rosettes on the arcade ceiling of the tower are indicative of Spanish Colonial Revival architecture. City officials desired that renovated markets like this one be visually impressive and symbolic of the city's progress.

Sam Stone, Jr. Office Records, Southeastern Architectural Archive, Tulane University Special Collections, Howard-Tilton Memorial Library.

however, were anything but benign. Renovations of the markets were also an attempt to control Black and white bodies, limiting their mobility and barring Black people from fully accessing the market's facilities.

The segregationist instinct, however, did not extend to the market stalls themselves, indicating that the purveying and purchasing of foods was not viewed as an intimate bodily act in the same way as eating, digesting, and defecating. Furthermore, because the city depended too heavily upon the exchange of food between the city's diverse populations, segregating the markets would not have been feasible. Feeding the city remained a priority even as segregation laws clenched tighter around other food spaces such as restaurants. Consequently, markets—particularly the French Market located in the city's historic core—remained meeting grounds for the entire city, an occasion to interact with people outside of one's immediate community.

Historically, the French Market drew diverse customers from across the city, whereas each neighborhood market was tied more closely to the ethnic, racial, and socioeconomic identity of its particular locality. In the Jim Crow era, New Orleanians tended to live intimate lives, ones that functioned within the bounds of their immediate communities. Shopping at the public markets disrupted that tendency. Millie McClellan Charles, a Black New Orleanian who lived uptown, recalled how she rarely came downtown, "except for with my grandmother who went to the French Market every Saturday."[121] The French Market broke the cycle of isolation and the instinct to stay within one's neighborhood.

Although the renovations ensured the public markets' multiethnic and multiracial body of customers, the enclosures excluded itinerant vendors, many of whom were Black. Those physical changes, therefore, robbed Black entrepreneurs of business opportunities and spaces to build social bonds through the daily acts of provisioning a community. Black street vendors were all too aware of the ways in which local officials passed laws and enacted changes to the built environment that stymied their abilities to grow their businesses, support their families, and build community. These conditions were reflective of a much broader sweep of barriers and injustices that Black community members faced on a daily basis. J. N. Brown, a peanut vendor living in Arkansas, explained in an interview with WPA employee Bernice Bowden,

> We colored people are livin' under the law, but we don't make no laws. You take a one-armed man and he can't do what a two-armed man can. The colored man in the south is a one-armed man, but of course the

colored man can't get along without the white folks. But I've lived in
this world long enough to know what the cause is—I know why the
colored man is a one-armed man.[122]

In this dialogue, Brown defined how his livelihood was bound by laws not of
his own choosing or making. As a Black man, he operated and lived in a world
where he was politically and legally disenfranchised and was reluctantly
dependent upon white community members to speak on his behalf in those
arenas. In New Orleans, too, the changes to the physical layout and manipula-
tion of the market environment are just a few examples of the many ways in
which local lawmakers and their constituents purposefully tried to close
Black people out of certain sectors of the public food culture.

For vendors like Harriet Camille, who was born into slavery, putting food
on her own table proved increasingly difficult by 1940. According to the notes
of Maude Wallace, an employee of the Louisiana Writers' Project who interviewed Camille, at around eighty years old Camille could no longer hold
regular employment. But she was able to make ends meet by peddling on the
streets. As recorded by Wallace, "Every morning, rain or shine, she takes her
little basket on her arm and goes on down the Bayou Road to Esplanade, selling a little parsley or onions if she has them." Her route took her near the St.
Bernard and Tremé Markets, where there were guaranteed to be potential customers. She was not only looking to sell her wares, but also ask for charity,
according to Wallace. Sometimes, Camille was successful, bringing home
"cold food or pennies." "In this way they live," observed Wallace, making do
on the fringes of the city's public food culture.[123]

Faced with more and more barriers, physical and otherwise, street vendors of
all races relied on the tried-and-true methods of their industry to attract
customers and try to scrape by in the Jim Crow era. In and outside of New
Orleans, these small-scale entrepreneurs wielded their charisma to attract and
maintain customers. First-person accounts from Clyde "Kingfish" Smith of
New York and John Evans of North Carolina provide insights into the creative strategies vendors employed across the country. Although similar
first-person accounts from New Orleans–based vendors are difficult to come
by, folklore compendiums like *Gumbo Ya-Ya* (1945) provide some insights
into the business strategies, particularly street vendor cries, of twentieth-
century New Orleans vendors.

Like other pieces of literature from the time, *Gumbo Ya-Ya* is both romantic and nostalgic, casting New Orleans in a particular light to appeal to a
national audience primed to see the city as both "antiquated" and "other"; yet

within those pages, too, are glimmers of New Orleans' actual street food culture and the businessmen and businesswomen who made a living by hawking wares. Key to their efforts were street cries, which, as in generations past, resounded throughout the city streets.

In the midst of the Great Depression, Clyde "Kingfish" Smith, with limited options for work, began peddling fish in New York City in 1932. In that year, competition among vendors, whose numbers were robust, was fierce. As had long been the case, when other industries shut people out, street vending was always something to fall back on, and after the Great Crash of 1929 many people, including some in New Orleans, turned to peddling.

As Smith told two WPA interviewers, "There were quite a few peddlers and somebody has to have something extra to attract attention." For Smith, that "something extra" was his creative approach to his street cry, the song that alerted customers to his presence, the wares he was selling, and other useful information like pricing and point of origin for products. He recalled a general rule: "One of the first things I learned about peddling was to be any success at all, you had to have an original cry." Too often he had seen new vendors, including himself, struggle on the streets with cries that merely stated what they were selling or what their specialty was, like newly minted fish vendors crying out, "Old Fish Man."[124]

Taking a different tack, Smith began experimenting with rhyming, thinking that he could beat out the competition and attract more customers through a lively, lighthearted approach. Although over time he became skilled at improvisation, his streets cries were carefully crafted through trial and error, tested out on the streets themselves, and judged by how large a crowd or how many customers he could attract. His earliest success was his "fish cry," which eventually became twenty-four lines long. The opening lines of it are ripe with ear-catching rhyme:

> Yo, ho, ho, fish man!
> Bring down your dishpan!
> Fish ain't but five cents a pound.
> So come on down,
> And gather around,
> I got the best fish
> That's in this town.[125]

Smith recalled how he tested out this cry on a few city blocks that several fish vendors had already passed through; on that day, it was not clear to Smith if his rhyme-centric cry would be interesting enough to garner any new customers. But he soon found out that his creative vocalizing did, in fact, bring them in. The key? Getting them to laugh and look at the goods he was offering, and then they would start buying, he recalled. Braiding essential information into his cry, Smith enumerated the kinds of fish he had for sale that day (porgies, Crockers) and their preparation (fried, broiled). He also emphasized their limited availability, perhaps to entice potential customers to buy sooner rather than later:

> I got porgies,
> Crockers too.
> I ain't got but a few,
> So you know what to do.
> Come on down,
> And gather round,
> Cause my fish ain't
> But five cents a pound.[126]

Smith sang out these cries all day long. He noted: "The average day I cover about eight blocks and spend about an hour in each block, sometimes longer."[127]

There were practical reasons that vendors like Smith and countless others in New Orleans and across the country may have chosen to sing rather than yell or call out about their products. In fact, singing might have been the most sensible choice in that it can prevent the voice from tiring. Singing engages the diaphragm, using muscles to support the careful flow of breath through the vocal cords and out of the mouth. Engaging the diaphragm places less strain on the vocal cords, thus prolonging one's ability to keep singing and selling wares. The longer one can sing, the more money one can potentially make. So, singing made good business sense. Vendors like Smith may not have made a conscious decision to preserve their voices in this way, but through example, by observing other vendors, singing became a popular means of communicating. Singing was also advantageous to those working in a particularly crowded soundscape, especially those who could sing in a higher register. Falsetto voices, or male voices sung in a higher range, as well as women's voices, which are typically higher than men's, would have carried over the general din of the crowd—a sweeping melody that may have been more easily heard than those of their competitors.

Gumbo Ya-Ya shares in its pages dozens of cries inspired by, and perhaps accurately capturing, the vocalizations of New Orleans' street vendors; like

Smith's, these cries also reflect an intentional use of rhyme to compellingly communicate what goods were for sale; and also like Smith, the cries employ a bit of humor and directly engage with potential customers, calling them to action.

To start a dialogue, one New Orleanian vendor called attention to a customer's presence and seamlessly incorporated her into the existing rhythm, rhyme, and repetition of his call.[128] This form of improvisation demonstrates another artistic skill strongly associated with the music traditions of New Orleans, including what would eventually become its most famous cultural products: jazz. In this street cry, the vendor candidly and playfully engages a potential customer:

> Watermelon! Watermelon! Red to the rind,
> If you don't believe me jest pull down your blind!
>
> I sell to the rich, I sell to the po';
> I'm gonna sell the lady
> Standin' in that do'.
>
> Watermelon, Lady!
> Come and git your nice red watermelon, Lady!
> Red to the rind, Lady!
> Come on, Lady, and get 'em!
> Gotta make the picnic fo' two o'clock,
> No flat tires today!
> Come on, Lady![129]

Specifically, the vendor directed his call at a woman customer, alluding to the fact that most purchasers of food in twentieth-century New Orleans were, in fact, women—some of the very same women who advocated for changes to New Orleans' public food culture that would physically cut off street vendors from the previously porous perimeters of the public markets. One sees this direct engagement with women in many cries from *Gumbo Ya-Ya*: "Come and gettum, Lady! I got green peppers, snapbeans, and tur-nips!" And, "I got blackber—reeeees, Lady!" or "I got strawberries, Lady!"[130]

The watermelon vendor not only addressed potential customers directly, encouraging them to engage in a two-way conversation; he also described the quality of his produce, simultaneously promoting his product. The watermelon was "Red to the rind"—a guarantee of quality; Smith, too, had emphasized the quality of his product stating in his cry, "I got the best fish / That's in this town." Their cries were a verbal guarantee—a promise of quality. To further impress upon the potential buyer the excellence of his produce, the New Orleanian vendor may have sliced open a melon for display so that customers could visually inspect and smell the product, using their senses to make an informed decision. He may have arranged the wares to allow for this kind of sensory interaction, helping to ease any skepticism from prospective buyers. His cry also created desire for the watermelon. Mouthwatering with anticipation, the listeners may have had a greater longing for the ripe, bright, sweet flavor of the fruit after having heard the song. These descriptive tactics influenced potential customers, drawing some to the vendors' businesses, and strengthening their economic and cultural presence in the community.

Smith and some of the New Orleans vendors featured in *Gumbo Ya-Ya* clearly cultivated a certain magnetism when they cried out about their wares. Years into the business, Smith noted, "When I sing, a certain amount of people will be standing around, looking and listening, and that attracts more people." In this sense, he was giving a street performance as much as he was selling wares. He went on to discuss why gathering a crowd is crucial to a successful sale: "Whenever people see a crowd they think it's a bargain so they want to get in on it."[131]

Smith made sure that he gathered a crowd not only through witty, memorable lyrics, but also by projecting his voice out into the neighborhood so that it pierced through windows and walls of surrounding domiciles. The sonic waves of his street cry literally penetrated the barriers that stood between the public and private spheres. The ability of Smith's cries, and those of countless vendors in New Orleans, to pass through seemingly solid walls demonstrates that the line between public and private spaces was porous. Smith and other vendors took advantage of this phenomenon to announce their presence to customers inside their homes. Smith reflected, "When I sing it will be so loud that people come to the windows and look out. They come down with bedroom shoes on, with bathrobes, and some have pans or newspapers to put the fish in."[132] In other words, they rushed down from their homes to make sure they could get product from Smith before he ran out or moved on down the block.

Soon Smith learned that to maintain the attention of customers, he had to keep creating new material for his cries. And so he developed new iterations of his "fish cry," finding inspiration in popular music of the era. Whereas his first "fish cry" followed a melody of his own making, his second utilized the tune of "the most popular song hit of that time" in Smith's estimation: "Jumpin' Jive." The first few lines of the fifteen-line song are as follows:

Jim, jam, jump, jumpin jive
Make you buy yo fish on the East Side,
Oh, boy,
What you gonna say there cats?
Jim, jam, jump, jumpin jive.
When you eat my fish,
You'll eat four or five.[133]

The newly adapted "fish cry," according to Smith, was a huge success.

Smith began experimenting with other well-known tunes. But he took things one step further, adapting his street cries to the cultural touchstones of the different communities in which he worked. Clarifying his approach, he explained, "I put the words to the tune, to fit the occasion, to fit the neighborhood. If I go to a Jewish neighborhood, I sing songs like 'Bei Mir Bist Du Shon.' In a colored neighborhood they like something swingy. I might sing the same song but I put it in a swing tune. I go into a Spanish neighborhood, I speak to them in Spanish."[134] Smith applied well-known business principles, including adjusting marketing campaigns to fit different communities, to build a solid street vending business. As a racially and ethnically diverse city with a pension for music, New Orleans likely echoed with similarly creative street vendor cries. In New York, Smith was so successful at garnering customer loyalty that he began noticing that repeat customers would wait until they heard his street cry to come buy fish (instead of buying from the first vendor that came through the neighborhood).

John Evans, too, had an electric personality; people gravitated toward him just like they did to Smith and some of the more memorable vendors referenced in *Gumbo Ya-Ya*. It was likely this gravitas that made him a known and beloved figure in Wrightsville Beach, North Carolina, for some odd fifty years, and helped him earn his livelihood as a vendor. According to his interview with the Federal Writers' Project, Evans had been a fisherman and huckster in his youth, after federal emancipation. Evans recalled, "I made enough sellin' fish to the summer folk all along Wrightsville and Greenville Sounds to keep me all winter." He undoubtedly deployed his deep and resonant voice to capture the attention of passersby and charmed them with his wordsmithing. Allegedly, he could vocalize for an astonishing two or three minutes without taking a breath, suggesting that he could cry out about his wares at length, increasing his reach to potential customers; these skills were how he made a way out of no way.[135]

Although Smith and Evans appear to have worked solo; other vendors teamed up with each other. As recorded in *Gumbo Ya-Ya*, some New Orleanian vendors vocalized in pairs—an innovative approach that could expand the reach of their businesses. One pair of vendors combined their street cries in a duet that may have drawn upon the Black vocal tradition of call and response, which has roots in African musical traditions.[136]

> 1st: *Calas, Calas,*—all nice and hot
> *Calas, Calas,*—all nice and hot
>
> 2nd: Lady, me I have *calas!* Laaa-dy, me I have *calas!*
> All nice 'n hot—all nice 'n hot—all nice 'n hot...[137]

Working the streets in pairs was not only a means to create dynamic performances, but also a means of extending the reach of one's business, potentially making it more profitable—a necessary step when competition was so high among vendors. For a pair of calas sellers, one could stand at the furnace preparing the rice fritters while the other took the piping hot products out in the streets to catch people who might not pass directly in front of the stand. Other vendors, too, worked in pairs, including young Black vendors, who, according to *Gumbo Ya-Ya*, each took one side of the street, carrying their wares and crying out at the same time or alternating: "I got mustard greens 'n Creole cabbage! Come on, Lady. Look what I got!" Another pair cried out, "Irish pota-tahs! Dime a bucket! Lady, you oughta see my nice Irish po-ta-tahs!"[138]

Teamwork enabled these vendors to cover more ground as they moved down a street or across a town square, which proved to be an effective marketing strategy. They needed to employ these strategies, and many others, to get by in a local food economy that seemed pitted against them. Local officials more often than not were more concerned with the well-being of customers and public market vendors, leaving street food vendors with a predictably unstable environment within which to build their businesses. What's more, in the opening decades of the twentieth century, women consumer-activists seemed determined to cut off street vendors from the public markets through their plans to enclose the structures either through screening them in or renovating them entirely into walled buildings. And that is exactly what happened in the 1930s, cleaving the crucial physical connection between street vendors and their customers who frequented the public markets.

Although physically separated from the markets—structures that had come to represent the city's unique brand of American progressivism—street food vendors remained a substantial part of New Orleans' public food culture through the 1930s. In fact, the particularities of the city's progressivism, so steeped in tradition, still allowed the continued presence of street vendors in the city's commercial and residential neighborhoods—a type of food enterprise that had nourished the city since the colonial period. Street vendors may have been physically cut off from the public markets, but their businesses could still legally operate, and in some cases thrive, in the surrounding throughways and parks. For the foreseeable future, then, New Orleans' public food culture would continue to rely on both public markets and street food vendors even as new models of provisioning centered around private markets flourished across the United States.

In the late 1930s and 1940s, it was not traditional street food vending, but the rehabilitated public markets that New Orleanians would call into question. Once renovations were finally complete in 1940, they almost immediately lost favor among city officials and New Orleans residents alike. Throughout the 1940s, state, city, and local officials and their constituents hotly debated whether or not the city should finally abandon the public markets despite the major overall of the market facilities. Once again, grassroots activism, including that among white women's groups, would play a key role in deciding the fate of New Orleans' public food culture.

6

The Rise of Convenience Culture in New Orleans, 1940–1950

IN THE FALL of 1941, Effie Fisher, president of the Garden District Homemakers' Club of New Orleans, was fed up with the culture of grocery shopping.[1] "As a housewife," she said, "I want to take advantage of every modern development, and I can see no reason why I should have to make two trips [one to the public market and one to the grocer], when I could get everything I want in one place."[2] For many city residents like Fisher, one-stop shopping was impossible because of local laws.

For generations, the city government had stalwartly protected the public markets from private grocers by making it illegal for the latter to sell fresh food (meat, seafood, and produce) within a certain radius of any public market. In 1941, private grocers could not sell fresh meat or seafood within three thousand feet (nine blocks) or fresh produce within six hundred feet (two blocks) of any public market. It was also illegal for any vendor to sell grocery items in the public markets.[3]

Unlike Fisher, families living on the outskirts of the city or in the suburbs, far away from the public markets, enjoyed a culture of convenience where they could acquire everything they needed at one retailer: staple groceries, fruit, vegetables, fresh meats, and other commodities.[4] As the *New Orleans Item* noted, "The classes who can call from place to place in their automobiles" did not suffer the same hardships as those women like Fisher who shopped in their own neighborhood in New Orleans.[5] Fisher craved a similar kind of convenience as the women who could afford to live in the suburbs or had access to automobiles and could drive to the supermarket.

Mrs. J. E. Davidson, chairman of the Consumer Education Division of the Woman Citizen's Union, was one such woman with access to a car and therefore could exercise consumer choice.[6] She found the public markets antiquated and inconvenient. Speaking out against their monopoly over food provisioning in the city, she claimed: "I don't deal with the public markets for

the simple reason that I prefer the 'one stop' place. This is 1941, not 1841."[7]
Hers was a lifestyle choice made by more and more New Orleanians, at least
those with the means to do so; their decisions heralded major changes to New
Orleans' public culture of food.

Having finally finished the decade-long renovation of its sixteen remaining public markets by 1940, city officials quickly found that their efforts to
attract vendors and customers back into the markets were in vain.[8] What they
envisioned as a renaissance in modern public provisioning turned out quite
differently. The recently renovated municipal spaces were now sanitary and
aesthetically modern, yes, but compared to private greengrocers and supermarkets on the outskirts of the city, they offered a comparatively limited
selection. Many people, like Fisher and Davidson, found shopping for fresh
food at the public markets inconvenient. Instead of a renaissance in the 1940s,
therefore, New Orleans' public markets experienced a decade of dissolution.

Over the course of the 1940s, New Orleans' public markets slowly slid into
oblivion as more and more New Orleanians embraced a national consumer
culture embodied in supermarkets.[9] As New Orleanians' allegiance to the
public markets faltered, street vendors returned to populate the city streets,
sidewalks, and other public spaces, selling their wares as they had since the
colonial period and bringing renewed energy to New Orleans' postwar public
food culture. The fall of the public markets, the rise of the supermarket, and
the resurgence of street food vending demonstrate core principles of provisioning in mid-century New Orleans: that a healthy local economy simultaneously provides convenience and builds community while braiding together
local and national food cultures.

After the major renovations of the 1930s, the municipal markets failed to live
up to city officials' and residents' expectations of modern provisioning.
Although their architecture embodied urban ideals of cleanliness and new
technologies, the public markets experienced a serious decline in tenants. As
reported in the *New Orleans Item*: "Stalls are empty, space unused, elaborate
refrigeration equipment idle."[10] In 1940, 38 of the city's 125 meat stalls (30
percent) were unoccupied. Almost half of the poultry stalls were unoccupied,
likewise. Seven of the city's twenty-seven fish stalls (26 percent), and 27 percent of vegetable stalls were also empty. The *New Orleans Item* revealed that
one of the public markets had just three tenants. And in Jefferson Market,
"Pipes and wiring for six or seven additional stalls were placed but the units
never were completed because of lack of tenants."[11] These bleak conditions
signaled the public markets' general unprofitability. Revenues declined

significantly in the years leading up to 1940, from $153,290 to $109,423, an almost 30 percent decrease.[12] In fact, several of the markets had been operating at a loss for years.

City officials attempted to repurpose unused market space for other government needs. Starting in 1940, the Louisiana State Department of Labor used one of the two buildings that made up Dryades Market for office space because there were not enough tenants to justify keeping both sides open.[13] A year later, the city declassified the Maestri Market; that is, it stopped treating the building as a public market and opened the space to private use. In the case of the Maestri Market's declassification, the city leased the building out to a group of vendors who were going to operate private businesses out of it—ones that existed outside of the public market system.[14] Such measures and conditions demonstrate that many of the city's public markets—even ones that had for so long been flagships of the public market system, such as Dryades—were locked in a downward spiral of economic unviability. In other words, the market renovations of the 1930s failed to revive public provisioning in New Orleans. Why? Because of the radius law that prohibited customers like Fisher and Davidson from one-stop shopping.

In the early 1940s, New Orleans' local food economy was unusual in comparison to the rest of the United States. Theodore Grunewald, director of the Department of Public Markets, acknowledged that distinctiveness when enumerating the damage that the zoning laws did to private entrepreneurs and urban shoppers: "No other American city has a public market system with far-reaching restrictions on grocery operations in the neighborhood of meat markets." Across the country, he explained, the one-stop store was trending, while New Orleans' local food economy remained largely unchanged.[15] In fact, in the 1940s, national supermarket chains like A&P, Safeway, and Kroger exercised considerable power in the American economy, broadening consumer access to a wide array of largely affordable products.[16] New Orleans law, however, kept national trends and chains at bay by protecting the public markets from competition.

A longtime proponent of looking to other cities for inspiration and guidance for how to manage New Orleans' provisioning system, Grunewald believed that private grocers, market vendors, and customers would benefit from lifting the market ordinance restrictions. Without these restrictions, grocers could sell fresh foods and market vendors could sell grocery items. He claimed that grocers and market vendors would witness increased sales, while customers would save time. Grunewald not only described the benefits of lifting the law, he also explained why there was no reason that the city should protect butchers' businesses any longer with the nine-block radius rule. Why grant butchers protection, he asked, if the city did not grant similar protection to say, drugstore operators, candy stores, or any other merchants? As the local food economy currently stood, Grunewald saw "no real benefit to the public or anybody else." He pointed out that cities across the country "are dropping their public markets generally" and are "turning them over to private interests and groups of merchants." In his estimation, it was time for New Orleans to follow suit. Voicing his opinion, however, did not result in immediate change to New Orleans' local law or traditional food economy.[17]

Outside of the city center, where these laws did not apply, middle-class, predominantly white shoppers had access to one-stop shops. Some were mom-and-pop stores with one or two locations and whose design and setup perhaps aligned more with the historic grocery stores in the city center than the behemoth supermarkets that would supersede them. Compared to supermarkets, these one-stop grocery stores (i.e., greengrocers) were smaller buildings with narrower aisles. Possibly they had a parking lot, but not necessarily. Yet they still offered far more product and greater convenience to customers than the grocers operating within the restricted zones who could not sell fresh foods.

Some of the one-stop grocery stores grew into chain stores and operated several locations. W. A. Green operated one such group of stores, including Green's Super Markets and Green's Piggly Wiggly No. 3 and No. 4 outside of the restricted zones.[18] The latter two stores were part of the Piggly Wiggly grocery store chain that originated in Memphis, Tennessee. At a Green's Super Market in New Orleans, customers could experience the convenience so many urban New Orleanians were craving. According to a store advertisement, shoppers could buy pork chops, apple-strawberry two-layer cake, cornflakes, flour, toilet paper, bunches of fresh watercress, broccoli, carrots, and much more, all in one trip.[19]

Convenience was king at these midsize retailers, and for customers that meant selecting their own groceries off shelves rather than having to go through a store clerk. As an advertisement for the opening of Green's Piggly Wiggly store No. 3 proudly announced, Piggly Wiggly "scientifically improved" their self-service "to make shopping a minimum of trouble and a maximum of pleasure." The advertisement pronounced that at the new store one can "really learn what it means to shop conveniently," imploring potential customers to "take as much time or as little as you please, never waiting for assistance . . . paying for everything once, as you leave!" Driving home the message, the advertisement claims, "This is the MODERN way to shop—and once you've tried it, noted the convenience, time-saving and money-saving, you'll be another Piggly Wiggly enthusiast."[20]

For mid-century shoppers, convenience came in the form of buying necessities in one place and at their own pace, yes, but convenience also came from the prepacked and prepared goods for which those stores were known.[21] With frozen dinners and other convenience foods now made on an industrial scale, customers could reduce the time they spent in the kitchen. This ethos of expediency became synonymous with chains like Piggly Wiggly. Nellie Gondran, a local resident, suggested in an advice column that her fellow New Orleanians abandon making "canapes, sandwiches or other refreshments ahead of time for a party." Instead, she advised them to "serve 'Piggly Wiggly style'" by arranging different types of store-bought spreads, cheeses, cut olives, pecan halves, "or what have you" in festive dishes.[22] In the minds of more and more New Orleanians, "Piggly Wiggly style" was a desirable new way of life.[23]

In time, Piggly Wiggly and other grocery store chains in New Orleans and across the country would undergo a transformation as they began to open the warehouse-sized retail spaces we know today as supermarkets. Broadly speaking, in early 1940s American supermarkets were a relatively new shopping experience for the primarily white and middle-class Americans who had moved out of city centers and into rapidly expanding suburbs. The food cultures that they fostered were different from New Orleans' public market culture. Unlike the public market, which had deep roots in the colonial Atlantic world, the supermarket was distinctly American and forged during the Jim Crow era. As a result, one of the more dramatic differences between the establishment of the supermarket and the public markets in New Orleans was the near total absence of Black Americans, other people of color, and poor whites as customers of the former. In moving out of the city center, the food economy of the greater New Orleans area readily adopted this broader American culture, as defined and perpetuated by wealthier white Americans. That culture reflected—and exacerbated—de facto segregation and economic disparity between urban and suburban communities. As a national food culture grew stronger in New Orleans, it contributed to the marginalization of some local food traditions, including the public food culture.

Unlike public markets, supermarkets were not crowded by street traffic. Rather, they had parking lots to accommodate cars and control the flow of traffic.[24] That these stores occupied plots large enough to accommodate parking lots in addition to more expansive buildings demonstrates the stark differences between urban and suburban food spaces in the postwar period. It also underscores the impact of car culture on shopping habits.[25] The average public

The Schwegmann Bros. Giant Supermarket in Metairie, Louisiana, enjoyed a full parking lot around 1950. Supermarkets like this one were designed specifically with car access and parking in mind to make it convenient for shoppers to transport groceries home.

Charles L. Franck Studio Collection at The Historic New Orleans Collection, Acc. No. 1979.325.4039.

market in New Orleans was roughly the size of a tennis court, with other businesses closely clustered around it. Although there was street parking, there were no parking lots because the public market system had been conceived as one driven by pedestrian traffic. Public market customers carried baskets on their arms and bought a relatively small number of foodstuffs they could carry home with the intention of consuming them that day. Even if customers had a car and wanted to drive to the public market, there would not necessarily be a convenient space to park. Supermarket shoppers, by contrast, could drive to the store, easily park, and use shopping carts to purchase items in bulk for several days or even the entire week. With access to a car, they could haul their hefty supplies back home and simply store perishables in their refrigerator and freezer, which were increasingly common features in homes across the United States.

Supermarket buildings were enclosed and not exposed to most forms of nature or industrial waste, as New Orleans' pavilion-style public markets had been in the past. Thus, their environments were comparatively sterile and aesthetically modern. Overhead lighting illuminated the aisles. Products were refrigerated. Even the stores themselves were air conditioned to keep shoppers comfortable. Public market renovations in the 1930s resulted in the enclosure of the buildings and the implementation of better electrical technologies, including lighting and refrigerated storage; however, the public markets had a dark past riddled with unsanitary conditions that could not be easily erased from shoppers' minds. Even though the city had equipped the public markets with the latest technologies, there were certain ones, like air conditioning, that did not make it into the 1930s renovations, creating noticeable differences between public markets and supermarkets.

Other than the hum of refrigerators, the supermarkets were quiet compared to the raucous public markets or even private markets in bustling urban neighborhoods. There were no vendors crying out prices. There were no heated negotiations taking place between vendors and customers. The price was the price. Simple as that. Spatially, supermarkets were organized and uniform. Shelves of groceries were conveniently displayed and easy to reach. Without the interference of zoning ordinances, prepackaged meats, canned goods, baking mixes, and frozen dinners were neatly arranged near one another.

In some instances, akin to the shopping culture at Green's Piggly Wiggly, customers no longer had to interact with employees when shopping at supermarkets. Shoppers were independent and free from the task of outsmarting predatory vendors in the public markets and in the city streets. They no longer had to ask for the assistance of a private grocer to retrieve, pack, and deliver grocery items to them. Instead, at their leisure, shoppers could identify items and place them in shopping carts or baskets on their own accord. This was the height of modern, convenience shopping in the mid-century United States.[26]

Bearing witness to the freedom of suburban shoppers (and city residents with access to vehicles or other modes of ground transportation), urban residents living in the restricted zones became increasingly discontent with New Orleans' public food culture. For many New Orleanians, the neighborhood public markets no longer served (or needed to serve) as an economic and community center. This attitude change happened to coincide with the enclosure of the public market buildings from the streets in the first half of the twentieth century. That enclosure marked the buildings as distinct economic spaces in what had been a multidimensional, albeit at times chaotic, public food culture grounded in the city streets. In this sense, the construction of walls around the markets symbolized a fissure not only with the streets, but also with the surrounding community. Those same walls came to symbolize a growing resemblance between public and private markets, creating new opportunities for direct comparison now that they were both enclosed retail spaces. Such comparisons found the public markets wanting and the local laws that protected them constraining to customers that were more and more enamored with convenience shopping.[27]

In contrast to the entrepreneurs who operated supermarkets in the suburbs and the customers who had access to their businesses, New Orleanians who continued to work and shop in the city were not happy with the state of urban food provisioning. As in decades past, discontented New Orleanians— retailers and shoppers alike—took their complaints and proposed solutions to their local representatives. In 1940, for example, private grocers reinvigo- rated their long-standing campaign to repeal the radius law, which would enable them to operate anywhere in the city and sell both grocery items and fresh food. Tensions escalated in August 1941 when debates over the public markets made the front page of the *New Orleans Item*, including Grunewald's criticisms of the radius rule. Of a mind similar to Grunewald, grocer Ben Haney called the public markets antiquated. He explained, "The world has changed. The retail business of dealing with the housewife has revolutionized. But New Orleans has stayed behind the times," and grocers and consumers suffered as a result. Haney estimated that about 60 percent of New Orleans' population lived within the restricted zones where private grocers were not permitted to sell fresh meat and seafood. He also observed that, at the time, there were only about eighty-five butchers operating in the public markets, but there were sixteen hundred independent grocers operating around the city, many of whom were interested in selling fresh products but were unable to because of local law. For Haney, city officials' prioritization of the dwin- dling numbers of butchers was an example of a failing democracy: "I don't see any democracy in that arrangement. No group of merchants, no matter who they are, are entitled to that favor."[28]

In Haney's estimation, it was egregious not only that the city so fiercely protected butchers, but that it did so to the disadvantage of shoppers. He made the point that customers living in the urban core did not have the same food choices or access as those living on the outer rim of the city or in the neighboring suburbs: "The housewife in some of the outlying areas has the opportunity to buy her meat and fish at 'one stop' groceries, which can locate wherever the business warrants it." But "The housewife in the older sections [of the city] is deprived of this chance" because of the radius law.[29]

The next day, the voices of women like Effie Fisher—who patronized the public markets and whose food choices were limited—rang out on the front page of the *New Orleans Item*.[30] They expressed their frustration with the local law that forced them to shop at several businesses to acquire all that they needed for the week. Like the grocers, Fisher did not approve of butchers' protection under local law, asking that if the butchers "can't make a go of matters in real competition, why should they get a monopoly?" Similarly, Mrs. J. E. Davidson spoke out against the butchers, calling their business practices obsolete. She drew attention to the fact that if the radius rule was lifted, vendors in the public markets could then sell grocery items, which she saw as a distinct advantage: "I should think that the butchers are being pretty short-sighted. I should think that if they added groceries they would sell a larger bulk of foodstuffs, and perhaps more meat as well, when they drew housewives to the markets."[31]

Butchers, historically the most politically connected and vocal vendors in the public markets, fiercely opposed lifting the radius law that protected their businesses from competition. They maintained that, as small business owners, they were struggling to make a living even with the protective laws in place. Mr. Wolf, for example, described himself not as a successful business owner with a strong monopoly over the city's local food scene but as a struggling one barely able to make ends meet. Some of his grievances echoed those of generations of butchers before him: "We have to pay rents that are out of all proportion." He continued: "And the city doesn't enforce the restrictive zone fairly. There are violations all around us, with places selling meat that shouldn't, and peddlers allowed to sell practically under our noses."[32]

Wolf elaborated on his struggles and stated that rental fees were higher than ever. What many butchers had advocated for ten years prior was now a hindrance: a modern and costly retail space. In 1941, Wolf paid $17.64 a week to retain his stall at the public market, and, he noted, "Before the city modernized the markets and gave us the improved refrigeration and everything else, my costs were about one-third of what they are now." Paying a total of $70.56 a month in rental fees at the time, Wolf suggested that a fair rate for most butchers would be more in the range of $30 a month. Even then, Wolf argued, the butchers would still need the zoning rule to stay competitive.[33]

Further, Wolf saw the suggestion that butchers begin vending groceries as asinine: "These two things don't go together at all," he said; Wolf argued that he had trained his entire life to be a butcher, not a grocer, and that assuming that butchers could easily take on the mantle of an entirely different business model was ridiculous. He implored customers to recognize the artisanry and skill of trained butchers in preparing and selling the best-quality product. After all, many of them had been in the trade for years, if not generations.

According to Wolf, they "know good meat" and "know how to cut it." And as a result of their commitment to selling quality product, he argued, they also had higher safety standards and more sanitary retail spaces than private stores that "sell stuff that sometimes isn't properly prepared; and their sanitation can't match ours."[34] Reports in the local newspaper corroborated Wolf's claims. Earlier that year, the Bureau of Sanitation found Peter J. Piazza's fish market sorely in need of improvements, identifying several elements that needed to be installed or repaired: "Side walks must be repaired and painted; establishment must be screened; running hot water supply must be installed in shop; toilet must be repaired and kept in proper condition at all times."[35] Some private markets were dangerous.

Wolf's criticisms of the private markets were backed by his fellow butchers, including Robert Cazaubon, who brought concerns of public health to the forefront of the radius debates. Cazaubon contended that there was a "purpose and a reason" backing the zoning rules: public health. Thanks to the city's renovation project, the butchers now had state-of-the-art equipment that included hot and cold running water, washroom facilities, and refrigeration to meet public health criteria. By contrast, he asserted, "The store that sells meat as a side line simply sets aside a small part of the floor, puts in a chopping block and a display case, and goes right ahead."[36] A fellow butcher who operated out of the Dryades Market, Thomas Rooney, contributed a stomach-turning image of the potential goings-on at private grocers: "You know that in groceries, clerks handle oil, potatoes that have worms in them, onions, maybe even shoes and stockings that they fit to people's feet. Then they handle the meat. That's not clean, is it?" The butchers, by contrast, "have to be clean" because they are regularly inspected by city officials. Cazaubon added that the retention of the radius law would ensure that butchers could continue to offer affordable prices: "Our meat prices generally are the lowest in the country, and the reason is—the public markets."[37] He argued that if the radius were lifted, butchers in the public markets would certainly go out of business, and private grocers would shoot up meat prices "sky-high."[38] According to these butchers, protecting the public markets was really a means of protecting New Orleanians' access to affordable, safe food.

The points that the butchers made largely reflect arguments made by earlier generations in their trade; however, one issue raised was specific to recent changes in the New Orleans area's food economy: the proliferation of chain stores. As larger businesses, chain stores generally had more capital to invest in tactics to break their competition, butchers among them. They could place certain popular items on sale and sell them at a loss to incentivize shoppers to patronize their business, a pricing strategy known as a "loss leader." A super-market, for example, might sell chicken at a loss in the hope that a customer would also purchase various canned goods, produce, dairy products, and snacks whose total profit to the store would outweigh the loss on the chicken. Witness to the implementation of such practices, the butchers exclaimed: "We face ruinous competition from the chain stores that use loss leaders and other tactics to defeat us unfairly."[39]

New Orleans' butchers were not the only food entrepreneurs concerned with chain stores' abilities to offer food at discount prices to entice customers. Mom-and-pop corner grocers, too, saw the looming threat; it was hard not to when companies like A&P were already running 4,638 stores across the country by 1920. In the following decades, to stay competitive, small-scale grocers joined trade groups like the Independent Grocers Alliance and the Retail Grocers' Association that enabled them to acquire goods wholesale at the same price as chain stores like A&P; similarly, mom-and-pop grocers used these groups to lobby for price controls on key staples to mitigate the discounts chain stores could offer. Without price controls in place, they insisted, there was no way their businesses could survive.[40]

Disheartened by the same trends mom-and-pop grocers observed, butchers like Wolf understood all too well that they were in a dying trade—one that could not survive the wave of progress and culture of convenience that had taken hold across the country, including the greater New Orleans area. As he pointed out, there were fewer and fewer butchers in the city. Many butchers had or were on the cusp of retiring, and many in the younger generations did not express interest in learning the trade. The one young person he did train ended up working for a private store because that job offered higher wages. Looking back on the past several years, Wolf's future appeared dark to him. Knowing that he was fighting against the tide of popular opinion, he glumly concluded by saying, "I guess we're doomed."[41]

New Orleanians agreed with Wolf's woeful prediction. With the market debate making headlines for weeks, word of the radius law's demise continued to spread throughout the city. As reported by the *New Orleans Item*, "The consumers interviewed by The Item were unanimous in their expression of the opinion that the restrictions should be removed. They said they wanted 'one-stop' stores and that the restrictions prevent this in many sections of the city, and serve no useful purpose." Making no attempt to appear objective, the *New Orleans Item* author stated plainly, "We agree with them."[42]

The public commentary shared in the *New Orleans Item*, along with the continued protest and activist measures taken by proponents from both sides of the market debate, generated significant attention. In response, a special Association of Commerce committee formed to assess the prohibition of fresh meat and seafood within nine blocks of any public market.[43] The committee met with public market vendors, private store owners, city officials, women's civic organizations, and a number of other players with vested interest in New Orleans' public food culture. It ultimately recommended that the city lift the radius restrictions.[44] Committee members decided that concerns over sanitation that had originally animated the public markets and radius restrictions were no longer relevant in the modern era because all purveyors of meat were subject to health inspections.[45] Further, shopping habits had evolved over time. Gone were the days in which the "housekeeper made morning pilgrimages to vegetable stalls, butchers' stalls, fish stalls and then the grocery stores, with a servant to carry the basket." In the committee's estimation, "the old need for immediate sale of each day's supply" was no longer necessary.[46]

Although the committee recommended lifting the radius rule, its recommendation was not taken up by the city council, as local officials turned their attention to World War II and domestic efforts to support soldiers and allies abroad; nevertheless, business prospects were bleak for the public markets. Market vendors launched new marketing campaigns to drum up business, including running advertisements in the same newspaper that published the major stories critical of their enterprises, the *New Orleans Item*. In May 1942, a large print ad ran on page 4 of the newspaper calling readers to "Patronize the Public Market in Your Neighborhood." The print ad shows community members flocking on foot to a bustling market interior. Its message reinforced two major points: that the markets were under "constant supervision of State and City Boards of Health" and that they were surrounded by diverse stores and were therefore a "One-Stop Shopping Center." The retailers co-opted the very language of their opponents, who often criticized them for not being a "one-stop" shop, and rebranded the term for their own purposes. Rather than focusing solely on the public markets, they defined the commercial corridors along which the public markets sat as a "shopping center"—a savvy, yet largely unsuccessful attempt at rebranding; public opinion had already coalesced around the idea of the public markets as an inconvenient shopping experience, and no amount of advertising could change that.[47]

Details about the lived experiences of market vendors and their customers are somewhat obscure during World War II. Where debates over the public markets filled the city's papers through the spring of 1942, in the following months the local papers rarely mentioned the public markets or market vendors. Additionally, the existing records of the Department of Public Markets during the war are thin; only a few documents reference structural maintenance and the regulation of newly opened private markets.[48] One can surmise, however, that as New Orleans became an important manufacturing center and port for the war effort, some individuals and families once employed in the local food economy likely transitioned into the wartime industrial sector, a phenomenon documented across the country.[49] Others were likely drafted into or joined the military, leaving their positions as vendors to train and eventually deploy abroad.

As a result, the public markets' operations, along with sectors within the local food economy, shrank significantly. Take, for example, the fishermen shortage in the winter of 1943 that led to a seafood shortage in New Orleans' public markets and other retail spaces. The *New Orleans Item* reported that there was a "man power shortage" and few people to staff fishing boats because many of them had been drafted, after which they "belong to Uncle Sam." Still other fishermen left their jobs to go work in the shipyards to facilitate the movement of goods for the war. As a result, "About 100 Louisiana fishing boats are tied up by the man power shortage," leading to scarcity in New Orleans. As reported in the *New Orleans Item*, the French Market "had one good fish day last week," but "there isn't any in sight for this week."[50]

Shortages, from meat and seafood to agricultural products, continued to affect food-retailing spaces, including the public markets, and the communities they served throughout the war.[51] In response to food shortages, the national government worked to create food relief programs. New Orleans' newspapers detailed those plans for readers, as was the case for the federal government's plan to head off an anticipated produce shortage in the fall of 1943. Articles reported a plan to encourage southern agricultural states, Louisiana among them, to "raise as many vegetables as possible" to supply the nation.[52] These articles indicate a significant decrease of fresh food distribution in communities, including New Orleans. That meant there was less fresh food moving through the public markets, which hurt vendors and customers alike.

To compensate, in addition to working with farmers, the national government struck up a victory garden campaign to encourage Americans to grow their own produce. At the same time, it implemented a national rationing system to curb consumption of meat and other products, notably dairy and sugar.[53] As reported in the *Times-Picayune*, the US secretary of agriculture encouraged Americans in urban and suburban communities, who had either their own plot of land or a communal one, to actively partake in a victory garden program. Like people across the country, New Orleanians took up the call and grew vegetables to support the war effort.[54] These combined conditions and measures, ranging from labor shortages to alternative food procurement strategies, corroded the economic and cultural importance of the public markets as Americans were forced to become more self-sufficient and less reliant on the public food culture to sustain themselves.

During the war, city officials made little progress reforming the market ordinances, and the radius rule remained in place. But the Department of Public Markets worked with the city surveyor to map out the proposed location of new private markets to ensure that they were not in violation of the radius rule.[55] Additionally, city officials discussed ways to declassify unprofitable public markets. Prior to the war, the city had divested itself of the Maestri Market. With that precedent in mind, in September 1944, Grunewald successfully encouraged the city to divest itself of the Rocheblave Market.[56]

After declassifying the Rocheblave Market, the city leased the building to the Victory Land Company at a yearly rental of $3,000 starting November 1, 1944, for five years. The original market vendors were able to stay in the building and continue selling their wares. The butchers and seafood vendor paid $15 a week in rent, and the fruit stand $22.50 a week, which matched public market rental fees around that time.[57] Thus day-to-day operations of the vendors remained fairly stable despite the change from public to private enterprise. However, they found themselves on the other side of the market wars, working as private vendors—the very group of entrepreneurs that many of them had fought against for years. No longer protected by the public markets' ordinances, these newly minted private vendors faced new threats within the recently declassified market: eviction.

Just over a year later, the Victory Land Company, with the permission of the City Commission Council, decided to sublease the building to DeLatour, Simoneaux and Bergeron, Inc. "for the purpose of installing a super food store." The sublease had a devastating impact on the market vendors who were suddenly left without a place to operate their businesses. There were five butcher stands, one seafood stand, and one fruit stand at the market. Many of the vendors had been operating there for more than twenty years.[58] Shocked by news of the sublease and their pending removal, butcher Nick Schilleci said that he was going to seek legal aid to prevent their eviction, feeling like they were being put "out in the cold." They had ten days' notice to pack up their businesses, but as one of the other butchers Simon Courrege explained, "You can't do anything in 10 days." He elaborated: "You've got to have a rat-proofed building, then make it sanitary before you can move. There is no place to move, and we couldn't buy equipment anyway. All of us are citizens and all have families." In his mind, the eviction was a grievous offense that violated vendors' rights and endangered their families.[59]

For decades, Schilleci, Courrege, and their fellow vendors had had relatively secure access to operate in the market, and historically city officials had fought hard to protect their businesses from competitors. Within a matter of years, however, those dynamics completely shifted as the city endeavored to declassify more and more public markets, placing vendors in an incredibly vulnerable position without guarantees to a retail space or a way to continue operating their businesses.

Their eviction notice raised many questions. Without the public market, where would they build those crucial connections with neighbors that sustained their businesses? Could they afford to branch out on their own? Could they access the capital necessary to open a brick-and-mortar location, or would structural inequalities and discrimination continue to bar them from those essential loans? The market vendors faced a world of unknowns as they broke down their stalls to make room for their Goliath: the supermarket.

World War II was an equally devastating and uncertain time for New Orleans' street food vendors. Local residents estimated that of the approximate four thousand vegetable peddlers serving the city before the war, only a handful remained by the summer of 1944. Remarking on the increasing impact the war was having on daily life in New Orleans, journalist John Collier observed: "The war has finally left its imprint on that most untouchable of New Orleans traditions—the vegetable peddler." He went on to describe how "the familiar cries of 'I gotta da tomatah' or 'stwabewwies,'" which had echoed down city streets for generations, were no longer heard in certain neighborhoods because many of the street vendors had joined the service; they were fighting abroad or working in plants building ships, tanks, planes, and other equipment needed for the war effort.[60]

Collier interviewed community members about their impressions of the war's impact on the local public culture of food. One interviewee remarked that the French Market complex, where many vendors procured their products to peddle in the streets, was completely different. Before the war, the market was abuzz with commercial and social activity, whereas in that moment, "It's almost deserted." Collier found that city-issued licenses were dropping off significantly: "Records at City Hall showed that only three peddlers have gotten licenses so far this month [August], and only 25 in the last four months, compared with 35 who got licenses in January alone."[61]

Collier observed that although New Orleanians had patronized street vendors' businesses for generations, many did not know about the details of their work: how, when, and where they procured their product, and so on. Perhaps foreseeing a limited future for street food culture in the coming years and wanting to preserve a record of it, Collier sought to write down and share a few details about the daily routines of an average New Orleanian street food vendor. His preservation efforts echoed those of generations past, especially in the years following the Civil War and Reconstruction.

According to Collier, the peddler woke up around four o'clock in the morning and drove his wagon up to the curb stalls at the French Market, where "he is met by farmers who have driven their trucks in from the country the previous night and have arrayed their wares on the sidewalk." And when they meet, they begin bargaining. The whole process "is much like an old-time auction." There was a strong culture of negotiation between the two parties, each suggesting a price "about 50 percent higher than what he is willing to accept or give," but the two parties would eventually come to an agreement after "a little wrangling." With their wares in carts, they would head out into the streets to do business starting no later than eight o'clock in the morning, often selling until six o'clock in the evening or later.[62]

Collier acknowledged that it was not a very lucrative business, with peddlers making about fifteen to twenty dollars a week, "a small consideration these days," but one that provided them employment they might not have been able to find elsewhere.[63] Around 1944, a peddler could make about the same amount of money as some workers in the sugar and related industries of New Orleans working a forty-hour week.[64] These sugar workers were known to be underpaid, struggling to keep up with the rising cost of living.[65] Street vendors, therefore, were in a similarly precarious situation. With the near disappearance of street vendors during the war, their cries once described as "blood curdling" by some, became much more palatable in the midst of war, when many residents craved a return to normalcy. Feeling that moment of loss, Collier described the once common cry of "I gotta da bana-nah" as "sweet music to every housewife's ear."[66]

Some street food vendors found work in different industries, including military service, during World War II; in their new jobs, perhaps they experienced an increase in their standard of living and heightened expectations for the future. Some switched industries when the war ended, while others returned to their prewar work. Prior to the war, Alexander Granderson, a Black New Orleanian, peddled fruits and vegetables when he lived uptown with his wife, mother, and siblings.[67] The archival record does not reveal much about what he did during the war years, but afterward, he remained in the peddling business for some time before eventually becoming a mechanic for an Oldsmobile dealership.[68]

William Stock, a white New Orleanian, also worked as fruit and vegetable peddler pre- and postwar, eventually marrying Katie Coates and starting a family in the years following the war.[69] Decades later, Stock's daughter Marguerite would take over the family business, operating a much-beloved and award-winning fruit and vegetable stand on River Road (not too far from New Orleans' uptown neighborhoods) with her husband, Jerry Burns. In 1988, after operating that stand for over thirty years, she recalled, "My daddy, William Stock, started the business with a horse and wagon. Then we had a fruit truck that went into the neighborhoods. I learned the business from my parents."[70]

For Marguerite Stock Burns, the family's stand was more than a business; it was a community meeting ground ripe with conversation and hospitality: "Friends stop by all the time just to talk and to visit. We hear about their troubles and good times, and we tell them about ours. We see people here we don't see anywhere else. We know all about them and they know all about us."[71] So adored was their business by local clientele, a friend and customer composed a song, "The DeWitt River Road Fruit Stand Blues," whose sheet music he presented to Burns and her husband.[72] Their social network also extended to the wholesalers at the French Market from whom they bought most of their produce. To this day, the produce stand remains a family business that New Orleanians proudly patronize. One of those customers, Janice Sayas, remarked on the friendly relationship she has with the current owner, Dewitt Burns: "Every time we pass his stand, we can't help but pull over," she said. "He's just like a neighbor to us."[73] So Stock's peddling work before and after the war, provided a foundation upon which his daughter and her descendants would go on to support themselves while simultaneously building decades-long relationships, including friendships, with loyal customers.

As the public markets and street vendors nearly disappeared during the war, city officials scrambled to come up with alternative modes of public provisioning. They experimented with opening what was largely considered to be an antiquated market style: a curb market. Curb markets, as indicated by their name, were set up on a street curb. Throughout the country's history, curb markets had been decried as a public nuisance that crowded city streets, blocking both vehicular and pedestrian traffic. Then in the 1940s, Theodore Grunewald, as director of the Department of Public Markets, proposed reinvigorating a model that had largely been abandoned generations prior.

Grunewald wanted to support local growers who had lost direct access to customers in the French Market. The curb market allowed them to re-engage with residents across the city, offering lower prices (reduced by about 30 percent) for fresh foods because middlemen and middlewomen (the market vendors and private retailers) were cut out of the picture. Grunewald saw their direct engagement with customers as key to a healthy public food culture. Grunewald's return to historic market models was made possible by the food shortages and economic hardship caused by World War II. Whereas prior to the war, local officials would have vehemently opposed supporting any business that might compete with the vendors in the public markets, the war effort necessitated the permissibility of pop-up markets that sold affordable, fresh food directly to customers. During the war at least, many customers' arguments about convenience shopping and whether to abandon the public markets system altogether were set aside as basic food access became the priority.

On April 30, 1943, the first "farmers' curb market" opened on the road median on Melpomene Street at the intersection of Claiborne on the back corner of Faubourg Lafayette, upriver of the French Quarter. It was sponsored by the War Emergency Food Association in New Orleans. The group's goal, according to member Kitty Monroe Westfeldt, "was to help the farmer market his produce and to aid the housewife in obtaining adequate supplies of fresh vegetables at reasonable prices."[74] Women activists played a major role in organizing the pop-up market and had reached out to farmers to tell them about the opportunity.

For the pop-up market, farmers operating on the outskirts of town brought in truckloads of fresh produce. Two trucks were present that first day.[75] Their goods were desperately needed by the New Orleans population; the *New Orleans Item* reported that "there were more customers than produce" and that the first truck to arrive "couldn't sell fast enough to meet demand." The four farmers selling out of the truck sold half of their product in an hour. The second truck, which arrived later, sold eggs and potatoes, "and the eggs were gone before half the people were waited on." The customers were diverse because nearly all members of the war-wearied populace were desperate for fresh food. "Society women, civic leaders and uptown housewives arrived by street car and automobile with market baskets or shopping bags on their arms, and pushed their way through the throngs of Negroes and neighborhood shoppers, who were also trying to get at the produce." The purchasing environment at the first market was chaotic, with customers weighing their own produce under the watchful eye of one of Grunewald's staff, but even that staff member could not ensure that both farmers and customers were treated fairly.[76]

Given the evident demand for the curb market after the first day, Grunewald agreed to ask the city to construct a shed over it where trucks could pull up and display their wares—not dissimilar to the pavilion-style markets prevalent in the city in the nineteenth and early twentieth centuries. Grunewald did not expect any resistance from the city as, according to the paper: "Mayor Maestri had already expressed his intention of co-operating fully with the new curb market as a war measure." With the support of city officials, the market ran every Friday from eight o'clock in the morning to one o'clock in the afternoon.[77] The city provided wooden tables for farmers to display their produce and eventually built a metal awning to protect farmers and their customers from the elements.[78] The curb market (later rebranded the Melpomene St. Farmers' Curb Market) expanded over time, and eventually came to operate on both Tuesdays and Fridays.[79]

In May 1944, the War Emergency Food Association partnered with Grunewald to propose a second curb market at Carrollton and St. Charles Avenue, far uptown above Tulane University.[80] Grunewald was supportive of the activism of the women's associations behind the idea: "My department will offer its co-operation to the ladies sponsoring the opening of this market place which will aid farmers and housewives in solving the problem of marketing vegetables."[81] The plan for the second curb market went forward, and as with the first one, the city built a pavilion at the new location.[82] As in years past, women's grassroots activism played a crucial role in shaping the public culture of food in New Orleans, demonstrating the power of local consumer-activists in the making of local infrastructure.

In the wake of World War II, supermarkets became increasingly strong competitors in the New Orleans area food economy. In many ways, their success served as the final nail in the coffin for the public market system. Schwegmann Brothers Giant Supermarkets, known colloquially as Schwegmann's, was one such business whose initial supermarket venture and subsequent growth coincided with the final years of the public markets. The first Schwegmann's supermarket opened at the intersection of St. Claude and Elysian Fields in 1946—serving the Marigny community downriver of the French Quarter.[83] The Schwegmann family had been in the grocery business for generations, dating back to 1869. But by the end of World War II, John Schwegmann Jr. had declared that "the era of supermarkets was well under way," and decided to embrace the supermarket model. That new model was strikingly different from the family's previous grocery stores in terms of sheer size. Whereas those original stores were about thirty feet wide, the supermarket on St. Claude was one hundred feet by one hundred twenty-five feet. Schwegmann recalled one customer at the new supermarket asking in awe, "John, do you mean to say a customer will come in to buy a loaf of bread and walk 100 feet to get a quart of milk?"[84]

The Schwegmann's supermarket adopted the self-service model that was increasingly popular in the city. Schwegmann recalled how transitioning from clerk service to self-service was not easy for all their customers. In fact, at his father's old grocery store on Piety and Burgundy, there was a contingent of customers who resisted that transition. Schwegmann identified them as "oldtimers"—"the ones who got up at 4:30 in the morning and were at the store at 5:30 with their market baskets." These were customers who had grown up going to the public markets and were accustomed to showing up at dawn to have their pick of the choicest, freshest products at market vendors' stalls. When the Schwegmann family transitioned the old store to a completely self-service model, eliminating the clerk stalls, some of those "oldtimers" expressed their discontent. Schwegman remembered, "I will never forget how some of the older elderly women in the neighborhood, the ones who wore bonnets and carried the market baskets, spoke to me and said, 'John, you mean I have to look all over this place for what I need—if you don't put those counters back, I'm going to buy at Eicke's,'" that is, Schwegmann's local competitor. So Schwegmann's father put one counter back to appease those customers, while keeping the rest of the store self-service.[85]

Schwegmann Sr. convinced those customers to switch to self-service by offering a larger discount on the items they procured themselves. For example, canned tomatoes sold by a store clerk were eight cents a can, whereas they were only six cents a can via self-service. People love a good bargain, so much so that even the most stubborn of customers were willing to change their ingrained shopping habits. Witness to the successful implementation of self-service in the old store, Schwegmann Jr. brought the culture of self-service and low prices to his supermarket, which attracted hordes of customers. As he recalled, "From the day our store opened, the people came in to shop in capacity crowds."[86]

Schwegmann Jr. attributed the success of his first supermarket to several factors, including the company's commitment to selling certain items at bargain prices. Schwegmann Jr. recalled, "Large volume and low mark-ups were our established policy from the beginning, regardless of how scarce the merchandise was." His strategy demonstrates how large-volume supermarkets could undercut smaller mom-and-pop shops, which lacked the buying power to purchase in bulk and were forced to charge higher prices.[87] And, because they switched to a self-service model, they significantly reduced labor costs. Further, Schwegmann's sold house-brand products—everything from beer and whiskey to coffee—allowing the company to sell a relatively more afford-able version of a product compared to their name-brand alternatives. Although many of its innovations increased shopper independence and reduced interactions with staff, some additions, like the inclusion of a bar in various store locations, afforded opportunities for community members, especially men, to mingle as their partners shopped. These were but a handful of innovations that Schwegmann's invented or adopted in their stores.[88] So successful was the Schwegmann's supermarket model that by 1986 the chain consisted of twelve stores, employed over four thousand people, and soon became the largest grocer in the New Orleans area.[89]

Although the first Schwegmann's supermarket opened within the bounds of the city, the company quickly expanded out into the suburbs. Their next store on Airline Highway was eighty-six thousand square feet. Even more impressive, the store on Old Gentilly Road boasted, for a time, the title of largest supermarket in America at one hundred fifty-five thousand square feet.[90] In preparation for the store's opening in late November 1957, store clerks fully stocked aisles, anticipating the mass movement of people and products. On opening day, New Orleans area residents flocked to the store, waiting in checkout lines eight people deep. The company marketed its stores as an ingenious example of modern distribution methods in the country, directly juxtaposing itself against the historic public food culture of New Orleans.[91] That message resonated with customers who sought a shopping experience quite different from what they had grown up with in the city.

In 1946, the city government finally began dissolving its monopoly over food provisioning after more than 150 years of trying to maintain control over it. In May, city officials were seriously contemplating a plan to lease or sell all the public markets for private operation except for the French Market. The city would retain that market, according to Public Property Commissioner Hotard, because of "its historic value."[92] The *New Orleans States* applauded Hotard's proposal to keep the French Market, noting that city residents would meet Hotard's idea with "universal approval," as the city shared a united opin-ion that "the market should stand as a public monument as long as the Vieux Carré endures."[93]

The shelves of the spice section at the Schwegmann Bros. Supermarket in Gentilly, Louisiana, were fully stocked on opening day on November 25, 1957. These orderly and abundant groceries signaled to shoppers that the new supermarket could meet all their shopping needs.
Charles L. Franck Studio Collection at The Historic New Orleans Collection, Acc. No. 1994.94.1665.

For the neighborhood markets, however, the end-of-year revenues spoke volumes about the city's failing experiment in modern public provisioning. As Hotard put it, "We have no business being in markets and operating at a loss."[94] In 1945, only three of the remaining fourteen markets still under city control were profitable that year: St. Roch Market at $2,144, Magazine Market at $223.86, and Jefferson Market at $214.86. The other eleven markets' losses totaled $22,063.54.[95] As the *New Orleans Item* opined, "They are a white elephant supported by the machine.... They have mostly been ill managed and do nobody any good."[96] Given the cultural significance of the French Market, however, it would continue to operate at a loss, which in 1945 totaled $6,479.03.[97]

Although the neighborhood markets retained little or no favor, the oldest market, arguably one of the most recognizable landmarks in New Orleans to this day, retained a place of importance in the hearts and minds of New

Customers with full shopping carts wait in long lines to check out on opening day at the Schwegmann Bros. Supermarket in Gentilly, Louisiana, on November 25, 1957. The sheer number of customers reflected the community's enthusiasm for the opening of this super-market location.

Charles L. Franck Studio Collection at The Historic New Orleans Collection, Acc. No. 1994.94.2.1663.

Orleanians. By naming the historic value of the French Market, and not simi-larly doing so for the neighborhood public markets, Hotard tacitly confirmed that those facilities were no longer operating as the center of economic and community life in their neighborhoods. Those nourishing networks had, for the most part, collapsed, and their value to the community disintegrated.

There was a belief among New Orleanians, however, that the neighbor-hood markets could have maintained economic and cultural value to the city if Grunewald had managed them more effectively. Some people felt that if the city had truly clamped down on the spread of private retailers, the public mar-kets could have thrived. Others argued that if the city had eliminated the radius rule earlier, integrating grocery and fresh food shopping, the public markets would have done better. Still others' criticisms of the public markets' management went back decades, arguing that if the city had renovated the entire public market system a generation earlier, they would have remained essential to local economy and culture. The *New Orleans States* wrote that, had the city managed the neighborhood markets more effectively, "there would likely be, today, scattered over New Orleans, 16 splendid little copies of French Market, each hallowed also by tradition and historic worth."[98] Therefore, it was not the idea of public markets, necessarily, that was off-putting to some community members, but rather their mishandling by city officials.

In hopes of recouping some costs, city officials continued to declassify public markets and lease them out to private retailers. By 1947, the Le Breton, Keller, Lautenschlaeger, Mid-City, and Tremé Markets had become private retail spaces, and city officials were in the midst of reviewing ordinances to declassify more of the markets. The city prioritized leasing to current tenants, allowing them to stay put. According to the *Times-Picayune*, "To date all markets leased under the present policy have been leased to tenants, and the city has obtained agreement by the lessees to permit all tenants to remain in these markets at current rates." And at that date Grunewald noted that the public markets were no longer operating at a loss.[99] Local officials continued to prioritize leasing to present tenants as they declassified more markets. In December, the city leased the St. Roch Market to the St. Roch Super Market, Inc., a corporation composed of present tenants of the market, and Ninth Street to the Ninth Street Market Corporation, which was likewise composed of market tenants.[100] In doing so, the city had declassified fifteen of the sixteen public markets; the last remaining was the Jefferson Market, and it was soon to be leased.

City officials, though, did not want to stop with just leasing the buildings. Mayor Chep Morrison declared that he wanted the city "out of the real estate business" all together and proposed that the city sell all sixteen city-owned structures that used to be public markets. He argued that with the high real estate value at the time, the buildings would bring more than $1 million if sold, which could then be used to improve the city streets. Further, he noted that by selling the buildings to private owners, thus putting them back on the tax assessment rolls, the city would gain about an additional $40,000 annually in taxes.[101] Some residents disagreed with the mayor's proposal to sell the markets. Leon Bryer maintained that "if the public markets lost their value on account of the big super markets, they can be easily used for some other public needs, welfare and education centers."[102] Many other residents, however, were in agreement with the mayor and city council that the city should sell off the structures.

By 1948, the city council nixed the public markets from the annual budget, abolished the Department of Public Markets, and laid off or reassigned its twenty-nine remaining employees.[103] The mayor noted that as the city began selling off the structures, those people who took out a five-year lease on the buildings could retain those even if the properties were sold.[104] The first buildings went up for auction in August 1948.[105] After the abolishment of his department, Grunewald was reassigned to help with the sale of the buildings, although he died before the process was complete.[106]

By March 1950, most of the structures had been sold.[107] The three remaining ones included the lower half of the Dryades Markets as well as the Prytania and St. Roch Markets. Of the latter two, the local paper stated that they would not be sold because "they stand on property which the city needs."[108] The city demolished the Prytania Market around 1954 to create a parking lot for the growing commercial corridor around the historic market structure.[109] Car culture and parking lots, which prior to the war had largely been characteristic of the suburbs and supermarkets, were now seeping into urban life. That the city prioritized a parking lot over a market structure is representative of how quickly life in New Orleans was changing in the postwar period. In this instance, car culture literally destroyed vestiges of the public market culture.

In 1958, the State Department of Health, which had occupied the lower Dryades Market building for years, was preparing to move to the new Civic Center, and the city was preparing to auction off the last Dryades building. Even though city officials and residents had moved on from the neighborhood public markets, news coverage of the sale revealed lingering nostalgia and recognition of the vital economic and community role the Dryades Market had once played. An article in the *Times-Picayune* retraced the history of the public amenity back to 1848, more than a century earlier, and noted: "It may be premature to bid a respectful adieu to 'Dryades,' but the respect itself it is entitled to."[110] The building sold in October 1958, marking the end of the city's ties to the historic neighborhood market structure.[111] Perhaps it was those last remnants of appreciation and nostalgia, combined with a desire to hold on to valuable property, that incentivized city officials never to sell the St. Roch Market structure, the last neighborhood market hall still in city possession to this day.

After the war, roadside produce stands popped up across the city, reinvigorating street food culture through the 1950s and into the 1960s. Some of these postwar stands were extensions of shops and stores; many others were operated by vendors without access to storefronts. Their stands were clustered on busy pedestrian thoroughfares in the French Quarter and along Canal Street, taking advantage of passersby in these major shopping districts. These pop-up retail spaces were technically illegal. According to City Ordinance No. 4797 A.S., it was "unlawful for any person or persons to encumber or obstruct any of the streets, gutters, public roads, public grounds, public squares, public places or promenades, banquettes or sidewalks of the city by depositing in or on the same any box, bale, hogshead, barrel, or any goods, wares or merchandise, or any article whatsoever, except for the necessary time of loading and unloading same." Yet that did not stop local growers from acquiring vendor permits from the city and hawking their wares. In fact, their numbers were so great that prior to his death, Grunewald had conducted several campaigns against the daily "sidewalk squatters." However, "The drive failed to correct the evils," reported the *New Orleans States*, "because property owners permitted them to conduct such business, despite the fact it's still a violation." Further, New Orleanians patronized these street vendors' businesses. Grunewald and his team, therefore, were battling an entrenched entity that many people had little problem with, and if they did, they did not voice it to local officials.[112]

Even after the complete abandonment of the public markets, street food vendors continued to make a living along the city's thoroughfares. Their ranks included not only those vendors who set up roadside stands, but also itinerant hawkers who moved through different neighborhoods. Some of the more mobile vendors continued to carry baskets in their arms and on their heads, while others used wheelbarrows and mule-drawn carts. Still others, who could afford to do so, used trucks. Their goal—to distribute food to eke out a living—was strikingly similar to their forebears: generations of vendors who had traversed the city streets, setting up temporary stalls in public spaces, and acquiring new customers and building up an existing customer base by employing a particular set of business tactics and strategies. Their historic yet ever-relevant businesses chipped away at and ultimately outlasted the public markets.

In this way, street food vendors remained an anchor of the city's public food culture into the 1960s even as supermarkets, new food technologies, and an increasingly delocalized food system took hold in the United States. Even New Orleans' urban grocers, who had fought so fiercely for and eventually won the rights to sell fresh produce in their establishments across the city, struggled in the postwar period. Like the public markets, they lost clientele to the suburbs and could not compete with the supermarkets across the greater New Orleans area. They also faced increasingly restrictive zoning ordinances that converted previously mixed-used neighborhoods into solely residential ones, forcing greengrocers and other shopkeepers to move their businesses to newly formed commercial sectors in the city. Within these new sectors, competition among greengrocers was fierce, and many struggled to survive; as small-scale greengrocers waned, supermarkets continued to thrive.[113]

Ever adaptable and able to fill in the gaps in New Orleans' local economy left by the public markets and greengrocers, street vendors kept New Orleans' public food culture alive. They did so even as more and more shoppers turned to the novel ease of frozen meals and other prepared foods in the second half of the twentieth century. Street vendors filled a need that dated back to the very founding of the city to contribute to the nourishment of its population through personal, intimate, and quotidian interactions. Their role was particularly important for communities without easy access to a retail supermarket; they helped extend networks of exchange into neighborhoods that might otherwise have very limited options for nutrient-dense, fresh, affordable food.

Even as some New Orleanians slid a Swanson's TV dinner into the oven or heated a can of Campbell's soup on the stovetop, they could still, as generations had done before them, answer the call of the passing vendor—"Come and gettum, Lady! I got green peppers, snapbeans, tur-nips! I got oranges! I got celery! I got fine ripe yellow banana! Tur-nips, Lady! Ba-na-na, Lady!"—and buy a bunch of bananas for the household while exchanging a few tidbits of neighborhood gossip.[114] The sonorous calls of these postwar vendors were perhaps best captured in the 1958 film *King Creole*, starring Elvis Presley and set in New Orleans, which has a long opening sequence featuring the city's street vendors and their cries. As in the film, New Orleans' nourishing networks continued through the 1960s, fed by everyday yet significant relationships between vendors and customers as they bought and sold fresh and prepared food in the city streets. Yet even those seemingly strong relationships would eventually wither in the ensuing decades.

7

Reimagining Public Food Culture in Modern New Orleans

WHEN THE CITY of New Orleans said goodbye to Arthur Robinson, beloved street food vendor known as Mr. Okra, it did so in the only way that made sense to New Orleanians: through food and music. On the afternoon of Sunday, February 25, 2018, friends, family, customers, and neighbors congregated at the Marigny Opera House. Some of them carried fresh produce in their arms to contribute to the growing cornucopia of fruits and veggies lovingly arranged around his casket—a sacred ring of pineapples, broccoli, apples, and oranges. Even the floral arrangements filling the space featured the hallmarks of Robinson's trade: carrots, bananas, and lemons. "Rest in abundance," the room seemed to sing.[1]

After the viewing came to a close, community members gathered in the street behind the Kinfolk Brass Band, forming a "second line," a traditional funerary parade, especially within New Orleans' Black community.[2] Robinson's family—in solidarity sporting matching green Mr. Okra T-shirts—squeezed into his polychromatic truck. They found seats in between the kaleidoscopic mounds of fresh produce they had skillfully and artfully displayed, just as Robinson would have done. Following suit was a procession of friends and neighbors clad in produce-themed ensembles, some donning Mr. Okra aprons and others carrying Mr. Okra umbrellas. Then the second line began to roll, moving slowly at first as the brass band played a dirge, but then picking up as the musicians transitioned to upbeat New Orleans classics like "Over in the Glory Land," "Little Liza Jane," and "Iko Iko."[3]

For almost two hours, second liners walked along the oak-lined streets of the Crescent City, allowing familiar rhythms and melodies to ease the ache in their hearts. Neighbors gathered on their front stoops or in their yards along the parade route, holding up signs, and waving as the second line passed by. Still others settled in at the end of the route, B.J.'s Lounge, waiting to comfort Robinson's family and honor his memory through good food and good music—a true celebration of his life.[4]

When Robinson passed away that February, many thought he was the last of New Orleans' street food vendors.[5] But he would not be the last. On the day of her father's funeral, Sergio Robinson, who had long worked alongside her father, shared her plans to continue his business. And she did just that, driving his iconic, eye-catching truck for a few years after his death to continue catering to their long-standing customer base. By doing so, she (and a smattering of remaining street food vendors) brought fresh produce to urban neighborhoods, many of which lacked supermarkets. For some, her wares were the only fresh food they could easily access, and so she played a crucial role in providing nutrient-dense foods to community members who desired reliable access to them.[6]

Like her father, Sergio sang into the truck's megaphone, announcing her presence as she wended her way along streets lined with vibrantly painted houses: "I've got bananas. I've got eating pears. I've got strawberries, onions and tomatoes." In the months immediately following her father's death, New Orleanians were delighted to hear the familiar street cry—one they thought was lost when they lost Arthur Robinson. Rushing to greet Sergio, her customers told her they were mourning too. They also shared their joy that she was continuing the family business accompanied by many hugs and handshakes. Building on those crucial connections, she would warmly greet them and ask after their families: "Hello, love." "How are you today, baby?" "How's your momma?"[7]

Sergio also cultivated new customers, many of whom reached out to her directly. "People are still coming out and we get calls now too," she noted. "People want us to come out to the East to the West Bank. You can't really make that work for what we're selling, but it's amazing because people come to us. They'll find us on the route [and] wait for us." Determined to build a relationship with Sergio, who had then become known as Ms. Okra in New Orleans, customers were willing to sacrifice convenience for connection.[8] For Sergio's clientele, old and new alike, it was through the seemingly mundane act of purchasing food that they formed social bonds and a sense of connection with her and each other. Street food was woven into the tapestry of their daily lives. Street food mattered. More importantly, street vendors like Arthur and Sergio Robinson mattered.

Public food culture plays a critical role in the creation and growth of urban communities. That same culture plays an equally important role in sustaining cities by providing affordable, safe, culturally meaningful foods for community members. Further, a strong public food culture can bring economic stability to communities by employing local people and generating entrepreneurial opportunities for them. In this way, if a city were to abandon or lose its public food culture entirely, a crucial force would be lost—not just a means of nourishing the body, but a means of fostering community and empowerment through food. When New Orleans city council members deprioritized and eventually abandoned the public markets, they were also giving up on the idea that the government should ensure that New Orleans' residents had access to affordable, safe food. Instead, they left private enterprises to provision the city. The networks of capitalism that drove their businesses, though, were rarely nourishing for historically marginalized and disenfranchised people.

Throughout the second half of the twentieth century, city residents faced an increasingly dysfunctional urban food economy—one that did not provide equal and just food access for all New Orleanians. Although faced with the realities of an unequitable food system, community members fiercely protected local culinary traditions. They did so while also patronizing remaining supermarket chains and national fast-food restaurants with greater frequency. In this period, New Orleanians' identities were not defined by rigid demarcations between the national and the local: a New Orleanian could be someone who cooked gumbo at home one night and got McDonald's take-out the next. Yet over time, industrialized, processed, nutrient-poor foods began to crowd out historic ones. And like many Americans, regardless of race or class or socioeconomic status, New Orleanians grew to enjoy and develop a preference for convenience foods.[9]

At the same time, community members found it difficult to find fresh produce and familiar prepared foods. Supermarkets and a handful of remaining corner grocery stores were pulling out of economically disadvantaged communities in favor of building their businesses in the more lucrative suburbs. Additionally, the remaining street food vendors passed through residential neighborhoods with less and less frequency. Those that were car-less, especially the elderly, had few options to travel to the suburbs to find provisions and became increasingly underserved and isolated. As a result of public and private sector abandonment, a "food apartheid" took hold in certain New Orleans neighborhoods, closing off food access to communities, especially communities of color.[10] Some scholars and community advocates use "food apartheid" instead of "food desert," a more widely known term, to draw attention to systemic racism and structural inequalities that create food access issues for communities of color.

How pervasive are these inequities? In 2014, a study found that majority Black neighborhoods (80 percent of the population identified as Black) and racially mixed neighborhoods in New Orleans both had food access issues. In that year, 36 percent of majority Black neighborhoods and 25 percent of racially mixed neighborhoods did not have access to a single grocery store. And a quarter of majority Black neighborhoods and racially mixed neighborhoods had only one supermarket in their community, demonstrating a lack of consumer choice.[11] Sociologist Kenneth H. Kolb has identified this phenomenon as "retail inequality" where residents do not have the same ability to shop at food purveyors as everyone else. This unequal access to food not only impacts the health and nutrition of residents but exacerbates the inequalities they experience in all areas of life.[12]

Addressing retail inequality has been challenging, with many programs failing to provide communities with the support they need. In the 2010s, policymakers attempted to combat food deserts by funding grocery stores in underprivileged communities, increasing the availability of healthy food options, and teaching community members about shopping and cooking techniques that would improve their nutrition and overall health.[13] However, a study that Kolb conducted in two historically Black neighborhoods in Greenville, South Carolina, from 2014 to 2019, has shown that this approach was not effective as it did not improve community members' overall health by any significant measure. Ultimately, many experts, ranging from scholars to policy advocates, failed to recognize the underlying issues for people facing retail inequality. The Greenville residents who participated in the study were not actually asking for government support to change what they were eating. They liked what they ate and shared that the opening of a grocery store in their neighborhood would not likely change their eating habits.[14] They wanted something much bigger: improvements in every sector of their lives, including living and retail conditions.[15]

Specific to retail needs, including food procurement, the Greenville community members desired access to retailers offering a large variety of goods and services who would engage with them directly, understand their needs as consumers, and value them as customers despite their limited economic means.[16] After decades of neglect, they wanted to see retailers, city officials, and other Greenville residents invest in their neighborhoods and in them.[17] Apparently, they were craving something more akin to the nourishing networks New Orleanians had access to historically when public markets and street food vendors were abundant and central to the daily routines of city residents. That food system was not without its flaws, but one thing was clear: social bonds sat at its foundation. Within our modern context, Greenville residents saw value in fostering strong social ties between retailers and their customers, believing those nourishing networks to be key to the better quality of life they so desired.

Unfortunately, those social ties are too often strained and brittle in communities facing retail inequality in the twenty-first century. A fall 2012 and spring 2013 study of the Hollygrove neighborhood in New Orleans by Laura McKinney and Yuki Kato sheds light on the fractured nature of social bonds among its residents, 92 percent of whom were African American. At the time of their study, the working-class neighborhood had been designated as a food desert. The mean tenure of Hollygrove residents participating in the study was 37.5 years, with a majority having lived there for more than forty years; yet the researchers remarked that at the pre-study information session, only a few of them knew each other. McKinney and Kato clarified: "Even those who acknowledged 'having seen' each other had never made an interpersonal connection. Particularly striking was the revelation that some had lived just a few doors down from each other for years, but still had not exchanged basic introductions."[18]

What if Hollygrove community members had access to a public food market, mom-and-pop grocers, and street food vendors, as New Orleanians had in the nineteenth and early twentieth centuries? Perhaps they would have more opportunities to interact with one another and build social ties not only between customer and vendor, but among fellow customers who are also their neighbors. In the past, the nearest public markets to Hollygrove were the two along the Carrollton Avenue corridor on which the neighborhood abuts. The Carrollton Market was about two miles away from Hollygrove and the Suburban Market was about a mile and a half away from Hollygrove. Both markets were accessible via the streetcar line and motor bus on Carrollton in the 1920s.[19] In 1937, there were at least ten grocery stores and other food stores in the Hollygrove neighborhood—an abundance of retail options.[20] Not to mention the itinerant street vendors who increased access to fresh and prepared food. Had these small-scale retailers and public markets remained operational and lucrative with the support of public and private partnerships, maybe Hollygrove residents' social networks would have strengthened over time instead of weaking and disappearing almost entirely among some members of the community.

Fostering social ties among community members is, to be sure, not a cure-all for systemic inequities. The realities of retail inequality are too complex for such a simple solution. But cultivating stronger ties among retailers and their customers, and between neighbors as well, might be a step in the right direction to improving the overall health and well-being of those battling retail inequality.

New Orleanians have recognized the power of encouraging community through food and have sought to create environments where social bonds can form. Since the collapse of New Orleans' public market system in the mid-twentieth century, some city residents have created alternative food-provisioning models that have a focus on nurturing social ties. These new permutations of New Orleans' public food culture include the adoption of farmers' markets in the mid-1990s, food trucks in the late-2000s, and fine food halls in the 2010s. Their emergence signals a return and reimagining of historic public food culture to fit modern New Orleanians' needs and desires to reconnect with local businesspeople and community members.

Despite this reimagining, however, food justice has not yet been achieved. Community members still go hungry and without job opportunities. Many have limited retail options. The city's modern public food culture is not yet large and broad enough to combat the negative effects of industrialization and globalization on our food systems. These effects are compounded by systemic poverty in Louisiana, much of which is inextricably bound with race. In southern Louisiana, one in seven people and one in four children struggled with hunger in 2023, a situation tied to New Orleans' consistent rankings as having one of the highest metropolitan poverty rates in the country.[21] Looking to the past for lessons learned and a path forward for building a more robust and sustainable local food economy is paramount to addressing retail inequality in the present moment.

Although there was a surge in street vending in postwar New Orleans, after the 1960s the number of vendors working in the city street dwindled. Very few street food vendors remain. Even so, the memory of them is strong. New Orleanians who grew up in the postwar period can easily recall the street vendors of their youth and can, on request, sing the cries of the Clothes Pole Man, Buglin' Sam, the Waffle Man, and the Rag Man.[22] The hallmarks of their trade—their street cries—currently live on in New Orleanians' memories.

Although few in number, some remaining vendors have embraced the traditional nature of their trade and have woven it into their business strategies. They are skillfully playing off their historic ties to the past to amplify their appeal to nostalgic customers who are looking for an alternative to globalized commercial food cultures. Ron Kottemann is one such vendor who has stewarded his family's Roman Candy (taffy) business through these strategies. The candy is special to customers like Brett Rettman who grew up snacking on it. Now, as an adult, eating the candy, like Proust's madeleine, transports him back to his early childhood when he used to enjoy the treat with his mother.[23] The Kottemann family operates two Roman Candy wagons, one that moves throughout the city and one that since 1985 has been permanently stationed at the Audubon Zoo, where a steady stream of families buys their candies.[24]

Kottemann celebrated the centennial of his family's business by making taffy at the 2015 New Orleans Jazz and Heritage Festival; he was sixty-five years old at the time. At Jazz Fest, you could spot him and his son Daniel, then thirty-three, in the hundred-year-old white wagon making and selling candy. The family candy recipe had not changed in those one hundred years and was first imagined and created by his Sicilian great-grandmother, Angelina Napoli Cortese, for celebrations at home.[25]

The business they continue to operate certainly has deep traditions, but it is by no means static. The family has adapted its business practices to fit the modern moment and the changing needs and desires of their clientele. They now sell their products on their website and are doing "a prodigious online business," discovering that their candy is popular for weddings, baby showers, and other large-group gatherings that want to highlight New Orleans' culture.[26] Gabrielle Jones, a loyal customer, found online ordering particularly convenient when Covid-19 precautions prevented her from heading to the zoo location for what she sees as "the best candy ever."[27]

The Kottemanns not only sell their family's historic candies online but continue to build and share their brand by selling merchandise too. Such trinkets include a Roman Candy cross-stitch wagon magnet for eight dollars, a Roman Candy onesie for babies for twenty-five dollars, and a $120 model of the original mule-drawn Roman Candy wagon. Each of these items prominently displays images or figures of the mule-drawn cart, tying the business to its early nineteenth-century history and lasting connection to the public culture of food in New Orleans.[28] The target audience? The nostalgic New Orleanian, and also tourists who may have caught a glimpse of the historic white wagon ambling down the city streets on the Travel Channel or Food Network. Like generations of tourists before them, they want to bring a piece of New Orleans' "authentic" street food culture home with them.

In this way, some modern street vendors, like their antecedents, continue to shape Americans' perception of New Orleans as a place rooted in nineteenth-century culture and somewhat resistant to the sweeping changes brought about by industrialization and globalization in the twentieth century. The reality, contrary to what the mule-drawn cart might signal, is quite different, as indicated by the changes the Kottemanns have made over time. Their flexibility and willingness to experiment with new business models has enabled their business to survive, but their path has not been without its challenges or their success possible without the support from other community members.

Part of the family's lasting business success, according to Ron Kottemann, was the food truck boom of the 2010s. That boom "helped traditional street operators" because it "created solidarity for what was once a dying form of food vending," Kottemann observed.[29] Like other cities across the United States, after the 2008 financial crises New Orleans saw an uptick in food trucks, especially gourmet food trucks, as it became difficult to secure capital for brick-and-mortar restaurant locations; the food truck was a more affordable option than a traditional restaurant. For many entrepreneurs, opening a food truck became a way to keep a food career alive or start one from scratch despite the recession.

Kottemann pointed out that with the increase in food trucks there were more mobile food vendors in the streets. "And in numbers you have a bit of protection," he noted, from what he saw as the city's heavy-handed regulation of street food.[30] Those city regulations limited where and when mobile vendors could operate their businesses and prioritized the protection of brick-and-mortar competitors like restaurants. Mobile vendors, for example, could not operate within six hundred feet of any brick-and-mortar restaurant—a radius law that echoed those that had protected the public markets for generations. As in the city's past, it was street food vendors—with limited access to private property (i.e., a storefront)—who found themselves deprioritized and struggling to make a living in public spaces.

Throughout New Orleans' history, community members who had the ear of local officials were better able to get their needs met. Unlike street food vendors in the nineteenth and early twentieth century, twenty-first-century gourmet food truck owners tended to have access to more capital and political networks; they therefore exercised more influence over New Orleans' local law. The food truck vendors took their case to the city council and argued for greater support for their businesses, which they noted were struggling under the regulations of the day.

Amenable to their case, city council President Stacy Head introduced an ordinance in January 2013 that would increase the number of food truck permits in the city. Additionally, it would allow food truck operators to park within fifty feet of any restaurant and also park closer to the Central Business District (CBD), but not within its limits.[31] The food truck operators' ability to gain the attention of the city council marked a distinct shift in the legal influence of street vendors whose voices and opinions had so often been omitted from the archival record in the past.

With the proposal to shrink the radius to fifty feet, restaurant owners voiced their concerns about losing business. Restaurateur Robert Laws, for example, wrote a petition outlining his grievances with the proposed law, which 280 people signed. Excerpts from it read:

> Restaurant owners in the CBD are about to have their sales invaded on by the food truck industry should new legislation get passed in February.... Restaurateurs have made great investments in their product and have worked hard to build a following of customers in their area. To think that a food truck can soon park 50 feet from our doors and sell food during peak hours of business for 4 hours is truly concerning!!!!! This legislation should be stopped immediately!!!!!!!"[32]

Countering Laws' petition, the New Orleans Food Truck Coalition, a group of food truck operators, released its own petition, which five hundred people signed. Their petition noted that there "is no doubt that thriving food truck cultures coexist with vibrant restaurant scenes [across the country], and New Orleans is no different." Naming themselves as part of the restaurant culture of New Orleans, the food truck operators noted that "there are over 1,300 restaurants in New Orleans today—an increase of over 50% since Hurricane Katrina—yet business is better than ever. Consumers are attracted by competition and choice."[33] In other words, supporting their businesses through modifying and updating local laws would benefit the community on the whole. Their arguments reflect those made by private grocers and shoppers in the first half of the twentieth century when they pleaded with the city government to lift the public markets' monopoly over local provisioning.

Debates between the two factions and their local representatives peppered the city's newspaper through the spring of 2013, and the city council and Mayor Mitch Landrieu also butted heads over the proposed radius or "buffer zone" that would protect the city's restaurants. Landrieu did not want a buffer to exist at all; and he got his way in July 2013 when a revised ordinance came in front of the city council and passed, allowing mobile food vendors to operate anywhere as long as they did not impede "the ingress or egress of any operating building or structure during its operating hours." In addition, the ordinance enabled the city to give out one hundred permits specifically to food trucks in addition to the one hundred permits that could be given out to all types of mobile food sellers. The modified mobile food vendor law not only impacted the livelihoods of street food truck owners, but also people like Kottemann and produce truck operators like Arthur and Sergio Robinson.[34]

By 2021, Sergio Robinson was no longer operating her family's produce truck business. She did not publicly share why she made that decision. Community members have had to turn elsewhere to access fresh food and build important bonds with food vendors. Although the discontinuation of Robinson's family business marked for many the end of a street-peddling era in New Orleans, around the same time, new iterations and forms of historic public food culture began to emerge. Their advent demonstrates community members' continued need and desire for a robust public culture of food. And in a surprising twist of fate, iterations and reimaginings of the city's public markets began to re-emerge in the 2010s.

In the decades following the city's dispossession of the public markets, some of the buildings were converted into privately owned grocery stores and supermarkets. A few of them still operate, including the Circle Food Store and the Algiers Central Market, which occupy the old St. Bernard Market in the Seventh Ward and Foto Market in Algiers, respectively. Many of New Orleans' historic market buildings were, however, renovated and repurposed as commercial, educational, and residential spaces. The Jefferson Market on Magazine Street now operates as the gymnasium for St. George's Episcopal School. The squeak of tennis shoes on varnished floors creates a soundscape very different from the vendor calls that used to echo in the cavernous ceiling of this historic market building. The exterior of the building, however, still prominently features the historic market's name above the main doors.

Even the French Market underwent changes, at one point completely abandoning the sale of fresh foods. In 1975, the French Market Corporation, which managed the historic market, decided to modernize the retail space, which had not been refurbished since the 1930s. The corporation's understanding of a "modern" market was quite different from that of local officials in the 1930s. Instead of trying to create a space to provision community members with fresh, affordable, safe food using the latest technologies, the corporation took a different approach. It sought to convert the historic market structure into a venue for boutique shops selling knickknacks—like bejeweled Mardi Gras masks and prepackaged praline candies—and restaurants offering such iconic Creole dishes as red beans and rice, gumbo, and po'boys. The corporation did so by partitioning off and enclosing historic vendor stalls into distinct retail spaces.

By converting the covered stalls into walled shops, the corporation continued the enclosure process of the 1910s to 1930s in which city officials sought to close off the public markets from what they saw as the more chaotic and less controllable city streets. During the 1970s renovations, the corporation was not only creating a physical barrier between the market and public thoroughfares, but between one retailer and the next. In doing so, it created more fissures in the city's public food culture. Over time, those renovations led to the proliferation of specialty shops and the complete erasure of fresh food purveyors. As radio producer Nina Feldman observed in 2014, the French Market had not sold fresh produce since 2005; as a result, "For the past 10 years, the French Market has felt more like a mall than a market, specializing in souvenirs and specialty items for tourists."[35]

Restaurateur Dickie Brennan also witnessed that change in New Orleans' local food economy over the course of his lifetime. In adulthood, he noted that the French Market he had known in his youth had disappeared and the supermarkets that rose to prominence sold processed foods and produce not from Louisiana growers or in season locally, but from California and places beyond—changes that took hold in the 1940s and 1950s and quickly expanded from there. That transformation certainly offered shoppers convenience, but, in the process, meaningful connections to people and the land were largely lost in his estimation.[36]

Over the course of Brennan's adult life, the tides have turned once again. New Orleanians are now seeking a stronger connection to locally sourced goods produced and sold by community members. Brennan has contributed to and has been shaped by the change; he is committing to using locally sourced seafood for his restaurants, for example, and supporting Louisiana-based vendors.[37]

It was not just in the restaurants that these changes took hold. As Brennan noted, in the 1990s, New Orleanians were clamoring for a retail space that sold fresh, local food. The Crescent City Farmer' Market (CCFM) was founded to meet those needs. The CCFM was established in 1995 as part of the Twomey Center for Peace Through Justice at Loyola University New Orleans and operated under the historic premise that public markets are for the public good. The CCFM is currently part of a larger nonprofit, Market Umbrella, of which the CCFM is the public face. According to its website, the CCFM has played an important role in repairing and fostering sound economic development and community relations: "By providing a public market where consumers and producers come together over food—a powerful cultural common denominator in the New Orleans region—the Crescent City Farmers Market promotes good health among citizens, greater social interaction between communities and sustainable economic development."[38]

From its first day in October 1995, the market drew large crowds eager to patronize local purveyors, so much so that all vendors had sold out of their stock within thirty minutes of the market's opening.[39] That first market was located in a parking lot in the Warehouse District just upriver from the French Quarter.[40] Whereas decades prior, in 1954, the historic Prytania Market building had been bulldozed to create a parking lot, in the mid-1990s, once a week, the CCFM transformed a parking lot back into a community market.[41] Residents' enthusiasm for the CCFM grew over time, and the market was expanded to operate several times a week in different parts of the city, building and increasing access to fresh food. Several years later, an opportunity arose for the CCFM to operate a market in the French Market.

In 2014, under the supervision of executive director John Smith, the French Market Corporation partnered with the CCFM to, once again, become a space for community members to purchase fresh food from local farmers and purveyors. Starting in the fall, the CCFM hosted a fresh food market there on Wednesday evenings. Prior to opening the new market, the CCFM conducted market research revealing that locals "wanted produce first and foremost" and that tourists wanted "grab and go [food] items."[42] Catering to the needs of French Quarter residents, vendors sold local produce from farms like Tommott's Cajun Farm and Perrilloux Farms, while other vendors offered premade foodstuffs to satiate hungry tourists. Later that year, the French Market gained a gourmet food stall, Continental Provisions, which featured cheeses from the St. James Cheese Co., meats from Cleaver & Co., and breads from Bellegarde Bakery—all local institutions.

To increase community members' access to food sold at all locations of the CCFM, Market Umbrella offers the Market Match program. Through this initiative, people enrolled in the Supplemental Nutrition Assistance Program (SNAP)—the federal program also known as food stamps—can use their Electronic Benefit Transfer card (EBT) to purchase wooden tokens at the market's welcome tent. They can then spend those tokens at the market. Speaking to the importance of shoppers interacting with local purveyors, the CCFM explained that by participating in Market Match, "Participants can enjoy the magic of farmers markets by actively purchasing local foods directly from farmers and fishers." What the CCFM identified as the "magic" of the farmers' market is precisely the nourishing networks that bring community members together to build crucial social bonds through the exchange of food.[43]

In addition to the CCFM at the French Market, other historic public market structures in the city have also seen a revival and return to fresh foods more recently. The St. Roch Market structure, the only neighborhood market building that the city held onto after it sold all the others, reopened its doors as a fine food hall in the spring of 2015. Fine food halls, broadly defined, are businesses that host numerous tenants operating independent food businesses within a single structure; these enterprises range from restaurants and coffee bars to butcher stalls and bakeries. Fine food halls do not tend to host fast-food chains, but rather focus on local, artisanal, and boutique businesses to foster those critical connections between community members. New Orleans is one of numerous cities across the country that have adopted the fine food hall business model in the twenty-first century.

The year St. Roch opened as a gourmet food hall, the company's website paid homage to the market's historic importance, stating that it was a "main-stay of the turn-of-the-century creole neighborhood carrying the same name."[44] Patrons of the St. Roch Market could purchase locally inspired foods from thirteen different vendors, including Elysian Seafood, Shank Charcuterie, and Koreole. More than half of the businesses were women- or minority owned. For some neighboring residents, the restored market was a symbol of New Orleans' economic revival and cultural resilience after the devastating impacts of Hurricane Katrina in 2005. For others, St. Roch was a harbinger of gentrification, and not the kind of business of which the Bywater neighborhood was in desperate need: a store that sold affordable, safe, and cultural meaningful foods.[45]

After a year of operation, some community members' concerns remained in place. St. Roch vendors held a community meeting to learn what locals needed and wanted from the fine food hall. Taking seriously their community members' needs, vendors adjusted their retailing practices to offer goods like rice, beans, and pasta at prices that matched grocery stores in the area; they also rearranged how they placed products around the hall, making it easier for customers to find staples like fresh produce, seafood, and shelf-stable items. And although St. Roch had intended to open with the ability to accept SNAP, federal requirements outlining what businesses could participate did not accommodate the fine food hall model. That model—echoing how the historic St. Roch Market had operated—featured a collection of independent vendors operating within a larger business framework.[46] Both St. Roch Market and the US Department of Agriculture had to make adjustments to accommodate this food provisioning model in the twenty-first century.

By 2023, the Bywater neighborhood had gentrified and had become a well-established tourist destination. The St. Roch Market, in response, broadcast a slightly different message on its website, stating that it was a "destination for the culinary curious," while linking to several feature articles that appeared in *Food & Wine*, *Travel + Leisure*, *Architectural Digest*, and the *New*

York Times, among others. Playing off its historic roots, the website prominently displayed quotations from various publications. One from *Southern Living* stated, "St. Roch generates the nostalgia of bygone time and place suddenly not so far away"; another, from the Zagat guide, exclaimed, "An Absolute must visit." St. Roch consisted of several restaurants, a coffee shop, and a bar in 2023. As food businesses in the city had done for generations, the vendors at St. Roch played on tourists' desires to engage with New Orleans' past through food. They did so to bring attention and awareness to their businesses, whose vendors, eight in total, still included Jennifer Sherrod and Brandon Blackwell of Elysian Seafood and many additional faces, some of whom were chefs who had emigrated from other countries.[47] After 2023, St. Roch Market said goodbye to more of its founding businesses and welcomed several others—changes that reflect the constantly shifting nature of New Orleans' food culture and economy.

Today, as with generations past, recent immigrants' food businesses are providing them with an economic toehold. Than Lin Regules offers Malaysian and Burmese cuisine at her stall, Laksa NOLA, which she opened in St. Roch Market after a year of hosting pop-ups around the city.[48] Not unlike street food vendors in the past who eventually built a strong following and accessed enough capital to lease their own stand in one of the public markets or open their own storefront, Regules built her reputation through pop-up collaborations with NOLA Distillery and the Drifter Hotel. Then she launched Laska NOLA. Now St. Roch Market serves as an incubator space for her new restaurant concept, providing her with an opportunity to continue to grow her business, and perhaps open her own brick-and-mortar location.

Some vendors have already demonstrated how the St. Roch Market concept can help launch their own brick-and-mortar businesses, as was the case for Charly Pierre and Minerva Chereches. In the spring of 2021, the co-owners were operating Fritai as a stand at the St. Roch Market. There, they sold "Haitian street food for the soul" that captivated locals and tourists alike.[49] When observed through a historical lens, Pierre and Chereches combined street food culture and public market culture—whose vendors were so often in competition and at odds with one another—together at St. Roch. What would have been incongruent in 1830 or 1930 was a combination that appealed to the sensibilities of twenty-first-century culinary enthusiasts who not only wanted to enjoy delicious street food but also wanted to support companies that, in turn, supported local communities. As an *Eater* profile said of Fritai, "The duo only hires locals, especially those 'who really need help and especially those without a chance.'"[50] Their pledge to provide job opportunities for their neighbors appealed to consumer-conscious patrons who were aware that New Orleans is a city that depends heavily on the service industry for employment.

Having found success at St. Roch, Pierre and Chereches left the incubator to launch Fritai as a stand-alone restaurant on Basin Street in the Tremé. There, they continued to draw the attention of the food world. *NOLA Eater* named Fritai Restaurant of the Year in 2021 and the James Beard Foundation named it a semifinalist for Best New Restaurant in 2022.[51] In 2023, Pierre recalled, "Fritai has been a crazy experience. We started out at a little food hall" and had become and award-winning restaurant, which journalist Nylah Burton described as "bursting with flavor, community, and innovation."[52]

Whereas St. Roch has been rebranded as a fine food hall, the Dryades Market has been renovated and reopened as a cultural center dedicated to preserving and sharing the history of New Orleans and the South, more broadly. Originally opened in 1849, the Dryades Market became the home of the Southern Food & Beverage Museum (SoFAB) in 2014, after the organization renovated the market's upper building with historic preservation principles in mind. When visiting SoFAB, looking at the interior floor, you can still see imprints of where the stall dividers were once located—a physical marker of the building's historic past. And that past is ever-present in the museum, which seeks to honor the building's history as a public market. Elizabeth Williams, the founder of SoFAB, highlights how the structure is tied to the museum's mission to discover, understand, and celebrate "food, drink and its related culture and folklife in America and the world."[53]

The main hall of SoFAB, which was once the home of many butchers, now houses the Leah Chase Gallery, an exhibit space dedicated to the foodways of the American South, and for several years included an exhibit about the history of the Dryades Market.[54] Installed in a glass-walled corner of the renovated building from 2015 to 2017, the exhibit enabled visitors to read about the historic structure while also seeing its sister structure across the street.[55] On the other side of the museum, in what was once the seafood section of the Dryades Market, now stands the Rouses Culinary Innovation Center. Museum visitors can sign up to take cooking classes in this space, once again bringing food and community back into the historic market structure. Through public programming and exhibit installations, SoFAB endeavors to reintroduce the New Orleans community to its rich public market history and the role those spaces played in the creation of the city's cuisine.[56] In this way, the Dryades Market is once again a community center that fosters a sense of shared history among New Orleanians.

Despite the industrialization and globalization of the city's food culture over the course of the twentieth and twenty-first centuries, there remains a need for a hyper-local, community-driven public food culture. More and more people are interested in supporting locally owned businesses that in turn support local producers and distributors. Those same customers enjoy celebrating and honoring local traditions through the purchase and consumption of regional foods all the while knowing that their purchases are supporting the city's economy, which provides jobs to people in their community. At the moment, this modern public food culture is not overtaking and replacing industrialized and globalized food cultures, but rather coexists alongside those more expansive, delocalized systems. At first glance, the two systems appear to satiate some shoppers' dual desires for convenience, yes, but also a strong sense of community and place. A closer look, however, shows that there is still much work to be done to create a food system that simultaneously fosters community and honors local traditions, enables consumer choice, and offers convenience for all community members.

A robust local food system engineered to create jobs and provide affordable, fresh, and locally sourced foods may hold the key to repairing our food system, but only if we take lessons from the history of the public culture of food, both its triumphs and failures. What are those lessons? For one, retail equality, including access to diverse food purveyors, is crucial for the health and well-being of communities. Second, local governments can play an instrumental role in building, maintaining, operating, and regulating food distribution centers, like public markets and farmers' markets, that support local entrepreneurs and their customers. Third, the local governments themselves must be monitored to ensure that community members have access to both sell and purchase wares in those spaces. And finally, local governments must give local leaders and community members the space and time to build crucial relationships with one another through the exchange of food. These are some, but certainly not all, of the pillars of nourishing networks that community leaders have and continue to fight for not only in New Orleans but across the country, as we strive for a more just food future.

Notes

ABBREVIATIONS

BPC II-23   Building Plans Collection, Number II-23, City Archives & Special Collections, New Orleans Public Library, New Orleans, LA

DPM   Department of Public Markets Miscellaneous Files ca. 1923–1949, City Archives & Special Collections, New Orleans Public Library, New Orleans, LA

HNOC   Williams Research Center, The Historic New Orleans Collection, New Orleans, LA

LaRC   Louisiana Research Collection, Howard-Tilton Memorial Library, Tulane University, New Orleans, LA

LOC   Library of Congress, Washington, DC

MCR   Market Committee Records, 1913–1916, Louisiana Research Collection, Howard-Tilton Memorial Library, Tulane University, New Orleans, LA

NOPL   City Archives & Special Collections, New Orleans Public Library, New Orleans, LA

SEEA   Southeastern Architectural Archive, Tulane University, New Orleans, LA

SNP   Born in Slavery: Slave Narratives from the Federal Writers' Project, 1936 to 1938, Library of Congress, Washington, DC

INTRODUCTION

1. Elizabeth Mullener, "The Fruit Peddler: Arthur 'Mr. Okra' Robinson of New Orleans," *Times-Picayune*, August 28, 2005; Chris Bynum, "Even Fruit Vendor Has a Song at Jazz Fest," *Times-Picayune*, April 25, 2009; Mike Scott, "More 'Okra,' Please,—A Documentary About the Iconic Local Produce Vendor Will Add Some New Orleans Flavor to the Sundance Film Festival," *Times-Picayune*, January 19, 2013.

2. Mark Guarino, "He Has mangos," *New Orleans Advocate*, April 28, 2015; Scott, "More 'Okra,' Please."

3. Mullener, "The Fruit Peddler."

4. Mullener, "The Fruit Peddler"; Alison Festerstock, "I Have Music for Mr. Okra!— Iconic Produce Peddler Arthur Robinson's Truck Died. A Group of Local Musicians Hope to Sing Him a New Set of Wheels," *Times-Picayune*, May 19, 2010.

5. As quoted in Campbell Robertson, "Arthur J. Robinson, Known as 'Mr. Okra' to New Orleans, Dies at 74," *New York Times*, February 19, 2018.

6. Mullener, "The Fruit Peddler."

7. Ian McNulty, "Mr. Okra, New Orleans' Iconic Singing Produce Vendor, Dies Thursday Evening," *New Orleans Advocate*, February 15, 2018.

8. Mullener, "The Fruit Peddler."

9. Bynum, "Even Fruit Vendor."

10. Judy Walker, "Mr. Okra Is at New Orleans Jazz Fest," *Nola.com*, May 6, 2011.

11. Judy Walker, "Mr. Okra's Is the Latest Voice 'In Your Pocket,'" *Times-Picayune*, May 20, 2013.

12. Lashon Daley, *Mr. Okra Sells Fresh Fruits and Vegetables* (Gretna, LA: Pelican Publishing Company, 2015); "Native Produces NYC Award-Winning Film," *Franklin Banner-Tribune*, July 30, 2009; Scott, "More 'Okra,' Please"; Festerstock, "I Have Music."

13. This following anecdote is drawn from my personal experiences during 2014 Mardi Gras season, when I witnessed community members and tourists, alike, interacting with fellow Mardi Gras revelers, including those dressed as "Mr. Okra" and produce.

14. Scott, "More 'Okra,' Please."

15. Ann Maloney, "Arthur 'Mr. Okra' Robinson, Who Died Thursday, Remembered," *Times-Picayune*, February 16, 2018.

16. *New Orleans Food Memories*, produced/narrated by Peggy Scott Laborde (2009; New Orleans: WYES, 2025), streamed documentary.

17. "Jazz & Razz," *Times-Picayune*, May 20, 2010.

18. Mark Guarino, "Mr. Okra Is Still the Freshest Thing Going at Fest," *New Orleans Advocate*, April 26, 2015.

19. Doug MacCash, "Mr. Okra Among Southern Living Magazine's Southerners of the Year 2017," *Times-Picayune*, November 17, 2017.

20. Robertson, "Arthur J. Robinson."

21. Ann Maloney, "Why 'Mr. Okra's' Death Matters: The End of an Era in New Orleans," *Nola.com*, February 17, 2018.

22. Spiro Kostof, *The City Assembled: The Elements of Urban Form Through History* (London: Thames and Hudson, 1992), 123.

CHAPTER 1

1. The details of this vignette and Catherine's story are drawn from "$100 Reward," *Daily Picayune*, January 4, 1844.

2. For detailed explorations of Louisiana's population of free people of color, see Arnold R. Hirsch and Joseph Logsdon, eds., *Creole New Orleans: Race and Americanization* (Baton Rouge: Louisiana State University Press, 1992); Sybil Kein, ed., *Creole: The History and Legacy of Louisiana's Free People of Color* (Baton Rouge: Louisiana University Press, 2000); Judith Kelleher Schafer, *Becoming Free, Remaining Free: Manumission and Enslavement in New Orleans, 1846–1862* (Baton Rouge: Louisiana State University Press, 2003).

3. For an in-depth study of enslaved people working to purchase their freedom, see Schafer, *Becoming Free*, 45–58.

4. "$100 Reward," *Daily Picayune*, April 11, 1844.

5. For works further exploring the connections made between African American people on rivers and along waterways, see Thomas C. Buchanan, *Black Life on the Mississippi: Slave, Free Blacks, and the Western Steamboat World* (Chapel Hill: University of North Carolina Press, 2004); Alisha Hines, "Geographies of Freedom: Black Women's Mobility and the Making of the Western River World, 1814–1865" (PhD diss., Duke University, 2018).

6. "Levee Scenes," *Daily Picayune*, November 18, 1856.

7. In 1803, Napoleon Bonaparte sold the territory of Louisiana to the United States. In December of that year, New Orleans' first city council replaced the Spanish Cabildo, the major governing body of the city during Spanish rule (1769–1803). In 1805, under a new city charter, the Conseil de Ville was created and replaced the interim government established in 1803. The US territory of Orleans, in which New Orleans was located, became the state of Louisiana in April 1812.

8. For a more detailed exploration of colonial public food culture in New Orleans and Louisiana, more broadly, see Ashley Rose Young, "Nourishing Networks: The Public Culture of Food in Nineteenth-Century America" (PhD diss., Duke University, 2017), 20–75; Daniel H. Usner, Jr., *Indians, Settlers, & Slaves in a Frontier Exchange Economy: The Lower Mississippi Valley Before 1783* (Chapel Hill: University of North Carolina Press, 1992); Shannon Lee Dawdy, "'A Wild Taste': Food and Colonialism in Eighteenth-Century Louisiana," *Ethnohistory* 57, no. 3 (2010): 389–414.

9. Usner, *Indians, Settlers, & Slaves*, 199.

10. Pierre Le Moyne d'Iberville, *Iberville's Gulf Journals*, ed. Richebourg Gaillard McWilliams (Tuscaloosa: University of Alabama Press, 1980), 70.

11. Lawrence N. Powell, *The Accidental City: Improvising New Orleans* (Cambridge, MA: Harvard University Press, 2012), 95, 113; Usner, *Indians, Settlers, & Slaves*, 161–67, 214–17, 286; Ira Berlin, *Many Thousands Gone: The First Two Centuries of Slavery in North America* (Cambridge, MA: Belknap Press of Harvard University Press, 1998), 200–202.

12. Marie-Madeleine Hachard, *Relation du Voyage des Dames Religieuses Ursulines de Rouen a La Nouvelle-Orléans*, ed. Gabriel Gravier (Paris: Maisonneuve, 1872), 30.

13. Food, Fuel and General Supplies, Book 1, 41, 10/5/1770, Alphabetical and Chronological Digest of the Acts and Deliberations of the Cabildo, 1769–1803 (hereafter cited as Digest of the Cabildo, 1769–1803), City Archives & Special Collections, New Orleans Public Library, New Orleans, LA (hereafter cited as NOPL), accessed November 3, 2014, http://nutrias.org/~nopl/inv/digest/digest32.htm.

14. Spanish colonial administrations were known to have built environments and created legal structures that enabled surveillance of and control over colonial subjects. For more on this subject, see Rob Man, "Plazas and Power: Canary Islanders at Galveztown, an Eighteenth-Century Spanish Colonial Outpost in Louisiana," *Historical Archaeology* 46, no. 1 (2012): 49–61.

15. For studies of moral economy in and outside of the United States and also within public markets, see E. P. Thompson, "The Moral Economy of the English Crowd in the Eighteenth Century," *Past & Present*, no. 50 (February 1971): 76–136; E. P. Thompson, *Customs in Common* (New York: New Press, 1991), 336–51; William J. Novak, *The People's Welfare: Law and Regulation in Nineteenth-Century America* (Chapel Hill: University of North Carolina Press, 1996); William J. Novak, "Public Economy and the Well-Ordered Market: Law and Economic Regulation in Nineteenth-Century America," *Law and Social Inquiry* 18 (Winter 1993): 1–32.

16. Food, Fuel and General Supplies, Book 1, 41, 10/5/1770, Digest of the Cabildo, 1769–1803, NOPL.

17. Food, Fuel and General Supplies, Book 1, 51, 1/11/1771, Digest of the Cabildo, 1769–1803, NOPL, accessed November 3, 2014, http://nutrias.org/~nopl/inv/digest/digest32.htm.

18. Weights and Measures, Book 1, 110, 12/4/1772; Weights and Measures, Book 1, 121, 3/5/1773; Digest of the Cabildo, 1769–1803, NOPL, accessed November 3, 2014, http://nutrias.org/~nopl/inv/digest/digest74.htm.

19. Food, Fuel and General Supplies, Book 1, 41, 10/5/1770, Digest of the Cabildo, 1769–1803, NOPL.

20. Markets, Book 1, 39, 9/14/1770; Markets, Book 2, 139, 9/13/1782, Digest of the Cabildo, 1769–1803, NOPL, accessed November 3, 2014, http://nutrias.org/~nopl/inv/digest/digest51.htm; Beth A. Jacob, "New Orleans' Historic Public Markets: Reviving Neighborhood Landmarks Through Adaptive Reuse" (master's thesis, Tulane University, 2012), 53; Richard Campanella, *Bienville's Dilemma: A Historical Geography of New Orleans* (Lafayette: Center for Louisiana Studies, University of Louisiana at Lafayette, 2008), 243.

21. In September 1770, a group of four butchers approached the Cabildo to create a contract, which, according to the Digest of the Acts and Deliberations of the Cabildo, the commissioners approved. Later, the Digest refers to "the public meat market, established by O'Reilly in favor of the City Treasury," confirming the idea that the Cabildo and governor approved the proposed contract of the butchers and

created a public meat market. Markets, Book 1, 39, 9/14/1770; Markets, Book 1, 68, 8/2/1771, Digest of the Cabildo, 1769–1803, NOPL.

22. Records and Deliberations of the Cabildo, 1769–1803, vol. 1, May 21, 1779, 317–18, microfilm Set 690 as cited in Robert A. Sauder, "The Origin and Spread of the Public Market System in New Orleans," *Journal of Louisiana History* 22, no. 3 (Summer 1981): 282.

23. Records and Deliberations of the Cabildo, 1769–1803, vol. 3, September 10, 1784, 18, microfilm Set 690 as cited in Sauder, "The Origin and Spread," 282.

24. Campanella, *Bienville's Dilemma*, 24.

25. Markets, Book 4, vol. 2, 174, 10/13/1798; Markets, Book 4, vol. 2, 180, 11/23/1798; Markets, Book 4, vol. 2, 191, 12/15/1798; Markets, Book 4, vol. 3, 38, 6/14/1799; Markets, Book 4, vol. 3, 71, 9/20/1799; Markets, Book 4, vol. 3, 112, 11/29/1799; Markets, Book 4, vol. 3, 143, 2/21/1800, Digest of the Cabildo, 1769–1803, NOPL, accessed November 3, 2014, http://nutrias.org/~nopl/inv/digest/digest51.htm.

26. Cindy R. Lobel, *Urban Appetites: Food & Culture in Nineteenth-Century New York* (Chicago: University of Chicago Press, 2014), 18.

27. Donatien Augustin, *A General Digest of the Ordinances and Resolutions of the Corporation of New-Orleans* (New Orleans: J. Bayon, 1831), 189.

28. Augustin, *A General Digest*, 119–23. Note: According to the Digest, the ordinance was approved on December 10, 1834.

29. For a Manhattan-based case study of market vendor stall placements, see Gergely Baics, *Feeding Gotham: The Political Economy and Geography of Food in New York, 1790–1860* (Princeton, NJ: Princeton University Press, 2016), 138.

30. "ROBT. HAMET BREEDIN," *Daily Picayune*, March 1, 1837; "BRANDRETH'S VEGETABLE UNIVERSAL PILLS," *Daily Picayune*, September 20, 1838.

31. Anne Newport Royall, *Mrs. Royall's Southern Tour*, vol. 3 (Washington, DC, 1831), 18–19.

32. Interview with M. S. Fayman, around 1936–38, vol. 8, Maryland, Brooks-Williams, Born in Slavery: Slave Narratives from the Federal Writers' Project, 1936 to 1938 (hereafter cited as SNP), Library of Congress, Washington, DC (hereafter cited as LOC), accessed March 15, 2023, https://www.loc.gov/item/mesn080/. Note: The interviews collected and transcribed by Federal Writers' Project employees, a majority of whom were white, are inherently problematic sources that skew the memories and perspectives of Black interviewees. Most of the interviews date between 1937 and 1939. Within the Federal Writers' Project, there were state-based projects, and state units had a fair bit of autonomy in what they documented, although the Central Office sent example interview questions to all interviewers. For additional discussion of the WPA slave narratives as a source, see Jerrold Hirsch, "Toward a Marriage of True Minds: The Federal Writers' Project and the Writing of Southern History," in *The Adaptable South: Essays in Honor of George Brown Tindall*, ed. Elizabeth Jacoway et al. (Baton Rouge: Louisiana State University Press, 1991), 148–75.

33. Arthur Singleton, *Letters from the South and West* (Boston: Richardson and Lord, 1824), 124.

34. Singleton, *Letters from the* South, 123.

35. Basil Hall, *Travels in North America in the Years 1827 and 1828*, vol. 3, 2nd ed. (Edinburgh: Cadell and Co.; London: Simpkin and Marshall, 1830), 330–32.

36. Susan Tucker, with Cynthia LeJeune Nobles, Karen Trahan Leathem, and Sharon Stallworth Nossiter, "Setting the Table in New Orleans," in *New Orleans Cuisine: Fourteen Signature Dishes and Their Histories*, ed. Susan Tucker (Jackson: University of Mississippi Press, 2009), 13; Campanella, *Bienville's Dilemma*, 250–51.

37. James Stuart, *Three Years in North America*, vol. 2 (Edinburgh: Printed for R. Cadell, 1833), 235.

38. Claire Robertson and Iris Berger, eds., *Women and Class in Africa* (New York: Africana Publishing, 1986); Catherine Coquery-Vidrovitch, *African Women: A Modern History*, trans. Beth Gillian Raps (Boulder, CO: Westview Press, 1997); Bessie House-Midamba and Fliex K. Ekechi, eds., *African Market Women and Economic Power: The Role of Women in African Economic Development* (Westport, CT: Greenwood Press, 1995).

39. Alisha Cromwell, "A Form of Skilled Labor: Entrepreneurial Gullah Geechee Women and 'Head Carrying'" (paper presented at the International Gullah Geechee and African Diaspora Conference, Conway, South Carolina, March 4–7, 2020).

40. Augustin, *A General Digest*, 155. Note: According to the Digest, the ordinance was approved on February 18, 1831. See pages 158–59.

41. Vernon Valentine Palmer, "The Customs of Slavery: The War Without Arms," *American Journal of Legal History* 48, no. 2 (April 2006): 192–97; Paul Alliot, *Louisiana Under the Rule of Spain, France, and the United States, 1875–1807*, trans. James Alexander Robertson (Cleveland, OH: Arthur H. Clark Company, 1911), 61–63.

42. Augustin, *A General Digest*, 203.

43. Augustin, *A General Digest*, 155; *A Digest of the Ordinances, Resolutions, by-laws and Regulations of the Corporation of New Orleans: and a Collection of the Laws of the Legislature Relative to Said City* (New Orleans: Gaston Brusle, 1836), xix–xxi, 97, 137.

44. Augustin, *A General Digest*, 203.

45. The listed recipients of the indemnity are Pertonille H. Jean, Pauline Frouby, f. d. c. l., T. B. Debuc, Catherine Godof, Victoire Champiaux, [?] Belmont, Antoinette Gilbert, Mrs. Ambroise, Sanibe Reynold, Paul Gaulet, Maria Acori, Marie Jacques Vassale, Rosalie [?], Emilie Belisse, Thiat, Joseph Avril, Jeanne Duharlay, F. L. Petard, Widow Coeur de Roi, Francisco Diaz, Placide Bueno, T. Damery, Sabino Jiminez, Desire' Carcassone, Philips Cale, Bonito Ferres, Simon Petavin, Medie' Daviau, Paignon Guichard, Pierre Pinet, Manual Creci, Moses Plumer, Pigeon, Daniel Clements, and a person whose name is illegible. "Session of Wednesday, January 18, 1832," Ordinances and resolutions (translations), 1805–1832, New Orleans (La.) Conseil de Ville, NOPL.

46. "Session of Saturday, February 25, 1832" and "Session of April 18, 1832," Ordinances and resolutions (translations), 1805–1832, New Orleans (La.) Conseil de Ville, NOPL.

47. Augustin, *A General Digest*, 157.

48. Pralines are candies made of caramelized sugar and toasted pecans. In the nineteenth century, there were different kinds of pralines ranging in color from pink to white to caramel. In addition to caramel pralines, the ones that you can still purchase in the French Quarter today, there were also "cream pralines." A favorite among the upper echelons of New Orleans society, cream pralines were made up of two shelled pecans held together with a creamy meringue filling. "The Revival of the Cream Praline," *Daily Picayune*, November 1, 1896.

49. Mung Park, a Scottish missionary who traveled in Senegambia and inland along the Niger River in the late eighteenth century, notes a similarly fermented dish made from sour milk and cornmeal, which he ate near Doolinkeaboo. Jessica B. Harris, *High on the Hog: A Culinary Journey from Africa to America* (New York: Bloomsbury, 2011), 55.

50. For an analysis of the ways in which enslaved food vendors navigated marketplaces in New Orleans and built economic and social networks, see Rashauana Johnson, *Slavery's Metropolis: Unfree Labor in New Orleans During the Age of Revolution* (Cambridge: Cambridge University Press, 2016), 65–75.

51. Hall, *Travels in North America*, 332.

52. Royall, *Mrs. Royall's Southern Tour*, 19.

53. Ellen Call Long, *Florida Breezes, or, Florida, New and Old* (1883; reprint, Gainesville: University of Florida Press, 1962), 26–27.

54. Robert Olwell, "'Loose, Idle and Disorderly': Slave Women in the Eighteenth-Century Charleston Marketplace," in *More Than Chattel: Black Women and Slavery in the Americas*, ed. David Barry Gaspar and Darlene Clark Hine (Bloomington: Indiana University Press, 1996), 97–110; Cynthia M. Kennedy, *Braided Relations, Entwined Lives: The Women of Charleston's Urban Slave Society* (Bloomington: Indiana University Press, 2005), 138–40.

55. Baics, *Feeding Gotham*, 121–25.

56. Interview with Pierre Aucuin as cited in Ronnie W. Clayton, ed., *Mother Wit: The Ex-Slave Narratives of the Louisiana Writers' Project* (New York: Peter Lang, 1990), 21. Note: Unlike the other state projects participating in the Federal Writers' Project, which conducted a majority of interviews between 1937 and 1939, the Louisiana Writers' Project collected most of its interviews between 1940 and 1941.

57. Interview with Catherine Cornelius as cited in Clayton, *Mother Wit*, 46.

58. Interview with Willis Cozart, May 12, 1937, vol. 11, North Carolina, Part 1, Adams-Hunter, SNP, LOC, accessed March 15, 2023, https://www.loc.gov/item/mesn111/.

59. Interview with Henry Wright, around 1936–38, vol. 4, Georgia, Part 4, Telfair-Young, SNP, LOC, accessed March 16, 2023, https://www.loc.gov/item/mesn044/.

60. Interview with Marshal Butler, around 1936–38, vol. 4, Georgia, Part 1, Adams-Furr, SNP, LOC, March 16, 2023, https://www.loc.gov/item/mesno41/.

61. Interview with Phil Town, around 1936–38, vol. 4, Georgia, Part 4, Telfair-Young, SNP, LOC, March 16, 2023, https://www.loc.gov/item/mesno44/.

62. Interview with Hal Hutson, around 1936–38, vol. 13, Oklahoma, Adams-Young, SNP, LOC, March 16, 2023, https://www.loc.gov/item/mesn130/.

63. Thavolia Glymph, *Out of the House of Bondage: The Transformation of the Plantation Household* (New York: Cambridge University Press, 2008), 12–17, 9–10.

64. "15 Dollars Reward," *Bee*, February 19, 1828. Note: Nancy may have used her social networks to find allies and set herself up for a successful escape from slavery, as postulated by Rashauana Johnson. Johnson, *Slavery's Metropolis*, 71.

65. Interview with George Bollinger, around 1936–38, vol. 10, Missouri, Abbot-Younger, SNP, LOC, March 16, 2023, https://www.loc.gov/item/mesn100/.

66. Interview with Easter Huff, around 1936–38, vol. 4, Georgia, Part 2, Garey-Jones, SNP, LOC, March 16, 2023, https://www.loc.gov/item/mesno42/. Note: The phrase "self-manumitted" is my own formulation that I later discovered already existed in the historiography. See, for example, John Lovell's work. The phrase "self-liberated" is a formulation of Greg Alan Beaman, a New Orleans historian. I first heard the term during a conversation with him about enslaved people running for their freedom. Greg Beaman, discussion with the author, May 17, 2023. John Lovell, "Youth Programs of Negro Improvement Group," *Journal of Negro Education* 9, no. 3 (1940): 379–87.

67. "$20 Reward," *Daily Picayune*, November 26, 1840; "$20 Reward," *Daily Picayune*, March 2, 1844.

68. "Five Dollars Reward," *Daily Picayune*, June 11, 1854.

69. "10 Reward," *Daily Picayune*, November 13, 1844.

70. Royall, *Mrs. Royall's Southern Tour*, 18.

71. Royall, *Mrs. Royall's Southern Tour*, 70.

72. Rashauna Johnson uses the concept of "confined cosmopolitanism" to explore how people of African descent moved throughout the Atlantic world as they represented their enslavers' interests, thus affording them unusual mobility. A similar situation existed within New Orleans' public food culture, in which enslaved Black women experienced certain protections and freedoms usually not granted to them because they represented their enslavers' interests in the marketplace. My work, therefore, is an extension of Johnson's, adding another dimension to the study of urban slavery in the Atlantic world. Johnson, *Slavery's Metropolis*.

73. *Bee*, October 13, 1835, as cited in Roger A. Fischer, "Racial Segregation in Ante Bellum New Orleans," *American Historical Review* 74, no. 3 (1969): 292.

74. Louis Moreau Lislet, *A General Digest of Acts of the Legislature of Louisiana* (New Orleans: Benjamin Levy, 1828), 102.

75. Johnson, *Slavery's Metropolis*, 70. Note: According to the Digest, the Black Code was passed on June 7, 1806.

76. Local laws across the country regulated middlemen and middlewomen's ability to sell goods at a markup. Novak, "Public Economy," 18.

77. Lobel, *Urban Appetites*, 18, 26.

78. For a deeper exploration of the petition and how vendors expressed their vision for a more equitable marketplace, see Candice L. Harrison, " 'Free Trade and Hucksters' Rights!' Envisioning Economic Democracy in the Early Republic," *Pennsylvania Magazine of History and Biography* 137, no. 2 (April 2013): 171–72. For a similar example of women hucksters petitioning their local government after the implementation of new city ordinances that disproportionately impacted their livelihoods, see Seth Rockman, *Scraping By: Wage Labor, Slavery, and Survival in Early Baltimore* (Baltimore: Johns Hopkins University Press, 2009), 100–101, 127–29.

79. Petition of the Hucksters, December 18, 1805, 31, Philadelphia (Pa.). City Council. Petitions to the Select and Common Councils, Box 1, Folder 11, Historical Society of Pennsylvania, Philadelphia, PA.

80. For an analogous case study of Charleston's laws, see Olwell, " 'Loose, Idle and Disorderly,' " 100.

81. For examples of illicit trading and property owners' complaints of such economic transactions, see Johnson, *Slavery's Metropolis*, 73–74.

82. "$10 Reward," *Daily Picayune*, August 8, 1846.

83. It appears that Charleston was the only city to implement the metal badge system—the oldest badge dating to 1800. These badges came in different shapes and sizes and were composed of different metals. Sometimes the shape of the badge correlated to the skill set or role of the wearer: fisher, huckster, fruiterer, and blacksmith, among others. The fact remains, though, that many economic transactions were performed illegally, between unlicensed food vendors and customers, suggesting that the need to feed that city outweighed the need to abide local law. Harlan Greene and Harry Hutchins, *Slave Badges and the Slave-Hire System in Charleston, South Carolina, 1783–1865* (Jefferson, NC: McFarland, 2004).

84. Benjamin Latrobe, *Impressions Respecting New Orleans*, ed. Samuel Wilson Jr. (New York: Columbia University Press, 1951), 101.

85. Virginia Meacham Gould, " 'If I Can't Have My Rights, I Can Have My Pleasures, and If They Won't Give Me Wages, I Can Take Them': Gender and Slave Labor in Antebellum New Orleans," in *Discovering the Women in Slavery*, ed. Patricia Morton (Athens: University of Georgia Press, 1996), 184.

86. Royall, *Mrs. Royall's Southern Tour*, 71.

87. Royall, *Mrs. Royall's Southern Tour*, 70.

88. Printed Bond issued to Juan Gomez permitting him to have a private market cart, January 31, 1843, CFH09.02.2.025N, Charles F. Heartman Manuscripts of Slavery Collection, Xavier University of Louisiana Library, New Orleans, Louisiana; s.v. "Juan Gomez," in *Gardner's New Orleans Directory for 1861* (New Orleans: Charles Gardner, 1861), 196.

89. Printed Bond issued to Widow Mathé permitting her to have a private market cart, September 16, 1843, CFH09.02.2.025X, Charles F. Heartman Manuscripts of Slavery Collection, Xavier University of Louisiana Library, New Orleans, Louisiana; s.v. "Widow Mathé," in US census of 1850; "Female Enterprise: Josephine Tassy Mathé," NOPL, accessed August 5, 2023, http://archives.nolalibrary.org/~nopl/exhibits/fe/mathe.htm.

90. Josephine Tassy Mathé purchased a person listed as "Louise" on August 3, 1813. Gwendolyn Midlo Hall, comp., s.v. "Louise" and "Josephine, Fwoc Tassy," in *Afro-Louisiana History and Genealogy, 1719–1820*, accessed August 5, 2023, http://www.ibiblio.org/laslave/.

91. For discussions of New Orleans' streets, their condition, and the way people navigated them, see Richard Campanella, *Bourbon Street: A History* (Baton Rouge: Louisiana State University Press, 2014), especially Chapter 4.

92. Campanella, *Bourbon Street*, 46.

93. "We Have Been Requested," *New Orleans Argus*, July 21, 1829.

94. "Regulating the Currency," *Daily Picayune*, October 30, 1841.

95. "$100 Reward," *Daily Picayune*, January 4, 1844.

96. Royall, *Mrs. Royall's Southern Tour*, 70.

97. Royall, *Mrs. Royall's Southern Tour*, 69.

98. Cromwell, "A Form of Skilled Labor."

99. "The Mustard Dealer," *Daily Picayune*, December 29, 1846.

100. Augustin, *A General Digest*, 213–17. Note: According to the Digest, the ordinance was approved on August 24, 1829.

101. "Oysters," *Daily Picayune*, October 4, 1837.

102. "Oysters," *Daily Picayune*, October 4, 1837.

103. Walt Whitman, *Complete Prose Works: Specimen Days and Collect, November Boughs and Good Bye My Fancy* (Boston: Small, Maynard & Co, 1901), 440.

104. Anne C. Bailey, *African Voices of the Atlantic Slave Trade: Beyond the Silence and the Shame* (Boston: Beacon Press, 2005); Bruce Boyd Raeburn, "Reflections of Senegambia in New Orleans Jazz," in *New Orleans, Louisiana & Saint-Louis, Senegal: Mirror Cities in the Atlantic World, 1659–2000s*, ed. Emily Clark, Ibrahima Thioub, and Cécile Vidal (Baton Rouge: Louisiana State University Press, 2019).

105. Singleton, *Letters from the South*, 130.

106. As noted by linguist Richard W. Bailey, New Orleans was a multilingual city in the antebellum period: "Amerindian and African languages, Caribbean creoles, German, Spanish, French, and English were all routinely spoken by persons permanently resident in New Orleans—and the brisk trading along the levee brought still more languages." Richard W. Bailey, "The Foundation of English in the Louisiana Purchase: New Orleans, 1800–1850," *American Speech* 78 (2003): 365.

107. Mark Smith, *Sensing the Past: Seeing, Hearing, Smelling, Tasting, and Touching in History* (Berkeley: University of California Press, 2007), 44. See also Aimée Boutin's study of the soundscape of Paris and the integral role that street vendors

played in organizing life in a major European city: Aimée Boutin, *City of Noise: Sound and Nineteenth-Century Paris* (Urbana: University of Illinois Press, 2015).

108. Richard Cullen Rath, *How Early America Sounded* (Ithaca, NY: Cornell University Press, 2003), 66.

109. Latrobe, *Impressions Respecting*, 25.

110. Campanella, *Bienville's Dilemma*, 27.

111. Hirsch and Logsdon, *Creole New Orleans*, 192.

112. Alice Moore Dunbar-Nelson, "People of Color in Louisiana," in Kein, *Creole*, 8.

113. Mary Gehman, "Visible Means of Support: Business, Professions, and Trades of Free People of Color," in Kein, *Creole*, 212.

114. Whitney Nell Stewart, "Fashioning Frenchness: *Gens de Couleur Libres* and the Cultural Struggle for Power in Antebellum New Orleans," *Journal of Social History* 51, no. 3 (Winter 2017): 526–56.

115. Royall, *Mrs. Royall's Southern Tour*, 70.

116. "Street Hawkers," *Daily Picayune*, June 26, 1846.

117. "The Candy Man," *Daily Picayune*, July 15, 1846.

118. Benjamin Latrobe, *The Journal of Benjamin Latrobe, 1799–1820: From Philadelphia to New Orleans*, ed. Edward C. Carter II, John C. Van Horne, and Lee Formwalt (New Haven: Yale University Press, 1980), 204.

CHAPTER 2

1. Fredrika Bremer, *The Homes of the New World: Impressions of America*, vol. 2 (New York: Harper & Bros., 1853), 213.

2. Bremer, *Homes of the New World*, 213. For a work highlighting the underexamined presence of African and African-descent peoples in Europe, see Olivette Otele, *African European: An Untold History* (London: Hurst, 2020).

3. Bremer, *Homes of the New World*, 213.

4. Campanella, *Bienville's Dilemma*, 171.

5. Richard Campanella, "Culture Wars, Ethnic Rivalry and New Orleans' Messy Municipality Era," *Times-Picayune*, March 11, 2016.

6. Thomas Ashe, *Travels in America Performed in the Year 1806* (London: Printed for Richard Phillips, 1809), 310.

7. In the late antebellum period, New Orleans was the second-largest immigrant port city in the country after New York. Campanella, *Bienville's Dilemma*, 170–71.

8. When I use "German," "Irish," "French," and other European nation state identities, I do so with some trepidation and with an underlying understanding that regional cultures were still powerful and that identities continued to emerge from both regional and national cultures. In federal census data, from the period, for example, individuals or families who were recent immigrants sometimes listed the state rather than the country from which they had emigrated from. One might have listed Baden, Hesse, or Bavaria, all German states, instead of Germany.

Or one might have listed Alsace, a region over which France had sovereignty in this period, instead of France. Still others, even ones from those regions, chose the national rather than state category. To create some consistency among the data, I have opted to use the broader national categories instead of the state-based ones.

9. *Gibson's Guide and Directory of the State of Louisiana, and the Cities of New Orleans and LaFayette* (New Orleans: J. Gibson, 1838), 313.

10. *Gibson's Guide and Directory*, 313.

11. Joseph Pilié, an immigrant from French colonial Saint-Domingue, was an engineer and surveyor for the city of New Orleans. Stanley Clisby Arthur, *Old New Orleans: A History of the Vieux Carré, Its Ancient and Historical Buildings* (New Orleans: Harmanson, 1936), 137; *Gibson's Guide and Directory*, 313. Note: As the city constructed the Vegetable Market as part of the French Market complex, one city resident complained about the construction's impact on her property value. Adelaide Segond Carrick, a white woman who owned several lots and buildings neighboring the French Market complex, petitioned the city council to halt construction and take down the preliminary structures of the Vegetable Market. Having received no response from the council, she wrote a second letter reiterating her demands, but to no avail. Letter from Adelaide Segond Carrick to the Conseil de Ville, October 20, 1823, #689, New Orleans (La.) Conseil de Ville., Letters, Petitions, and Reports, 1804–1835, vol. 3, NOPL.

12. *Gibson's Guide and Directory*, 312; "City Council, Saturday, 30th January 1836," *New Orleans Commercial Bulletin*, February 1, 1836.

13. Rosemary Wakeman, "Fascinating Les Halles," *French Politics, Culture & Society* 25, no. 2 (Summer 2007): 51; James Schmiechen and Kenneth Carls, *The British Market Hall: A Social and Architectural History* (New Haven: Yale University Press, 1999), 47–60.

14. Lobel, *Urban Appetites*, 18.

15. Lobel, *Urban Appetites*, 18.

16. Lobel, *Urban Appetites*, 18.

17. Helen Tangires, *Public Markets and Civic Culture in Nineteenth-Century America* (Baltimore: Johns Hopkins University Press, 2003), 40.

18. Interview with Nellie Smith, around 1936–38, vol. 4, Georgia, Part 3, Kendricks-Styles, SNP, LOC, March 20, 2023, https://www.loc.gov/item/mesn043/.

19. Lobel, *Urban Appetites*, 18.

20. Baics, *Feeding Gotham*, 20.

21. John Pintard, *Letters from John Pintard to His Daughter Eliza Noel Pintard Davidson, 1816–1833*, vol. 2 (New York: New-York Historical Society, 1941), 124.

22. Gabrielle O. Begue, "Considering the New Orleans Corner Store: The Architectural Origins, Development, and Preservation of an Endangered Vernacular Tradition" (master's thesis, Tulane University, 2012), 59.

23. Begue, "Considering the New Orleans Corner Store," 60.

24. Campanella, "Culture Wars."

25. Campanella, "Culture Wars."

26. *Gibson's Guide and Directory*, 312.

27. Campanella, *Bienville's Dilemma*, 174.

28. Campanella, "Culture Wars."

29. "The Third Municipality," *Daily Picayune*, January 20, 1838.

30. *Gibson's Guide and Directory*, 312–13.

31. *Gibson's Guide and Directory*, 311–12.

32. *Gibson's Guide and Directory*, 311.

33. In 1840, the city's population consisted of 59,519 white people, 23,448 enslaved Black people, and 19,226 free people of color. Campanella, *Bienville's Dilemma*, 32–33.

34. Campanella, *Bienville's Dilemma*, 155.

35. New Orleans annexed Lafayette City in 1852, Jefferson City in 1870, and the town of Carrollton in 1874. Richard Campanella, "When Carrollton Became New Orleans," *Cityscapes: A Geographer's View on the New Orleans Area*, September 8, 2017, https://richcampanella.com/wp-content/uploads/2020/02/Picayune_Cityscapes_2017_09_Annexation-of-Carrollton.pdf.

36. For foundational texts in conceptions of property law and citizenship, see Morton J. Horwitz, *The Transformation of American Law, 1780–1860* (Cambridge, MA: Harvard University Press, 1977); Lawrence Friedman, *A History of American Law* (New York: Simon & Schuster, 1973). See also a relatively more recent work on the topic: Jedediah Purdy, *The Meaning of Property: Freedom, Community, and the Legal Imagination* (New Haven: Yale University Press, 2010).

37. See, for example, Justin A. Nystrom's work on the immigrant Italian population in the food industries of New Orleans: Justin A. Nystrom, *Creole Italian: Sicilian Immigrants and the Shaping of New Orleans Food Culture* (Athens: University of Georgia Press, 2018).

38. Eugenié Lavedan Maylié, *Maylié's Table D'Hote Recipes and the History and Some Facts Concerning "La Maison Maylié et Esparbé"* (Maylié's Restaurant, n.d.).

39. "H.F. Pilster," *Daily Picayune*, December 6, 1838.

40. "Premium Beef," *Daily Picayune*, November 14, 1840.

41. Schafer, *Becoming Free*, 46.

42. Schafer, *Becoming Free*, xiv.

43. The archival record does not reveal exactly how enslaved people paid their attorneys, or if they, in fact, paid them at all. Legal historian Judith Kelleher Schafer surmised that perhaps the free Black community, or their relatives, may have helped pay fees; or it is possible that attorneys waived their fees. Judith Kelleher Schafer, *Slavery, the Civil Law, and the Supreme Court of Louisiana* (Baton Rouge: Louisiana State University Press, 1994), 92.

44. *Fanny (Phany) c.w. v. Desdunes Poincy and Widow N. Bouny*, 1421 (1st D. Ct. New Orleans, October 18, 1847–June 2, 1848) and *Arsène v. Pineguy*, 434 (1st D. Ct. New Orleans, November 5, 1846–June 1, 1847), NOPL as cited in Alexandra T. Havrylyshyn, "Free for a Moment in France: How Enslaved Women and Girls Claimed Liberty in the Courts of New Orleans (1835–1857)" (PhD diss., University of California, Berkeley, 2018), 63.

45. *Naba, f.m.c., v. Derbigny, f.m.c.*, 9252 (2nd D. Ct. New Orleans, November 7, 1855) and *Naba, f.m.c. v. State*, 9723 (2nd D. Ct. New Orleans, February 13, 1856), NOPL as cited in Schafer, *Becoming Free*, 77.

46. Schafer, *Becoming Free*, xiv.

47. Gehman, "Visible Means of Support," 213.

48. Hirsch and Logsdon, *Creole New Orleans*, 192.

49. As of 2024, these streets were named Oretha Castle Haley Boulevard and Martin Luther King Jr. Boulevard, respectively.

50. Campanella, *Bienville's Dilemma*, 170–75.

51. "The Neighborhood of Dryades Market," *New Orleans Times*, November 5, 1865.

52. In 1807, when he laid out the Faubourg de la Course, Barthelemy Lafon named the streets after figures in classical European mythology: Rue de Driades, Rue Hercule, and Cours des Tritons, for example. The Dryades neighborhood, therefore, was aptly named and fit in with the existing nomenclature of that area of town. "The Neighborhood of Dryades Market," *New Orleans Times*, November 5, 1865.

53. Early investors included Thomas Banks, James H. Caldwell, and Maunsel White. "The Neighborhood of Dryades Market," *New Orleans Times*, November 5, 1865; "New Orleans, the Dual City," *Times-Picayune*, March 4, 1934.

54. "City Intelligence," *Daily Picayune*, January 11, 1849.

55. "Rear of the First District," *Daily Picayune*, December 28, 1852.

56. "City Intelligence," *Daily Picayune*, January 10, 1849.

57. "City Intelligence," *Daily Picayune*, January 10, 1849.

58. Augustin, *A General Digest*, 199.

59. "Second Municipality: Weekly Report of the Treasurer," *Daily Picayune*, July 16, 1840.

60. "Second Municipality: Weekly Report of the Treasurer," *Daily Picayune*, July 23, 1840.

61. "Second Municipality Resolutions," *Daily Picayune*, July 26, 1840.

62. "Rear of the First District," *Daily Picayune*, December 28, 1852.

63. The Dryades Market would, from that day forward, consist of two structures on opposite sides of Melpomene Street.

64. "City Intelligence," *Daily Picayune*, January 11, 1849.

65. In 1907, for example, the Commercial-Germania Trust & Savings Banks had branches "Near All the Principle Markets," which included locations at the Dryades, Poydras, Magazine, Tremé, and French markets among other commercial districts. "Commercial-Germania Trust and Savings Banks," *New Orleans Item*, December 12, 1907; "Dollar Deposits Welcome," *Daily Picayune*, January 20, 1907. See also Alvin P. Howard's study of branch banking in New Orleans in which he argues that, as in Europe, New Orleans' commercial centers were neighborhood-based economies, in which neighborhoods were loosely grouped around the food market: Alvin P. Howard, "Branch Banking in New Orleans," *Bankers Magazine* 102 (1921): 762.

66. Jacob, "New Orleans' Historic Public Markets," 73–74.

67. Coffeehouses had many functions. Often, they served alcohol in addition to coffee. For further discussion on the history of these spaces, including bars, in America, see Christine Sismondo, *America Walks into a Bar: A Spirited History of Taverns and Saloons, Speakeasies, and Grog Shops* (New York: Oxford University Press, 2011).

68. "Grocery Store for Sale," *Daily Picayune*, March 17, 1848.

69. "Desirable Lots in the Gregory Square," *Daily Picayune*, December 18, 1847.

70. "A School Jubilee," *Daily Picayune*, November 14, 1904.

71. "Dryades Street Has Steady Patient Growth," *Times-Picayune*, October 2, 1926.

72. Patrick Irwin built a stand at the corner of Melpomene and Dryades Streets where patrons could purchase tickets for transportation services. "Old Time Bus-Lines and Street Cars in New Orleans," *Daily Picayune*, July 30, 1911.

73. "Death of Patrick Irwin," *Daily Picayune*, April 26, 1878; "Old Time Bus-Lines and Street Cars in New Orleans," *Daily Picayune*, July 30, 1911. Note: It appears that the Dryades omnibus line was discontinued on July 8, 1862, under Union General Benjamin Butler's martial law. It is unclear if and when the line reopened. "Army of Occupation: History of Army and Navy Movement," *Daily Delta*, January 1, 1863.

74. After establishing the Dryades Market, opening two omnibus lines along Rampart and Carondelet Streets, and contributing to the construction of railroad lines in the city, Irwin turned to local politics. He became an alderman in 1853, a member of the legislature in 1854, and president of the Hibernia Bank in 1870 and later the president of the Hibernia Insurance Company. His personal history indicated the financial and political leverage that the public market system could afford investors. "Death of Patrick Irwin," *Daily Picayune*, April 26, 1878.

75. Historical preservationist Beth Jacob noted that the Magazine Street shopping corridor, typically thought of as one continuous commercial district, was actually composed of four commercial-social hubs, each oriented around one of the four public markets that operated on the street by 1860. The markets included St. Mary's, Magazine, Ninth Street, and Jefferson. These hubs represented individual nodes not only within the local food economy but also within the city's residential and social geospatial networks. Jacob, "New Orleans' Historic Public Markets," 72–73.

76. "For Rent," *Daily Picayune*, November 20, 1849.

77. "The Keller Market," *New Orleans Times*, April 5, 1867.

78. Campanella, "Culture Wars."

79. Campanella, *Bienville's Dilemma*, 36.

80. Preface to Henry Jefferson Leovy and Charles H. Luzenberg, *The Laws and General Ordinances of the City of New Orleans: Together with the Acts of the Legislature, Decisions of the Supreme Court, and Constitutional Provisions Relating to the City Government* (New Orleans: E. C. Wharton, 1857).

81. For a complete digest of the revised market ordinances, see Leovy and Luzenberg, *Laws and General Ordinances*, 146–57.

82. Revised City Ordinance No. 425 in Leovy and Luzenberg, *Laws and General Ordinances*, 147.

83. "Sale of Markets," *Daily Picayune*, December 6, 1859.

84. Revised City Ordinance No. 424 in Leovy and Luzenberg, *Laws and General Ordinances*, 147.

85. Revised City Ordinance No. 447 in Leovy and Luzenberg, *Laws and General Ordinances*, 151.

86. Revised City Ordinance No. 427 in Leovy and Luzenberg, *Laws and General Ordinances*, 148.

87. Revised City Ordinance No. 460 in Leovy and Luzenberg, *Laws and General Ordinances*, 153–54.

88. Revised City Ordinance No. 429 in Leovy and Luzenberg, *Laws and General Ordinances*, 148.

89. Agricultural Department of the United States, *Report of the Commissioner of Agriculture for the year 1870* (Washington, DC: Government Printing Office, 1871), 244.

90. "Local Intelligence: Open for Inspection," *Philadelphia Inquirer*, April 12, 1859; "The Western Market House," *Philadelphia Press*, April 20, 1859; Agricultural Department of the United States, *Report of the Commissioner*, 245.

91. Tangires, *Public Markets*, 98–99.

92. "Laying of the Corner Stone of the New Market House," in Charles A. Poulson, *Scrap-Books Consisting of Engravings, etc. and Newspaper Clippings Illustrative of Philadelphia*, vol. 10 (Philadelphia: Library Company of Philadelphia, c. 1824–1864), 66, as cited in Tangires, *Public Markets*, 112.

93. Tangires, *Public Markets*, 108.

94. Revised City Ordinance No. 432 in Leovy and Luzenberg, *Laws and General Ordinances*, 149.

95. Augustin, *A General Digest*, 155–59.

96. "Selling Without License," *Daily Picayune*, November 6, 1845.

97. "City Intelligence," *Daily Picayune*, December 29, 1846.

98. "Proceedings of the Council of the Second Municipality," *Daily Picayune*, January 7, 1841.

99. "Second Municipality Council," *Daily Picayune*, January 6, 1841.

100. The ordinance was passed on January 12, 1841, and approved by the mayor on January 13, 1841. "Proceedings of the Council of the Second Municipality," *Daily Picayune*, January 14, 1841; "No. 117. An Ordinance," *Daily Picayune*, January 30, 1841.

101. "No. 117. An Ordinance," *Daily Picayune*, January 30, 1841.

102. "No. 117. An Ordinance," *Daily Picayune*, January 30, 1841.

103. "Proceedings of the Council of the Second Municipality," *Daily Picayune*, January 14, 1841.

104. Lyle Saxon, *Gumbo Ya-Ya: Folk Tales of Louisiana* (Boston: Houghton Mifflin, 1945), 29.

105. "A Police Officer…" *Daily Picayune*, February 6, 1841.

106. "Peddling Without License," *Daily Picayune*, December 3, 1852.

107. Campanella, *Bienville's Dilemma*, 32–33.

108. "Peddling," *Daily Picayune*, October 13, 1842. Note: Richard Riker, referred to as Dickey Riker in the *Daily Picayune*, was a lawyer and politicians who, over the course of his career, served as the district attorney of Manhattan and also served three nonconsecutive terms as the recorder of New York City. He was a known abuser of the Fugitive Slave Act, sending free Black people to the South to be enslaved. When he passed away in 1842, the *Daily Picayune* described him as "a human judge and an honest man." "Death of Richard Riker," *Daily Picayune*, October 6, 1842.

109. For a study of Know-Nothingism in New Orleans, and Louisiana more broadly, see Marius M. Marriere, *The Know Nothings in Louisiana* (Jackson: University Press of Mississippi, 2018).

110. Campanella, *Bienville's Dilemma*, 35.

111. Beyond those listed has a "huckster" or "peddler" in the 1860 US federal census, there are other examples of free people of color working in the food industry. One such person was F. S. Durel, a free woman of color, who was born in Africa around 1786. The census listed her as a "Vegetable Dealer" who owned $300 of real estate and lived in the 5th Ward of New Orleans. She perhaps operated her own produce stand in one of the municipal markets or may have been a wholesaler. S.v. "F.S. Durel," in the census of 1860.

112. Anthony G. Barthélémy, "Light Bright, Damn *Near* White: Race, the Politics of Genealogy, and the Strange Case of Susie Guillory," in Kein, *Creole*, 257.

113. Stewart, "Fashioning Frenchness," 527.

114. Schafer, *Becoming Free*, xxi.

115. S.v. "Augustin Ben," in US census of 1860.

116. S.v. "Mary Ben," in US census of 1860.

117. S.v. "Augustin Ben," in US census of 1850.

118. S.v. "Louis John," "Rosine John," and "Zuline John," in US census of 1860.

119. Interview with Pierce Cody, around 1936–38, vol. 4, Georgia, Part 1, Adams-Furr, SNP, LOC, April 4, 2023, https://www.loc.gov/item/mesn041/.

120. For a postbellum example of the role of vendors as knowledge keepers who carried and shared information, see works focusing on Chinese vendor experiences in the postwar South: Lucy M. Cohen, *Chinese in the Post–Civil War South: A People Without a History* (Baton Rouge: Louisiana State University Press, 1984), 83; Kathleen López, *Chinese Cubans: A Transnational History* (Chapel Hill: University of North Carolina Press, 2013), 78.

121. Andrew Smith, *Starving the South: How the North Won the Civil War* (New York: St. Martin's, 2011).

CHAPTER 3

1. " 'Toto,' the Old Praline Woman of Canal Street," *Daily Picayune*, August 5, 1894.

2. " 'Toto,' the Old Praline Woman of Canal Street," *Daily Picayune*, August 5, 1894.

3. Reconstruction arguably began in New Orleans when the city to fell to Union forces in 1862 and lasted through 1877, when federal troops finally pulled out of the city. For a nuanced study of Reconstruction in New Orleans and the major political players who shaped the period, see Justin A. Nystrom, *New Orleans After the Civil War: Race, Politics, and a New Birth of Freedom* (Baltimore: Johns Hopkins University Press, 2010).

4. "In an Article," *Daily Picayune*, August 27, 1867.

5. "Encourage the Private Markets," *Daily Picayune*, February 17, 1868.

6. "One of the Advantages," *Daily Picayune*, October 9, 1866.

7. "Improved Market System," *Daily True Delta*, March 22, 1866; Sauder, "The Origin and Spread," 286.

8. Revised Markets Ordinance Art. 596 in Henry Jefferson Leovy and Charles H. Luzenberg, *The laws and general ordinances of the city of New Orleans: together with the acts of the Legislature, decisions of the Supreme Court, and constitutional provisions relating to the city government* (New Orleans: Simmons & Co., 1870), 226.

9. Despite my best research efforts, I could not find the given names of Mrs. Simon, Mrs. LaCaz, or Mrs. Christian in the archival record.

10. Rose Nicaud's witness statement from the official court documents of *State of Louisiana v. Arthur Guerin*, 571 (2nd D. Ct. New Orleans, October 28, 1868), NOPL as cited in Robyn Rene Andermann, "Brewed Awakening: Re-Imagining Education in Three Nineteenth-Century New Orleans Coffee Houses" (PhD diss., Louisiana State University, 2018), 196.

11. Andermann, "Brewed Awakening," 162–200. Note: Rose Nicaud started as an itinerant coffee vendor before launching her open-air coffee stand in the French Market, which she operated roughly from the 1850s through the 1870s. Mary Gehman has credited Nicaud with kick-starting the sale of freshly brewed coffee in the public markets, although the archival record remains mum on the topic. At her French Market coffee stand, Nicaud grew a national reputation immortalized by writer Catherine Cole. Born into slavery in 1812, Nicaud had gained her freedom by 1840, although the means through which she did so is not revealed in the archival record. In her biographical sketch of Nicaud, Cole claims that the vendor had purchased her own freedom by selling one cup of coffee at a time—a slow march toward freedom even in a city with a robust coffee culture. What we can infer, though, is that Nicaud supported herself in freedom through her coffee business. Mary Gehman, *The Free People of Color of New Orleans: An Introduction* (New Orleans: Margaret Media, 1994), 56.

12. "Private Markets," *Daily Picayune*, December 14, 1867.

13. "Private Markets," *Daily Picayune*, December 14, 1867.

14. "Private Markets," *Daily Picayune*, December 14, 1867.

15. "Encourage the Private Markets," *Daily Picayune*, February 17, 1868.

16. Begue, "Considering the New Orleans Corner Store," 77.

17. "The Kellog Legislature: The House," *Daily Picayune*, January 25, 1874.

18. "Butchers' Meeting at Magazine Market," *Daily Picayune*, February 6, 1874.

19. "Members in the Louisiana House of Representatives 1812–2024," David R. Poynter Legislative Research Library, Louisiana House of Representatives, July 11, 2023, https://house.louisiana.gov/H_PDFdocs/HouseMembership_History_CURRENT.pdf.

20. "Butchers' Meeting at Magazine Market," *Daily Picayune*, February 6, 1874.

21. Act No. 31 in *Acts Passed by the General Assembly of the State of Louisiana at the Second Session of the Third Legislature, Begun and Held in New Orleans, January 5, 1874* (New Orleans: Republican Office, 1874), 65–66.

22. "Opened Up Again," *Daily Picayune*, July 28, 1877. Note: The number of private markets grew during the second half of the nineteenth century, but not to the extent that you see in cities like Boston where deregulation and privatization flourished. "Official Journal of the House of Representatives of the State of Louisiana," *Daily Advocate*, June 16, 1900.

23. City officials approved the construction of the Le Breton Market and the Keller Market around 1867, the St. John Market around 1872, the Second Street Market around 1873, and the St. Roch Market around 1875.

24. "Municipal Brevities," *Daily Picayune*, April 28, 1878.

25. "The New Second Street Market," *Daily Picayune*, April 7, 1873.

26. For an in-depth accounting of the White League's coup, see Nystrom, *New Orleans After the Civil War*, 160–85.

27. Nystrom, *New Orleans After the Civil War*, 176–77.

28. Nystrom, *New Orleans After the Civil War*, 175–85.

29. "Address of the National Party of Louisiana to the People," *Daily Picayune*, November 3, 1878.

30. Nystrom, *New Orleans After the Civil War*, 188–89.

31. Nystrom, *New Orleans After the Civil War*, 192, 199.

32. "Address of the National Party of Louisiana to the People," *Daily Picayune*, November 3, 1878.

33. Joy Jackson argued that the 1884 World's Fair was a critical event that marked New Orleans' re-emergence as a competitive, noteworthy city in the late nineteenth century. Building upon Jackson's work, Samuel Shepherd suggested that the exposition's importance stretched beyond rebuilding the city's reputation. He argued that it provided American tourists and Louisianans alike "a glimmer of hope for the future." According to him, the World's Exposition and the city of New Orleans became symbolic of the New South—a region that was unearthing itself from debris of the Civil War and Reconstruction by promoting both commercial and industrial development. Joy Jackson, *New Orleans in the Gilded Age: Politics and Urban Progress, 1880–1896* (Baton Rouge: Published by Louisiana State University Press for the Louisiana Historical Association, 1969), 204–6; Samuel Shepherd, "A Glimmer of Hope: The World's Industrial and Cotton Centennial Exposition, New Orleans, 1884–1885," *Louisiana History*, 26, no. 3 (Summer 1985): 271–90.

34. Lydia Strawn, *Illinois Central World's Exposition Messenger* (c. 1884), 11–13, Fairs & Festival World's Fair (1884), Folder 1, Louisiana Research Collection, Howard-Tilton Memorial Library, Tulane University, New Orleans, LA (hereafter cited as LaRC).

35. For works that explore Americans' romanticization of the South, see Karen L. Cox, *Dreaming of Dixie: How the South Was Created in American Popular Culture* (Chapel Hill: University of North Carolina Press, 2011); Emily Epstein Landau, *Spectacular Wickedness: Sex, Race, and Memory in Storyville, New Orleans* (Baton Rouge: Louisiana State University Press, 2013); Kevin Fox Gotham, *Authentic New Orleans: Tourism, Culture, and Race in the Big Easy* (New York: New York University Press, 2007); Anthony Stanonis, *Creating the Big Easy: New Orleans and the Emergence of Modern Tourism, 1918–1945* (Athens: University of Georgia Press, 2006).

36. *Our Great All Around Tour* (New York: Leve & Alden Printing Company, 1884), 23, Fairs & Festival World's Fair (1884), Folder 1, LaRC.

37. Gotham, *Authentic New Orleans*, 46.

38. New Orleans and other American cities had poor reputations in the nineteenth century. Americans saw urban centers as dangerous and dirty. During the late nineteenth century, however, Americans slowly changed their perceptions of American cities and began to see their cultural worth. Stanonis, *Creating the Big Easy*, 4; Cox, *Dreaming of Dixie*, 109.

39. Examples of promotional pamphlets include Strawn, *Illinois Central*; *Our Great All Around Tour*; *Visitors' Guide to The World's Industrial and Cotton Centennial Exposition* (Louisville, KY: Courier-Journal Printing Co., 1884), Fairs & Festival World's Fair (1884), Folder 1, LaRC.

40. Strawn, *Illinois Central*.

41. "New Orleans City Worthies," *Daily Picayune*, March 26, 1837.

42. Introduction to *Historical Sketchbook and Guide to New Orleans and Environs* (New York: Will H. Coleman, 1885).

43. Lafcadio Hearn, "At the Gate of the Tropics," in *Inventing New Orleans: Writings of Lafcadio Hearn*, ed. S. Frederick Starr (Jackson: University Press of Mississippi, 2001), 7.

44. *New York Commercial Advertiser* excerpted in *New Orleans Times-Democrat*, December 22, 1884 as cited in Gotham, *Authentic New Orleans*, 55. Note: Gotham cited the original newspaper as *New York Commercial Advisor*, but I believe the source may have been the *New Orleans Commercial Advertiser*.

45. Lafcadio Hearn, "A Creole Type," *The Selected Writings of Lafcadio Hearn*, ed. Henry Goodman (New York: Citadel Press, 1971), 260. Note: Other southern port towns were described as "sleepy." See descriptions of Charleston in Harriette Kershaw Leiding, *Street Cries of an Old Southern City* (Charleston: Daggett Printing Co., 1910). When writers described the American Sector, they regularly fixated on Canal Street, which abuts the French Quarter. This was the city's main

shopping district and thus had the most recently updated amenities like electricity and public transportation. Postcards that feature Canal Street in the first half of the twentieth century, for example, show the street lined with electric lights and the towering buildings flanking it ablaze with light bulbs. Postcard of Canal Street by Night, Box: Louisiana, U.S. Postcards, Postcard Collection, David M. Rubenstein Rare Book & Manuscript Library, Duke University, Durham, NC (hereafter cited as Rubenstein).

46. Stephanie Foote, *Regional Fictions: Culture and Identity in Nineteenth-Century American Literature* (Madison: University of Wisconsin Press, 2001), 3.

47. This cultural mingling was often captured and represented on postcards, which tourists sent to friends and family back home. See, for example, the following postcards: "Interior—French Market—New Orleans, LA. 36"; "Vestibule French Market, New Orleans, LA"; "Famous Old French Market, New Orleans, La.—11," Box: Louisiana U.S. Postcards, Postcard Collection, Rubenstein.

48. Lafcadio Hearn, "Voices of Dawn," in *Selected Writings*, 266–68.

49. For additional examples of calas vendors speaking and singing in Creole, see Saxon, *Gumbo Ya-Ya*, 33–34; Federal Writers' Project, *New Orleans City Guide*, ed. Delia LaBarre (Boston: Houghton Mifflin, 1938), 165; Howard Mitcham, *Creole Gumbo and All That Jazz* (Gretna, LA: Pelican, 1992), 27–28.

50. Grace King, *New Orleans: The Place and the People* (New York: Macmillan, 1895), 264–65.

51. Hearn, "Voices of Dawn," 266–68.

52. For studies of white Americans' consumption of Black bodies in literature and other works of culture, see Kyla Wazana Tompkins, *Racial Indigestion: Eating Bodies in the 19th Century* (New York: New York University Press, 2012) and Theresa McCulla, *Insatiable City: Food and Race in New Orleans* (Chicago: University of Chicago Press, 2024).

53. The image of the French mustard seller can be found between pages 124 and 125. Célestine Eustis, *Cooking in the Old Créole Days: La Cuisine Créole à l'Usage des Petits Menages* (New York, R. H. Russell, 1903).

54. My translation.

55. The image of the young calas girl can be found between pages 101 and 102. Eustis, *Cooking in the Old Créole Days*.

56. Tanya Sheehan wrote of the photographic smile in the early twentieth century and how white Americans sought to imitate Black expression in photographs to momentarily partake in the Black lived experience, and in particular Black people's emotions and physicality. Tanya Sheehan, "Looking Pleasant, Feeling White: The Social Politics of the Photographic Smile," in *Feeling Photography*, ed. Elspeth H. Brown and Thy Phu (Durham, NC: Duke University Press, 2014): 127–57.

57. Sheehan, "Looking Pleasant," 152.

58. Sheehan, "Looking Pleasant," 146.

59. Sheehan, "Looking Pleasant," 148.

60. Interview with W. L. Bost, around 1936–38, vol. 11, North Carolina, Part 1, Adams-Hunter, SNP, LOC, April 4, 2023, https://www.loc.gov/item/mesn111/.

61. Interview with Perry McGee, around 1936–38, vol. 10, Missouri, Abbot-Younger, SNP, LOC, April 4, 2023, https://www.loc.gov/item/mesn100/.

62. The St. Louis hotel opened in 1838.

63. "'Toto,' the Old Praline Woman of Canal Street," *Daily Picayune*, August 5, 1894. Note: The *Springfield Republican* republished the article a few weeks later, suggesting that its Massachusetts-based readership would have been interested in learning more about Toto and the mythologized food culture of New Orleans. "Toto the Creole Praline Woman," *Springfield Republican*, August 20, 1894.

64. For works on various forms of resistance within slave society, see Berlin, *Many Thousands Gone*; John W. Blassingame, *The Slave Community: Plantation Life in the Antebellum South* (New York: Oxford University Press, 1979); Eugene D. Genovese, *Roll, Jordan, Roll: The World the Slaves Made* (New York: Pantheon, 1974); Glymph, *Out of the House of Bondage*; Herbert G. Gutman, *The Black Family in Slavery and Freedom, 1750–1925* (New York: Pantheon, 1976); Charles W. Joyner, *Down by the Riverside: A South Carolina Slave Community* (Urbana: University of Illinois Press, 1984); Lawrence W. Levine, *Black Culture and Black Consciousness: Afro-American Folk Thought from Slavery to Freedom* (Oxford; New York: Oxford University Press, 1978); Deborah Gray White, *Ar'n't I a Woman? Female Slaves in the Plantation South* (New York: Norton, 1999).

65. For works that critically examine Black mammy figures and their roles in influencing American perceptions of the South, see Kenneth W. Goings, *Mammy and Uncle Mose: Black Collectibles and American Stereotyping* (Bloomington: Indiana University Press, 1994); Micki McElya, *Clinging to Mammy: The Faithful Slave in Twentieth-Century America* (Cambridge, MA: Harvard University Press, 2007); Jo-Ann Morgan, "Mammy the Huckster: Selling the Old South for the New Century," *American Arts* 9, no. 1 (Spring 1995): 87–109; Patricia A. Turner, *Ceramic Uncles & Celluloid Mammies: Black Images and Their Influence on Culture* (Charlottesville: University of Virginia Press, 2002); Tompkins, *Racial Indigestion*.

66. "Black Mammy," 14–15. Folder 5: Plantations and Planters of Louisiana, undated, Box 13, Lyle Saxon Papers, LaRC.

67. Praline vendor postcard, item number: 959.2.349, Postcards Book 08: Markets & Vendors French Market (hereafter cited as Postcards Book 08), Williams Research Center, The Historic New Orleans Collection, New Orleans, LA (hereafter cited as HNOC).

68. Praline vendor postcard, item number: 1983.10, Postcards Book 08, HNOC. Note: The image on this postcard was also featured in the following cookbook: *A Book of Famous Old New Orleans Recipes Used in the South for More Than 200 Years* (New Orleans: Peerless Printing Co., 1900).

69. *A Book of Famous Old New Orleans Recipes.*

70. Praline vendor postcard, item number: 959.2.349, Postcards Book 08, HNOC.

71. "'Toto,' the Old Praline Woman of Canal Street," *Daily Picayune*, August 5, 1894.

72. "'Toto,' the Old Praline Woman of Canal Street," *Daily Picayune*, August 5, 1894.

73. Gotham, *Authentic New Orleans*, 54.

74. Fascination with street food vendors was not a new phenomenon. For centuries, Europeans had recorded the images, voices, and culinary traditions of itinerant vendors on the page. Compendiums of street cries and accompanying images and prose text were also popular. Some of the compendiums included William Marshall Craig, *The Itinerant Traders of London* (London: Richland Phillips, 1804); Thomas Rowlandson, *Characteristic Sketches of the Lower Orders* (London: L. Harrison for Samuel Leigh, 1820); Thomas Rowlandson and H. Merke, *Cries of London* (London: R. Ackermann, 1799). A number of books in this genre were written specifically for children: Sam Syntax, *Description of the Cries of London* (London: John Harris, 1821); *Scenes and Cries of London* (London: Dean and Son, Juvenile and Educational Book Warehouse, 1861).

75. Psyche A. Williams-Forson, *Building Houses Out of Chicken Legs: Black Women, Food, & Power* (Chapel Hill: University of North Carolina Press, 2006), 20.

76. "'Toto,' the Old Praline Woman of Canal Street," *Daily Picayune*, August 5, 1894.

77. For works discussing the ways in which women exercised power through their clothing and costumes in New Orleans and the nation, see Stewart, "Fashioning Frenchness"; Laura F. Edwards, *Only the Clothes on her Back: Clothing and the Hidden History of Power in the Nineteenth-Century United States* (New York: Oxford University Press, 2022).

78. "A Relic of the Past: Pen Sketches Along Canal Street Boulevard in New Orleans," *Boston Daily Advertiser* August 29, 1887.

79. "'Toto,' the Old Praline Woman of Canal Street," *Daily Picayune*, August 5, 1894.

80. See, for example, photograph of a praline vendor with the title, "Makin' a Living," printed from the original 1939 negative, Artist Files, Folder: Luria, Corinna Morgiana, HNOC. See also the reference to praline vendors in *Gumbo Ya-Ya*: "Today they [praline vendors] appear, garbed in gingham and starched white aprons and *tignon*, usually in the Vieux Carré, though now they represent modern candy shops." Saxon, *Gumbo Ya-Ya*, 37.

81. "'Toto,' the Old Praline Woman of Canal Street," *Daily Picayune*, August 5, 1894.

82. "Are Pralines Losing Ground?," *Daily Picayune*, November 13, 1893.

83. Saxon, *Gumbo Ya-Ya*, 43–44; Catherine Cole, *The Story of the French Market* (New Orleans: New Orleans Coffee Company, 1916).

84. Cole, *The Story of the French Market*.

85. Martha Reinhard Smallwood Field wrote under the pen name of Catherine Cole. Although the New Orleans Coffee Company published her story in 1916, Field wrote it years prior, around 1884, and several years after Nicaud's death in 1880. Field, born in 1855, may very well have witnessed Nicaud's entrepreneurship firsthand and based her writings on those memories. Andermann, "Brewed Awakening," 184–85.

86. Interview with Anita Fonvergne as cited in Clayton, *Mother Wit*, 77.

87. Interview with Anita Fonvergne as cited in Clayton, *Mother Wit*, 77.

88. "Sale of the Revenues of the Public Markets For the Year 1879," *Daily Picayune*, December 19, 1878; Jacob, "New Orleans' Historic Public Markets," 63.

89. "Sixth District Court: The Private Markets," *Daily Picayune*, March 20, 1878; "Public and Private Markets," *Daily Picayune*, June 4, 1900; "The Market Question Plainly Set Forth," *Daily Picayune*, January 8, 1901.

90. "The House," *Daily Picayune*, February 28, 1878.

91. "The Private Markets," *Daily Picayune*, April 22, 1878; "Not a Religious War, but One Involving a Question of Meat," *Daily Picayune*, April 23, 1878.

92. S.v. "Bernard Barthe," in US census of 1870.

93. "Sixth District Court: The Private Markets," *Daily Picayune*, March 21, 1878.

94. "City Hall Affairs: Cost of Recorder's Courts—the Market War," *Daily Picayune*, April 28, 1879.

95. Jacob, "New Orleans' Historic Public Markets," 64.

96. "The Private Market Trouble Breaks Out in a New Place," *Daily Picayune*, April 7, 1878; "The Private Market Question," *Daily Picayune*, April 9, 1878; "The Vegetable Market War," *Daily Picayune*, April 11, 1878.

97. "The Vegetable Market War," *Daily Picayune*, April 11, 1878.

98. Agricultural Department of the United States, *Report of the Commissioner*, 242.

99. For a study of the evolution of middlemen in the US food industry in the nineteenth century, see Helen Tangires, *Public Markets and Civic Culture in Nineteenth-Century America* (Baltimore: Johns Hopkins University Press, 2003), 21–63.

100. Agricultural Department of the United States, *Report of the Commissioner*, 242–43, 247.

101. "Municipal Affairs," *Daily Picayune*, April 1, 1878.

102. "Sixth District Court," *Daily Picayune*, January 27, 1878.

103. "Municipal Affairs," *Daily Picayune*, April 1, 1878.

104. S.v. "Victor Anseman," in US census of 1900.

105. S.v. "Magdeline Ansemann," in US census of 1880.

106. Despite my best research efforts, I could not find Mrs. H. Dumestre's given name in the archival record.

107. "The Private Market Trouble Breaks Out in a New Place," *Daily Picayune*, April 7, 1878; "The Private Market Question," *Daily Picayune*, April 9, 1878; "The Vegetable Market War," *Daily Picayune*, April 11, 1878.

108. "The Vegetable Market War," *Daily Picayune*, April 11, 1878.

109. "On Trial: A Practical Case Respecting Fruit Vending," *Daily Picayune*, April 4, 1878.

110. "Municipal Brevities," *Daily Picayune*, April 21, 1878.

111. Letter from hucksters in Portsmouth, Virginia, to General Oliver Otis Howard, May 21, 1866, NMAHC.FB.M752, File 2.7.8, Registers and Letters Received by the Commissioner of the Bureau of Refugees, Freedmen, and Abandoned Lands, 1865–1872, National Museum of African American History and Culture, Washington, DC.

112. Letter from hucksters in Portsmouth, Virginia, Registers and Letters Received by the Commissioner of the Bureau of Refugees, Freedmen, and Abandoned Lands, 1865–1872.

113. Letter from hucksters in Portsmouth, Virginia, Registers and Letters Received by the Commissioner of the Bureau of Refugees, Freedmen, and Abandoned Lands, 1865–1872.

114. Letter from hucksters in Portsmouth, Virginia, Registers and Letters Received by the Commissioner of the Bureau of Refugees, Freedmen, and Abandoned Lands, 1865–1872.

115. Letter from hucksters in Portsmouth, Virginia, Registers and Letters Received by the Commissioner of the Bureau of Refugees, Freedmen, and Abandoned Lands, 1865–1872.

116. Letter from hucksters in Portsmouth, Virginia, Registers and Letters Received by the Commissioner of the Bureau of Refugees, Freedmen, and Abandoned Lands, 1865–1872. Note: For a study of northern planters' role in the revitalization of the southern agricultural economy and the problematic use of Black labor to perpetuate an abusive plantation economy in the Reconstruction era, see Lawrence N. Powell, *New Masters: Northern Planters During the Civil War and Reconstruction* (New Haven: Yale University Press, 1980).

117. Letter from hucksters in Portsmouth, Virginia, Registers and Letters Received by the Commissioner of the Bureau of Refugees, Freedmen, and Abandoned Lands, 1865–1872.

118. Letter from hucksters in Portsmouth, Virginia, Registers and Letters Received by the Commissioner of the Bureau of Refugees, Freedmen, and Abandoned Lands, 1865–1872.

119. Letter from hucksters in Portsmouth, Virginia, Registers and Letters Received by the Commissioner of the Bureau of Refugees, Freedmen, and Abandoned Lands, 1865–1872.

120. Dominique M. Hawkins and Catherine E. Barrier, "Bywater Historic District," *nola.gov*, City of New Orleans Historic Landmarks Commission, May 2011, https://www.nola.gov/nola/media/HDLC/Historic%20Districts/Bywater.pdf.

121. In the postbellum period, elites moved away from the inner city and resettled near City Park, uptown along St. Charles Avenue (around the modern-day campus of Tulane University), and also along Esplanade Avenue. Campanella, *Bienville's Dilemma*, 175. Note: "Garden suburb" is a term used among historical geographers to describe urban areas that are "leafier and more bucolic that the congested urban core." Richard Campanella, direct message on X to Ashley Rose Young, August 15, 2023.

122. Campanella, *Bienville's Dilemma*, 176.

123. Nystrom, *Creole Italian*, 75; Richard Campanella, *Geographies of New Orleans: Urban Fabrics Before the Storm* (Lafayette: University of Louisiana at Lafayette Center for Louisiana Studies, 2006), 200.

124. Campanella, *Geographies of New Orleans*, 315.

125. Campanella, *Bienville's Dilemma*, 176.

126. S.v. "Torre Gracia" and "Lina Gracia," in US census of 1880.

127. S.v. "Nenette Lecausse," in US census of 1880.

128. S.v. "Lucie Luccassio," "Joseph Luccassio," "Mary Luccassio," and "Nicolas Colessi," in US census of 1880.

129. S.v. "Nicholas Clesi" and "Mary Clesi," in US census of 1910; s.v. "Nicholas Clesi" and "Mary Clesi," in US census of 1920.

130. Nystrom, *Creole Italian*, 70.

131. Hearn, "Voices of Dawn," 266–68.

132. Lafcadio Hearn, *The New Orleans of Lafcadio Hearn: Illustrated Sketches from the Daily City Item*, ed. Delia LaBarre (Baton Rouge: Louisiana State University Press, 2007), 81.

133. "Peddling Pests," *Daily Picayune*, April 4, 1889.

134. "Noises of the Dawn," *Daily Picayune*, May 25, 1900.

135. For a study of racial identity, and its ambiguity, among Italian and Italian American communities in the Gulf South, see Jessica Barbata Jackson, *Sicilians, Race, and Citizenship in the Jim Crow Gulf South* (Baton Rouge: Louisiana State University Press, 2020).

136. For works that examine the fear that some white Americans held of Black men and the means by which they attempted to control Black bodies, see Crystal Nicole Feimster, *Southern Horrors: Women and the Politics of Rape and Lynching* (Cambridge, MA: Harvard University Press, 2009); Danielle L. McGuire, *At the Dark End of the Street: Black Women, Rape, and Resistance: A New History of the Civil Rights Movement, from Rosa Parks to the Rise of Black Power* (New York: Alfred A. Knopf, 2010); Hannah Rosén, *Terror in the Heart of Freedom: Citizenship, Sexual Violence, and the Meaning of Race in the Postemancipation South* (Chapel Hill: University of North Carolina Press, 2009). For additional relevant works on gender and race in the American South, see Gail Bederman, *Manliness & Civilization: A Cultural History of Gender and Race in the United States, 1880–1917* (Chicago: University of Chicago Press, 1995); Glenda Gilmore, *Gender and Jim Crow: Women and the Politics of White Supremacy in North Carolina, 1896–1920* (Chapel Hill: University of North Carolina Press, 1996).

137. New Orleans, La., City Ordinance 356, N.C.S. (1900).

138. *City of New Orleans v. Fargot*, 116 La., 370–71 (1906).

139. In 1911, the city amended the ordinance permitting street vendors, once again, to vocalize and to knock on doors and ring door bells "during the hours allowed by law for peddling and hawking," that is, not between six in the morning and noon when the public markets were open for business. The modified law went into effect January 1, 1912. New Orleans, La., City Ordinance 7741, N.C.S. (1911).

140. "Peddlers Become Too Boisterous: Six Men Fined by Recorder Hughes," *New Orleans Item*, July 21, 1904. Note: New Orleans' recorders were city officials with the power to fine and imprison people who broke the law. The Recorders Courts operated without the aid of a jury.

141. *City of New Orleans v. Tony Renfero, Nicola Aranda, Tony Latriglio, Sam Carruso, Emile Martin and Charlie Mayensa* (First Recorder's Court of the City of New Orleans, July 21, 1904), NOPL. Note: These archival materials are included in a Criminal District Court case that was perhaps an appeal to the original Recorder's Court case, according to NOPL archivist Brittanny Silva. For the District Court case, see *State v. Renfero, Tony et al.*, 33547 (Orleans Parish Criminal District Court, Section A), NOPL.

142. "Peddlers Become Too Boisterous: Six Men Fined by Recorder Hughes," *New Orleans Item*, July 21, 1904. Note: The archival record indicates slight variations in the vendors' names. There are, for example, some difference between what was reported in the newspaper versus the court records.

143. "Peddlers Arrested," *Daily Picayune*, June 30, 1905.

144. "Peddlers Arrested," *Daily Picayune*, June 30, 1905.

145. Nystrom, *Creole Italian*, 88.

146. Campanella, *Bienville's Dilemma*, 94, 311.

CHAPTER 4

1. "Inviting the Cholera," *Daily Picayune*, July 13, 1884.

2. "Inviting the Cholera," *Daily Picayune*, July 13, 1884; "The Dryades Market," *Daily Picayune*, July 16, 1884.

3. "An Attack on the Private Markets," *Daily Picayune*, May 24, 1900.

4. For the year of 1879, for example, the city leased out the market revenues for the Fruits and Vegetable Markets in the French Market complex, the French Meat Market, and the Poydras, Pilie, Tremé, Washington, Port, St. Bernard, Le Breton, St. Mary's, Jefferson, Sorapuru, Ninth Street, Algiers, Claiborne, and Dryades Markets. "Sale of the Revenues of the Public Markets for the Year 1879," *Daily Picayune*, December 19, 1878.

5. Prior to 1885, the city government shutdown and demolished the Port Market. Jacob, "New Orleans' Historic Public Markets," 114.

6. "Wayside Notes," *Daily City Item*, February 2, 1891.

7. "The Suburban Market," *Daily Picayune*, September 6, 1896.

8. "Looking Through the Markets," *Daily Picayune*, July 3, 1883; "Misdeeds and Mishaps," *Daily Picayune*, July 18, 1882; "A Tumbling Market," *Daily Picayune*, November 30, 1885.

9. "Merchant Near Public Markets Hold Meeting Last Night and Appoint Delegations to Go to Baton Rouge," *Daily Picayune*, June 12, 1900.

10. Sauder, "The Origin and Spread," 287–88.

11. *The Picayune's Creole Cook Book*, 2nd ed. (New Orleans: Picayune Publishing Company, 1901), 35.

12. "M'Donogh Has His Eye on the Ball," *Daily Picayune*, April 22, 1900; "A Discussion on the Public and Private Markets," *Daily Picayune*, May 24, 1900.

13. "A Discussion on the Public and Private Markets," *Daily Picayune*, May 24, 1900.

14. "Favors Private Markets and Peddlers," *Daily Picayune*, June 5, 1900.

15. "City Hall: Matters for Legislation to Be Considered Monday Night," *Daily Picayune*, April 8, 1900.

16. "Petitions," *Daily Picayune*, April 4, 1900. Note: There is inconsistency in the historic record regarding the length of the radius rules. Some sources approximated nine blocks as thirty-two hundred feet and others as three thousand feet. For an example of the latter, see "Elimination of Odd Law on City Market Restrictions Held Needed," *New Orleans Item*, August 27, 1941.

17. "An Attack on the Private Markets," *Daily Picayune*, May 24, 1900; "The Market Question Plainly Set Forth," *Daily Picayune*, January 8, 1901.

18. "Legislative Committee," *Daily Picayune*, May 18, 1900; "An Attack on the Private Markets," *Daily Picayune*, May 24, 1900.

19. "An Attack on the Private Markets," *Daily Picayune*, May 24, 1900; s.v. "Frank Zenglel," in US census of 1900.

20. "An Attack on the Private Markets," *Daily Picayune*, May 24, 1900.

21. "The Legislative Committee," *Daily Picayune*, April 10, 1900.

22. "An Attack on the Private Markets," *Daily Picayune*, May 24, 1900; "Rabito," *Daily Picayune*, October 2, 1903; s.v. "Anthony P Rabito," in US census of 1900.

23. "A.P. Rabito," *Daily Item*, February 8, 1901.

24. "Favors Private Markets and Peddlers," *Daily Picayune*, June 5, 1900.

25. "An Attack on the Private Markets," *Daily Picayune*, May 24, 1900; s.v. "McCaleb E. Howard, jr.," in *Soards' New Orleans City Directory* (New Orleans: Soards Directory Co., 1900), 560.

26. "An Attack on the Private Markets," *Daily Picayune*, May 24, 1900.

27. The city government passed the peddler ordinance on November 14, 1900; "The Market Ordinance," *Times-Picayune*, January 8, 1901.

28. New Orleans, La., City Ordinance 356, N.C.S. (1900).

29. "The Market Question Plainly Set Forth," *Daily Picayune*, January 8, 1901.

30. "The Market Question Plainly Set Forth," *Daily Picayune*, January 8, 1901.

31. New Orleans, La., City Ordinance 7741, N.C.S. (1911).

32. For an in-depth study of corner grocery stores in New Orleans, see Begue, "Considering the New Orleans Corner Store."

33. The ordinance was passed on October 24, 1900, see New Orleans, La., City Ordinance 312, N.C.S (1900).

34. "The Market Question Plainly Set Forth," *Daily Picayune*, January 8, 1901.

35. "The Market Ordinance," *Daily Picayune*, January 8, 1901; "The Market Question Plainly Set Forth," January 8, 1901, 9.

36. "The Market Question Plainly Set Forth," *Daily Picayune*, January 8, 1901.

37. "An Attack on the Private Markets," *Daily Picayune*, May 24, 1900.

38. "The Market Question Plainly Set Forth," *Daily Picayune*, January 8, 1901.

39. "The Market Ordinance," *Daily Picayune*, January 8, 1901.

40. "The Market Question Plainly Set Forth," *Daily Picayune*, January 8, 1901.

41. "Zengel Market," *Daily Picayune*, January 7, 1900.

42. "The 'Quasi' Market Facts and Figures," *Daily Picayune*, January 24, 1901.

43. "Zengel Market," *Daily Picayune*, January 7, 1900.

44. The local newspapers referred to Agatha Bertucci by her married name, Mrs. Anthony Bertucci. "Death of Mrs. Anthony Bertucci," *Daily Picayune*, April 29, 1911.

45. S.v. "Hattie Bertucci," in US censuses of 1900 and 1910.

46. "The Shrimp Law," *Daily Picayune*, June 4, 1906; s.v. "Annie W. Rabito," in US census of 1900.

47. "Rabito," *Daily Picayune*, October 2, 1903.

48. "The 'Quasi' Market Facts and Figures," *Daily Picayune*, January 24, 1901.

49. "The 'Quasi' Market Facts and Figures," *Daily Picayune*, January 24, 1901.

50. "The 'Quasi' Market Facts and Figures," *Daily Picayune*, January 24, 1901.

51. "Mayor's Regular Message," *Daily Picayune*, January 10, 1906; "Looking Up Public Markets," *Daily Picayune*, January 14, 1906; "The Mayor's Message," *Daily Picayune*, January 30, 1907.

52. "Keep Off the Sidewalks," *Daily Picayune*, September 2, 1905.

53. Sauder, "The Origin and Spread," 287–88.

54. "Progressive and Popular Merchants of Dryades St.," *Daily States*, October 25, 1903.

55. "Leading Merchants 9th Street Market District," *Daily States*, November 29, 1903.

56. "Dryades Market Continued," *Daily States*, November 22, 1903.

57. Flettrich's efforts to maintain his stand paid off. Lawrence's Coffee Stand reportedly served one thousand customers a day in 1903. "The Leading Merchants of Poydras Market," *Daily States*, December 20, 1903.

58. James Harvey Young, *Pure Food: Securing the Federal Food and Drug Act of 1906* (Princeton, NJ: Princeton University Press, 1989), 40–52.

59. Young, *Pure Food*, 40–52.

60. For key works on the history of the Pure Food Movement, see Philip J. Hilts, *Protecting America's Health: The FDA, Business, and One Hundred Years of Regulation* (Chapel Hill: University of North Carolina Press, 2004); Young, *Pure Food*; Lorine Goodwin, *The Pure Food, Drink and Drug Crusaders* (Jefferson, NC: McFarland, 1999).

61. "The Pure Food Bill," *Daily Picayune*, February 26, 1906.

62. "Enforcing the Pure Food Law," *Daily Picayune*, July 4, 1906.

63. "A Market Raid," *Daily Picayune*, November 21, 1908.

64. "Rotten Meat in Markets," *Daily Picayune*, August 24, 1906.

65. "Will Prosecute Meat Dealers," *Daily Picayune*, August 3, 1907.

66. "Will Prosecute Meat Dealers," *Daily Picayune*, August 3, 1907; "A Market Raid," *Daily Picayune*, November 21, 1908.

67. "Dryades St. and Market—the Daily States Publishes a Page for the Benefit of the Market and Street Every Sunday.—Warmly Supported by Businessmen—Readers Invited to Peruse the Announcements and Visit the Advertisers All Lines of Trace Represented Here," *Daily States*, October 25, 1903.

68. I paired information in the *Daily States* profiles with city directories to map out where vendors lived, therefore determining their proximity to the public markets.

69. "Ninth St. Market District Makes a Grand Showing—the Leading Merchants Advertise in the Sunday Morning States—They Wish to Make Known the Advantages of Trading at This Important Center of Commerce—Every Business Extensively Represented and Their Trading Capacity Fully Set Forth," *Daily States*, November 15, 1903.

70. "Progressive and Popular Merchants of Dryades St.," *Daily States*, October 25, 1903.

71. "Dryades Market Continued," *Daily States*, November 1, 1903; s.v. "Bradburn Marshall M.," in *Soards' New Orleans City Directory for 1903*, vol. 30 (New Orleans: Soards Directory Co., 1903), 1038.

72. "Dryades Market Continued," *Daily States*, November 8, 1903; s.v. "Leidenheimer George H," in *Soards' New Orleans City Directory for 1903*, vol. 30, 545.

73. "Dryades Market Continued," *Daily States*, November 8, 1903; s.v. "Charles A. Kaufman," in *Soards' New Orleans City Directory for 1903*, vol. 30, 489.

74. Campanella, *Bienville's Dilemma*, 170.

75. Jacob Brener owned a clothing store on Dryades Street and lived at 1401 Baronne Street. His relation, Philip Brener, was listed in the city directory as living at the same residence and having the occupation of a peddler. The Brenner residence was about a seven-minute walk from Kaufman's grand home on St. Charles Avenue. S.v. "Brener Jacob" and "Brener Philip," in *Soards' New Orleans City Directory for 1903*, vol. 30, 152.

76. "Dryades Market Continued," *Daily States*, November 1, 1903; s.v. "Flettrich Lawrence" and "Flettrich Philip," in *Soards' New Orleans City Directory for 1903*, vol. 30, 337.

77. "Dryades Market District Continued," *Daily States*, January 10, 1904.

78. Jessica Williams, "Mayor Cantrell Apologizes for 1891 Italian-American Lynchings in New Orleans," *New Orleans Advocate*, April 12, 2019.

79. "Poydras Market Continued," *Daily States*, January 10, 1904.

80. "Some of the Leading and Progressive Merchants of the Great Historical French Market and Its Surroundings," *Daily States*, December 20, 1902.

81. "Progressive and Popular Merchants of Dryades St.," *Daily States*, December 27, 1903.

82. "Poydras Market Continued," *Daily States*, January 10, 1904.

83. S.v. "Paul St. Philip," in US census of 1900.

84. "Some of the Leading and Progressive Merchants of the Great Historical French Market and Its Surroundings," *Daily States*, December 27, 1903; s.v. "Henry J. Schenck," US census of 1900.

85. "Progressive and Popular Merchants of Dryades St.," *Daily States*, January 10, 1904.

86. Eugenia Marine Lacarra, interviewed by Artheé A. Anthony, New Orleans, December 9, 1977 as cited in Artheé A. Anthony, "'Lost Boundaries': Racial Passing and Poverty in Segregated New Orleans," in Kein, *Creole*, 303.

87. James M. Montoya Sr., interviewed by Artheé A. Anthony, New Orleans, March 15, 1977 as cited in Anthony, " 'Lost Boundaries,' " 310.

88. "The Ewing Market," *Daily Picayune*, October 18, 1907.

89. "Ewing Market Named with Pretty Ceremony," *Daily Picayune*, October 24, 1907.

90. "Health Campaign," *Daily Picayune*, October 4, 1907.

91. "Health Campaign," *Daily Picayune*, October 4, 1907.

92. "Doullut Market Accepted by the City Favored," *Daily Picayune*, May 31, 1907; "Behrman Quasi Public Market," *Daily Picayune*, February 27, 1901.

93. In architectural terms, the markets were open-sided front gable structures with wide awnings over the sidewalks. They were about two bays wide by five bays deep. Louvered vents occupied the upper portion of each bay. "Doullut Market Accepted by the City Favored," *Daily Picayune*, May 31, 1907; "Theodore Foto Market," *Times-Picayune*, July 31, 1910, 7.

94. The Port, Washington, and St. John Markets had been demolished by 1911, but the communities that had lived near these razed structures had similarly convenient access to more recently built public markets, including the St. John, Zengel, and Lautenschlaeger Markets. Jacob, "New Orleans' Historic Public Markets," 107.

95. New Orleans' system paralleled those of several major European cities that had a central wholesale-retail market and a series of auxiliary markets. Antwerp, for example, had a robust system consisting of twenty-one markets in the early twentieth century. Such parallels existed because major European cities drew inspiration from each other's public market cultures, especially that of Paris. Clyde Lyndon King, "Municipal Markets," *Annals of the American Academy of Political and Social Science* 50 (November 1913): 110.

96. King, "Municipal Markets," 110.

97. Speech made at Round Table Club, around 1915, Market Committee Records, 1913–1916 (hereafter cited as MCR), Box 1, Folder 985-1-5, LaRC.

CHAPTER 5

1. The local newspapers referred to Lucia Sargent by her married name, Mrs. Gordon Sargent.

2. Notes from State Board of Health 1912, MCR, Box 1, Folder 985-1-1, LaRC.

3. Notes from State Board of Health 1912, MCR, Box 1, Folder 985-1-1, LaRC.

4. Saxon, *Gumbo Ya-Ya*, 27.

5. "Fly Ordinance Again," *Daily Picayune*, March 21, 1911; "Crescent City Notes," *New Advocate*, March 21, 1911; "Fly Ordinance Finds No Favor," *Daily Picayune*, March 24, 1911.

6. "Modern Model Public Markets: Dryades to Be First Rebuilt," *Daily Picayune*, July 31, 1910. Note: New Orleanians dealt with frequent disease outbreaks beyond salmonella, like yellow fever, typhoid, malaria, cholera, among others, some of which residents also tied back to the poor sanitary conditions around food distribution.

Over the course of the nineteenth century, thousands of New Orleanians died from these diseases. Campanella, *Bienville's Dilemma*, 94, 311.

7. See Anne Hardy's work on Great Britain as a case study for the scientific and cultural awareness of germ theory and specifically how it impacted cultures of consumption at the turn of the twentieth century. Anne Hardy, *Salmonella Infections, Networks of Knowledge, and Public Health in Britain, 1880–1975* (Oxford: Oxford University Press, 2015), 69–71.

8. "Fly Ordinance Finds No Favor," *Daily Picayune*, March 24, 1911.

9. "Fly Ordinance Finds No Favor," *Daily Picayune*, March 24, 1911.

10. "Fly Ordinance Again," *Daily Picayune*, March 21, 1911.

11. "McCue Market First to Screen Itself," *Daily Picayune*, July 19, 1912.

12. "Doullut Market Accepted by the City Favored," *Daily Picayune*, May 31, 1907.

13. "Modern Model Public Markets: Dryades to Be First Rebuilt," *Daily Picayune*, July 31, 1910; "Paving Progress Has Been Made," *Daily Picayune*, September 1, 1913.

14. For works on the City Beautiful movement and the history of urban planning in the United States, in general, see Carl S. Smith, *The Plan of Chicago: Daniel Burnham and the Remaking of the American City* (Chicago: University of Chicago Press, 2006); Jon A. Peterson, *The Birth of City Planning in the United States, 1840–1917* (Baltimore: Johns Hopkins University Press, 2003).

15. "Fly Ordinance Again," *Daily Picayune*, March 21, 1911.

16. "Modern Model Public Markets: Dryades to Be First Rebuilt," *Daily Picayune*, July 31, 1910. Note: The city government also focused on technological improvements in its public campaign to renovate the market, noting that the new Dryades Market would be screened and would have a system of exhaust fans to keep air flowing through the building.

17. "Modern Model Public Markets: Dryades to Be First Rebuilt," *Daily Picayune*, July 31, 1910; "Budget Committee Matters," *Daily Picayune*, November 12, 1910; "New Dryades Market," *Daily Picayune*, September 8, 1911; "Mayor Behrman Urges Acceptance of Delgado Trade School Bequest: Dryades Market Refrigerator," *Daily Picayune*, March 27, 1912; Notes from State Board of Health 1912, MCR, Box 1, Folder 985-1-1, LaRC; Beth A. Jacob, "Seated at the Table: The Southern Food and Beverage Museum's New Home on Oretha Castle Haley Boulevard," *Preservation in Print* 41, no. 8 (November, 2014): 22–23.

18. Roof Plan of Dryades Market Building A, Building Plans Collection, Number II-23 (hereafter cited as BPC II-23), NOPL.

19. Cross Section of Dryades Market Building A, BPC II-23, NOPL.

20. Front Elevation of the Dryades Market Building A and Side Elevation of Arcade Between Building A and B, BPC II-23, NOPL.

21. "Views of New Market House That Was Opened Yesterday," *Plain Dealer*, November 5, 1912. For works analyzing the evolution and significance of hospital architecture as it relates to increased understandings of sanitation, cleanliness, and germ theory, see Jeanne Kisacky, "Germs Are in the Details: Aseptic Design and

General Constructors at the Lying-In Hospital of the City of New York, 1897–1901," *Construction History* 28, no. 1 (2013): 83–106; Jeanne Kisacky, *Rise of the Modern Hospital: An Architectural History of Health and Healing, 1870–1940* (Pittsburgh: University of Pittsburgh Press, 2017), 56–57; Christine Stevenson, *Medicine and Magnificence: British Hospital and Asylum Architecture, 1660–1815* (New Haven: Yale University Press, 2000); Leslie Topp, *Freedom and the Cage: Modern Architecture and Psychiatry in Central Europe, 1890–1914* (University Park: Penn State University Press, 2017).

22. Notes from State Board of Health 1912, MCR, Box 1, Folder 985-1-1, LaRC.

23. For example works highlighting the history of consumer activism, see National Consumers Committee for Research and Education and Consumers Union Foundation, *Consumer Activists: They Made a Difference. A History of Consumer Action Related by Leaders in the Consumer Movement* (Mount Vernon, NY: Consumers Union Foundation, 1982); Emily E. LaBarbera-Twarog, *Politics of the Pantry: Housewives, Food, and Consumer Protest in Twentieth-Century America* (Oxford: Oxford University Press, 2017).

24. Pamela Tyler, *Silk Stockings and Ballot Boxes: Women and Politics in New Orleans, 1920–1963* (Athens: University of Georgia Press, 1996), 3.

25. For an excellent analysis of how women consumer-activists used rhetoric around public health crises to further marginalize Black New Orleanians in the municipal markets of New Orleans, see Theresa McCulla, "Consumable City: Race, Ethnicity, and Food in Modern New Orleans" (PhD diss., Harvard University, 2017), 112–23.

26. The Pure Food and Drug Act of 1906, which prevented the distribution and sale of adulterated or harmful foods as well as drugs, medicine, and liquor in the United States, was a major example of the growing federal presence in communities across the country. For works focusing on the role of grassroots activism in shaping public health, and those efforts' connections to women's enfranchisement in the Progressive Era, see Maureen A. Flanagan, *Seeing with Their Hearts: Chicago Women and the Vision of the Good City, 1871–1933* (Princeton, NJ: Princeton University Press, 2002); Jennifer Lisa Koslow, *Cultivating Health: Los Angeles Women and Public Health Reform* (New Brunswick, NJ: Rutgers University Press, 2009).

27. For a work focusing on the role of women in perpetuating white supremacy through grassroots activism, see Elizabeth Gillespie McRae, *Mothers of Massive Resistance: White Women and the Politics of White Supremacy* (New York: Oxford University Press, 2018).

28. "Brave Dr. Dowling," *Daily Picayune*, December 16, 1912.

29. "Editor's Point of View: A City Federation," *New Orleans Item*, June 9, 1912.

30. Report of the Market Committee, Housewives' League Division, City Federation of Clubs, March 24, 1914 ((hereafter cited as Report of the Market Committee), MCR, Box 1, Folder 985-1-2, LaRC.

31. "Women's Work to Cheapen Living," *Times-Picayune*, January 21, 1914; Report of the Market Committee, MCR, Box 1, Folder 985-1-2, LaRC.

32. "Women's Work to Cheapen Living," *Times-Picayune*, January 21, 1914.

33. Report of the Market Committee, MCR, Box 1, Folder 985-1-2, LaRC.

34. New Orleans, La., City Ordinances 1231 and 1221, C.C.S. (1914).

35. "Market Criticism Taken as Meant, Says Lafaye," *New Orleans Item*, February 21, 1915.

36. "Markets to Be Open at All Hours of Day," *Times-Picayune*, December 16, 1914; "Full Time Markets," *Times-Picayune*, January 6, 1915.

37. Report of the Market Committee, MCR, Box 1, Folder 985-1-2, LaRC.

38. New Orleans, La., City Ordinance 1231, C.C.S. (1914). Note: 18 mesh bronze wire has 18 openings per linear inch. "Mesh, Mesh Count," Darby Wire Mesh, accessed May 12, 2023, https://www.darbywiremesh.com/wire-mesh-glossary/; "How to Screen in a Porch: Types of Screen Material," Home Depot, accessed May 12, 2023, https://www.homedepot.com/c/ah/how-to-screen-in-a-porch/9ba683603be9fa5 395fab9012167af12.

39. For works that interpret the significance of the color white in architecture, see Suellen Hoy, "Whiter Than White—and a Glimmer of Green," in *Chasing Dirt: The American Pursuit of Cleanliness* (New York: Oxford University Press, 1995); Mark Wigley, *White Walls, Designer Dresses: The Fashioning of Modern Architecture* (Cambridge, MA: MIT Press, 1995).

40. New Orleans, La., City Ordinance 1231, C.C.S. (1914).

41. Report of the Market Committee, MCR, Box 1, Folder 985-1-2, LaRC.

42. Report of the Market Committee, MCR, Box 1, Folder 985-1-2, LaRC.

43. Report of the Market Committee, MCR, Box 1, Folder 985-1-2, LaRC.

44. "Housewives' League of City Federation of Women' Clubs," *Times-Picayune*, December 27, 1914.

45. The development of residential real estate nearer the shores of Lake Pontchartrain, for example, was in large part due to technological advancements that enabled developers to tame the lakeshore by constructing a seawall; that seawall opened up two thousand acres of prime real estate that resulted in a building boom in the 1920s. Hirsch and Logsdon, *Creole New Orleans*, 198.

46. These lakeshore communities developed almost exclusively as spaces for white residents. Building homes out near Lake Pontchartrain was expensive and cost prohibitive for New Orleans' working poor population of diverse racial backgrounds. Further, "explicit racial prohibitions" ensured that Black community members could not live in these communities. Hirsch and Logsdon, *Creole New Orleans*, 198–99.

47. "L. and N. Shops to Be Fully Rat-Proofed," *New Orleans Item*, August 3, 1914.

48. Richard Campanella, "How New Orleans Handled an Outbreak of Bubonic Plague in 1914," *Preservation in Print*, April 1, 2020, https://prcno.org/how-new-orleans-handled-an-outbreak-of-bubonic-plague-in-1914/.

49. "Educational Work in Rat Campaign Going Merrily On," *Times-Picayune*, July 18, 1914.

50. Sauder, "The Origin and Spread," 288.

51. In 1914, the city government invested in screening in key markets: the Le Breton, St. Bernard, St. Roch, and Ninth Street Markets. According to the US Bureau of the Census report of 1918, six of New Orleans' markets were enclosed at the time the report was published and the other twenty-two markets, including the nine quasi-public ones, were open air. "Improving Markets," *Times-Picayune*, January 17, 1914; "Ninth Street Market," *Times-Picayune*, February 5, 1914; United States Bureau of the Census, *Municipal Markets in Cities Having a Population of over 30,000: 1918* (Washington, DC: Government Printing Office, 1919), 29; Sauder, "The Origin and Spread," 288; Jacob, "New Orleans' Historic Public Markets," 68, 139.

52. "Board Now After Keller Market," *Times-Picayune*, January 11, 1920; Sauder, "The Origin and Spread," 289.

53. "Public Market Reorganization Plans Outlined," *Times-Picayune*, December 17, 1930.

54. "Klorer Submits Plan to Rebuild Public Markets," *Times-Picayune*, March 20, 1930.

55. "Mayor Appoints Group to Study Market Problem," *Times-Picayune*, April 4, 1930.

56. "Klorer Submits Plan to Rebuild Public Markets," *Times-Picayune*, March 20, 1930.

57. Andrew Fitzpatrick, "To the People of New Orleans," *New Orleans States*, March 20, 1930.

58. The twenty-three public markets were the French Market complex as well as the Claiborne, Dryades, Ewing, Foto, Guillotte, Jefferson, Keller, Lautenschlaeger, Le Breton, Magazine, Maestri, Mehle, Memory, Ninth Street, Poydras, Rocheblave, Second Street, St. Bernard, St. Roch, Suburban, Tremé, and Zengel Markets. This list of twenty-three facilities does not include quasi-public markets.

59. Fitzpatrick, "To the People of New Orleans," 13.

60. Although the "Klorer ordinance" made the front page of the *Times-Picayune* and the *Daily States*, I did not find similar coverage of the proposed plan on the front page of the *Louisiana Weekly*, one of New Orleans' historically Black newspapers.

61. "Council Expected to Reject Klorer Market Proposal," *Times-Picayune*, March 28, 1930.

62. "Reject It," *New Orleans States*, April 2, 1930.

63. "Market Leasing Plan Is Scored," *New Orleans States*, April 1, 1930.

64. "Council Expected to Reject Klorer Market Proposal," *Times-Picayune*, March 28, 1930.

65. "Grunewald Mart Report Will Be Studies [*sic*] Today," *Times-Picayune*, January 21, 1931.

66. "Grunewald Mart Report Will Be Studies [*sic*] Today," *Times-Picayune*, January 21, 1931; "Entire Markets Committee Will Conducting Hearing," *Times-Picayune*, January 22, 1931.

67. The federal government's renewed fervor in public markets only lasted so long. Signaling its growing disinterest and investment in public markets, the federal

government folded the Bureau of Markets into the Bureau of Agricultural Economics in 1922. The latter bureau eventually dissolved in 1953. Jacob, "New Orleans' Historic Public Markets," 41–44.

68. "Mayor Appoints Group to Study Market Problem," *Times-Picayune*, April 4, 1930.

69. "Grunewald, Civic Leader, Dies at 77," *New Orleans Item*, July 25, 1949.

70. "Grunewald—," *New Orleans States*, July 25, 1949.

71. "Grunewald, Civic Leader, Dies at 77," *New Orleans Item*, July 25, 1949.

72. "A Builder Passes," *New Orleans Item*, July 26, 1949.

73. "Grunewald—," *New Orleans States*, July 25, 1949.

74. The local newspapers referred to Aurelie Benedict by her married name, Mrs. J. T. Benedict.

75. "Organization Also Gives Endorsement to Public Markets," *Times-Picayune*, April 12, 1930.

76. "Grunewald Back from Market Tour," *Times-Picayune*, June 22, 1930.

77. "Grunewald Market Report Will Be Studies [*sic*] Today," *Times-Picayune*, January 21, 1931.

78. "Grunewald Back from Market Tour," *Times-Picayune*, June 22, 1930.

79. "Report on Survey Made in Seven Cities Delivered by Grunewald," *Times-Picayune*, June 25, 1930.

80. "Public Market Reorganization Plans Outlined," *Times-Picayune*, December 17, 1930.

81. "Public Market Reorganization Plans Outlined," *Times-Picayune*, December 17, 1930.

82. The local newspapers referred to Henrietta Porteous by her married name, Mrs. William A. Porteous.

83. "Public Market Reorganization Plans Outlined," *Times-Picayune*, December 17, 1930.

84. "Public Market Reorganization Plans Outlined," *Times-Picayune*, December 17, 1930.

85. "Organization Also Gives Endorsement to Public Markets," *Times-Picayune*, April 12, 1930.

86. As with the outcries against the "Klorer ordinance" several months earlier, opposition to Grunewald's plan did not make front-page news of the *Louisiana Weekly*, one of the city's historically Black newspapers.

87. "Pratt Firm for Public Markets," *New Orleans States*, December 17, 1930.

88. "Plan for Private Markets Lease Denied by Pratt," *Times-Picayune*, December 18, 1930.

89. "Letters from Readers: Public Market Problem," *Times-Picayune*, December 21, 1930.

90. "Public Markets Rehabilitation Plans Opposed," *Times-Picayune*, December 31, 1930.

91. "Grunewald Market Plan Denounced as Menace to Independent Business," *Times-Picayune*, January 6, 1931.

92. "Grunewald Again Urged to Speed Markets Report," *Times-Picayune*, January 7, 1931.

93. "Grunewald Market Plan Denounced as Menace to Independent Business," *Times-Picayune*, January 6, 1931.

94. "Council Expected to Approve Grunewald," *New Orleans States*, July 21, 1931.

95. "Mayor to Call Markets Board for Conference," *Times-Picayune*, September 19, 1931.

96. "Housewives League to Hear Three Speakers," *New Orleans States*, April 3, 1932; "League Opposes Grocery Sales in Public Marts," *Times-Picayune*, April 9, 1932.

97. "Housewives Plan to File Protest on Bread Quality," *Times-Picayune*, October 14, 1933.

98. "Mrs. Benedict's Funeral Today," *New Orleans Item*, January 20, 1934.

99. "Market Repairs to Be Discussed: Proposal to Seek WPA Funds Will Feature Conference," *Times-Picayune*, October 24, 1935; "Market Repairs Planned by City: Skelly Says Work Depends on Assistance of WPA," *Times-Picayune*, October 26, 1935. For key works on the role of the WPA in funding civic projects in American cities, see *Jobs: The WPA Way* (Washington DC: Works Progress Administration, 1936); David A. Horowitz, "The New Deal and People's Art: Market Planners and Radical Artists," *Oregon Historical Quarterly* 109, no. 2 (Summer 2008): 318–28; Nick Taylor, *American-Made: The Enduring Legacy of the WPA: When FDR Put the Nation to Work* (New York: Bantam, 2008).

100. "Funds for Markets Approved," *Sunday Item-Tribune*, February 27, 1938; "City Market Is 'Before and After' Picture In Itself," *New Orleans Item*, October 13, 1938. Note: The *Times-Picayune* highlighted the municipal government's intention to renovate the Foto Market, but I have not been able to confirm that officials carried out those renovations in the 1930s. "Seven Markets Singled Out for Rehabilitation," *Times-Picayune*, March 11, 1931.

101. "Will Raze 3 Markets Soon: Wreckers to Get Busy on Claiborne, Second St., Guillot [*sic*] Structures," *Item-Tribune*, May 24, 1931, 7; "Poydras Mart to Be Razed," *Item-Tribune*, February 21, 1932; "Group Asks Library," *New Orleans Item*, February 8, 1938; "Ordinance Is Introduced Regarding Property in Council," *Times-Picayune*, March 22, 1939.

102. The total number of operational public markets reported around 1940 varies among the city's newspapers and city directories from sixteen to twenty facilities. Some of these publications include a number of the quasi-public markets in their tallies, while others do not. The city directories, in particular, were known to have listed buildings as "public markets" that no longer operated as such (even if they had been part of the public market overhaul project). In 1940, at least sixteen renovated public markets remained operational according to Mayor Robert S. Maestri's annual message to the commission council. "Text of Mayor's Annual Message Before Council," *Times-Picayune*, August 16, 1940.

103. "Mayor Recounts City's Advances in Past 3 Years," *Times-Picayune*, August 13, 1939.

104. "Business Starts Today at City's Six New Markets," *Times-Picayune*, June 27, 1932; "Grunewald, 76, Former Market Director, Dies," *New Orleans States*, July 25, 1949.

105. "A Builder Passes," *New Orleans Item*, July 26, 1949.

106. Department of Public Markets City of New Orleans, Reports of Custodial Worker (St. Bernard Market) around 1948, Department of Public Markets Miscellaneous Files ca. 1923–1949 (hereafter cited as DPM), Box 1, Folder City Board of Health Reports—Private Markets, Department of Public Markets Old Records, NOPL.

107. At the City Archives & Special Collections at the New Orleans Public Library and the Southeastern Architectural Archive at Tulane University, I have examined the detailed architectural plans created by Sam Stone Jr. & Co. for the following eight markets: Dryades, Magazine, Suburban, Zengel, Ewing, Jefferson, Ninth Street, and Maestri markets.

108. Rental Plan, "Dryades Market—Bldg. A"; Rental Plan, "Suburban"; Fixtures Vegetable Stalls Plan, "Dryades—Bldg. A, Magazine, Ninth St., St. Bernard, Zengel, Ewing, Suburban," Sam Stone, Jr. Office Records, Southeastern Architectural Archive, Tulane University, New Orleans, LA (hereafter cited as SEAA).

109. "Business Starts Today at City's Six New Markets," *Times-Picayune*, June 27, 1932.

110. Joseph Maresca, *WPA Buildings: Architecture and Art of the New Deal* (Atglen, PA: Schiffer Publishing, 2016), 11.

111. "Funds for Markets Approved," *New Orleans Item*, February 27, 1938.

112. "French Market Contracts Let; Total Is $201,886," *Times-Picayune*, June 9, 1936. Note: The French Market was not the only renovated public market to raise concerns for New Orleanians. After the unveiling of the Magazine Market in 1932, the vendors working within the Spanish Colonial Revival building, which had both commercial and community meeting spaces, described its multiuse design as "neither a market nor a house, but a freak of architecture." But more concerning to them than the aesthetic were problems with its functionality as a retail space. They argued that there was not enough room to accommodate the vendors' businesses, nor were there enough electrical appliances or refrigeration facilities. "New Mart 'Freak of Architecture,' Aver Merchants," *Times-Picayune*, July 15, 1932.

113. Richard Striner, "Art Deco: Polemics and Synthesis," *Winterthur Portfolio* 25, no. 1 (1990): 21.

114. Maresca, *WPA Buildings*, 9, 112.

115. C. Matlack Price, "Italian Derivations in American Architecture: The Revival of Architectural Ideals of the Renaissance," *Arts & Decoration* 3, no. 7 (May 1913): 242.

116. David Gebhard, "The Spanish Colonial Revival in Southern California (1895–1930)," *Journal of the Society of Architectural Historians* 26, no. 2 (1967): 131. Note: Spanish Colonial Revival architecture was also popular in Florida at this time, and, as in California, the buildings had very few historic ties to the state.

117. In the early twentieth century, the patronage of restaurants in the American South was dictated more by class than by race. However, the major customer base were white residents, and mainly men. At that time, it was not customary for women to eat with men, although some establishments were defying those social conventions. Typically, though, public eateries were seen as places where white women could be exposed to what were thought to be inappropriate behaviors, "race mixing," among them. As restaurant culture changed approaching mid-century and women dined with men on a regular basis, the popular belief that public dining should remain racially segregated stayed in place. Angela Jill Cooley, *To Live and Dine in Dixie* (Athens: University of Georgia Press, 2015), 47.

118. The architectural plans for the Maestri Market also show racially segregated men's and women's restrooms as well as vestibules.

119. Floor Plan, "Additions to Bldg. 'B' Dryades Market," Nov. 19, 1931, Revised Dec 30, 1931; Floor Plan, "Additions to Bldg. 'B' Dryades Market," Jan. 21, 1932, Revised Jan 21, 1932, Revised Feb 5, 1932; Features, "Showing Addition to & Changes in Floor Layout-Bldg.—'B,'" June 20, 1931; Floor Plan, "Additions to Bldg. 'B' Dryades Market," Jan. 21, 1932. Revised March 2, 1932 and March 9, 1932, Sam Stone, Jr. Office Records, SEAA.

120. The phrase "segregationist instinct" is a formulation of Richard Campanella's. I first saw the term during an exchange we had about racial segregation in New Orleans. Richard Campanella, direct message on Twitter to Ashley Rose Young, August 20, 2016.

121. Millie McClellan Charles, interviewed by Felix Armfield, July 12, 1994 as cited in Lakisha Michelle Simmons, *Crescent City Girls: The Lives of Young Black Women in Segregated New Orleans* (Chapel Hill: University of North Carolina Press, 2015), 31.

122. Interview with J. N. Brown, November-December 1938, vol. 2, Arkansas, Part 1, Abbott-Byrd, SNP, LOC, June 7, 2023, https://www.loc.gov/item/mesn021/.

123. Interview with Harrison Camille as cited in Clayton, *Mother Wit*, 39.

124. Clyde "Kingfish" Smith, interviewed by Herbert Halpert, February 1979 (hereafter cited as Clyde "Kingfish" Smith) as cited in Anna Banks, *First-Person America* (New York: Alfred A. Knopf, 1980), 237.

125. Clyde "Kingfish" Smith as cited in Banks, *First-Person America*, 241.

126. Clyde "Kingfish" Smith as cited in Banks, *First-Person America*, 241.

127. Clyde "Kingfish" Smith as cited in Banks, *First-Person America*, 238.

128. I experienced this kind of business strategy when shopping in the vegetable hall of Cleveland's West Side Market in 2014. I was wearing a Yale University sweatshirt that morning. As I listened to vendors calling out about their wares, I heard one advertising blackberries: "Blackberries! Blackberries! Two cartons for six dollars!" When he spotted me, he modified his street cry: "Yalies love blackberries too! Two cartons for six dollars! C'mon Yalie! Buy some beautiful blackberries!" The parallel between the strategies of twentieth-century Cleveland and nineteenth-century New Orleans was uncanny, demonstrating the continuities that exist in street food culture across temporal and geographic planes.

129. Saxon, *Gumbo Ya-Ya*, 27.

130. There are similarities in how vendors sang their cries across generations suggesting a strong continuity in New Orleans' street crying tradition. For example, the street vendor in Lafcadio Hearn's work cried out, "Black-Breees!" and exaggerated the last syllable. So too did the vendor whose cry was recorded in *Gumbo Ya-Ya*: "Blackber—reeees!" Hearn, "Voices of Dawn," 266–68; Saxon, *Gumbo Ya-Ya*, 28–29.

131. Clyde "Kingfish" Smith as cited in Banks, *First-Person America*, 237.

132. Clyde "Kingfish" Smith as cited in Banks, *First-Person America*, 237–38.

133. Clyde "Kingfish" Smith as cited in Banks, *First-Person America*, 241.

134. Clyde "Kingfish" Smith as cited in Banks, *First-Person America*, 237.

135. Interview with John Evans, around 1936–38, vol. 11, North Carolina, Part 1, Adams-Hunter, SNP, LOC, June 8, 2023, https://www.loc.gov/item/mesn111/.

136. For works that discuss African and Caribbean musical and sonic traditions in slave societies, see Bailey, *African Voices*; Ronald Radano, "Black Music Labor and the Animated Properties of Slave Sound," *Boundary 2* 43, no. 1 (2016): 173–208; Shane White and Graham J. White, *The Sounds of Slavery: Discovering African American History Through Songs, Sermons, and Speech* (Boston: Beacon Press, 2005).

137. Saxon, *Gumbo Ya-Ya*, 35.

138. Saxon, *Gumbo Ya-Ya*, 29.

CHAPTER 6

1. The local newspapers referred to Effie Fisher by her married name, Mrs. G. W. Fisher.

2. Harnett T. Kane, "Orleans' Housewives Want 'One Stop' Stores," *New Orleans Item*, August 29, 1941.

3. Harnett T. Kane, "City's Manner of Handling Food Sales to Housewives Ruled by Unique Law," *New Orleans Item*, August 27, 1941.

4. "Merchants Attack Law on Markets," *New Orleans Item*, July 29, 1940.

5. "The Public Markets," *New Orleans Item*, September 2, 1941.

6. Despite my best research efforts, I could not find Mrs. J. E. Davidson's given name in the archival record.

7. Harnett T. Kane, "Orleans Housewives on Stores," *New Orleans Item*, August 29, 1941.

8. "Text of Mayor's Annual Message Before Council," *Times-Picayune*, August 16, 1940.

9. For key works exploring consumerism in the mid-twentieth-century United States, see Susan Porter Benson, *Household Accounts: Working-Class Family Economies in the Interwar United States* (Ithaca, NY: Cornell University Press, 2007); Lizabeth Cohen, *A Consumers' Republic: The Politics of Mass Consumption in Postwar America* (New York: Knopf, 2003); Meg Jacobs, *Pocketbook Politics: Economic Citizenship in Twentieth-Century America* (Princeton, NJ: Princeton University Press, 2005); William Leach, *Land of Desire: Merchants, Power, and the Rise of a New American Culture* (New York: Pantheon, 1993); Roland Marchand, *Advertising the American Dream: Making Way for Modernity, 1920–1940* (Berkeley: University of California Press, 1985); Kathy Peiss, *Hope in a Jar: The Making of America's Beauty Culture* (New York: Metropolitan Books, 1998); Susan Strasser, *Satisfaction Guaranteed: The Making of the American Mass Market* (New York: Pantheon, 1989); Sharon Zukin, *Point of Purchase: How Shopping Changed American Culture* (New York: Routledge, 2004).

10. Harnett T. Kane, "Food Sales Methods Get Attention," *New Orleans Item*, August 27, 1941.
11. "Merchants Attack Law on Markets," *New Orleans Item*, July 29, 1940.
12. Kane, "Food Sales Methods Get Attention."
13. "Merchants Attack Law on Markets," *New Orleans Item*, July 29, 1940.
14. Kane, "Food Sales Methods Get Attention."
15. Kane, "Food Sales Methods Get Attention." Note: For more insights into the spread of supermarket culture in the United States, see Tracey Deutsch, *Building a Housewife's Paradise: Gender, Politics, and American Grocery Stores in the Twentieth Century* (Chapel Hill: University of North Carolina Press, 2010); Susanne Freidberg, *Fresh: A Perishable History* (Cambridge, MA: Belknap Press of Harvard University Press, 2009); Shane Hamilton, *Supermarket USA: Food and Power in the Cold War Farms Race* (New Haven: Yale University Press, 2018); Benjamin Lorr, *The Secret Life of Groceries: The Dark Miracle of the American Supermarket* (New York: Avery, 2020); Ellen M. Plante, *The American Kitchen: 1700 to Present* (New York: Facts on File, 1995); Andrew Seth and Geoffrey Randall, *The Grocers: The Rise and Rise of Supermarket Chains* (London: Kogan Page, 1998).
16. Hamilton, *Supermarket USA*, 7. Note: A&P, Safeway, and Kroger were grocery store chains before adopting the supermarket model in the 1930s. A&P and Kroger were established in the nineteenth century, slowly evolving from smaller retail grocers into larger grocery stores and then eventually supermarkets. Safeway, established in the 1920s, underwent a more rapid transformation from grocery store to supermarket chain.
17. Kane, "Food Sales Methods Get Attention."
18. "Green's Super Food Stores," *New Orleans Item*, September 17, 1942.
19. "Green's Super Markets," *Times-Picayune*, March 13, 1942.
20. "Announcing the Opening of a New Piggly Wiggly Store," *New Orleans Item*, January 3, 1941.
21. Laura Shapiro, *Something from the Oven: Reinventing Dinner in 1950s America* (New York: Penguin, 2005), xvi–xvii.
22. The local newspapers referred to Nellie Gondran by her married name, Mrs. McCormick Gondran.
23. "Select 3 Best 'Discoveries': Helpful Household Hints Win $1 Prizes," *New Orleans Item*, March 12, 1942.
24. "Ernst Food Market," *New Orleans Item*, March 12, 1942. Note: Ernst Food Market was located at 3901 Washington Ave. in New Orleans.
25. For a study of the interconnectivity of car culture and urban and suburban spaces in America, see Richard W. Longstreth, *The Drive-In, the Supermarket, and the Transformation of Commercial Space in Los Angeles, 1914–1941* (Cambridge, MA: MIT Press, 1999).
26. Elizabeth M. Williams, *New Orleans: A Food Biography* (New York: Altamira Press, 2013), 89–90.

27. For a study of the growing importance of convenience as tied to a larger consumer culture in postwar America, see Cohen, *A Consumers' Republic*.

28. Harnett T. Kane, " 'Free Trade' for All Meat Markets, Groceries Urged," *New Orleans Item*, August 28, 1941.

29. Harnett T. Kane, "Free Trade for Marts," *New Orleans Item*, August 28, 1941.

30. For a related work that explores the role and politics of women consumer-activists in the 1930s through the end of the twentieth century, see LaBarbera-Twarog, *Politics of the Pantry*.

31. Kane, "Orleans' Housewives Want 'One Stop' Stores."

32. Kane, "Orleans Housewives on Stores."

33. Kane, "Orleans Housewives on Stores."

34. Kane, "Orleans Housewives on Stores."

35. Official notice from Dr. John M. Whitney to Mr. Peter J. Piazza, May 6, 1941, DPM, Box 1, Folder City Board of Health Reports—Private Markets, Department of Public Markets Old Records, NOPL.

36. Harnett T. Kane, "Meat Law Is Protection for Butchers, Says Head," *New Orleans Item*, September 3, 1941.

37. Kane, "Meat Law Is Protection."

38. "Remove the Restrictions," *New Orleans Item*, September 4, 1941.

39. Kane, "Orleans Housewives on Stores."

40. Jenny McTaggart, "1920s: A Decade of Promise," *Progressive Grocer*, December 31, 2011, https://progressivegrocer.com/1920s-decade-promise; Marc Levinson, *The Great A&P and the Struggle for Small Business in America* (New York: Hill and Wang, 2011), 144.

41. Kane, "Orleans Housewives on Stores."

42. "Remove the Restrictions," *New Orleans Item*, September 4, 1941.

43. "Full Hearing on Markets," *New Orleans Item*, October 1, 1941.

44. "Markets," *New Orleans States*, March 24, 1942.

45. "Revision of Rule on City Markets Urged by A. of C.," *Times-Picayune*, March 25, 1942.

46. "Bow to the Inevitable," *New Orleans Item*, March 26, 1942.

47. "Patronize the Public Market," *New Orleans Item*, May 15, 1942.

48. Structural maintenance report examples include roof repair estimates from 1944 and 1945, DPM, Box 2, Folder Roof Repairs—Miscellaneous Market Supervisor (Current) and Folder Private Market Surveys—Department of Public Markets Old Records, NOPL.

49. Amy Bentley, *Eating for Victory: Food Rationing and the Politics of Domesticity* (Urbana: University of Illinois Press, 1998), 10–11.

50. "Committee Will Study Fish Lack," *New Orleans Item*, February 11, 1943. Note: What many of the Louisiana fishermen did not realize was that fishing was categorized an essential industry; they could have retained their jobs instead of joining the military, but that categorization was not common knowledge.

51. "Cut in Live Stock [*sic*] in Area Possible," *Times-Picayune*, June 29, 1943.

52. "Plan Advanced by Farm Group: Program Aims at Relief of Food Shortage," *Times-Picayune*, June 25, 1943.

53. For an in-depth exploration of World War II victory gardens and their significance in American life, see Bentley, *Eating for Victory*.

54. "Victory Gardens Are Urged by Wickard," *Times-Picayune*, January 22, 1943.

55. City surveyor report, October 24, 1944, of a proposed private market located at 139 S. Cortes Street in relationship to the Suburban Market, DPM, Box 2, Folder Private Market Surveys—Department of Public Markets Old Records, NOPL.

56. "Drinkless V-Day Resolution Up," *New Orleans States*, September 18, 1944; "Market Tenants Oppose Eviction," *Times-Picayune*, February 22, 1946.

57. "Butchers," *New Orleans States*, February 21, 1946; Kane, "Orleans Housewives on Stores."

58. "Rocheblave Mart Tenants Protest Eviction Order," *New Orleans States*, February 21, 1946.

59. "Butchers," *New Orleans States*, February 21, 1946.

60. John Collier, "Ears Rest as Peddler Goes to War," *New Orleans Item*, August 30, 1944.

61. Collier, "Ears Rest as Peddler Goes to War," 17.

62. Collier, "Ears Rest as Peddler Goes to War," 17.

63. Collier, "Ears Rest as Peddler Goes to War," 17.

64. In 1943, employees of the sugar and related products industry made thirty cents an hour, and their representatives were asking for a wage increase of forty cents per hour. Those advocates noted that in the North, people working in the same industry made sixty to sixty-five cents per hour. "Asks Sugar Pay Raise Immediately," *New Orleans Item*, March 5, 1943.

65. "Asks Sugar Pay Raise Immediately," *New Orleans Item*, March 5, 1943.

66. Collier, "Ears Rest as Peddler Goes to War," 17.

67. S.v. "Alexander Granderson," in US census of 1940; s.v. "Alex Granderson," in US census of 1950.

68. "Your Car Is Always Important," *New Orleans States-Item*, February 17, 1972.

69. "Deaths," *New Orleans States-Item*, January 8, 1978; s.v. "William Stock," in US census of 1940; s.v. "William C Stock," in US census of 1950.

70. James A. Perry, "Couple's Stand on Quality Bears Fruit," *Times-Picayune*, December 12, 1988.

71. Perry, "Couple's Stand on Quality Bears Fruit," 43.

72. Gayle Ashton, "Fruit Juice Runs in Schaub Blood," *Times-Picayune*, June 22, 1984.

73. Christina Ferrari, " 'It's Down to Me Now': Jefferson Roadside Vegetable Stand Is a Family Legacy for Dewitt Burns," *Nola.com*, July 20, 2023.

74. "Farmers, Clubs Organize New Curb Market Here; to Be Opened Friday," *New Orleans Item*, April 29, 1943.

75. Growers and farmers on the outskirts of New Orleans operated what locals called "truck farms," which largely grew fresh produce. Locals often referred to their produce as "truck." For a history of truck farms in the greater New Orleans area, see Richard Campanella, "Now Forgotten, 'Truck Farms' Once Dotted New Orleans, but Were Overtaken by Urban Growth," *Nola.com*, October 1, 2020.

76. Frances Bryson, "Farmers' Curb Market Swamped in Bargain-Hungers' Holiday," *New Orleans Item*, April 30, 1943.

77. Bryson, "Farmers' Curb Market Swamped."

78. "Here and There," *New Orleans Item*, May 22, 1943.

79. "Extend Hours of Curb Market," *New Orleans Item*, February 17, 1945.

80. "Here and There," *New Orleans Item*, May 5, 1944.

81. "Another Farmers' Market Favored," *New Orleans Item*, May 5, 1944.

82. "Plan Ceremony at Curb Market," *Times-Picayune*, October 11, 1944.

83. Ed Anderson, "John G. Schwegmann: The Times-Picayune Cover 175 years of New Orleans History," *Times-Picayune*, January 29, 2012.

84. "Just Like Meeting an Old Friend," *Times-Picayune*, May 21, 1967.

85. "How Time Does Fly," *Times-Picayune*, August 20, 1962.

86. "How Time Does Fly," *Times-Picayune*, August 20, 1962.

87. "How Time Does Fly," *Times-Picayune*, August 20, 1962.

88. Williams, *New Orleans: A Food Biography*, 90.

89. National Register of Historic Places Registration Form for Schwegmann Bros. Giant Supermarket No. 1, National Register of Historic Places Program, May 1, 2014, https://www.nps.gov/nr/feature/places/pdfs/14000314.pdf.

90. Williams, *New Orleans: A Food Biography*, 89–90.

91. "MARCH of PROGRESS," *Times-Picayune*, January 25, 1953.

92. "City Market Shift Pondered," *New Orleans Item*, May 27, 1946.

93. "Public Markets Go," *New Orleans States*, May 30, 1946.

94. "City Market Shift Pondered," *New Orleans Item*, May 27, 1946.

95. "Bureau Asks French Mart Control Shift," *New Orleans Item*, May 29, 1946.

96. "City Market Program," *New Orleans Item*, May 30, 1946.

97. "Bureau Asks French Mart Control Shift," *New Orleans Item*, May 29, 1946.

98. "Public Markets Go," *New Orleans States*, May 30, 1946.

99. James Gillis, "Third of Public Markets Leased to Other Operators," *Times-Picayune*, May 18, 1947.

100. "Market Occupants Purchase Leases," *Times-Picayune*, December 2, 1947.

101. Jack Dempsey, "Proposes Markets' Sale to Get Street Repair Fund," *New Orleans States*, December 11, 1947.

102. "Views on Sundry," *Times-Picayune*, March 17, 1948.

103. Dempsey, "Proposes Markets' Sale"; "No Padding of Pay Rolls, Declares Research Bureau," *Times-Picayune*, February 19, 1948.

104. Dempsey, "Proposes Markets' Sale."

105. "Sale Date Is Set for Public Marts," *New Orleans States*, August 148, 1948.

106. "New Branch Library Is Being Sought," *New Orleans Item*, May 15, 1948; "Grunewald Rites Slated Thursday," *Times-Picayune*, July 26, 1949.

107. "New Department's Duties Vague," *Times-Picayune*, March 27, 1950.

108. "Only Three Left," *Times-Picayune*, October 1, 1950; "Dryades Market," *Times-Picayune*, June 24, 1958.

109. "Report of Councilman A. Brown Moore," *New Orleans Item*, October 10, 1956.

110. "Dryades Market," *Times-Picayune*, June 24, 1958.

111. "Agreeable Offer," *Times-Picayune*, October 31, 1958.

112. "All Sidewalk Stands Are Illegal—yet They Flourish in New Orleans," *New Orleans States*, December 6, 1945.

113. Begue, "Considering the New Orleans Corner Store," 103–6.

114. Dreyer, Saxon, and Tallant, *Gumbo Ya-Ya*, 28.

CHAPTER 7

1. Ann Maloney, "Friends, Family Send Off Mr. Okra," *Times-Picayune*, February 26, 2018.

2. In modern New Orleans, some community members and tourists participate in derivations of second lines that are not confined to a funerary practice but are used to celebrate weddings or are part of festivals and community events; these iterations of the second line do not typically include the dirge and focus more on celebratory music, dancing, and singing.

3. Maloney, "Friends, Family Send Off Mr. Okra."

4. Maloney, "Friends, Family Send Off Mr. Okra."

5. Ann Maloney, "The Last Peddler Passes On," *Nola.com*, February 21, 2018.

6. Guarino, "Mr. Okra Is Still."

7. Ann Maloney, "Sergio 'Ms. Okra' Robinson Keeps New Orleans Street Peddling Tradition Rolling," *Nola.com*, April 30, 2018.

8. Ian McNulty, "Call Her Ms. Okra: Daughter Keeps Street Vendor's Legacy Rolling On at Jazz Fest, and Gratitude Flows Back," *New Orleans Advocate*, April 29, 2018.

9. Kenneth H. Kolb, *Retail Inequality: Reframing the Food Desert Debate* (Oakland: University of California Press, 2021), 194.

10. For an in-depth discussion of food apartheid, see Ashanté M. Reese, *Black Food Geographies: Race, Self-Reliance, and Food Access in Washington, D.C.* (Chapel Hill: University of North Carolina Press, 2019), 28–29.

11. Adrienne R. Mundorf and Amelia Willits-Smith, "10 Years Later: Changes in Food Access Disparities in New Orleans Since Hurricane Katrina," *Journal of Urban Health*, 92, no. 4 (2015): 607.

12. Kolb, *Retail Inequality*, 2.

13. Kolb, *Retail Inequality*, 11.

14. Kolb, *Retail Inequality*, 188, 195.

15. Kolb, *Retail Inequality*, 1.

16. Kolb, *Retail Inequality*, 215.

17. Kolb, *Retail Inequality*, 196.

18. Laura McKinney and Yuki Kato, "Community Context of Food Justice: Reflections on a Free Local Produce Program in a New Orleans Food Desert," *AIMS Agriculture and Food* 2, no. 2 (2017): 190.

19. Richard Campanella, direct message on X to Ashley Rose Young, July 27, 2023.

20. Richard Campanella shared 1937 data on Italian-owned businesses in New Orleans to formulate the number of food-related retail stores in Hollygrove. Richard Campanella, direct message on X to Ashley Rose Young, July 27, 2023.

21. "Second Harvest Food Bank of Greater New Orleans and Acadiana," Feeding America, accessed March 11, 2023, https://www.feedingamerica.org/find-your-local-foodbank/second-harvest-food-bank-of-greater-new-orleans-and-acadiana; "QuickFacts: New Orleans City, Louisiana," US Bureau of the Census, accessed March 11, 2023, https://www.census.gov/quickfacts/neworleanscitylouisiana.

22. Maloney, "Why 'Mr. Okra's' Death."

23. Brett Rettman, review of Roman Candy Company, *Google Maps*, accessed March 11, 2023, https://goo.gl/maps/150HUQmu3ZoPcctF6.

24. Ron Kotteman, phone conversation with Ashley Rose Young, August 12, 2023.

25. Mark Guarino, "A Jazz Fest Regular, Roman Candy Quietly Marks 100 Years," *New Orleans Advocate*, April 30, 2015.

26. Guarino, "A Jazz Fest Regular."

27. Gabrielle Jones, review of Roman Candy Company, *Google Maps*, accessed March 11, 2023, https://goo.gl/maps/dkTctzayuifWTMzN8.

28. "Order Roman Candy Gifts Online," *Roman Candy Company*, accessed March 11, 2023, https://romancandy.com/merchandise.

29. Guarino, "A Jazz Fest Regular."

30. Guarino, "A Jazz Fest Regular."

31. Danny Monteverde, "Dueling Petitions Address Food Truck Status," *New Orleans Advocate*, January 29, 2013.

32. As quoted in Monteverde, "Dueling Petitions."

33. As quoted in Monteverde, "Dueling Petitions."

34. Jaquetta White in "Council Passes Food Truck Rules," *New Orleans Advocate*, July 26, 2013.

35. Nina Feldman, "New Farmers Market Brings Fresh Produce Back to Historic French Market," *All Things New Orleans*, New Orleans Public Radio, New Orleans, LA: WWNO, October 15, 2014.

36. Dickie Brennan, interviewed by Ashley Rose Young, New Orleans, May 20, 2019.

37. Dickie Brennan, interviewed by Ashley Rose Young, New Orleans, May 20, 2019.

38. "About Us," Crescent City Farmers Market, accessed February 8, 2021, https://www.crescentcityfarmersmarket.org/about-us.

39. Jeanne Hardy, "Market Milestone," *Times-Picayune*, October 18, 1996.

40. "Farmers' Market Going Strong a Year Later," *Times-Picayune*, October 18, 1996.

41. "Report of Councilman A. Brown Moore," *New Orleans Item*, October 10, 1956.

42. Feldman, "New Farmers Market."

43. "Market Match: Meeting Shoppers Halfway," Crescent City Farmers Market, accessed February 24, 2021, https://crescentcityfarmersmarket.org/market-match.

44. "St. Roch Market," St. Roch Market, accessed October 15, 2015, http://www.strochmarket.com.

45. Richard A. Webster, "Residents Help with Repairs to Vandalized Market—the Debate over Gentrification Erupts in St. Roch (or Is It New Marigny?)," *Times-Picayune*, June 14, 2015.

46. Todd A. Price, "Between—St. Roch and a Hard Place—Market Operators Make Changes in and for the Neighborhood," *Times-Picayune*, July 10, 2015.

47. "St. Roch Market," St. Roch Market, accessed March 11, 2023, http://www.strochmarket.com.

48. "Laksa NOLA," St. Roch Market, accessed March 11, 2023, http://www.strochmarket.com/laksanola.

49. "Fritai," St. Roch Market, accessed February 1, 2021, http://www.strochmarket.com/fritai.

50. Stephanie Carter, "Charly Pierre and Minerva Chereches Are Blending Haitian Flavors in New Orleans," *Eater*, June 22, 2017.

51. Clair Lorell, "Here Are New Orleans's 2021 Eater Award Winners," *NOLA Eater*, December 8, 2021; "Here Are the 2022 James Beard Awards Restaurant and Chef Semifinalists," *Eater*, February 23, 2022.

52. Nylah Burton, "Chef Charly Pierre Pays Homage to Haitian Street Food in His New Orleans Restaurant," *Andscape*, January 19, 2023.

53. "Mission," Southern Food & Beverage Museum, accessed February 8, 2021, https://southernfood.org/mission-history.

54. I was a member of the team that curated the *Dryades Street Market* exhibit.

55. The city rehabilitated and reopened the other Dryades Market building in 2015 as the New Orleans Jazz Market, a cultural center dedicated to the music genre.

56. For example, in 2015, a partnership with the Subnature and Culinary Culture project at Duke University led to the installation of an exhibit, *Taste Terroir Tapestries: Interactive Consumption Histories*, which endeavored to re-engage museum visitors with the city's historic public food culture. The tapestries consisted of paper placemats that were previously used during community meals where participants learned about and tasted historic street foods including calas, the sugary rice fritter sold by Black women in nineteenth-century New Orleans. The placemats were printed with historic images of street vendors and public markets as well as street vendors' cries and historic figures' impressions and memories of the city's nineteenth-century street foods. After tasting what was for many unfamiliar historic foods, participants at the community meals were then asked to write their own impressions of the flavors and textures of those dishes on the placemats, thus bringing

together the experiences of eaters, past and present, on one piece of paper. The placemats were then stitched together and hung in columns to create a tapestry of eaters' impressions of the city's public food culture. Once hung in the Leah Chase Gallery, the tapestries brought into conversation images, text, and even the food particles and stains of the city's street food with the historic market structure in which they hung. While museum visitors contemplated the tapestries, smells and sounds could also be heard emanating from the Rouses Culinary Innovation Center, which added layers of sensory engagement to the museum-goer's experience. For more on the Terroir Tapestries, see Jennifer Jacqueline Stratton and Ashley Rose Young, "Terroir Tapestries: An Interactive Consumption Project," in *Food and Museums*, ed. Nina Levent and Dr. Irina Mihalache (New York: Bloomsbury Academic, 2016).

Bibliography

PRIMARY SOURCES
Manuscript Materials

Durham, NC
> David M. Rubenstein Rare Book & Manuscript Library, Duke University
>> Postcard Collection, circa 1893–2000s

New Orleans, LA
> City Archives & Special Collections, New Orleans Public Library
>> Acts and Deliberations of the Cabildo, 1769–1803 (AB300)
>> Alphabetical and Chronological Digest of the Acts and Deliberations of the Cabildo, 1769–1803
>> Building Plans Collection
>> Department of Public Markets Miscellaneous Files ca. 1923–1949
>> New Orleans (La.) Conseil de Ville. Letters, Petitions, and Reports, 1804–1835 (AB320)
>> Ordinances and resolutions (translations), 1805–1832, New Orleans Conseil de Ville (AB311)

Louisiana Research Collection, Tulane University Special Collections, Howard-Tilton Memorial Library
> Folders (Loose)
>> Fairs & Festival World's Fair (1884)
> Lyle Saxon Papers, 1879–1949 (Manuscript Collection 4)
> Market Committee Records, 1913–1916 (Manuscript Collection 985)

Southeastern Architectural Archive, Tulane University Special Collections, Howard-Tilton Memorial Library
> Sam Stone, Jr. Office Records (Collection 85)

Williams Research Center, Historic New Orleans Collection
    Artist Files
    Charles L. Franck Studio Collection
    Postcards Book 08: Markets & Vendors French Market
Xavier University of Louisiana Library
    Charles F. Heartman Manuscripts of Slavery Collection
Pennsylvania
    Historical Society of Pennsylvania
        Philadelphia. City Council. Petitions to the Select and
        Common Councils (Collection 1002)
Washington, DC
    Manuscript Division, Library of Congress
        Born in Slavery: Slave Narratives from the Federal Writers' Project, 1936 to 1938
    National Museum of African American History and Culture, Smithsonian
    Institution
        Registers and Letters Received by the Commissioner of the Bureau of Refugees,
        Freedmen, and Abandoned Lands, 1865–1872

Newspapers

Massachusetts
    Boston Daily Advertiser
    Daily Advocate
    Springfield Republican
Louisiana
    Bee
    Daily City Item
    Daily Delta
    Daily Item
    Daily Picayune
    Daily States
    Daily True Delta
    Item-Tribune
    New Advocate
    New Orleans Advocate
    New Orleans Argus
    New Orleans Commercial Bulletin
    New Orleans Item
    New Orleans States
    New Orleans Times
    Nola.com
    Plain Dealer
    Sunday Item-Tribune

Times-Democrat
Times-Picayune
New York
   New York Commercial Advertiser
Pennsylvania
   Philadelphia Inquirer
   Philadelphia Press

PUBLISHED PRIMARY SOURCES

Acts Passed by the General Assembly of the State of Louisiana at the Second Session of the Third Legislature, Begun and Held in New Orleans, January 5, 1874. New Orleans: Republican Office, 1874.

Agriculture Department of the United States. *Report of the Commissioner of Agriculture for the Year 1870.* Washington, DC: Government Printing Office, 1871.

Ashe, Thomas. *Travels in America Performed in the Year 1806.* London: Printed for Richard Phillips, 1809.

Augustin, Donatien. *A General Digest of the Ordinances and Resolutions of the Corporation of New-Orleans.* New Orleans: Printed by J. Bayon, 1831.

Banks, Anna, ed. *First-Person America.* New York: Alfred A. Knopf, 1980.

A Book of Famous Old New Orleans Recipes Used in the South for More Than 200 Years. New Orleans: Peerless Publishing Co., 1900.

Bremer, Frederika. *The Homes of the New World: Impressions of America.* Vol. 2. New York: Harper & Bros., 1863.

Clayton, Ronnie W., ed. *Mother Wit: The Ex-Slave Narratives of the Louisiana Writers' Project.* New York: Peter Lang, 1990.

Cole, Catherine. *The Story of the French Market.* New Orleans: New Orleans Coffee Company, 1916.

Craig, William Marshall, *The Itinerant Traders of London.* London: Richland Phillips, 1804.

De Caro, F. A., ed. *Louisiana Sojourns: Travelers' Tales and Literary Journeys.* Baton Rouge: Louisiana State University Press, 1998.

A Digest of the Ordinances, Resolutions, by-Laws and Regulations of the Corporation of New Orleans: And a Collection of the Laws of the Legislature Relative to the Said City. New Orleans: Gaston Brusle, 1836.

Eustis, Célestine. *Cooking in the Old Créole Days: La Cuisine Créole à l'Usage des Petits Menages.* New York: R.H. Russell, 1903.

Federal Writers' Project. *New Orleans City Guide.* Edited by Delia LaBarre. Boston: Houghton Mifflin, 1938.

Ferris, Marcie Cohen. *The Edible South: The Power of Food and the Making of an American Region.* Chapel Hill: University of North Carolina Press, 2014.

Ferris, Marcie Cohen. *Matzoh Ball Gumbo: Culinary Tales of the Jewish South.* Chapel Hill: University of North Carolina Press, 2005.

Fournel, Victor. *Les Cris de Paris: Types et Physionomies d'Autrefois*. Paris: Firmin-Didot, 1887.

Gibson's Guide and Directory of the State of Louisiana, and the Cities of New Orleans and LaFayette. New Orleans: J. Gibson, 1838.

Hachard, Marie-Madeleine. *Relation du Voyage des Dames Religieuses Ursulines de Rouen a La Nouvelle-Orleans*. Edited by Gabriel Gravier and Mère St. Agustin de Tranchepain. Paris: Maisonneuve, 1872.

Hall, Basil. *Travels in North America in the Years 1827 and 1828*. Edinburgh: Robert Cadell, 1830.

Hearn, Lafcadio. *Inventing New Orleans: Writings of Lafcadio Hearn*. Edited by S. Frederick Starr. Jackson: University Press of Mississippi, 2001.

Hearn, Lafcadio. *The New Orleans of Lafcadio Hearn: Illustrated Sketches from the Daily City Item*. Edited by Delia LaBarre. Baton Rouge: Louisiana State University Press, 2007.

Hearn, Lafcadio. *The Selected Writings of Lafcadio Hearn*. Edited by Henry Goodman. New York: Citadel Press, 1971.

Historical Sketchbook and Guide to New Orleans and Environs. New York: Will H. Coleman, 1885.

King, Grace. *New Orleans: The Place and the People*. New York: Macmillan, 1895.

Latrobe, Benjamin. *Impressions Respecting New Orleans*. Edited by Samuel Wilson Jr. New York: Columbia University Press, 1951.

Latrobe, Benjamin. *The Journal of Benjamin Latrobe, 1799–1820: From Philadelphia to New Orleans*. Edited by Edward C. Carter II, John C. Van Horne, and Lee Formwalt. New Haven: Yale University Press, 1980.

Le Moyne d'Iberville, Pierre. *Iberville's Gulf Journals*. Edited by Richebourg Gaillard McWilliams. Tuscaloosa: University of Alabama Press, 1980.

Leiding, Harriette Kershaw. *Street Cries of an Old Southern City*. Charleston: Daggett Printing Co., 1910.

Leovy, Henry Jefferson and Charles H. Luzenberg. *The laws and general ordinances of the city of New Orleans: together with the acts of the Legislature, decisions of the Supreme Court, and constitutional provisions relating to the city government*. New Orleans: E. C. Wharton, 1857.

Leovy, Henry Jefferson and Charles H. Luzenberg. *The laws and general ordinances of the city of New Orleans: together with the acts of the Legislature, decisions of the Supreme Court, and constitutional provisions relating to the city government*. New Orleans: Simmons & Co., 1870.

Lislet, Louis Moreau. *A General Digest of Acts of the Legislature of Louisiana*. New Orleans: Benjamin Levy, 1828.

Long, Ellen Call. *Florida Breezes, or, Florida, New and Old*. 1883. Reprint, Gainesville: University of Florida Press, 1962.

Maylié, Eugenié Lavedan. *Maylié's Table D'Hote Recipes and the History and Some Facts Concerning "La Maison Maylié et Esparbé."* Maylié's Restaurant, n.d.

Mitcham, Howard. *Creole Gumbo and All That Jazz: A New Orleans Seafood Cookbook.* Gretna, LA: Pelican, 1992.

Our Great All Around Tour. New York: Leve & Alden Printing Company, 1884.

The Picayune's Creole Cook Book. 2nd ed. New Orleans: Picayune Publishing Company, 1901.

Pintard, John. *Letters from John Pintard to His Daughter Eliza Noel Pintard Davidson, 1816–1833.* Vol. 2. New York: New-York Historical Society, 1941.

Rowlandson, Thomas. *Characteristic Sketches of the Lower Orders.* London: L. Harrison for Samuel Leigh, 1820.

Rowlandson, Thomas and H. Merke. *Cries of London.* London: R. Ackermann, 1799.

Royall, Anne Newport. *Mrs. Royall's Southern Tour.* Vol. 3. Washington, DC: n.p., 1831.

Scenes and Cries of London. London: Dean and Son, Juvenile and Educational Book Warehouse, 1861.

Singleton, Arthur. *Letters from the South and West.* Boston: Richardson and Lord, 1824.

Soards' New Orleans City Directory. New Orleans: Soards Directory Co., 1900.

Soards' New Orleans City Directory for 1903. Vol. 30. New Orleans: Soards Directory Co., 1903.

Strawn, Lydia. *Illinois Central World's Exposition Messenger.* c 1884.

Stuart, James. *Three Years in North America.* Vol. II. Edinburgh: Printed for R. Cadell, 1833.

Syntax, Sam. *Description of the Cries of London.* London: John Harris, 1821.

Visitors' Guide to The World's Industrial and Cotton Centennial Exposition. Louisville, KY: Courier-Journal Printing Co., 1884.

Whitman, Walt. *Complete Prose Works: Specimen Days and Collect, November Boughs and Good Bye My Fancy.* Boston: Small, Maynard & Co., 1901.

SECONDARY SOURCES

Agyeman, Julian, Caitlin Matthews, and Hannah Sobel, eds. *Food Trucks, Cultural Identity, and Social Justice from Loncheras to Lobsta Love.* Cambridge, MA: MIT Press, 2017.

Alliot, Pual. *Louisiana Under the Rule of Spain, France, and the United States, 1875–1807.* Translated by James Alexander Robertson. Cleveland, OH: The Arthur H. Clark Company, 1911.

Andermann, Robyn Rene. "Brewed Awakening: Re-imagining Education in Three Nineteenth-Century New Orleans Coffee Houses." PhD diss., Louisiana State University, 2018.

Arthur, Stanley Clisby. *Old New Orleans: A History of the Vieux Carré, Its Ancient and Historical Buildings.* New Orleans, Harmanson, 1936.

Baics, Gergely. *Feeding Gotham: The Political Economy and Geography of Food in New York City, 1790–1860.* Princeton, NJ: Princeton University Press, 2016.

Bailey, Anne C. *African Voices of the Atlantic Slave Trade: Beyond the Silence and the Shame.* Boston: Beacon Press, 2005.

Bailey, Richard W. "The Foundation of English in the Louisiana Purchase: New Orleans, 1800–1850." *American Speech* 78 (2003): 363–84.

Baraka, Amiri. *Blues People: Negro Music in White America*. Westport, CT: Greenwood Press, 1980.

Beaman, Greg Alan. "Slavery in the Suburbs: A History of Real Estate and Slavery in the Faubourgs of New Orleans, 1788–1852." PhD diss., Georgetown University, 2023.

Beckles, Hilary McD. "An Economic Life of Their Own: Slaves as Commodity Producers and Distributors in Barbados." In *The Slaves Economy: Independent Production by Slaves in the Americas*, edited by Ira Berlin and Philip Morgan, 31–47. Frank Cass, 1991.

Beckles, Hilary McD. *Natural Rebels: A Social History of Enslaved Black Women in Barbados*. New Brunswick, NJ: Rutgers University Press, 1989.

Bederman, Gail. *Manliness & Civilization: A Cultural History of Gender and Race in the United States, 1880–1917*. Chicago: University of Chicago Press, 1995.

Begue, Gabrielle O. "Considering the New Orleans Corner Store: The Architectural Origins, Development, and Preservation of an Endangered Vernacular Tradition." Master's thesis, Tulane University, 2012.

Benson, Susan Porter. *Household Accounts: Working-Class Family Economies in the Interwar United States*. Ithaca, NY: Cornell University Press, 2007.

Bentley, Amy. *Eating for Victory: Food Rationing and the Politics of Domesticity*. Urbana: University of Illinois Press, 1998.

Berlin, Ira. *Many Thousands Gone: The First Two Centuries of Slavery in North America*. Cambridge, MA: Belknap Press of Harvard University Press, 1998.

Besson, Jean. "Gender and Development in the Jamaican Small-Scale Marketing System: From the 1660s to the Millennium and Beyond." In *Resources, Planning and Environmental Management in a Changing Caribbean*, edited by David Barker and Duncan McGregor, 11–35. Kingston: University of West Indies Press, 2003.

Blassingame, John W. *The Slave Community: Plantation Life in the Antebellum South*. New York: Oxford University Press, 1979.

Boutin, Aimée. *City of Noise: Sound and Nineteenth-Century Paris*. Urbana: University of Illinois Press, 2015.

Buchanan, Thomas C. *Black Life on the Mississippi: Slave, Free Blacks, and the Western Steamboat World*. Chapel Hill: University of North Carolina Press, 2004.

Bullard, Robert D. and Beverly Wright, eds. *Race, Place, and Environmental Justice After Hurricane Katrina: Struggles to Reclaim, Rebuild, and Revitalize New Orleans and the Gulf Coast*. Boulder, CO: Westview Press, 2009.

Calhoun, Craig, ed. *Habermas and the Public Sphere*. Cambridge, MA: MIT Press, 1992.

Campanella, Richard. *Bienville's Dilemma: A Historical Geography of New Orleans*. Lafayette: University of Louisiana at Lafayette, 2008.

Campanella, Richard. *Bourbon Street: A History*. Baton Rouge: Louisiana State University Press, 2014.

Campanella, Richard. *Geographies of New Orleans: Urban Fabrics Before the Storm.* Lafayette: University of Louisiana at Lafayette Center for Louisiana Studies, 2006.

Campanella, Richard. "How New Orleans Handled An Outbreak of Bubonic Plague in 1914." *Preservation in Print.* April 1, 2020. https://prcno.org/how-new-orleans-handled-an-outbreak-of-bubonic-plague-in-1914/.

Cardoso, Ryzia De Cássia Vieira, Michèle Companion, and Stefano Roberto Marras, eds. *Street Food: Culture, Economy, Health and Governance.* London: Routledge, 2017.

Cohen, Lizabeth. *A Consumers' Republic: The Politics of Mass Consumption in Postwar America.* New York: Knopf, 2003.

Cohen, Lucy M. *Chinese in the Post–Civil War South: A People Without a History.* Baton Rouge: Louisiana State University Press, 1984.

Cooley, Angela Jill. *To Live and Dine in Dixie: The Evolution of Urban Food Culture in the Jim Crow South.* Athens: University of Georgia Press, 2015.

Coquery-Vidrovitch, Catherine. *African Women: A Modern History.* Translated by Beth Gillian Raps. Boulder, CO: Westview Press, 1997.

Cott, Nancy F. *The Bonds of Womanhood: "Woman's Sphere" in New England, 1780–1835.* New Haven: Yale University Press, 1997.

Cox, Karen L. *Dreaming of Dixie: How the South Was Created in American Popular Culture.* Chapel Hill: University of North Carolina Press, 2011.

Cromwell, Alisha Marie. "Complicating the Patriarchy: Elite and Enslaved Businesswomen in the Nineteenth Century Atlantic World." PhD diss., University of Georgia, 2017.

Cromwell, Alisha Marie. "A Form of Skilled Labor: Entrepreneurial Gullah Geechee Women and 'Head Carrying.'" Paper presented at the International Gullah Geechee and African Diaspora Conference, Conway, SC, March 4–7, 2020.

Dantas, Mariana L.R. "Miners, Farmers, and Market People: Women of African Descent and the Colonial Economy in Minas Gerais." *African Economic History* 43 (2015): 82–108.

Dawdy, Shannon Lee. "'A Wild Taste': Food and Colonialism in Eighteenth-Century Louisiana." *Ethnohistory* 57, no. 3 (2010): 389–414.

Debe, Demetri D. "Necessary Connections: Building Black Mobility in the Public Markets of the Circum-Caribbean, 1660–1815." PhD diss., University of Minnesota, in progress.

Deryugina, Tatyana, Laura Kawano, and Steven Levitt. "The Economic Impact of Hurricane Katrina on Its Victims: Evidence from Individual Tax Returns." *American Economic Journal: Applied Economics* 10, no. 2 (April 2018): 202–33.

Deutsch, Tracey. *Building a Housewife's Paradise: Gender, Politics, and American Grocery Stores in the Twentieth Century.* Chapel Hill: University of North Carolina Press, 2010.

Diner, Hasia R. *Hungering for America: Italian, Irish, and Jewish Foodways in the Age of Migration.* Cambridge, MA: Harvard University Press, 2001.

Diner, Hasia R. *Roads Taken: The Great Jewish Migrations to the New World and the Peddlers Who Forged the Way*. New Haven: Yale University Press, 2015.

Edwards, Laura F. *Only the Clothes on Her Back: Clothing and the Hidden History of Power in the Nineteenth-Century United States*. New York: Oxford University Press, 2022.

Edwards, Laura F. *The People and Their Peace: Legal Culture and the Transformation of Inequality in the Post-Revolutionary South*. Chapel Hill: University of North Carolina Press, 2009.

Farah, Leila Marie and Samantha L. Martin, eds. *Mobs and Microbes: Global Perspectives on Market Halls, Civic Order and Public Health*. Leuven: Leuven University Press, 2023.

Feimster, Crystal Nicole. *Southern Horrors: Women and the Politics of Rape and Lynching*. Cambridge, MA: Harvard University Press, 2009.

Fischer, Roger A. "Racial Segregation in Ante Bellum New Orleans." *American Historical Review* 74, no. 3 (1969): 926–37.

Flanagan, Maureen A. *Seeing with Their Hearts: Chicago Women and the Vision of the Good City, 1871–1933*. Princeton, NJ: Princeton University Press, 2002.

Foote, Stephanie. *Regional Fictions: Culture and Identity in Nineteenth-Century American Literature*. Madison: University of Wisconsin Press, 2001.

Fouts, Sarah. "Re-Regulating *Loncheras*, Food Trucks, and Their Clientele: Navigating Bureaucracy and Enforcement in New Orleans." *Gastronomica* 18, no. 3 (Fall 2018): 1–13.

Fox-Genovese, Elizabeth. *Within the Plantation Household: Black and White Women of the Old South*. Chapel Hill: University of North Carolina Press, 1988.

Freidberg, Susanne. *Fresh: A Perishable History*. Cambridge, MA: Belknap Press of Harvard University Press, 2009.

Friedman, Lawrence M. *A History of American Law*. New York: Simon and Schuster, 1973.

Frink, Sandra Margaret. "Spectacles of the Street: Performance, Power, and Public Space in Antebellum New Orleans." PhD diss., University of Texas, Austin, 2024.

Gaspar, David Barry. "Slavery, Amelioration, and Sunday Markets in Antigua, 1823–1831." *Slavery & Abolition* 9, no. 1 (1988): 1–26.

Gebhard, David. "The Spanish Colonial Revival in Southern California (1895–1930)." *Journal of the Society of Architectural Historians* 26, no. 2 (1967): 131–47.

Gehman, Mary. *The Free People of Color of New Orleans: An Introduction*. New Orleans: Margaret Media, 1994.

Genovese, Eugene D. *Roll, Jordan, Roll: The World the Slaves Made*. New York: Vintage Books, 1976.

Gilmore, Glenda Elizabeth. *Gender and Jim Crow: Women and the Politics of White Supremacy in North Carolina, 1896–1920*. Chapel Hill: University of North Carolina Press, 1996.

Glymph, Thavolia. *Out of the House of Bondage: The Transformation of the Plantation Household*. New York: Cambridge University Press, 2008.

Goings, Kenneth W. *Mammy and Uncle Mose: Black Collectibles and American Stereotyping*. Bloomington: Indiana University Press, 1994.

Goodwin, Lorine. *The Pure Food, Drink and Drug Crusaders*. Jefferson, NC: McFarland, 1999.

Gotham, Kevin Fox. *Authentic New Orleans: Tourism, Culture, and Race in the Big Easy*. New York: New York University Press, 2007.

Gotham, Kevin Fox and Richard Campanella. "Constructions of Resilience: Ethnoracial Diversity, Inequality, and Post-Katrina Recovery, the Case of New Orleans." *Social Sciences* 2 (2013): 298–317.

Gould, Virginia Meacham. "'If I Can't Have My Rights, I Can Have My Pleasures, and If They Won't Give Me Wages, I Can Take Them': Gender and Slave Labor in Antebellum New Orleans." In *Discovering the Women in Slavery*, edited by Patricia Morton, 179–201. Athens: University of Georgia Press, 1996.

Graham, Richard. *Feeding the City: From Street Market to Liberal Reform in Salvador, Brazil, 1780–1860*. Austin: University of Texas Press, 2010.

Greene, Harlan. *Slave Badges and the Slave-Hire System in Charleston, South Carolina, 1783–1865*. Edited by Brian E. Hutchins and Harry S. Hutchins. Jefferson, NC: McFarland, 2004.

Greenspan, Anna. "Moveable Feasts: Reflections on Shanghai's Street Food." *Food, Culture & Society* 21, no. 1 (2018): 75–88.

Guàrdia, Manuel and José L. Oyón, eds. *Making Cities Through Market Halls: Europe, 19th and 20th Centuries*. Barcelona: Museu d'Història de Barcelona, 2015.

Gutman, Herbert G. *The Black Family in Slavery and Freedom, 1750–1925*. New York: Pantheon, 1976.

Habermas, Jürgen. *The Structural Transformation of the Public Sphere: An Inquiry into a Category of Bourgeois Society*. Translated by Thomas Burger with the assistance of Frederick Lawrence. Cambridge, MA: MIT Press, 1989.

Hamilton, Shane. *Supermarket USA: Food and Power in the Cold War Farms Race*. New Haven: Yale University Press, 2018.

Hanser, Amy. "Street Politics: Street Vendors and Urban Governance in China." *China Quarterly* 226 (2016): 363–82.

Hardy, Anne. *Salmonella Infections, Networks of Knowledge, and Public Health in Britain, 1880–1975*. Oxford: Oxford University Press, 2015.

Harris, Jessica B. *High on the Hog: A Culinary Journey from Africa to America*. New York: Bloomsbury, 2011.

Harris, Jessica B. "'I'm Talkin' 'Bout the Food I Sells': African American Street Vendors and the Sound of Food from Noise to Nostalgia." In *The Larder: Food Studies Methods from the American South*, edited by John T. Edge, Elizabeth S. D. Engelhardt, and Ted Ownby, 333–42. Athens: University of Georgia Press, 2013.

Harrison, Candice L. "'Free Trade and Hucksters' Rights!': Envisioning Economic Democracy in the Early Republic." *Pennsylvania Magazine of History and Biography* 137, no. 2 (April 2013): 171–72.

Hartigan-O'Connor, Ellen. "The Measure of the Market: Women's Economic Lives in Charleston, South Carolina, and Newport, Rhode Island, 1750–1820." PhD diss., University of Michigan, 2003.

Havrylyshyn, Alexandra T. "Free for a Moment in France: How Enslaved Women and Girls Claimed Liberty in the Courts of New Orleans (1835–1857)." PhD diss., University of California, Berkeley, 2018.

Hines, Alisha. "Geographies of Freedom: Black Women's Mobility and the Making of the Western River World, 1814–1865." PhD diss., Duke University, 2018.

Hilts, Philip J. *Protecting America's Health: The FDA, Business, and One Hundred Years of Regulation*. New York: Alfred A. Knopf, 2003.

Hirsch, Arnold R. and Joseph Logsdon, eds. *Creole New Orleans: Race and Americanization*. Baton Rouge: Louisiana State University Press, 1992.

Hirsch, Jerrold. "Toward a Marriage of True Minds: The Federal Writers' Project and the Writing of Southern History." In *The Adaptable South: Essays in Honor of George Brown Tindall*, edited by Elizabeth Jacoway et al., 148–75. Baton Rouge: Louisiana State University Press, 1991.

Horowitz, David A. "The New Deal and People's Art: Market Planners and Radical Artists." *Oregon Historical Quarterly* 109, no. 2 (2008): 318–28.

Horowitz, Roger, Jeffrey M. Pilcher, and Sydney Watts. "Meat for the Multitudes: Market Culture in Paris, New York City, and Mexico City over the Long Nineteenth Century." *American Historical Review* 109, no. 4 (October 2004): 1055–83.

Horwitz, Morton J. *The Transformation of American Law, 1780–1860*. Cambridge, MA: Harvard University Press, 1977.

House-Midamba, Bessie and Felix K. Ekechi, eds. *African Market Women and Economic Power: The Role of Women in African Economic Development*. Westport, CT: Greenwood Press, 1995.

Howard, Alvin P. "Branch Banking in New Orleans." *Bankers Magazine* 102 (1921): 761–64.

Hoy, Suellen. *Chasing Dirt: The American Pursuit of Cleanliness*. New York: Oxford University Press, 1995.

Jackson, Jessica Barbata. *Sicilians, Race, and Citizenship in the Jim Crow Gulf South*. Baton Rouge: Louisiana State University Press, 2020.

Jackson, Joy. *New Orleans in the Gilded Age: Politics and Urban Progress, 1880–1896*. Baton Rouge: Published by Louisiana State University Press for the Louisiana Historical Association, 1969.

Jacob, Beth A. "New Orleans' Historic Public Markets: Reviving Neighborhood Landmarks Through Adaptive Reuse." Master's thesis, Tulane University, 2012.

Jacob, Beth A. "Seated at the Table: The Southern Food and Beverage Museum's New Home on Oretha Castle Haley Boulevard." *Preservation in Print* 41, no. 8 (November 2014): 22–23.

Jacobs, Meg. *Pocketbook Politics: Economic Citizenship in Twentieth-Century America*. Princeton, NJ: Princeton University Press, 2005.

Jacoway, Elizabeth, et al., eds. *The Adaptable South: Essays in Honor of George Brown Tindall*. Baton Rouge: Louisiana State University Press, 1991.

Jobs: The WPA Way. Washington, DC: Works Progress Administration, 1936.

Johnson, Rashauna. *Slavery's Metropolis: Unfree Labor in New Orleans During the Age of Revolutions*. New York: Cambridge University Press, 2016.

Johnson, Walter. *Soul by Soul: Life Inside the Antebellum Slave Market*. Cambridge, MA: Harvard University Press, 1999.

Jones, Martha S. *All Bound Up Together: The Woman Question in African American Public Culture, 1830–1900*. Chapel Hill: University of North Carolina Press, 2007.

Joyner, Charles W. *Down by the Riverside: A South Carolina Slave Community*. Urbana: University of Illinois Press, 1984.

Kapchan, Deborah A. "Performance." *Journal of American Folklore* 108 (1995): 479–508.

Kein, Sybil, ed. *Creole: The History and Legacy of Louisiana's Free People of Color*. Baton Rouge: Louisiana University Press, 2000.

Kennedy, Cynthia M. *Braided Relations, Entwined Lives: The Women of Charleston's Urban Slave Society*. Bloomington: Indiana University Press, 2005.

Kerber, Linda K. "Separate Spheres, Female Worlds, Woman's Place: The Rhetoric of Women's History." *Journal of American History* 75, no. 1 (June 1988): 9–39.

King, Clyde Lyndon. "Municipal Markets." *Annals of the American Academy of Political and Social Science* 50, no. 1 (1913): 102–17.

Kisacky, Jeanne. "Germs Are in the Details: Aseptic Design and General Constructors at the Lying-In Hospital of the City of New York, 1897–1901." *Construction History* 28, no. 1 (2013): 83–106.

Kisacky, Jeanne. *Rise of the Modern Hospital: An Architectural History of Health and Healing, 1870–1940*. Pittsburgh: University of Pittsburgh Press, 2017.

Kolb, Kenneth H. *Retail Inequality: Reframing the Food Desert Debate*. Oakland: University of California Press, 2021.

Koslow, Jennifer Lisa. *Cultivating Health: Los Angeles Women and Public Health Reform*. New Brunswick, NJ: Rutgers University Press, 2009.

Kostof, Spiro. *The City Assembled: The Elements of Urban Form Through History*. London: Thames and Hudson, 1992.

LaBarbera-Twarog, Emily E. *Politics of the Pantry: Housewives, Food, and Consumer Protest in Twentieth-Century America*. Oxford: Oxford University Press, 2017.

Landau, Emily Epstein. *Spectacular Wickedness: Sex, Race, and Memory in Storyville, New Orleans*. Baton Rouge: Louisiana State University Press, 2013.

Leach, William. *Land of Desire: Merchants, Power, and the Rise of a New American Culture*. New York: Pantheon, 1993.

Lemon, Robert. *The Taco Truck: How Mexican Street Food Is Transforming the American City*. Urbana: University of Illinois Press, 2019.

Levine, Lawrence W. *Black Culture and Black Consciousness: Afro-American Folk Thought from Slavery to Freedom*. New York: Oxford University Press, 1978.

Levinson, Marc. *The Great A&P and the Struggle for Small Business in America*. New York: Hill and Wang, 2011.

Levitt, Jeremy I. and Matthew C. Whitaker, eds. *Hurricane Katrina: America's Unnatural Disaster*. Lincoln: University of Nebraska Press, 2009.

Lobel, Cindy R. *Urban Appetites: Food & Culture in Nineteenth-Century New York*. Chicago: University of Chicago Press, 2014.

Longstreth, Richard W. *The Drive-In, the Supermarket, and the Transformation of Commercial Space in Los Angeles, 1914–1941*. Cambridge, MA: MIT Press, 1999.

López, Kathleen. *Chinese Cubans: A Transnational History*. Chapel Hill: University of North Carolina Press, 2013.

Lorr, Benjamin. *The Secret Life of Groceries: The Dark Miracle of the American Supermarket*. New York: Avery, 2020.

Lovell, John. "Youth Programs of Negro Improvement Group." *Journal of Negro Education* 9, no. 3 (1940): 379–87.

Man, Rob. "Plazas and Power: Canary Islanders at Galveztown, an Eighteenth-Century Spanish Colonial Outpost in Louisiana." *Historical Archaeology* 46, no. 1 (2012): 49–61.

Marchand, Roland. *Advertising the American Dream: Making Way for Modernity, 1920–1940*. Berkeley: University of California Press, 1985.

Maresca, Joseph. *WPA Buildings: Architecture and Art of the New Deal*. Atglen, PA: Schiffer Publishing, 2016.

Marriere, Marius M. *The Know Nothings in Louisiana*. Jackson: University Press of Mississippi, 2018.

McCulla, Theresa. "Consumable City: Race, Ethnicity, and Food in Modern New Orleans." PhD diss., Harvard University, 2017.

McCulla, Theresa. *Insatiable City: Food and Race in New Orleans*. Chicago: University of Chicago Press, 2024.

McElya, Micki. *Clinging to Mammy: The Faithful Slave in Twentieth-Century America*. Cambridge, MA: Harvard University Press, 2007.

McGuire, Danielle L. *At the Dark End of the Street: Black Women, Rape, and Resistance: A New History of the Civil Rights Movement, from Rosa Parks to the Rise of Black Power*. New York: Alfred A. Knopf, 2010.

McKinney, Laura and Yuki Kato. "Community Context of Food Justice: Reflections on a Free Local Produce Program in a New Orleans Food Desert." *AIMS Agriculture and Food* 2, no. 2 (2017): 183–200.

McRae, Elizabeth Gillespie. *Mothers of Massive Resistance: White Women and the Politics of White Supremacy*. New York: Oxford University Press, 2018.

McTaggart, Jenny. "1920s: A Decade of Promise." *Progressive Grocer*, December 31, 2011. https://progressivegrocer.com/1920s-decade-promise.

Mendiola García, Sandra C. *Street Democracy: Vendors, Violence, and Public Space in Late Twentieth-Century Mexico*. Lincoln: University of Nebraska Press, 2017.

Miller, Monserrat. *Feeding Barcelona, 1714–1975: Public Market Halls, Social Networks, and Consumer Culture*. Baton Rouge: Louisiana State University Press, 2015.

Morgan, Jo-Ann. "Mammy the Huckster: Selling the Old South for the New Century." *American Art* 9, no. 1 (1995): 87–109.

Mukhija, Vinit and Anastasia Loukaitou-Sideris, eds. *The Informal American City: Beyond Taco Trucks to Day Labor*. Cambridge, MA: MIT Press, 2014.

Mundorf, Adrienne R. and Amelia Willits-Smith. "10 Years Later: Changes in Food Access Disparities in New Orleans since Hurricane Katrina." *Journal of Urban Health* 92, no. 4 (2015): 605–10.

National Consumers Committee for Research and Education and Consumers Union Foundation. *Consumer Activists: They Made a Difference: A History of Consumer Action Related by Leaders in the Consumer Movement*. Mount Vernon, NY: Consumers Union Foundation, 1982.

Nelson, Stephen A. "Myths of Katrina: Field Notes from a Geoscientist." *Minnesota Review* 85 (2015): 60–68.

Novak, William J. *The People's Welfare: Law and Regulation in Nineteenth-Century America*. Chapel Hill: University of North Carolina Press, 1996.

Novak, William J. "Public Economy and the Well-Ordered Market: Law and Economic Regulation in 19th Century America." *Law and Social Inquiry* 18, no. 1 (Winter 1992): 1–32.

Nystrom, Justin A. *Creole Italian: Sicilian Immigrants and the Shaping of New Orleans Food Culture*. Athens: University of Georgia Press, 2018.

Nystrom, Justin A. *New Orleans After the Civil War: Race, Politics, and a New Birth of Freedom*. Baltimore: Johns Hopkins University Press, 2010.

Olwell, Robert. "'Loose, Idle and Disorderly': Slave Women in the Eighteenth-Century Charleston Marketplace." In *More Than Chattel: Black Women and Slavery in the Americas*, edited by David Barry Gaspar and Darlene Clark Hine, 97–110. Bloomington: Indiana University Press, 1996.

O'Neil, Joseph. "Sustenance and Survival: Women, Food, and Sovereignty in Postemancipation Tobago." *New West Indian Guide* 96, nos. 3–4 (2022): 266–89.

Otele, Olivette. *African European: An Untold History*. London: Hurst, 2020.

Palmer, Vernon Valentine. "The Customs of Slavery: The War Without Arms." *American Journal of Legal History* 48, no. 2 (April 2006): 177–218.

Peiss, Kathy Lee. *Hope in a Jar: The Making of America's Beauty Culture*. New York: Metropolitan Books, 1998.

Peterson, Jon A. *The Birth of City Planning in the United States, 1840–1917*. Baltimore: Johns Hopkins University Press, 2003.

Pilcher, Jeffrey M. *Planet Taco: A Global History of Mexican Food*. New York: Oxford University Press, 2012.

Plante, Ellen M., *The American Kitchen: 1700 to Present*. New York: Facts on File, 1995.

Poulson, Charles A. *Scrap-Books Consisting of Engravings, etc. and Newspaper Clippings Illustrative of Philadelphia*. Vol. 10. Philadelphia: Library Company of Philadelphia, c. 1824–64.

Powell, Lawrence N. *The Accidental City: Improvising New Orleans*. Cambridge, MA: Harvard University Press, 2012.

Powell, Lawrence N. *New Masters: Northern Planters During the Civil War and Reconstruction*. New Haven: Yale University Press, 1980.

Price, C. Matlack. "Italian Derivations in American Architecture: The Revival of Architectural Ideals of the Renaissance." *Arts & Decoration* 3, no. 7 (1913): 240–43.

Purdy, Jedediah. *The Meaning of Property: Freedom, Community, and the Legal Imagination*. New Haven: Yale University Press, 2010.

Radano, Ronald. "Black Music Labor and the Animated Properties of Slave Sound." *Boundary 2* 43, no. 1 (2016): 173–208.

Raeburn, Bruce Boyd. "Reflections of Senegambia in New Orleans Jazz." In *New Orleans, Louisiana & Saint-Louis, Senegal: Mirror Cities in the Atlantic World, 1659–2000s*, edited by Emily Clark, Ibrahima Thioub, and Cécile Vidal, 210–232. Baton Rouge: Louisiana State University Press, 2019.

Rath, Richard Cullen. *How Early America Sounded*. Ithaca, NY: Cornell University Press, 2003.

Ray, Krishnendu. *The Ethnic Restaurateur*. London: Bloomsbury Academic, 2016.

Reese, Ashanté M. *Black Food Geographies: Race, Self-Reliance, and Food Access in Washington, D.C.* Chapel Hill: University of North Carolina Press, 2019.

Reeves, Sally K. "Making Groceries: A History of New Orleans' Public Markets." *Louisiana Cultural Vistas*, Fall 2007, 24–35.

Richard, François G. "Thinking Through Vernacular Cosmopolitanisms: Historical Archaeology in Senegal and the Material Contours of the African Atlantic." *International Journal of Historical Archaeology* 17, no. 1 (2013): 40–71.

Riesman, David. *The Lonely Crowd: A Study of the Changing American Character*. New Haven: Yale University Press, 1950.

Robertson, Claire and Iris Berger, eds. *Women and Class in Africa*. New York: Africana Publishing, 1986.

Rockman, Seth. *Scraping By: Wage Labor, Slavery, and Survival in Early* Baltimore. Baltimore: Johns Hopkins University Press, 2009.

Rosén, Hannah. *Terror in the Heart of Freedom: Citizenship, Sexual Violence, and the Meaning of Race in the Postemancipation South*. Chapel Hill: University of North Carolina Press, 2009.

Sauder, Robert A. "Municipal Markets of New Orleans." *Journal of Cultural Geography* 2 (Fall–Winter 1981): 82–95.

Sauder, Robert A. "The Origin and Spread of the Public Market System in New Orleans." *Journal of the Louisiana History* 22, no. 3 (Summer 1981): 281–97.

Saxon, Lyle. *Gumbo Ya-Ya: Folk Tales of Louisiana*. Boston: Houghton Mifflin, 1945.

Schafer, Judith Kelleher. *Becoming Free, Remaining Free: Manumission and Enslavement in New Orleans, 1846–1862*. Baton Rouge: Louisiana State University Press, 2003.

Schafer, Judith Kelleher. *Slavery, the Civil Law, and the Supreme Court of Louisiana*. Baton Rouge: Louisiana State University Press, 1994.

Schmiechen, James and Kenneth Carls. *The British Market Hall: A Social and Architectural History*. New Haven: Yale University Press, 1999.

Scola, Roger. *Feeding the Victorian City: The Food Supply of Manchester, 1770–1870* Manchester: Manchester University Press, 1992.

Seth, Andrew and Geoffrey Randall. *The Grocers: The Rise and Rise of Supermarket Chains*. London: Kogan Page, 1998.

Sharp, Kelly Kean. "Planters Plots to Backlot Stewpots: Food, Race, and Labor in Charleston, South Carolina, 1780–1850." PhD diss., University of California at Davis, 2018.

Shapiro, Laura. *Something from the Oven: Reinventing Dinner in 1950s America*. New York: Penguin, 2004.

Sheehan, Tanya. "Looking Pleasant, Feeling White: The Social Politics of the Photographic Smile." In *Feeling Photography*, edited by Elspeth H. Brown and Thy Phu, 127–57. Durham, NC: Duke University Press, 2014.

Shepherd, Samuel C. "A Glimmer of Hope: The World's Industrial and Cotton Centennial Exposition, New Orleans, 1884–1885." *Journal of the Louisiana Historical Association* 26, no. 3 (1985): 271–90.

Simmons, LaKisha Michelle. *Crescent City Girls: The Lives of Young Black Women in Segregated New Orleans*. Chapel Hill: University of North Carolina Press, 2015.

Sismondo, Christine. *America Walks into a Bar: A Spirited History of Taverns and Saloons, Speakeasies and Grog Shops*. New York: Oxford University Press, 2011.

Smith, Andrew. *Starving the South: How the North Won the Civil War*. New York: St. Martin's, 2011.

Smith, Carl S. *The Plan of Chicago: Daniel Burnham and the Remaking of the American City*. Chicago: University of Chicago Press, 2006.

Smith, Colin. "The Wholesale and Retail Market of London, 1660–1840." *Economic History Review*, new series 55, no. 1 (2002): 31–50.

Smith, Mark M. *Sensing the Past: Seeing, Hearing, Smelling, Tasting, and Touching in History*. Berkeley: University of California Press, 2007.

Stanonis, Anthony. *Creating the Big Easy: New Orleans and the Emergence of Modern Tourism, 1918–1945*. Athens: University of Georgia Press, 2006.

Stevenson, Christine. *Medicine and Magnificence: British Hospital and Asylum Architecture, 1660–1815*. New Haven: Yale University Press, 2000.

Stewart, Whitney Nell. "Fashioning Frenchness: *Gens de Couleur Libres* and the Cultural Struggle for Power in Antebellum New Orleans." *Journal of Social History* 51, no. 3 (Winter 2017): 526–56.

Strasser, Susan. *Satisfaction Guaranteed: The Making of the American Mass Market*. New York: Pantheon, 1989.

Stratton, Jennifer Jacqueline and Ashley Rose Young. "Terroir Tapestries: An Interactive Consumption Project." In *Food and Museums*, edited by Nina Levent and Irina Mihalache, 193–200. New York: Bloomsbury Academic, 2017.

Striner, Richard. "Art Deco: Polemics and Synthesis." *Winterthur Portfolio* 25, no. 1 (1990): 21–34.

Sweeney, Shauna. "A Free Enterprise: Market Women, Insurgent Economies, and the Making of Atlantic World Freedom, 1790–1880." PhD diss., New York University, 2015.

Tangires, Helen. *Movable Markets: Food Wholesaling in the Twentieth-Century City.* Baltimore: Johns Hopkins University Press, 2019.

Tangires, Helen. *Public Markets and Civic Culture in Nineteenth-Century America.* Baltimore: Johns Hopkins University Press, 2003.

Taylor, Nick. *American-Made: The Enduring Legacy of the WPA. When FDR Put the Nation to Work.* New York: Bantam, 2008.

Thompson, E. P. *Customs in Common.* New York: New Press, 1991.

Thompson, E. P. "The Moral Economy of the English Crowd in the Eighteenth Century." *Past & Present,* no. 50 (February 1971): 76–136.

Tocqueville, Alexis de. *Democracy in America.* Edited by George Lawrence and J. P. Mayer. New York: Harper Perennial Modern Classics, 2006.

Tompkins, Kyla Wazana. *Racial Indigestion: Eating Bodies in the 19th Century.* New York: New York University Press, 2012.

Topp, Leslie. *Freedom and the Cage: Modern Architecture and Psychiatry in Central Europe, 1890–1914.* University Park: Penn State University Press, 2017.

Tranberg Hansen, Karen and Walter E. Little, eds. *Street Economies in the Urban Global South.* Sante Fe, NM: SAR Press, 2013.

Tucker, Susan, ed. *New Orleans Cuisine: Fourteen Signature Dishes and Their Histories.* Jackson: University of Mississippi Press, 2009.

Turner, Patricia A. *Ceramic Uncles & Celluloid Mammies: Black Images and Their Influence on Culture.* Charlottesville: University of Virginia Press, 2002.

Tyler, Pamela. *Silk Stockings and Ballot Boxes: Women and Politics in New Orleans, 1920–1963.* Athens: University of Georgia Press, 1996.

United States Bureau of the Census. *Municipal Markets in Cities Having a Population of over 30,000: 1918.* Washington, DC: Government Printing Office, 1918.

Usner, Daniel H., Jr. "Food Marketing and Interethnic Exchange in the 18th-Century Lower Mississippi Valley." *Food and Foodways* 1 (1986): 279–310.

Usner, Daniel H., Jr. *Indians, Settlers, & Slaves in a Frontier Exchange Economy: The Lower Mississippi Valley Before 1783.* Chapel Hill: University of North Carolina Press, 1992.

Wakeman, Rosemary. "Fascinating Les Halles." *French Politics, Culture & Society* 25, no. 2 (2007): 46–72.

Weber, Lynn and Lori Peek, eds. *Displaced: Life in the Katrina Diaspora.* Austin: University of Texas Press, 2012.

Welke, Barbara Young. *Law and the Borders of Belonging in the Long Nineteenth Century United States.* New York: Cambridge University Press, 2010.

White, Deborah Gray. *Ar'n't I a Woman? Female Slaves in the Plantation South.* New York: Norton, 1999.

White, Shane and Graham J. White. *The Sounds of Slavery: Discovering African American History Through Songs, Sermons, and Speech*. Boston: Beacon Press, 2005.

Wigley, Mark. *White Walls, Designer Dresses: The Fashioning of Modern Architecture*. Cambridge, MA: MIT Press, 1995.

Williams, Elizabeth M. *New Orleans: A Food Biography*. New York: Altamira Press, 2016.

Williams-Forson, Psyche A. *Building Houses out of Chicken Legs: Black Women, Food, and Power*. Chapel Hill: University of North Carolina Press, 2006.

Young, Ashley Rose. "Nourishing Networks: The Public Culture of Food in Nineteenth-Century America." PhD diss., Duke University, 2017.

Young, James Harvey. *Pure Food: Securing the Federal Food and Drugs Act of 1906*. Princeton, NJ: Princeton University Press, 1989.

Zanoni, Elizabeth. *Migrant Marketplaces: Food and Italians in North and South America*. Urbana: University of Illinois Press, 2018.

Zukin, Sharon. *Point of Purchase: How Shopping Changed American Culture*. New York: Routledge, 2004.

Index

For the benefit of digital users, indexed terms that span two pages (e.g., 52–53) may, on occasion, appear on only one of those pages.

Figures are indicated by an italic *f*